Edward M. Browder,
Dallas, Texas.
November 1st, 1903.

JOHN KNOX

AND THE

CHURCH OF ENGLAND

By the same Author.

PATRICK HAMILTON, THE FIRST PREACHER AND MARTYR OF THE SCOTTISH REFORMATION. Collected from Original Sources never before used. GRIFFIN & Co. London, 1857.

THE SCOTTISH REFORMATION. GRIFFIN & Co. London, 1860. Embracing many New Facts obtained by Original Research, especially with regard to Alexander Alesius Scotus and other Protestant Scottish Exiles who settled in England, Germany, and Denmark.

THE FUNCTION OF THE FOUR GOSPELS, viewed in connection with Recent Criticism. A College Lecture. Published by Request. NISBET & Co. London, 1869.

THE EVIDENTIAL VALUE OF THE EARLY EPISTLES OF ST. PAUL, viewed as Historical Documents. A Lecture. Published by THE CHRISTIAN EVIDENCE SOCIETY. HODDER & STOUGHTON. London, 1874.

JOHN KNOX

AND THE

CHURCH OF ENGLAND:

HIS WORK IN HER PULPIT AND HIS INFLUENCE UPON
HER LITURGY, ARTICLES, AND PARTIES

A MONOGRAPH

FOUNDED UPON SEVERAL IMPORTANT PAPERS OF KNOX
NEVER BEFORE PUBLISHED

BY

PETER LORIMER, D.D.

PROFESSOR OF THEOLOGY, ENGLISH PRESBYTERIAN COLLEGE
AUTHOR OF "PATRICK HAMILTON," "THE SCOTTISH REFORMATION," ETC.

Henry S. King & Co.
65 CORNHILL AND 12 PATERNOSTER ROW, LONDON
1875

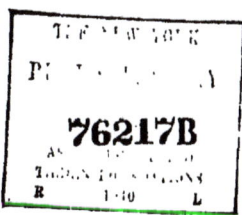

[All Rights Reserved.]

PREFACE.

ABOUT two years ago I was looking through the "Morrice" Collection of Manuscripts in Dr. Williams's Library, London, in search of unpublished papers bearing upon the history of the Elizabethan Puritans, when I came, quite unexpectedly, upon the Knox-Papers, which are here, for the first time, printed, and laid under contribution to the history of the English section of the Scottish Reformer's life and work.

It is very surprising that these Papers were not given to the world long ago, for they are included in the same collection from which Neal derived a large portion of his materials for the "History of the Puritans;" and they must have fallen under the eyes of Brooks, Price, and other original investigators in the same field, who all acknowledge their obligations to the same valuable repository. The explanation in regard to two of the Papers may probably be that the name of Knox appearing in the titles of them may have led these authors too hastily to conclude that they had already been published with his other writings, which were not, till lately, accessible in a collected form, and could not, therefore, be easily compared with the Papers; while in regard to another of the Papers—the most important of all—the absence from it of all names and dates may possibly have made the task of identification of authorship too difficult for investigators who, as English Nonconformists, not Scottish Presbyterians, were not sufficiently familiar with the literary characteristics of what Knox himself often calls "his rude hand." The Papers—four in number—are not "originals," but, in the judgment of Mr. Bond, Head of the Manuscript Department of the British Museum, they are contemporary transcripts. They exist in two sets of copies, both belonging to the "Morrice" Collection—the later set made in the last quarter of the seventeenth century, the earlier going back to the reigns of Edward VI. and Queen Elizabeth. The later copies were transcribed from the earlier, to which they give references, and are only useful as facilitating the reading of the older set.

The reader will find the Papers in the Second Part of the volume—reproduced from the older set of copies *verbatim et literatim*—accompanied with all the annotations, in the shape of Introduction and Notes, which seemed necessary and adequate to evince, both directly and indirectly, the genuineness and historical authority of the documents; and to indicate in the case of one of them, No. II., which appears to have been a joint production, the names of the men who in all probability associated themselves with Knox in drawing it up and presenting it to the Privy Council.

The amount of fresh biographical and historical material supplied by these Papers is so very considerable that it appeared to warrant and suggest a re-writing of the English chapter of Knox's life, especially when combined with the important letters of the period first given to the world by the late Mr. Tytler, in his "England under the Reigns of Edward VI. and Mary," and by the Rev. Thomas Walter Perry, in his work, published in 1863, entitled "Some Historical Considerations relating to the Declaration on

Kneeling, appended to the Communion Office of the English Book of Common Prayer," in which a highly valuable letter of Archbishop Cranmer to the Privy Council, bearing upon Knox, was first published. Having conceived this design, it became necessary to extend the range of my inquiries much beyond what was necessary to the elucidation of the Papers. The narrative portion of the volume ranges over the whole ten years of Knox's work in England and among Englishmen out of England, with which, of course, I have taken care to interweave all the material of a biographical and historical kind that has now, for the first time, become available. The effect of this is to exhibit all the new facts *in situ*, where they can be best appreciated and understood; these new facts supplementing the old ones, and the old facts so perfectly dovetailing with the new, as to authenticate them as true parts of the same story—links of it which have been long missing, but have at length been found.

The reader will please to note that the volume is offered not as a History but as a "Monograph." The rules which determine the forms and proportions of History are more stringent than those which apply to the somewhat indeterminate shapes proper or possible to the Monograph; and my chief reason, I confess, for preferring the latter form of composition was, that I wished to make larger and freer use of Knox's own writings, in the way of culling their most personal and characteristic passages, than would have been allowable in the case of a regular historical narrative. I wished, as much as possible, to let Knox himself be seen and heard in my book; and this all the more that it is wholly taken up with the English section of his life and teaching. Englishmen, of course, are not nearly so familiar with his true mind and character as Scotchmen may naturally be supposed to be, though very much has been done by two great writers of our own time—Mr. Carlyle and Mr. Froude—to explode the old misconceptions and prejudices of the English mind in regard to this grand historical figure. It seemed to me an appropriate aim, in drawing up a fuller account than has hitherto been possible of what this extraordinary Scotchman had been and had done in England, to endeavour to awaken among the English people a livelier interest in his person, and a higher degree of sympathy with his richly endowed and strongly marked nature; for his endowment was one of tenderness joined to strength—of humour as well as seriousness —of geniality and severity—of man-like sympathies added to godly zeal and fervour—and all this in a degree which is never imagined by any who have only read what others have written about him often under the influence of strong prejudice, instead of having looked into his own expressive face, and listened to his own many-toned voice, as these are only to be seen and heard in his own writings.

It is a singular coincidence that these Knox-Papers should have come to light, after an interval of more than three centuries, at a time of ecclesiastical agitation in the Church of England like the present, when they will naturally have a double degree of significance and interest. It is hoped that the fresh light which they throw upon the history of King Edward's Second Prayer Book, and his Forty-two Articles, will be equally welcome to all parties of the Anglican Church, however different may be the uses which they may be expected to make of the new facts now become available.

In my narrative of Knox's action and influence on this important field, I have not been careful, of course, to conceal on which side of the struggle of parties in which he figured my own sympathies lie; but I have not written polemically, nor have I indulged in commentary on persons or things beyond what was necessary in order to do justice either to the principles and views, or to the historical place and claims, of Knox himself.

I have freely and gratefully availed myself of all the help I could obtain from the best writers who have preceded me in the same field. I am under special obligations to Dr. M'Crie, the admirable biographer of Knox, and to Mr. Laing, the learned and elaborate editor of "Knox's Collected Works." Each of these authors has erected a noble and enduring literary monument to their illustrious countryman. What is here contributed to the same monumental use is but the adding of a few more stones to the two grand "cairns" which the admiration and gratitude of his country have already raised—the stones in this case, as in that of his "Life" and his "Works," being all brought from the same rich quarry of his own head, and heart, and work.

My best thanks are due and are cordially rendered to Mr. Hunter, of Dr. Williams's Library, for the ready access which he has always given me to its valuable MS. Collections, and to Mr. Bond for his learned judgment on the age and authority of the Knox-Papers.

THE AUTHOR.

English Presbyterian College:
1st January, 1875.

CONTENTS.

INTRODUCTION 1

PART FIRST.

KNOX'S WORK AND INFLUENCE IN THE CHURCH OF ENGLAND.

CHAPTER I.

KNOX'S WORK IN BERWICK, A.D. 1549-51—EARLIEST INTRODUCTION OF PURITAN WORSHIP INTO THE CHURCH OF ENGLAND . . 15

NOTE.—INFLUENCE OF BULLINGER ON CRANMER 48

CHAPTER II.

KNOX'S WORK IN NEWCASTLE, 1551-53—"VINDICATION OF THE DOCTRINE THAT THE MASS IS IDOLATRY"—KNOX APPOINTED ROYAL CHAPLAIN TO EDWARD VI. 51

SUPPLEMENT.—"THE REASONING BETWIXT KNOX AND THE ABBOTT OF CROSSRAGWELL" 88

CHAPTER III.

KNOX AS ROYAL CHAPLAIN AT THE COURT OF EDWARD VI.—HIS INFLUENCE UPON THE LITURGY AND ARTICLES OF THE ANGLICAN CHURCH, 1552 98

NOTES.—1. ON THE REGISTER OF PRIVY COUNCIL 137
   2. ON CERTAIN WRITINGS OF JOHN A'LASCO . . . 138
   3. ON THE EUCHARISTIC DOCTRINE OF THE EARLIEST HELVETIC CONFESSIONS 141

CHAPTER IV.

OFFER OF THE SEE OF ROCHESTER—EPISTLE TO THE CONGREGATION OF BERWICK 146

CHAPTER V.

THE LAST YEAR OF KNOX'S WORK IN ENGLAND—NEWCASTLE—
BUCKINGHAMSHIRE—KENT 162

CHAPTER VI.

KNOX IN FRANKFORT AND GENEVA—HIS INFLUENCE UPON THE
PURITAN PARTY OF THE CHURCH OF ENGLAND, 1554-59 . . 201

PART SECOND.

KNOX-PAPERS NEVER BEFORE PUBLISHED.

INTRODUCTORY NOTE ON "THE MORRICE COLLECTION OF MSS."
IN DR. WILLIAMS'S LIBRARY 245

I.

EPISTLE TO THE CONGREGATION OF BERWICK, 1552 . . . 251
NOTE 265

II.

MEMORIAL OR "CONFESSION" TO THE PRIVY COUNCIL OF EDWARD
VI., 1552 267
NOTES 275

III.

THE PRACTICE OF THE LORD'S SUPPER USED IN BERWICK BY JOHN
KNOX, 1550 290
NOTES 292

IV.

A LETTER WRITTEN TO KNOX FROM LONDON, 1566 . . . 298
NOTE 300

APPENDIX.

THE LIFE AND DEATH OF WILLIAM WHITTINGHAM, DEAN OF DUR-
HAM, FROM A MS. IN THE BODLEIAN LIBRARY . . . 303

JOHN KNOX

AND

THE CHURCH OF ENGLAND.

INTRODUCTION.

MEN are apt to think of John Knox too exclusively in connection with his work and success as the Reformer of Scotland. It is not usually remembered what a large portion of the best and most energetic part of his life was spent in England, and among Englishmen out of England. He first set foot in this country early in 1549. He was then in his forty-fifth year—in the full strength of manhood; and, having been welcomed by Cranmer and the Privy Council of Edward VI. as a seasonable addition to the small number of Reformation preachers who were then employed in proclaiming the gospel throughout the kingdom, he was immediately despatched on that service to the north of England; and he continued to be thus employed in the counties of Northumberland, Durham, and Cumberland, and afterwards in London, Buckinghamshire, and Kent, till several months after the accession of Mary, in 1553, when, his life being in danger, he was compelled to withdraw to the Continent. But on the Continent he spent much the greatest part of the five following years among the English Protestant exiles. One year out of the five was occupied in an important visit to Scotland, extending from September, 1555, to September, 1556; but during the rest of these years he was mainly engaged in ministering to the English congregations of Frankfort and Geneva. Thus for ten of the best years of his life and work he was chiefly in contact with English, not with Scottish, minds. Indeed, it is curious to observe how extensively he became connected with English life, not only in public matters, but by domestic ties and private friendships and correspondence. His first wife was an Englishwoman of good family in the county of Durham, whose father, Sir Richard Bowes, and uncle, Sir Robert Bowes, held important appointments under Government. Several of his private friends and correspondents were persons of high social standing in London, such as Mr. and Mrs. Locke—members of the same family which afterwards gave birth to the illustrious John Locke. In Frankfort and Geneva he was associated in the closest bonds of spiritual and personal communion with men like Bishop Coverdale, Bishop Bale, John Fox the martyrologist, William Whittingham, Dean of Durham, Goodman, Gilby, Sampson, and others, all eminent English Churchmen. All these circumstances show how closely the Scottish Reformer's life, both public and private, became interwoven with English society, and prepare us to understand how his personal influence should have availed for much in forming English opinion, and in infusing a "Knoxian" element into English Church life.

All that is known with certainty of Knox's life before he came into England may be told in little space. He was born in 1505, at Gifford Gate, Haddington. His father, William Knox, was able to give him a liberal education in the Grammar School of Haddington and at the University of Glasgow. He was about sixteen years of age when he became, in 1522, a student of philosophy, along with his celebrated countryman George Buchanan, under Dr. John Mair, or Major, who was one of the most famous scholastic doctors of the age. In the following year Major was transferred to St. Andrew's, and it is probable that Knox, as well as Buchanan, followed him thither. "From some unknown cause he left the University without qualifying himself to take the degree of Master of Arts, and for a period of nearly eighteen years we remain in complete ignorance of his course of life." It has been usual, indeed, to state that he taught philosophy and theology at St. Andrew's with even more credit for scholastic subtlety than his master, but "no evidence can be adduced to show that he was officially connected in any capacity whatever with that University. Not having a Master's degree would necessarily exclude him from acting as a Regent or Professor."*

---

* The statements quoted here and in the following paragraph are from the pen of Dr. Laing, the learned editor of Knox's Collected Works in 6 vols. They will be found in the Preface to vol. vi.

At the usual age he obtained orders in the Church of Rome as a secular priest, and there is some reason to think that he held the appointment of Chaplain or Rood-priest in the chapel of St. Nicholas at Samuelston, near Haddington, which he seems to have combined with the employment of private tutor in the family of the Kers of Samuelston. In the protocol books of Haddington his name occurs thrice—in 1540, 1541, and 1542, once under the style of *Schir* John Knox, as one of the Pope's knights, "being the usual designation of priests who had not attained the higher academical degree of Magister; and as late as March 27th, 1543, he pens and signs a notarial instrument of assignment as an apostolic notary, describing himself as "Joannes Knox, sacri altaris minister, sancti Andreae dioceseos, auctoritate apostolica notarius."*

These recent results of documentary research bring out for the first time the curious fact that, even as late as 1543, Knox still took the style and titles of a priest and official of Rome, a fact which shows how slowly his convictions as a Reformer must have grown to ripeness, and how tenacious he must have long been in defending those corruptions and superstitions, of which he afterwards became the most vehement and inexorable foe. As early as 1525, the books of Luther and Tyndale had found their way into the Scottish ports; as early as 1528 Patrick Hamilton had preached and died for the Reformation in St. Andrew's; and since then numerous distinguished converts to the same cause had been driven into exile, some of them never to return. But, singular to relate, Knox, who was destined to surpass all other Scottish Reformers in perfervid zeal and power, is still a Papist and a Papal functionary, at thirty-eight years of age, still signing himself a Minister of the "Sacred Altar,"—the same altar which, for the next thirty years of his life, he was loudly to denounce as an altar of sacrilege and idolatry. Of course, during all these years, he must have been studying deeply a question which was everywhere convulsing the world, although, unfortunately, nothing is known of the circumstances connected with his conversion to Reformation views, save the names of the two men who appear to have had most to do with gaining him to the cause of truth and liberty. These were Thomas Guillaume, one of the chaplains of

---

* "John Knox—Minister of the Sacred Altar, in the diocese of St. Andrew, by authority of the Apostolic see notary."

the Regent Arran during the brief period of his favour to the Evangelical cause in 1543—the first, according to Calderwood, "to give Knox a taste of the truth,"*—and the other the distinguished Preacher and Martyr, George Wishart, to whose person and preaching Knox attached himself with the warmest zeal as soon as Wishart appeared in Lothian in 1545, accompanying him from place to place in his preaching with a drawn sword over his shoulder, to protect him from the emissaries of Cardinal Beaton, and from whom he took his reluctant leave on the night of his apprehension by a band of horsemen at Ormiston, only on Wishart's insistance that he should return to his pupils at Langniddry, on the ground that "one was sufficient for the sacrifice."

The martyrdom of Wishart, in 1546, was the turning-point of Knox's life; and if, for some short time before that event, his new convictions had been gradually gathering strength, it was the profound impression made upon him by that tragedy which brought them to ripeness, and made him the successor as well as the disciple of that admirable Reformer. His desertion of "the sacred altar" was soon known to Beaton, and would have been speedily avenged if the Cardinal's own life had not been suddenly cut off by the conspiracy of Norman Lesley. That tragedy of vengeance, at once wickedly human and righteously divine, not only delivered him from immediate danger at the hand of the Cardinal, but ere long had the effect of converting the persecutor's stronghold in St. Andrews into a place of asylum for Knox and other Protestant refugees, upon whom the slaughter of Beaton was sought to be unrighteously avenged; and it was here that Knox was first summoned to undertake the office of a preacher and pastor by the collective voice of all the Protestants of the castle and city. It came upon him with a sudden surprise. He pleaded hard to be excused under a deep sense of unfitness; and when the preacher, John Rough, called upon him from the pulpit, in the hearing and in the name of the congregation, to come forward to the work, and would take no refusal, Knox was completely overcome by the conflict of his feelings, and, bursting into tears, hurried out

* Dr. McCrie remarks that Guillaume's name, after he repaired to England in 1544, does not again occur in history, but I have no doubt that the name "*Thomas Gilham, Scott,* Bachelor of Divinitie," which occurs on the list of preachers employed by the Privy Council, refers to the same individual. It stands very near to that of "John Ruthe, or Rough, Scottishman," who was his fellow chaplain in Regent Arran's court, and now shared his exile.

of the church. "His very first sermon," Dr. McCrie tells us, "made a great noise, and excited much speculation among all classes, and the fruit of a few weeks of labour was, that besides the garrison in the castle, a great number of the inhabitants of the town renounced Popery and made profession of the Protestant faith by participating of the Lord's Supper." *

The Papists of Scotland and France joined their forces to avenge the death of Beaton upon the Protestant garrison and refugees of St. Andrew's. By-and-by the city and castle were besieged by land and sea, and in the absence of expected relief from Henry VIII., the garrison was compelled to succumb after an obstinate defence. The French galleys bore away to France with the defeated and punished conspirators, and carrying with them Knox and other godly refugees; and for eighteen months thereafter the Reformer, yet new to his Evangelical faith, had to suffer for it a sore and ignominious bondage—chained as a galley-slave to the oar—"going in irons, miserably entreated, and sore troubled by corporeal infirmity." But during all those dismal months he never flinched nor faltered a jot. "Rejoicing in hope, patient in tribulation, continuing instant in prayer," he was content to bide his time, which to him was the Lord's own time; and at length, early in 1549, the hour of deliverance came; the day broke and the shadows fled away; and, released from his long durance by England's intercession, as it is thought, with the French King, he stood ready to repay the debt by years of zealous and devoted service to the cause of England's long postponed, long waited for, and still only commencing Reformation.

When Knox began his ministry in England he was already a Protestant of what afterwards came to be called the Puritan type, but what at that early date would have been described as Protestantism of the Zwinglian or Helvetic, as distinguished from the Lutheran or Saxon type. He had been, as we have seen, a devoted follower of Wishart, and Wishart was an admirer of the Helvetic churches, which he had visited in 1541-1542, and whose First Confession, that of 1537, he had translated into the Scottish tongue. Knox was a Reformer of the Swiss school long before he was personally acquainted with Calvin. His theology was formed upon the model of Zwingli, Œcololampadius and Bullinger, not upon that of Luther and

* Life of Knox, vol. i. p. 61.

Melancthon. In St. Andrew's he had said roundly of the Church of Rome, that "he no more doubted that it was the synagogue of Satan, and the head thereof, called the Pope, to be that man of sin of whom the Apostle spake, than he doubted that Jesus Christ suffered by the procurement of the visible church of Jerusalem. Yea, I offer myself," he continued, "by word or writing, to prove the Roman Church this day further degenerate from the purity which was in the days of the Apostles, than were the church of the Jews from the ordinances given by Moses, when they consented to the innocent death of Jesus Christ." This was bolder and more thorough-going Protestantism than had ever been heard before in Scotland. "Some said," as Knox himself tells us in his "History,"* "others hewed the branches of Papistry, but he striketh at the root to destroy the whole. Mr. George Wishart spake never so plainly." And he aimed at this "root and branch Reformation" because he had laid it down as a fundamental principle of revealed religion, "that in the worship of God, and especially in the administration of the Sacraments, the rule prescribed in Holy Scripture is to be observed without addition or diminution, and that the Church has no right to devise religious ceremonies and impose significations upon them." Luther and Melancthon had never laid down such an absolute principle as that. This was not Saxon, but Swiss Protestantism; not Anglican Protestantism, but Puritanism—and appropriately enough called Puritanism, when this name began to be given to it in mockery, because this fundamental principle was held by Puritans to be the only absolute test of what was pure and impure in religious and church life, the only Protestant purgatory in which all church corruptions and dross could be thoroughly purged away as by fire.

Only two years before his arrival in England—while he was still preaching to the garrison and citizens of St. Andrew's—in a convention of Gray and Black Friars, held by Dean Wynram, Subprior of the Abbey, Knox had been charged with holding and teaching the following articles:—

1. Man may neither make nor devise a religion that is acceptable to God; but man is bound to observe and keep the religion that from God is received, without chopping or changing thereof.

* "History of the Reformation in Scotland," in Knox's Works, vol. i. p. 192.

2. The Sacraments of the New Testament ought to be ministered as they were instituted by Christ Jesus, and practised by the Apostles; nothing ought to be added to them; nothing ought to be diminished from them.

3. The Mass is abominable idolatry, blasphemous to the death of Christ, and a profanation of the Lord's Supper.

"But why may not the Kirk," demanded Dean Wynram, "for good causes, devise ceremonies to decore [adorn] the Sacraments and other God's service?"

"Because the Kirk," answered Knox, "ought to do nothing but in faith, and ought not to go before, but is bound to follow, the voice of the true pastor. It is not enough that man invent a ceremony, and then give it a signification according to his pleasure; for so might the ceremonies of the Gentiles, and this day the ceremonies of Mahomet, be maintained. But if that anything proceed from faith, it must have the word of God for the assurance, for ye are not ignorant that faith comes by hearing, and hearing by the Word of God. Now, if ye will prove that your ceremonies proceed from faith, and do please God, ye must prove that God, in expressed words, has commanded them; or else shall ye never prove that they proceed from faith, nor yet that they please God, but that they are sin, and do displease him, according to the words of the Apostle, 'Whatsoever is not of faith is sin.'"

"Will ye bind us so strait," again interposed the Sub-prior, "that we may do nothing without the express word of God? What! if I ask a drink, think ye that I sin? and yet I have not God's word for me."

"I would not," rejoined the stern Reformer, "we should jest in so grave a matter. I wonder that ye compare things profane and holy things so indiscreetly together. The question was not nor is not of meat and drink, wherein the kingdom of God consists not, but the question is of God's true worshipping, without the which we can have no society with God. And here it is doubted if we may take the same freedom in the using of Christ's sacraments that we may do in eating and drinking; one meat I may eat, another I may refuse, and that without scruple of conscience. I may change one with another, even as oft as I please. Whether may we do the same in matters of religion? May we cast away what we please and retain what we please? If I be well remembered, Moses, in the name of God, says to the people of Israel, 'All that the Lord thy God commands thee to do, that do thou to the Lord thy God, add nothing to it, diminish nothing from it.' By this rule think I that the Kirk of God will measure God's religion, and not by that which seems good in their own eyes."

"Forgive me," said the Dean, who was not much in earnest to maintain his point, "I spake it but in jest, and I was dry; and now, Father," turning to Friar Arbuckill, "follow the argument—ye have heard what I have said, and what is answered to me again."

Then struck in Arbuckill, confident of victory, "I shall prove plainly that ceremonies are ordained by God."

"Such as God has ordained we allow," said Knox, quietly, "and with reverence we use them. But the question is of those that God has not ordained, such as in baptism are spittle, salt, candle, hood (except it be to keep the bairn from cold), hards, oil, and the rest of the Papisticall inventions."

Arbuckill.—"I will even prove these ye damn to be ordained of God."

Knox.—"The proof I would gladly hear."

Arbuckill.—"Says not St. Paul that another foundation than Jesus Christ may no man lay. But upon this foundation some build gold, silver, and precious stones; some hay, stubble, and wood. The gold, silver, and precious stones are the ceremonies of the Church, which do abide the fire and consume not away. This place of Scripture is most plain."

Knox.—"If I had sought the whole Scriptures I could not have produced a place more proper for my purpose, nor more potent to confound you. The ceremonies of the Kirk, say ye, are gold, silver, and precious stones, because they are able to abide the fire; but I would learn of you what fire it is which your ceremonies do abide. And in the meantime, till that ye be advised to answer, I will show my mind, and make an argument against yours upon the same text. I have heard this text adduced for a proof of purgatory, but for defence of ceremonies I never heard nor yet read it. But omitting whether ye understand the mind of the Apostle or not, I make my argument and say, that which may abide the fire may abide the word of God; but your ceremonies may not abide the word of God; ergo, they may not abide the fire; and if they may not abide the fire, then are they not gold, silver, nor precious stones.

Arbuckill.—" I deny your minor, to wit, that our ceremonies may not abide the trial of God's word."

Knox.—" That abides not the trial of God's word which God's word condemns. But as the thief abides the trial of the inquest, and thereby is condemned to be hanged, even so may your ceremonies abide the trial of God's word ; but not else. And now in few words to make plain that wherein ye may seem to doubt—to wit, that God's word damns your ceremonies, it is evident ; for the plain and straight commandment of God is, ' Not that thing which appears good in thy eyes shalt thou do to the Lord thy God, but what the Lord thy God has commanded thee, that do thou.' Now unless that ye be able to prove that God has commanded your ceremonies, this his former commandment will damn both you and them."

The conclusion of this debate was comical, and must be given in Knox's own words as a specimen of his characteristic vein of irony and humour :—

"The Friar, somewhat abashed what first to answer, while he wanders about in the mist, he falls in a foul mire ; for alleging that we may not be so bound to the word, he affirmed 'that the Apostles had not received the Holy Ghost when they did write their epistles, but after they received him, and then they did ordain the ceremonies.' (Few would have thought that so learned a man would have given so foolish an answer, and yet it is even as true as he bore a grey cowl.) John Knox hearing the answer, started and said, "If that be true I have long been in an error, and I think I shall die therein." The Sub-prior said to him, " Father ! what say ye ? God forbid that ye affirm that ! for then fareweel the ground of our faith." The Friar, astonished, made the best shift that he could to correct his fall—but it would not be. John Knox brought him oft again to the ground of the argument ; but he would never answer directly, but ever fled to the authority of the Kirk, whereto the said John answered oftener than once, "That the spouse of Christ had neither power nor authority against the word of God." Then said the Friar, " If so be, ye will leave us no Kirk." "Indeed," said the other, " In David I read that there is a church of the malignants, for he says *Odi Ecclesiam malignantium*. That church ye may have without the Word, and doing many things directly fighting against the Word of God. Of that church if ye will be, I cannot impede you. But as for me, I will be of none other church except of that which hath Christ Jesus to be pastor, which hears his voice, and will not hear a stranger."*

This passage from Knox's own pen is an apt introduction to that chapter of the History of the English Reformation which stands connected with his name. It paints very graphically the man as he was, and determines with the greatest precision the religious and ecclesiastical ground upon which he stood, at the time when, in the full maturity of his character and powers, he placed himself at the service of the Church of England, at the invitation of her Rulers.

The year in which Knox entered upon this service was a memorable epoch in the history of the English Reformation. Ever since the accession of Edward VI. the purification of the National Church from the corruptions of ages had been gradually but steadily advancing; and early in this year (1549) the first Prayerbook, called after the young King, received the sanction of Parliament, and was published for the use of the Church. Its earliest editions bear the date of the month of March. Exactly a year earlier the "Order of the Communion," which formed an important part of this book, had been issued by itself as a first step towards a Reformed Liturgy, accompanied with a Royal Proclamation, in which the young Monarch "willed all his loving subjects with such obedience and conformity to receive this our ordinance and most godly direction, that we may be encouraged from time to time further to travail for the Reformation, and setting forth of such godly orders as may be most to God's glory, the edifying of our subjects, and for the advancement of true religion—which thing we (by the help of God) most earnestly intend to bring to effect. God be praised, we know both what by his Word is meet to be redressed, and have an earnest mind, with all diligence and convenient speed, to set forth the same as it may most stand with God's glory and edifying and quietness of our people, which we doubt not but all our obedient and loving subjects will quietly and reverently tarry for." It was this Royal promise which was now fulfilled, in its first instalment, in the famous "Book of the Common Praier and administracion of the Sacramentes and other rites and ceremonies of the Churche, after the use of the Churche of Englande." Knox arrived in London just in time to obtain an

* Knox's "History of the Reformation in Scotland," Works, vol. i. pp. 194-200.

early copy of this important document—to which much of his coming action was to have reference—from the printing press of Richard Grafton, Printer to the King.

It was a highly important and valuable step in advance. What had long been "commonly called the Mass" was now called by preference "The Supper of the Lord and the Holy Communion," and was now to be ministered in England, as it had been for five-and-twenty years in the reformed churches of the Continent, "under both kinds." Many superstitious ceremonies and practises had been swept away, though not a little of this kind still remained for future retrenchment. The new Liturgy still lagged far behind the wishes and the views of the most zealous of the Reforming party—much as it outran the desires and shocked the prejudices of the opposite party who still formed the immense majority of the nation, and would have preferred the reconciliation of the kingdom to the Roman See. The book could not command the zealous service of more than half-a-dozen of the Bishops in introducing it into their dioceses; and during the whole brief reign of Edward there were several counties in the remoter parts of the kingdom where it was never introduced at all.

John Hooper, who returned from a two years' residence in Zurich a few months after Knox's arrival in England, and immediately became the most popular preacher in London, has left, in his letters to Bullinger, several graphic and highly interesting sketches of the strangely piebald and confused condition of ecclesiastical matters which then prevailed.

Writing to Bullinger from London, June 25, 1549, he says, "Great, great, I say, is the harvest, but the labourers are few. May our most indulgent Father send forth labourers into the harvest. Such is the maliciousness and wickedness of the bishops (referring to the Popish bishops, and especially to Bonner, Bishop of London) that the godly and learned men who would willingly labour in the Lord's harvest are hindered by them; and they neither preach themselves nor allow the liberty of preaching to others. For this reason there are some persons here who read and expound the holy Scriptures at a public lecture, two of whom read in St. Paul's Cathedral four times a week. I myself, too, as my slender abilities will allow me, having compassion upon the ignorance of my brethren, read a public lecture twice in the day to so numerous an audience that the church cannot contain them. The Anabaptists flock to the place, and give me much trouble with their opinions respecting the incarnation of the Lord, for they deny altogether that Christ was born of the Virgin Mary according to the flesh. . . . Although I am unable to satisfy their obstinacy, yet the Lord by his Word shuts their mouths, and their heresies are more and more detested by the people. How dangerously our England is afflicted by heresies of this kind God only knows; I am unable, indeed, from sorrow of heart, to express to your piety. . . . On the other hand, a great portion of the kingdom so adheres to the Popish faction as altogether to set at nought God and the lawful authority of the magistrates, so that I am greatly afraid of a rebellion and civil discord. May the Lord restrain restless spirits, and destroy the counsels of Achitophel. Do you, my venerable father, commend our King and the council of the nation, together with our Church, to God in your prayers."

In December of the same year he writes again to Zurich on the same subject: "Although our vessel is dangerously tossed about on all sides, yet God in his providence holds the helm, and raises up more favourers of his word in his Majesty's councils, who, with activity and courage, defend the cause of Christ. The Archbishop of Canterbury entertains right views as to the nature of Christ's presence in the Supper, and is now very friendly towards myself. He has some articles of religion, to which all preachers and lecturers in divinity are required to subscribe, or else a license for teaching is not granted them, and in these his sentiments respecting the Eucharist are pure and religious, and similar to yours in Switzerland. We desire nothing more for him than a firm and manly spirit. Like all the other bishops in this country, he is too fearful about what may happen to him. There are here six or seven bishops who comprehend the doctrine of Christ, as far as relates to the Lord's Supper, with as much clearness and piety as we could desire; and it is only the fear for their property that prevents them from reforming their churches, according to the rule of God's word. The altars are here in many churches changed into tables. The public celebration of the Lord's Supper is very far from the order and institution of our Lord. Although it is administered in both kinds, yet in some places the Supper is celebrated three times a day. Where they used, heretofore, to celebrate in the morning the *Mass* of the Apostles, they now have the *Communion* of the Apostles; where they had the Mass of the Blessed Virgin, they now have the Communion which they call the communion of the Virgin; where they had the principal or High Mass, they now have, as they call it, the High Communion. They still retain their vestments and the candles before the altars; in the churches they always chant the hours and other hymns relating to the Lord's Supper, but in our own language; and that Popery may not be lost, the Mass-priests, although they are compelled to discontinue the use of the Latin language, yet most carefully observe the same tone and manner of chanting to which they were heretofore accustomed in the Papacy. God knows to what perils and anxieties we are exposed by reason of men of this kind."

A few weeks later, he sends a third sketch, as lively as the other two:—"Now, as to what is doing in England. The Bishops of Canterbury, Rochester (Ridley), Ely (Goodrich), St. David's (Farrar), Lincoln (Holbrook), and Bath (Barlow), are all favourable to the cause of Christ, and, as far as I know, entertain right opinions in the matter of the Eucharist. I have freely conversed with all of them upon this subject, and have discerned nothing but what is pure and holy. . . . The Marquis of Dorset, the Earl of Warwick, and the greater part of the King's Council, favour the cause of Christ as much as they can. Our King is such an one for his age as the world has never seen. May the Lord preserve him. His sister, the daughter of the late King by Queen Ann, is influenced with the same zeal for the religion of Christ. She not only knows what the true religion is, but has acquired such proficiency in Greek and Latin that she is able to defend it by the most just arguments and the most happy talent; so that she encounters few adversaries whom she does not overcome. The people, however, that many-headed monster, is still wincing, partly through ignorance, and partly fascinated by the inveiglements of the bishops, and the malice and impiety of the Mass-priests. Such, then, is the present state of things in England."

Once more, in March, he writes as follows: "We do not water and plant in vain. God has given a sufficiently large and glorious increase to the seed sown by Peter and Paul. There has lately been appointed a new Bishop of London (Ridley), a pious and learned man, if only his new dignity do not change his conduct. He will, I hope, destroy the altars of Baal as he did heretofore in his Church when he was Bishop of Rochester. I cannot scarcely express to you under what difficulties and dangers we are labouring and struggling that the idol of the Mass may be thrown out. It is no small hindrance to our exertions, that the form which our Senate or Parliament, as we commonly call it, has prescribed for the whole realm is so very defective, and of doubtful construction, and in some respects, indeed, manifestly impious. I am so much offended with that book, and that not without abundant reason, that, if it be not corrected, I neither can nor will communicate with the Church in the administration of the Lord's Supper. Many altars have been destroyed in this city since I arrived here. . . . I am now engaged upon the eighth chapter of the Gospel of St. John. I freely held forth upon the sixth chapter to my audience, as God enabled me, respecting the Lord's Supper, for the space of three months, and lectured once or twice every day, and it pleased God to bless my exertions. A wonderful and most numerous concourse of people attended me, and God was with them, for he opened their hearts to understand the things which were spoken by me. But I incurred great odium and no less danger from the sixth chapter. The better cause, however, prevails; and during this Lent (1550) I have plainly and openly handled the same subject before the King and the nobility of the realm. In this city an individual of the name of Crane, a man of excellent erudition and holiness of life, a doctor in divinity, is combating my opinions in a public discourse. The Bishops of Winchester, London, and Worcester (Gardiner, Bonner, and Heath) are still in confinement, and maintain the Popish doctrines with all their might."*

Such is Hooper's description of the strange and disordered condition of the religious affairs of the kingdom during the first year of Knox's ministry as one of Cranmer's licensed preachers; and we may be sure that if Knox himself had described it to us, he would have set it in the same light, and judged it by the same standard. Hooper and Knox were men of kindred spirit and principles. Directly or indirectly, they had both drunk deep at the same Helvetic fount.

* "Original Letters relative to the English Reformation" (Parker Society), pp. 65, 71, 76, 79, 80.

PART FIRST.

KNOX'S WORK AND INFLUENCE IN THE CHURCH OF ENGLAND.

CHAPTER I.

KNOX'S WORK IN BERWICK, A.D. 1549-51.

THE earliest notice in the Public Records of the presence of John Knox in England is the following brief entry in the Register of the Privy Council of Edward VI.:—

"Sunday, the 7th Aprill, 1549.

"Warrant to the Receiver of the Duchy for 5 lib. to John Knock, preacher, by way of reward."

At that date he was already in the service of the Privy Council, as one of the Protestant ministers whom they employed to preach the doctrines of the Reformation throughout the kingdom. A list of these, containing eighty names—including many which afterwards became highly distinguished—has been preserved in the Record Office.* Knox's name appears among the rest—the sixty-fourth in chronological order—and not far from his stand the names of three other Scottish preachers who were closely associated with him at different periods of his public life—John Rough, John McBriar, and John Willock. The approximate date of his arrival in London from France was the preceding February or March; and in recommending him to the Privy Council for public

---

* This list may be seen in the Preface to the 6th vol. of Knox's Collected Works, edited by Dr. Laing, by whom it was first published.

employment, it is not improbable that Cranmer was influenced by what he had heard of the power and success of his short ministry at St. Andrews.*

In Knox's "History of the Reformation of Religion within the Realm of Scotland," which is to a considerable extent a history of his own life and work, he disposes of the English section of his life in less than half-a-dozen lines—"The said John was first appointed preacher to Berwick, then to Newcastle; last he was called to London, and the south parts of England, where he remained to the death of King Edward the Sixth." †

In one of the memorable dialogues, however, between him and the Scottish Queen, which he introduces into that history, there are some curious particulars preserved of the success of his work as a preacher in England, and of the deep but sinister impression which it had produced upon the minds of the English Papists. In an interview to which the Queen summoned him at Holyrood, in the autumn of 1561, she accused him, among other things, "that he had been the cause of great sedition and great slaughter in England, and that it was said to her that all which he did was by necromancy." To the which the said John answered, "Madam, it may please your Majesty patiently to hear my simple answers. . . . I heartily praise my God, through Jesus Christ, that Satan, the enemy of mankind, and the wicked of the world, have no other crimes to lay to my charge than such as the very world itself knoweth to be most false and vain. For in England I was resident only the space of five years. The places were Berwick, where I abode two years, so long in the Newcastle, and a year in London. Now, Madam, if in any of these places, during the time that I was there, any man shall be able to prove that there was either battle, sedition, or mutiny, I shall confess that I myself was the malefactor, and the shedder of the blood. I ashame not, Madam, further to affirm that God so blessed my weak labours that in Berwick (where commonly before there used to be slaughter by reason of quarrels that used to arise amongst soldiers) there was as great quietness all the

---

* Henry Balnaves, who had had much to do with Knox's sudden call to the ministry in St. Andrew's, was twice sent to London during the siege, to communicate with the Privy Council with the object of obtaining aid for the besieged; and the conjecture may be allowed that it was in this way that Knox's name first became known in the English capital.

† Works of Knox, vol. I. p. 231.

time that I remained there, as there is this day in Edinburgh. And whereas they slander me of magick, necromancy, or of any other art forbidden of God, I have witness, beside my own conscience, all congregations that ever heard me, what I spake both against such arts and against those that use such impiety. But seeing the wicked of the world said that my Master, the Lord Jesus, was possessed with Beelzebub, I must patiently bear, albeit that I, wretched sinner, be unjustly accused of those that never delighted in the verity." *

The Queen had, no doubt, heard these absurd accusations of magic and necromancy laid against the Reformer by the English and Scottish Papists at the French Court, from which she had recently returned to her own kingdom. But what must have been the strange power of his pulpit-eloquence, and what the marvellous effects which his preaching had wrought upon the minds and lives of men in England and his own country, when the Papists could only account for his success in pulling down the walls of their own Church, by referring it to the spells of the magician, or the unearthly power of the Great Enemy!

When Knox entered the pulpit of the old parish church of Berwick-on-Tweed, he found before him a mixed congregation of soldiers and civilians, like that to which he had first preached the Gospel in St. Andrew's. The great majority of his hearers were probably Papists, for as yet the Reformation had made very little way in the northern counties. Tunstall, the powerful Bishop of Durham, though no very zealous friend of Rome, was as lukewarm and dilatory as possible in giving effect to the new legislation; and the Council of the North were not very hotly urged by the Privy Council in London to carry out the new Ecclesiastical measures among a population who gave unmistakable signs of a spirit of disaffection and revolt. To add to the difficulty of the preacher's position, Berwick was at that very time the focus of a long and bloody war between the two Kingdoms—a war which had begun with the tremendous slaughter of the Scots at Pinkey, in the autumn of 1547, and in which the Scots, having received large assistance from France, were still able to maintain so vigorous a defence that there was no near prospect of a return of peace. The garrison of the border fortress was thus much larger than

* "Knox's Works," vol. ii. pp. 277-280.

usual, and doubtless in a condition of more than ordinary excitement. Quarrels and outbreaks among the soldiers were of frequent occurrence. Nor was there any better order among the townsmen than among the soldiers. John Brende, "Master of the Musters," sends word to the Protector Somerset, that "there is better order among the Tartars than in this town. No man can have anything unstolen; none but Scots can be harboured (allowed to lodge in the town) except by force; the price of victuals is excessive; the sick soldiers from Haddington, &c., are shut out of houses and die of want in the streets. The whole picture of the place is one of social disorder and the worst police. It will require a stern disciplinarian in the pulpit as well as a stirring preacher, to work out a moral and social reform."* The new preacher, besides—a Scotsman among Englishmen—has to deliver his message to hundreds of men who are inflamed with all the passions of war against his countrymen; and there is no saying what violence may be attempted against such a redoubtable assailant of the religion of Rome, when cooped up within narrow walls along with large numbers of armed Papists, who burn with a fiercer flame against the new "Gospellers" of England than even against the old Scottish foe. Knox's position is one of grave difficulty and danger. It needs all the courage of his heroic heart.

A document which he had joined with Henry Balnaves of Halhill, his fellow-exile in France, in sending only a few months before "to all Professors of Christ's true Evangell" in Scotland, leaves us in no doubt as to the exalted view he took of the duties incumbent upon every man called to the sacred office of a "bishop or minister of the word of God." In his "Brief Summarie" of his friend's learned and able treatise on "Justification and Good Works," he had declared "the principal office of a bishop to be to preach the true Evangell of Jesus

* State Papers—Domestic—Edward VI., Nov. 14, 1548. The "Scots," referred to in Brende's letter to Somerset, were natives of the neighbouring districts of the Merse and East Lothian, who had been compelled, at the sword's point, to accept an engagement to own the authority of the English King, and to serve under him against their own Regent, the Earl of Arran—and who had a claim, under the engagement, to be "harboured" in Berwick from the pursuit of their own countrymen. So that Knox must have had a sprinkling of "Scots" among his congregation, all wearing the red cross on their breasts as the King's cognizance.

Christ, knowing that if the flock perish the blood shall be required at his hands; and that he, neglecting the preaching of the Evangell, is no bishop, nor can do no work pleasant before God. And therefore no bishop should mix himself with temporal or secular business, for that is contrary to his vocation; but continually should preach, read, and exhort his flock to seek their spiritual food in the Scriptures. And so the tyrants in these days forbidding men to read the Scriptures, declare themselves wolves and no pastors; whom God shall shortly punish, because they have contemned his command, attending altogether upon their own vain superstitions; as He did Ely and his two sons under the law, and the whole priesthood after Jesus Christ."

Such was Knox's ideal of the office of a bishop or minister of the word of God, and we may be sure he did his utmost to realize it in his own person. For his soul was all on fire to resume the work which he had thus so recently described. In a prefatory epistle to the treatise just named, he exclaims, "O, blessed be thou, Eternal Father! which by thy only mercy hast preserved us to this day, and provided that the confession of our faith, which ever we desired all men to have known, should by this treatise come plainly to light. Continue, O Lord, and grant unto us that as now with pen and ink so shortly we may confess with voice and tongue the same before thy congregation; upon whom look, O Lord God, with the eyes of thy mercy; and suffer no more darkness to prevail." By a wonderful dispensation of Providence he now found himself, so "shortly" after he had uttered that prayer "an ambassador" no longer "in bonds"—free "with voice and tongue" to publish his confession before the congregation of God in England, under the sanction and protection of the rulers of the realm—the heads both of Church and State.

And what was the substance of this confession? What was his understanding of the "true Evangell of Jesus Christ" of which he spoke so warmly, and which he was now to preach again under auspices so favourable? We have only to look into the same treatise, in order to see that his "Confession of Faith" was identical with that of Luther, and Zwingli, and Calvin on the great articles of Justification and Good Works. It is a distinctively Reformation Confession. It is one of the purest expositions and ablest defences of Protestant doctrine ever written, and well worthy of careful study in our own time, when in many quarters reformation truth—the only true rendering of apostolic teaching—is so much decried. It was the work of Balnaves, and in Knox's judgment was "godly and perfite." He accepted it as his own confession, and arranged it for the press with chapters, annotations, preface, and summaries; and a few sentences taken from these summaries, written by the Reformer's own pen, may be given as a specimen of the whole:—

"The Faith of the Fathers, before Christ's coming in the flesh, and ours in the New Testament, was and is one thing. For they believed them to stand in the favour of God, by reason of that promised Seed which was to come, who, we believe, is come already, and hath fulfilled all which was spoken of him in the Law and the Prophets. By this Faith were the Fathers made safe, without all their works; and when our adversaries ask, What availed works? we answer that works are an outward testimony to faith, by which only man is first made just, and thereafter his works please God, because the person is acceptable. And so no godly man forbiddeth good works, but of necessity must they be excluded from the Justification of man. For Paul saith, If righteousness be of the Law, Christ's death is in vain. . . . The glory of works is excluded by the law of Faith. For in our Justification we only receive, as did our father Abraham (whose sons we are by faith), who was reckoned just before he wrought any good works. The verity of the Scripture proveth that the heritage cometh not by the law; for by the law Ishmael and Esau, the eldest sons, should have succeeded to the heritage, and not Isaac and Jacob, which were younger. And so by the promise cometh the heritage, and not by the law; for the law ever accuseth, and craveth more of us than we are able to pay; and therefore damnation abideth us, without we apprehend Jesus Christ, which payeth for us that which the law requireth. For he alone taketh away the sins of the world. He called all to himself, and sendeth none to the law to seek Justification. And, therefore, who seek any part therof by their works, spoile Christ of his office. . . . .

"After the Article of Justification, Christians should be instructed to do good works—not those which are invented by man, but which are commanded by God. . . . As the good tree beareth good fruits, so the just man worketh good works; but neither maketh the fruit the tree good, nor yet the works the man just;

for as the tree is before the fruit, so the man is just before the work be good. We should work good works because we, being sometime the sons of God's wrath, and subjects to Satan, are bought by the blood of Jesus Christ to serve in his kingdom—in the which rule faith, hope, and charity, ever working righteousness unto life. And so we owe obedience to Him whose servants we are. . . . After man is made just by faith, and possesseth Jesus Christ in his heart, then can he not be idle. For with true Faith is also given the Holy Spirit, which suffereth not man to be idle, but moveth him to all godly exercise of good works. The life of man is a perpetual battle upon earth, the law of the members ever warring against the law of the mind. The law of the mind, or of the Spirit, is the motion of the Holy Ghost stirring us up to all justice and righteousness—which we know to be good, and yet find no power in ourselves to perform the same. And this battle is most vehement in the most holy, as witnesseth Paul; and, therefore, to kill this outward man, which is our wit, reason, and will, we should offer our bodies (persons) unto God, in a quick, lively, and holy sacrifice. But before this sacrifice be pleasing to God, must the mind (which is the fountain of all good works) be renewed with the Spirit of God and made clean; which is when we cast from us our own wisdom, righteousness, holiness, and redemption, and receive the same from Jesus Christ."

Such was the wholesome Bible doctrine which sounded out from Knox's pulpit in Berwick, and the echoes of which soon began to be heard in all the country round. And as to the style and tone of his speech and delivery, we can easily judge from the specimens of his "vehemency of spirit" which we have already had before us. It can best be described and characterized as the martial or do-battle style of pulpit oratory—full of polemic fire, full of heroic courage. When the white-and-green-coated soldiers of King Edward[*] crowded to hear him in the old parish church, they heard, for the first time, a "Gospeller" who was as much "a good soldier" as the best of them—a redoubted man of war, who feared not the face of man—a warrior "clothed in the whole armour of God," and a

---

[*] In a curious document of that date preserved among the State Papers of Edward VI., and intituled "Statutes of Berwick," there is a Statute relating to this uniform, from which it appears that the soldier's "coat" at that period was of these colours—white, edged with green. "Coat money" is frequently mentioned as one of the allowances made at enlistment.

master of all his weapons—a preacher who seemed to have a special call to be an Evangelist to soldiers—for the language he liked best, and the figures of speech he made most use of, were those of soldiership and of battle.

We can imagine him repeating here, to that congregation of combatants the same martially oratorical harangue which he had only a few months before sent across the German Ocean from France to his old fellow-soldiers of Christ in Scotland : " I pray you pardon me, beloved brethren, that in this manner I thus digresse. Vehemency of spirit compelleth me thereto. The head of Satan shall be trodden down when he believeth surely to triumph. Therefore, most dear brethren (so call I all professing Christ's Evangell), continue in that purpose which ye have begun godly. Though the battle appear strong, your Captain is inexpugnable—to Him is given all power in heaven and earth. Abide, stand, and call for his support ; and so the enemies which now affray you shortly shall be confounded, and never again shall appear to molest you. . . . . Consider, brethren, it is no speculative Theologue which desireth to give you courage, but even your brother in affliction, which partly hath experience what Satan's wrath may do against the chosen of God. Rejoice yet, I say, spiritually, and be glad. The time of the battle is short, but the reward is eternal—victory is sure, without ye list to fly from Christ, which God forbid ! "

All that was necessary to enable a preacher who had such a Gospel to deliver, and who was in the habit of delivering it with such extraordinary power, to produce a deep and palpable impression upon his flock, was that he should not at once be silenced and driven away by those who had an interest in opposing his doctrine and his aims. But Knox came to Berwick under the appointment and protection of the King's Government. He was King Edward's commissioned agent as truly as any of the officers of the royal troops, and no resistance was offered to his continuance in the pulpit. He continued in Berwick for two years, with only a short interruption, when he was called to Newcastle in 1550 to give an account of his doctrine before the Council of the North; and the religious and moral effects of his ministry were of the most marked description. His biographer has recorded them in the following terms :—

"He had long thirsted for the opportunity which he now enjoyed. His love for the truth and his zeal against Popery had been inflamed during his captivity, and he spared neither time nor labour in the instruction of those to whom he was sent. Regarding the worship of the Church of Rome as idolatrous, and its doctrines as damnable, he attacked both with the utmost fervour, and exerted himself in drawing his hearers from the belief of the one and from the observance of the other, with as much eagerness as if he had been saving their lives from a devouring flame or flood. Nor were his efforts fruitless. During the two years that he continued in Berwick, numbers were converted by his ministry from ignorance and the errors of Popery; and a visible reformation of manners was produced upon the soldiers of the garrison."

What was the ordinary strain and style of Knox's ministry in Berwick we may gather with much probability from his "Declaration of the true Nature and Object of Prayer," a short tract, which, like several other of his smaller pieces, has all the appearance of having been preached in substance to his stated congregation, and which would seem, from several allusions contained in it to historical incidents whose dates are well known, to have been sent to the press either in 1549 or 1550, while the author was still in Berwick. The earliest edition, it is true, of which any copy has been preserved to our own time is that of 1554; but if the tract had been first prepared for that edition, the allusions referred to would have been quite inapposite and out of date—a circumstance which suggests that that edition of it was not the first, and was only a reprint designed to make the tract more extensively known, as its first circulation, before Knox's name had become famous, was probably confined to the border counties—a suggestion which is somewhat strengthened by the fact that, when it appeared in 1554, it was printed along with another of Knox's writings, his "Godly Letter to the Faithful," which is full of historical references to the latest events in the reign of Edward VI., and to the earliest incidents of that of Mary, his successor. A comparison of the two writings, in their whole tone and bearings, makes it plain that they could not both have sprung out of the same conditions of the Church and kingdom. It seems certain that the only date appropriate to the tract on Prayer is one or other of the two years already mentioned, for it was in the latter half of 1549 that the "intestine battle and domestical murder" referred to in the last paragraph of the piece as "*present signs* of God's wrath" took place, the reference being to the rebellions which broke out in that year in the western and eastern counties of the kingdom.

Assuming, as we safely may, that the substance of this Tract was delivered from Knox's pulpit in Berwick, it presents us with a very pleasing specimen of his average manner as a preacher, and of the instructive, edifying, and animated character of his ordinary ministration. It is entitled "A Declaration what true Prayer is; how we should pray, and for what we should pray, set forth by John Knox, preacher of God's Holy Word," and is arranged in a lucid series of "Observations," all expressed and illustrated in simple and perspicuous language, which frequently, however, rises into passages of genuine, inartificial eloquence. We limit ourselves to a few of the most interesting paragraphs, selecting them either for the way in which he illustrates his subject by his own life-experience, or as showing the manner in which he was in the habit of dealing, as a pastor " wise to win souls," with the superstitions to which many of his hearers were still clinging :—

"The Fourth Rule necessary to be followed in prayer is a *sure hope to obtain what we ask.* For nothing more offendeth God that that we ask doubting whether he will grant our petitions; for in so doing we doubt if God be true, if he be mighty and good. Such, sayeth James, obtene nothing of God. And therefore Jesus Christ commandeth that we firmly believe to obtene whatsoever we ask, for all things are possible to him that believeth. And therefore in our prayers always is to be expelled desperation. I mean not that any man in extremity of trouble can be without a present dolour, and without a greater fear of trouble to follow. Trouble and fear are very spurs to prayer; for when we are compassed about with vehement calamities, and, vexed with continual solicitude, having by help of man no hope of deliverance, with sore oppressed and punished heart, fearing also greater punishment to follow, from the deep pit of tribulation we call to God for comfort and support, such prayer ascendeth into God's presence and returneth not in vain. As David, in the vehement persecution of Saul, huntit and chasit from every hold, fearing that one day or other he should fall into the hands of his persecutors, after he had complained that no place of rest was left to him, vehemently prayed, saying, O Lord, whilk art my God, in whom I only trust, save me from them that persecute me, and deliver me from my enemies; let not this man (meaning Saul) devour my life as a lion doth his prey, for of none seek I comfort but of thee alone." In the midst of these anguishes the goodness of God sustained him, so that the present tribulation was tolerable, and the infallible promises of God so assured him of deliverance that fear was partly mitigate and gone, as plainly appeareth to such as diligently marketh the process of his prayers; for after long menacing and threatening made to him of his enemy, he concludeth with these words: "The dolour which he intended for me shall fall upon his own pate, and the violence wherewith he would have oppressit me shall cast down his own head. But I will magnify the Lord according to his justice, and shall praise the name of the Most Highest." This is not written for David only, but for all such as shall suffer tribulation to the end of the world. For I (let this be said to the laud and praise of God alone), in anguish of mind and vehement tribulation and affliction, called to the Lord not only when the ungodly, but even my faithful brethren, yea and my own self, that is, all natural understanding, judgit my cause to be irremediable. And yet, in my greatest calamity, and when my pains were most cruel, would the eternal wisdom that my hands should write far contrary to the judgment of carnal reason, that whilk his mercy hath proved true. Blessed be his holy name! And therefore dare I be bold, in the verity of God's word, to promise that, notwithstanding the vehemency of trouble, the long continuance thereof, the desperation of all men, the fearfulness, danger, dolour, and anguish of our own hearts, yet if we call constantly to God that beyond expectation of all men he shall deliver."

In these last sentences there is a plain allusion, as Dr. Laing remarks, "to his bodily and mental sufferings during the time of his confinement on board the French galley," and to the hope which he had by implication expressed in his "Epistle to the Congregation of the Castle of St. Andrews," before referred to, when he uttered that fervent prayer of thanksgiving and supplication which we have already quoted.

"The Fifth Observation which godly prayer requireth is *perfect knowledge of the Advocate, Intercessor, and Mediator.* For seeing no man is of himself worthy to compear or appear in God's presence, by reason that in all men continually resteth sin, whilk by itself doth offend the Majesty of God, raising all debate, strife, hatred, and division betwixt his inviolable justice and us. For the whilk, unless satisfaction be made by another than by ourselves, so little hope resteth that any thing from him we can obtain that no surety with him may we have at all. To exeme [deliver] us from this horrible confusion, our most merciful Father hath given unto us his only belovit Son to be unto us justice, wisdom, sanctification, and holiness. If in Him we faithfully believe, we are so clad that we may with boldness compear and appear before the throne of God's mercy, doubting nothing that whatsoever we ask by our Mediator that same we shall obtain most assuredly.

"Against such as depend upon the Intercession of Saints, no other ways will I contend, but shortly touch the properties of a perfect mediator. First are the words most sure of Paul, 'A mediator is not the mediator of one'—that is, wheresoever is required a mediator there are also two parties, to wit, one party offendant, and the other party which is offendit, whilk parties by themselves may in no wise be reconcilit. Secondly, the mediator which taketh upon him the reconciling of these two parties must be such an one as, having trust and favour of both parties, yet in some things must differ from both, and must be clear and innocent also of the crime committit against the party offendit. . . . . Who, then, shall here be found the Peace-Maker? Surely the infinite goodness and mercy of God might not suffer the perpetual loss and repudiation of his creatures, and therefore his eternal wisdom provided such a Mediator having wherewith to satisfy the justice of God—differing also from the Godhead—his only Son, clad in the nature of manhood, who interponit himself a Mediator. And not as man only; for the pure humanity of Christ, of itself, might neither make intercession nor satisfaction for us—but God and man. In that He is God He might complete the will of his Father; and in that He is man, pure and clean, without spot or sin, He might offer sacrifice for the purgation of our sins and satisfaction of God's justice. So without saints have these two—Godhead equal with the Father, and humanity without sin—the office of mediators saints may not usurp. . . . .

"But in so great light of the Gospel whilk now is beginning (praise be to the Omnipotent!), it is not necessary upon such matter long to remain. Some say, We will use but one Mediator Jesus Christ to God the Father, but we must have saints, and chiefly the Virgin Mary, the mother of Jesus Christ, to pray for us to Him. Alas! whosoever is so minded sheweth plainly themselves to know nothing of Jesus Christ rightly. Is He who descended from heaven, and vouchsafed to be conversant with sinners, commanding all sore vexit and sick to come unto Him (who, hanging upon the Cross, prayed first for his enemies), become now so untractable that he will not hear us without a person to be a mean? O Lord! open the eyes of such, that they may clearly perceive thy infinite kindness, gentleness, and love toward mankind!!

"*Where*, for *whom*, and at *what time* we ought to pray, is not to be passed over in silence.

"Private prayer, such as men secretly offer to God by themselves, requires no special place; although that Jesus Christ commandeth when we pray to enter into our chamber, and to close the door, and so to pray secretly unto our Father. Whereby he would that we should choose to our prayers such places as might offer least occasion to call us back from prayer, and also that we should expel forth of our minds, at time of our prayer, all vain cogitations. For, otherwise, Jesus Christ himself doth observe no special place of prayer, for we find him sometime pray on Mount Olivet; sometime in the desert; sometimes in the Temple, and in the Garden. And Peter coveteth to pray up on the top of the house. Paul prayed in prison, and was heard of God; who also commandeth men to pray in all places, lifting up unto God clean and pure hands, as we find that the Prophets and most holy men did, whensoever danger or necessity required.

"But public and common prayers should be used in places appointed for the assembly, from whence whosoever negligently extracteth themselves are in nowise excusable. I mean not that to absent from that place is sin because that place is more holy than another, for the haill earth created by God is equally holy. But the promise made that 'Wheresoever two or three be gathered together in my name, there shall I be in the middis of them,' condemneth all such as contemneth the congregation gathered in his name. But mark well the word 'gathered;' I mean not to hear piping, singing, or playing, nor to patter upon beads or books whereof they have no understanding; nor to commit idolatry, honouring that for God which is no God indeed. For with such will I neither join myself in common prayer, nor in receiving external sacraments; for, in so doing, I should affirm their superstition and abominable idolatry, whilk I, by God's grace, never will do, neither counsel other to do, to the end. This congregation whilk I mean should be gathered in the name of Jesus Christ—that is, to laud and magnify God the Father for the infinite benefits they have received by his only Son our Lord. In this congregation should be distributed the mystical and last Supper of Jesus Christ, without superstition, or any more ceremonies than He Himself used and his Apostles after Him. And, in distribution thereof in this congregation, should inquisition be made of the poor among them, and support provided until the time of their next convention, and it should be distributed amongst them. Also, in this congregation, should be made common prayers, such as all men hearing might understand, that the hearts of all, subscribing to the voice of one, might, with unfeigned and fervent mind, say Amen. Whosoever doth withdraw himself from such congregation (but, alas! where shall it be found?) do declare themselves to be no members of Christ's body.

"Now there remaineth for *whom* and at what *time* we should pray? For all men, and at all times, doth Paul command that we should pray. And principally for such of the household of faith as suffer persecution, and for commonwealths tyrannously oppressed, incessantly should we call that God, of his mercy and power, will withstand the violence of such tyrants. And when we see the plagues of God—as hunger, pestilence, or war coming, or appearing to reign, then should we, with lamentable voices and repenting hearts, call unto God, that it would please his infinite mercy to withdraw his hand; whilk thing, if we do unfeignedly, He will, without doubt, revoke his wrath, and in the midst of his fury think upon mercy, as we are taught in the Scripture by his infallible and eternal verities. As in Exodus, God saith, 'I shall destroy this nation from the face of the earth;' and when Moses addressit himself to pray for them, the Lord proceedeth, saying 'Suffer me that I may utterly destroy them.' And then Moses falleth down upon his face, and forty days continued in prayer for the safety of the people, for whom, at the last, he obtained forgiveness. David, in the vehement plague, lamentably callit unto God. And the King of Nineveh sayeth, 'Who can tell? God may turn and repent, and cease from his fierce wrath, that we perish not.' Whilk examples and Scriptures are not written in vain, but to certify us that God of his own native goodness, will mitigate the plagues (by our prayers offerit by Jesus Christ), although He hath threatened to punish or presently doth punish—whilk he doth testfy by his own words, saying, 'If I have prophesied against any nation or people that they shall be destroyit, if they repent of their iniquity it shall repent me of the evil whilk I have spoken against them.' This I speak, lamenting the great coldness of men, whilk, under so long scourges of God, are nothing kindled to pray by repentance, but carelessly sleepeth in a wicked life; even as though the continual wars, urgent famine, and quotidian [daily] plagues of pestilence, and other contagious, insolent [unusual] and strange maladies were not the present signs of God's wrath, provokit by our iniquities.

"O, England! let thy intestine battle and domestical murder provoke thee to purity of life, according to the word whilk openly hath been proclaimed in thee; otherwise, the cup of the Lord's wrath thou shalt drink. The multitude shall not escape, but shall drink the dregs, and have the cup broken upon their heads. For judgment beginneth in the house of the Lord, and commonly the least offender is first punished, to provoke the more wicked to repentance. But, O Lord, infinite in mercy, if thou shalt punish, make not consummation, but cut away the proud and luxuriant branches whilk bear no fruit, and preserve the commonwealth of such as give succour and harbour to thy contemned messengers, whilk long have suffered exile in desert. And let thy kingdom shortly come—that sin may be endit, death devourit, thy enemies confoundit; that we thy people, by thy Majesty delivered, may obtain everlasting joy and felicity, through Jesus Christ our Saviour, to whom be all honour and praise for ever.—Amen. Haisten, Lord, and tarie not."*

Strange as it may appear, Knox was left entirely to his own discretion, all the time he was in Berwick, as to his mode of conducting divine service and administering the sacraments. The first Book of Common Prayer, authorized by the Parliament of Edward VI., had not yet been introduced into the northern counties. Cuthbert Tunstall, bishop of the diocese, was no friend to the reforms of that reign; and the Council of the North, which might have disregarded his hostility, and insisted upon the introduction of the Book, conformably to law, had deemed it more prudent and politic to postpone that step till the preaching of

* "Knox's Works," vol. iii. pp. 83-105.

Reformation-truth had prepared the people of a long-neglected province to accept so great a change. When Knox, therefore, commenced his work in Berwick, he found the Reformation there no farther advanced than it had been in Henry VIII.'s time. The laws enacted in the late king's reign to regulate the services of the Church were no longer in force, and the new statutes of his successor on the same subject had not yet been carried out. He was thus left at full liberty to publish to the congregation his own views of what constituted purity of worship and sacramental adminstration; and, after gaining their assent to these views, to give effect to them in his liturgical practice.

All this is clear from the "Epistle to the Congregation of Berwick," which the reader will find in the second part of this volume, and which is now for the first time laid under contribution to the history of the Reformer's work in England. In the following sentences of the epistle Knox recalls the order of sacramental service which he had used among that people, and the circumstances in which they had accepted and followed the order:—

"In ceremonies and rites which I used in ministration of Christ's Sacraments, as I did observe the precepts and practice of Christ and his Apostles so nigh as the Holy Ghost did open unto me, so this day do I nothing repent of my enterprize and of your obedience; beseeching God, for Christ his Son's sake, that so the hearts of magistrates may be inclined to mercy, that what the empire of God's most sacred word did work in your hearts, without precept or law appointed by man, be not now hindered and pulled back again by rigour of law." He evidently wrote these words at a time—it was late in 1552—when it was in contemplation to enforce the rubrics of the Book of Common Prayer in the North as they had never been before, and it is to this previous immunity from liturgical control that he refers in another part of the epistle, in these words : " If ye shall be compelled by rigour of a law to alter that order, which of God's assured truth ye have learned and received, ye shall not damn yourselves as transgressors of any law, or violators of any common order, for that which before ye have godly used. For when ye followed and received Christ's simple institution—sitting at the table—there was no law (except the statute of that Roman Antichrist whom Christ Jesus shall confound, and all the maintainers of his abominations and idolatry contrair your faith); and therefore did ye not transgress, for where no law is there can be no transgression. And if now, by especial commandment of your upper powers, ye shall be compelled to observe the common order, God forbid that ye shall be damned or judged as shrinking from Christ," &c.

In another passage he refers to what had been his sacramental practice at Berwick in the following precise terms :—

"Kneeling at the Lord's Supper I have proved by my doctrine to be no convenient gesture for a table [a gesture], which hath been given in that action to such a presence of Christ as no place of God's Scripture doth teach unto us. And therefore kneeling in that action appearing to be joined with certain dangers, no less in maintaining superstition than in using Christ's holy institution with other gestures than either he used or commanded to be used, I thought good amongst you to avoid, and to use sitting at the Lord's Table, which ye did not refuse, but with all reverence and thanksgiving to God for his truth, knowing (as I suppose) ye confirmed the doctrine [teaching] with your gestures and confession."

Here, then, was the very beginning of Puritan practice in the Church of England in the administration of the Lord's Supper.

In both the formularies recently set forth—the "Order of Communion," in 1548—and the "Book of Common Prayer and Administration of the Sacraments," in 1549—the practice of kneeling in the Lord's Supper had been retained, along with the use of the same form of bread—the wafer form—which "heretofore hath been accustomed." But the practice of Knox in Berwick not only substituted common bread for "wafer-breads," thus anticipating by several years the same substitution as authorized by Edward's second Prayer-book, published in 1552, but gave the first example of the substitution of sitting instead of kneeling, in the act of communion, which has ever since continued to be a characteristic Puritan practice.

The reader will find in the second part of this volume a Paper, which remains as an interesting memorial of this feature of Knox's ministry in Berwick. It is entitled "The Practice of the Lord's Supper used in Berwick-upon-Tweed, by John Knox, Preacher to that Congregation in the Church there." Unfortunately it is only a fragment, and does not contain the most essential portion of his "Practice;" still it is of deep interest, so far as it goes, for it preserves the forms of prayer which Knox was accustomed to make use of in his administration of the

Sacrament—which have no resemblance whatever to those which were introduced into King Edward's "Order of the Communion," although it cannot be doubted that Knox had that "Order" in his hands. But he had a decided preference for a form of administration which he had made use of several years before in the Castle of St. Andrew's. And his "Practice," then in 1547, and now in 1549, is of equal interest to both countries, as the characteristic Puritan "Order" first introduced into both by Knox has continued in both down to the present day.

Nor was this beginning of Puritan worship slow to be followed up in England, even at that early date. We shall hear of it immediately as being introduced into Newcastle; and there is a remarkable passage in Becon's "Displaying of the Popish Mass," written in the days of Queen Mary, which makes it certain that in London itself, where Becon resided, it was no uncommon thing in King Edward's reign for the most zealous worshippers to receive the Communion in the sitting posture.

"O how oft have I seen, here in England, at the ministration of the Holy Communion, *people sitting at the Lord's table* after they have heard the sermon, or the godly exhortation set forth in the Book of Common Prayer read unto them by the minister, bitterly weep, heartily repent, and sorrowfully lament their too much unkindness and unthankfulness towards the Lord God for the death of his Son, Christ, and for his other benefits; again their negligence in doing their duty towards their poor neighbours! What free and large gifts also have I seen given to the poor men's box! What laying aside of all enmity, and renewing of unfeigned mutual reconciliation! . . . . What godliness also of life have I seen afterwards practised by them that were the communicants! What alteration of manners! what newness of conversation! . . . . by hearing the word of God preached, and by the worthy receiving of the Holy Communion, hath full oft been seen in England, when the doctrine of the Gospel flourished among us!"*

There is also a significant entry in Strype's Life of Parker (p. 25), which shows that the issue of Edward's first Prayer-book had not been followed by a universal compliance with the sacramental order therein enjoined :—

* Prayers and other Pieces of Thomas Becon, S.T.P., Chaplain to Archbishop Cranmer, Prebendary of Canterbury. Edited for the Parker Society, 1844, p. 256.

"Many also there were that administered the Sacraments in other manners than was prescribed by the Book of Common Prayer lately set forth by public authority. For the prevention of the spreading of these people, a commission was issued out in the month of January, 1550, to one-and-thirty persons, empowering them to correct and punish these men—five bishops, and divers other Protestant and learned men at Court."

"Sitting at the Lord's table," indeed, is not mentioned here as one of the non-conforming practices complained of, but in view both of Knox's and Becon's testimony, it was no doubt included among the rest; and Knox, when in London early in 1549, may even have seen it in use in some of the churches. But, so far as appears, his name is as yet the only one which can be distinctly associated with the introduction of this Helvetic form into the Anglican Church.

It is interesting to recall here the coincidence, which has already been suggested by the extracts given above from the letters of Hooper to Bullinger, that in the very same year that Knox the Puritan began his ministry at the northern extremity of the kingdom, Hooper the Puritan was commencing his in the capital. How much they resembled each other in their doctrine will appear by comparing what has just been quoted from Knox, with the following specimen of Hooper's preaching on the Book of Jonah before the King and his Court during Lent, in the following year, 1550. Limiting ourselves to his views on the right administration of the Sacraments, he spoke thus upon Baptism:—

"Baptism consisteth in two parts—the word and the element. The word is the preaching of the good and merciful promises of God's goodness, accepting us into his favour and grace for the merits of Christ; the which promises he briefly comprehended in these words: 'I baptize thee in the name of the Father, and of the Son, and of the Holy Ghost.' These words show the form of Baptism, and also that only men, reasonable creatures, should be baptized. So is condemned the gentilism and superstition that hath been used in the christening of bells. The matter and element of this Sacrament is pure water; whatsoever is added—oil, salt, cross, lights, and such other be the inventions of men; and better it were they were abolished than kept in the Church; for they obscure the simplicity and perfectness of Christ our Saviour's institution. I pray the King's Majesty and his most honourable

Council to prepare a ship, as soon as may be, to send them home again to their mother church, the bosom and breast of man."

On "The Form how to celebrate the Lord's Supper," Hooper is equally exacting for Scriptural simplicity, and an absolute return to Christ's own institution :—

"The outward preparation, the more simple it is, the better it is, and the nearer unto the institution of Christ and his Apostles. If the minister have bread, wine, a table, and a fair table-cloth, let him not be solicitous nor careful for the rest, seeing they be no things brought in by Christ, but by Popes; unto whom, if the King's Majesty and his honourable Council have good conscience, they must be restored again; and great shame it is for a noble king, emperor or magistrate, contrary unto God's word, to detain and keep from the devil or his minister any of their goods or treasure, as the candles, vestments, crosses, altars! For if they be kept in the Church as things indifferent, at length they will be maintained as things necessary. . . . . Thus should the perfection of Christ's institution be had in honour, . . . and nothing done in this Sacrament that had not God's word to bear it. But alas! God is accounted a fool; for men can use the Sacrament more religiously, devoutly, godly, and Christianly, than Christ, God's Son, as it appeareth. For his form and manner is put out, and man's device and wisdom is accepted for it."

The only difference between Hooper's Puritanism and Knox's was that Hooper was an Episcopalian Puritan, and accepted a bishopric, while Knox was a Presbyterian Puritan, and declined one; and thus they became the fathers and founders of the two chief varieties of Puritanism which emerged at the commencement of Elizabeth's reign, and the history of which forms so large a portion of its ecclesiastical annals. They were both, indeed, largely fitted to become ecclesiastical types and prototypes, for the description of Hooper drawn by Foxe the martyrologist would apply equally well to Knox. "Of body strong, his health whole and sound, his wit very pregnant, his invincible patience able to sustain whatsoever sinister fortune and adversity could do. In his doctrine he was earnest, in tongue eloquent, in the Scriptures perfect, in pains indefatigable. In his sermons, according to his accustomed manner, he corrected sin and sharply inveighed against the iniquity of the world and the corrupt abuse of the

Church."* And no less applicable to Knox than to Hooper was what the Papist Dr. Smith was compelled to say of Hooper's influence as a preacher, "that he was so admired by the people that they held him for a prophet."

It was an immense and astonishing success that Knox should have been able, in so short a time, to carry over the great bulk of his flock at Berwick from the practice of the Roman Mass to the observance of the Lord's Supper according to his own Puritan views. It is natural to inquire by what kinds of reasoning and appeal he could produce such a result in the course of less than twelve months; and, happily, we are in possession of one grand specimen of his logic and eloquence upon this theme, which was the great subject of controversy all over England in the years 1549, '50, and '51 ; the Convocation, the Universities, and the pulpits were all ringing with it. In April, 1550, Knox had to give, as we shall see in the next chapter, a public account of the doctrine which " he had constantly affirmed" in Berwick—" that the Mass was, and at all times had been, idolatry and abomination before God;" and there is one part of his "Vindication," uttered on that occasion, which we may here anticipate as the most popular part of it in point of style, and the most likely to have been a specimen of his manner of handling the subject in his pulpit at Berwick. It is the interesting and effective passage where he contrasts the Mass with the Lord's Supper, as follows :—

"Let no man intend to excuse the Masse with the pretext of the Lord's Supper. For now will I prove that thairwith it hath no congruence, but is express contrarie to it, and hath tackin the rememberance of the same out of mynd. And farther, it is blasphemous to the death of Jesus Chryst. First: Thai are contrarie in institutioun, for the Lord's Supper was instituted to be a perpetuall memorie of these benefittis whilk we have ressavit by Jesus Chryst, and by his death. And, first, we suld call to mynd in what estait we stude in the loynis of Adam, when that we all blasphemed the majestie of God in his face. Secondlie, that his owne incomprehensibill gudnes movit Him to love us maist wreachit and miserabill, yea, maist wickit and blasphemous ; and love most perfyte compellit Him to schow mercie. And mercie

* "Biographical Notice of Bishop Hooper," prefixed to his "Early Writings," p. 10.

pronouncit the sentence, whilk was that his only Sone suld pay the pryce of our redemptioun. Whilk thing, rychtlie callit to memorie in the present actioun of the Supper, culd not but move us to unfeaned thankisgeving unto God the Father, and to his onlye Sone, Jesus, who hath restorit us agane to libertie and lyfe; and this is it whilk Paule commandeth, saying: 'As oft as ye sall eat of this bread and drink of this cup, ye sall declair the Lordis death till He cum.' That is, ye sall laude, magnifie, and extoll the liberall kyndnes of God the Father, and the infinitt benefittis whilk ye have ressaveit by Chrystis death. But the Mass is instituted, as the plane wordis thairof and thair own lawis do witness, to be a sacrifice for the synnis of the quick and the dead; for doing of the whilk sacrifice God is bound not onlie to remit our synnis, but also to gif unto us whatever we will ask. And that sall testifie dyvers Massis celebratit for dyvers caussis; sum for peace in tyme of war; sum for raine, sum for fair weather; yea, and (allace, my hart abhorreth sic abominatioun!) sum for sickness of bestiall. Thay will say, thay severallie take prayeris for obteanyng sic thingis; and that is all whilk I desyre thay say; for the obteanyng sic vane triffellis destinat thay thair haill purpoise, and so prophane the Sacrament of Chrystis bodie and blude (yf that was any Sacrament which thai abused so) whilk suld never be usit but in memorie of Chrystis death. Then suld it not be useit to pray that the tuthe-acke be takin away from us; that oure oxen suld not tak the lowing ill, oure horse the spavin or farsye, and so of all maner diseasis for oure cattell. Yea, what was it whairfor ye wuld not say Mass, perversit preistis?

"But lat us hear more. The Supper of the Lord is the gift of Jesus Chryst, in whilk we suld laude the infinite mercie of God. The Masse is a sacrifice whilk we offer unto God, for doing whereof we alledge God suld love and commend us. "In the Supper of the Lord confes we ourselves redeamit from sin by the death and blud of Jesus Chryst onlie. In the Mass crave we remissioun of sinnes, yea, and whatsoever thing we list by working of that same work whilk we presentlie do ourself. And herein is the Mass blasphemous unto Chryst and his Passioun. For in so far as it offereth or permitteth remissioun of synnis, it imputeth imperfectioun upon Chryst and his sacrifice, affirmyng that all synnis were not remitted by his death, but that a great part are reservit to be purgeit by vertew and the value of the Masse; and also it is injurious unto Chryst Jesus, and not only speiking most falsely of Him, but also usurping to itself that whilk is proper to Him alone. For He affirmeth that He alone hath, by his own death, purged the synnis of the world, and that no part resteth to be changed by any other meanis. But the Masse singeth one other song, whilk is, that everie day, by that oblatioun offerit by the preistis, is sin purgeit and remission obteanit. Consider, Papistis, what honour your Masse giveth unto Chryst Jesus. Last, in the Supper of the Lord, we grant ourselves eternall dettouris to God, and unabill any way to mak satisfactioun for his infinit bennefittis whilk we have ressaveit. But in the Masse allege we God to be a dettour unto us, for oblatiouns of that sacrifice whilk we thair presentlie offer, and dar affirme that we thair mak satisfactioun by doing thairof for the synnis of ourself and of otheris. If these precedentis be not contrarie, lat men judge with indifferencie. . . .

· " They differ in use, for in the Lord's Supper the minister and congregatioun sat both at ane tabill, no difference betwix thame in pre-eminence nor habit as witnesseth Jesus Chryst with his discipillis, and the practise of the Apostillis after his death. But in the Papisticall Masse the preistis (so will thay be styllit) are placed by thameselves at ane altar. And I wold ask of the autoritie thairof, and what Scripture commandeth so to be done. Thay must be cled in a severall habit, whairof no mentioun is maid in the New Testament. It will not excuse thame to say, Paule commandit all to be done with ordour and decentlie. Dar thai be so bold as to affirme that the Supper of Jesus Chryst was done without ordour and undecentlie, whairin wer sene no suche disagysit vestamentis? Or will thai set up to us agane the Leviticall preisthood? Suld not all be taught by the plane word? . . .

" In the Supper of the Lord all were equallie participant, the bread being broken, and the cup being distributit amangis all, according to the holie commandement. In the Papisticall Mass the congregation get nothing except the beholding of your jukingis, noddingis, crossingis, turnyng, uplifting, whilk ar nothing but a diabolicall prophanation of Chrystis Supper. Now juke, cross, and nod as ye list, thai ar but your own inventionis. And finallie, brethrene, ye gat nothing but gaseit and beheld while that one did eat and drink all.

"It sall not excuse you to say, the congregatioun is participant spirituallie. O wickit Antichrystis! sayeth not Jesus Chryst, 'Eat of this, and drink of this, all do this in rememberance of me?' Chryst commandeth not that we suld gase upon it, bow, juke, and beck thaireto, but that we suld eat and drink thairof ourselves, and not that we suld behold utheris do the same, unless we wold confes the death of Jesus Chryst to apertaine nothing to us. . . . For when I eat and drink at that tabill, I opinlie confes the frute and vertew of Chrystis bodie, of his blude and passion, to aperteane to myself; and that I am a member of his mistical bodie and that God the Father is appeasit with me, notwithstanding my first corruptioun and present infirmities.

"Judge, brethrene, what comfort hath this takin frome us, whilk will that the sycht thairof sal be sufficient. I wold ask, first, yf the sycht of corporall meat or drink doeth feid or nurische the bodie? I think thai will say, Nay. And I affirme that na mair profit receaveth the soule in beholding ane other eat and drink the Lord's verie Supper (as for thair idolatrie, it is alwayis dampnable) than the bodie doeth in beholding ane other eate and drink, and thair receaving no part thairof."

During Knox's two years' ministry in Berwick his congregation was in a continual flux from the movement of troops. The war went on throughout the whole of 1549, and continued during some part of 1550; and when peace was proclaimed, towards midsummer of that year, great changes took place in the garrison. The advanced bodies of troops which had been stationed in Haddington and in the fort of Dunglass, half way between Haddington and Berwick, were marched back to the latter; and, in the autumn, many of the captains who had been engaged in the defence of Boulogne against the French were transferred, after the peace with France, along with 600 men, to the English borders; 200 of whom were sent into Berwick to labour upon the repair and enlargement of the fortifications. Knox must therefore have had, in the latter half of 1550, a very different congregation from what had listened to his rousing preaching in 1549. His range of usefulness was thus much enlarged, and many hundreds of fresh soldiers had the opportunity of listening to his faithful expositions of the Gospel of Jesus Christ, before he finally left the bustling town and castle. But before following him to Newcastle, late in the year, it is of some importance to mention an incident of his private life, of which Berwick was the scene, and which exercised a material influence not only upon his future domestic condition, but also upon the development of his Christian character and experience, and the spirit and power of his ministry.

"During Knox's ministrations at Berwick and Newcastle, he became acquainted," says Dr. Laing, "with the family of Bowes. Sir Ralph Bowes, of Streatham, had three sons, the eldest of whom, George, was knighted on the field of Flodden, in 1513. His third son, in 1550, is styled Richard Bowes of Aske, Captain of Norham Castle. He married Elizabeth, daughter and co-heir of Sir Roger Aske, of Aske, in Yorkshire, by whom he had two sons and several daughters." The second son of Sir Ralph was Sir Robert Bowes, who took a prominent part in the war with Scotland above referred to, and in 1550–51 was Acting Warden General of the North, under Dudley, the powerful Earl of Warwick, the same ambitious statesman who soon after was made Duke of Northumberland.

While Richard Bowes of Aske was Captain of Norham Castle, his lady and family resided either there or a few miles off, in Berwick. Mrs. Bowes was a lady of deep-toned piety, and had embraced Reformation truth some years before she heard Knox's preaching in 1549. His ministry instantly commended itself to her spiritual judgment, and she lost no time in making herself known to him, and introducing him to her family. This was the beginning of what he describes as a "great familiarity and long acquaintance, the cause of which was neither flesh nor blood, but a troubled conscience upon her part which never suffered her to rest but when she was in the company of the faithful, of whom (from the first hearing of the word at my mouth) she judged me to be one."

Mrs. Bowes had long been a sufferer from the morbid condition of mind known as "religious melancholy," and her case, from the account of Knox, who afterwards became her son-in-law, and studied and ministered to what he called her "tentation" with the most tender attention and assiduity for many years, would appear to have been one of a very obstinate and peculiar character. In one of his latest writings, penned in 1572, only a few months before his death,[*] he says of it, with deep feeling, "In Scotland, England, France, and Germany, I have heard the complaints of divers that

[*] "Knox's Works," vol. vi. p. 513.

feared God; but of the like conflict as she sustained, from the time of her first acquaintance and long before (as her own mouth oftener than once confessed to me) till this hour I have not known. For her tentation was not in the flesh, nor for anything that appertained to flesh (no, not when she was in greatest desolation), but it was in spirit. For Satan did continually buffet her that remission of sins in Christ Jesus appertained nothing unto her, by reason of her former idolatry and other iniquities; for the which, notwithstanding any worldly comfort, I have seen her (not for a start, but in long continuance) pour forth tears, and send to God dolorous complaints, ofter than ever I heard man or woman in my life. Her company to me was comfortable, yea, honourable and profitable, for she was to me and mine a mother—but yet it was not without some cross; for besides trouble and fasherie of body, sustained for her, my mind was seldom quiet, for doing somewhat for the comfort of her troubled conscience, whereof this rude letter is the least, and of basest [feeblest] argument amongst many which lye beside me."*

Of Knox's numerous epistles to Mrs. Bowes, it will be useful to quote here a portion of that which stands first in the printed collection, and which was written in London in the summer of 1553. It is quoted to show in a very authentic form the important influence which his long familiarity with this afflicted lady exercised upon his own spiritual character and ministry.

"Right dearly beloved Mother in our Saviour Jesus Christ,—When I call to mind and revolve with myself the troubles and afflictions of God's elect from the beginning (in which I do not forget you), there are within my heart two extreme contraries—a dolour almost unspeakable, and a joy and comfort which by man's senses cannot be comprehended nor understood. The chief causes of dolour be two: the one is the remembrance of sin which I daily feel remaining in this corrupt nature, which was and is so odious and detestable in the presence of our Heavenly Father that by no other sacrifice could or might the same be purged, except by the blood and death of the only innocent Son of God. When I deeply do consider the cause of Christ's death to have been sin, and sin

---

* The letter referred to here is the second in the interesting collection of "Epistles to Mrs. Bowes and her Daughter Marjory," published for the first time by Dr. Laing in Knox's Works, vol. iii. p. 343; and again, with some variation, vol. vi. p. 515.

yet to dwell in all flesh, with Paul I am compelled to sob and groan as a man under a heavy burden—yea, sometimes to cry, ' O wretched and miserable man that I am, who shall deliver me from this body of sin ?'

"The other cause of my dolour is, that such as most gladly would remain together for mutual comfort, one of another, cannot be suffered so to do. Since the first day that it pleased the Providence of God to bring you and me in familiarity, I have always delighted in your company ; and when labours would permit, ye know I have not spared hours to talk and commune with you, the fruit whereof I did not then fully understand nor perceive. But now absent, and so absent that by corporal presence neither of us can receive comfort of other, I call to mind how that oftimes when with dolorous hearts we have begun our talking, God hath sent great comfort unto both, which now, for my own part, I commonly want. The exposition of your troubles and acknowledging of your infirmities were first unto me a very mirror and glass wherein I beheld myself so rightly painted forth that nothing could be more evident to my own eyes. And then the searching of the Scriptures for God's sweet promises, and for his mercies freely given unto miserable offenders (for his nature delighteth to show mercy where most misery reigneth), the collection and applying of God's mercies, I say, were unto me as the breaking and handling with my own hands of the most sweet and delectable ointments, whereof I could not but receive some comfort by their natural sweet odours."

Then follows another remarkable paragraph which must not be withheld from the reader, as it is a kind of counterpart to what has now been given, showing, as it does, in a very striking way, how faithfully this true, strong man learned to deal with his own heart ; while the above shows how tenderly he touched and ministered to the hearts of others. He is usually thought of as a man only rough and stern of mind and speech ; he is seldom thought or spoken of as a hero who could be as tender as he was stern, and as gentle of sympathy and speech as he could be rough ; but these two paragraphs taken together will make it manifest that he could be as gentle and delicate in his handling of bowed-down weakness as he could be severe and unsparing in his face-to-face duels with arrogant or wicked strength ; and that if he was outspoken and uncourtly in reproving, by the authority of God's holy word, the open and flagrant sins of others, he was no less plain-spoken and unsparing in characterizing the most inward and secret of his own :—

"Albeit I never lack the presence and plain image of my own wretched infirmity, yet, seeing sin so manifestly abound in all estates, I am compelled to thunder out the threatenings of God against obstinate rebellers ; in doing whereof (albeit as God knoweth I am no malicious or obstinate sinner) I sometimes am wounded, knowing myself criminal and guilty in many, yea in all things (malicious obstinacy laid aside) that in others I reprehend. Judge not, mother, that I write these things debasing myself otherwise than I am ; no! I am worse than my pen can express. In body ye think I am no adulterer—let so be ; but the heart is infected with foul lusts, and *will* lust, albeit I lament never so much. Externally I commit no idolatry, but my wicked heart loveth the self, and cannot be refrained from vain imaginations—yea, not from such as were the fountain of all idolatry. I am no man-killer with my hands, but I help not my needy brother so liberally as I may and ought. I steal not horse, money, nor clothes from my neighbour; but that small portion of worldly substance I bestow not so rightly as his holy law requireth. I bear no false witness against my neighbour in judgment or otherwise before men, but I speak not the truth of God so boldly as it becometh his true messenger to do. And thus, in conclusion, there is no vice repugning to God's holy will expressed in his law wherewith my heart is not infected.

"Thus much written and indited before the receipt of your letters, which I received the 21st of June. They were unto my heart some comfort, for divers causes not necessary to be rehearsed, but most (as knoweth God) for that I find a congruence betwixt us in spirit, being so far distant in body. For when that digestly I did avyse with [examine and weigh] your letter, I did consider that I myself was complaining even the selfsame thing, at that very instant moment that I received your letter. By my pen, from a sorrowful heart, I could not but burst forth and say, 'O Lord ! how wonderful are thy works ! How dost Thou try and prove thy chosen children as gold by the fire ! How canst Thou in manner hide thy face from thy own spouse, that thy presence after may be more delectable ! How canst Thou bring thy saints low, that Thou mayest carry them to glory everlasting! How canst Thou suffer thy strong, faithful messengers in many things yet to wrestle with wretched infirmity and feeble weakness; yea, and sometimes permittest Thou them horribly to fall, partly that no flesh shall have whereof it may glory before Thee, and partly that others of smaller estate and meaner gifts in Thy Kirk might receive some consolation, albeit they find in themselves wicked motions which they are not able to expel.'"

For much more in the same tender and sympathetic strain, the reader is referred to the letter itself.* Enough has been quoted to verify the suggestion that this familiarity of Knox with Mrs. Bowes of Aske both by conversation and correspondence, of which so many memorials remain, had, no doubt, a powerful influence upon his mind and ministry. It served to cultivate and bring out the softer elements of his richly-endowed nature, and to provide a needful counterpoise of humility and sympathy to his heroic strength and self-assertion in the great battle of his life. It helped him to remember, amidst all his long struggles for the external success and victory of the kingdom of God—the wrestlings of a giant with giants, of a Samson Agonistes with a host of Philistines—that this kingdom of God is an inward as well as, and still more than, an outward reign; that it is in the hearts of God's children, the weakest as well as the strongest, the most bowed down as well as the most erect; and that its best and choicest riches are righteousness, peace, and joy in the Holy Ghost. The upshot was, to express it in the terms of Samson's riddle, that "out of the eater came forth meat, and out of the strong came forth sweetness;" and but for the key supplied by this religious intimacy of the strong man with a godly woman grieved in spirit, we could not "in three days have expounded the riddle."

These letters of Knox to Mrs. Bowes and his other English friends—almost the only portions of his private correspondence which have come down to us—deserve special attention in the treatment of the English portion of his life. They show that if he did much for the religion of the English people, the religion of the English people also did much for him. If he did much to brace and invigorate and exalt theirs theirs also did much in return to soften and sweeten his, and to make it more inward and sympathizing; very much the same reciprocal service which still passes

* "Knox's Works," iii. pp. 337-43.

and repasses between Scottish and English piety in our own day. Nor do any of his writings contribute more than these "Familiar Epistles" to confirm and illustrate the character drawn of this 'priest-hero' by his hero-loving countryman, Thomas Carlyle, when, in his own characteristic manner, he exclaims, "They go far wrong who think this Knox was a gloomy, spasmodic, shrieking fanatic. Not at all; he is one of the solidest of men, a most shrewd, observing, quietly discerning man; an honest-hearted, brotherly man—brother to the high, brother also to the low, sincere in his sympathy with both. A cheery, social man, with faces that loved him. An ill nature he decidedly had not. Kind, honest affections dwelt in the much-enduring, hard-worn, ever-battling man. Close at hand, he was found to be no mean, acrid man, but at heart a healthful, strong, sagacious man."

It was in May, or June, 1551, that Knox left Berwick to occupy a larger and more influential sphere in Newcastle, and it is extremely probable that one of the latest incidents of his life in the Border Town was his becoming acquainted for the first time with a countryman of his own, for whom he conceived the highest esteem and value, and who was destined in after years to be associated with him very closely in winning for the reformation of the Church of Scotland its final and complete victory. This was "that notable Man," as he calls him, John Willock. It was to him among other divines that John ab Ulmis, a Swiss student in Oxford, referred in one of his letters to Bullinger, dated London (probably in March), 1551, in which he informs Bullinger that "the Marquis" (meaning the excellent Marquis of Dorset, Henry Grey, the father of Lady Jane Grey) "is gone into Scotland with three hundred cavalry, and some good preachers, with the view principally of faithfully instructing and enlightening in religion that part of the country which has been subdued during the last few years. I think of joining him there in a few weeks." In another letter, dated after his return from Berwick, he writes: "Willock is preaching the word of God with much labour on the borders of Scotland;" and that this was Knox's future colleague, appears from the writer's having previously referred to him as the domestic chaplain of the Marquis, a position which we know from other sources that John Willock continued to occupy down to the accession of Mary. John ab Ulmis carried with him into Scotland two copies of Bullinger's "Fifth Decade," which the author had dedicated to the Marquis at his correspondent's suggestion, one of these being for the nobleman, and the other for Willock. He reached Berwick on the 1st of May, and presented the book "to his lordship in a numerous assemblage of persons; for at that time many of the Scottish nobility, with the Bishop of Argyle and the Lord Maxwell, had resorted to him at Berwick, with the view of making peace between both the kingdoms. Believe me it was most acceptable to the Marquis, and long and anxiously expected by him. I understand it was much approved by all, especially by the Bishop of Norwich (Thirlby), a very learned Englishman, and on the most intimate terms with our Marquis."*

That was probably the first time that any part of Bullinger's celebrated work had reached the north side of the Tweed; and as the "Fifth Decade" treated largely of the Lord's Supper, in the pure and true Helvetic sense, it was a singular coincidence that it should have been brought with so much despatch to that very spot of soil, where the Helvetic rite had first been fully carried out by a preacher who, as the scholar of Wishart who was the scholar of Bullinger, was himself, by only a single remove, a disciple of Zwingli's disciple and successor. It is every way probable that both Knox and Willock formed part of the assemblage which met in Berwick on that interesting occasion of renewed peace and amity between the two British kingdoms, which were destined ere many years passed over to be more closely allied by the bonds of the Gospel than ever they had been

---

* It was significant of the growing influence of Helvetic doctrine and practice upon the English Reformation, that John ab Ulmis, a disciple of Zwingli and Bullinger, should have been a protegé, at Oxford, of the Marquis of Dorset, who was now one of the most powerful members of the Privy Council, and inferior to none of the King's Councillors in Reformation zeal, and that Dorset should have received so graciously the dedication and present of Bullinger's work. That volume of the "Decades" had probably more influence in determining the changes introduced into the communion office of the Second Prayer-book of Edward, and in settling some points of the doctrine of the "Forty-two Articles of 1553," than any other single work that can be named. Arriving in England in the spring of 1551, it was just in time to make its influence felt in preparing, along with other factors both domestic and foreign, the second great stage of Anglican Reform, which dates in 1552. For further illustrations, and proofs upon this point, see note at the end of the chapter.

by political or dynastic ties. The Scottish Reformation at this very time was beginning to recover from the depression which had followed Wishart's martyrdom and Beaton's assassination; and John ab Ulmis, who seems to have been an enlightened as well as inquisitive observer, sent to Rudolph Gualter, of Zurich, Bullinger's colleague, some results of his observations on the Borders, which, as being of much historical and curious interest, may be here subjoined for the entertainment of the reader:—

"Bullinger dedicated, at my request, the Fifth Decade of his Sermons to the Marquis of Dorset, and wished me to present it to him as soon as published.

"The Marquis had gone to Berwick, a Scotch town, a little before the copies arrived in England, wherefore I thought it best for me to hasten to the utmost extremity of Britain, both for the sake of presenting the book to the Marquis, and also from a desire of seeing Scotland. Nor, indeed, do I repent me of a journey now almost completed, for not only was my visit very gratifying to the Marquis, but in the meantime I acquired a knowledge of those things, an opportunity of observing which could scarcely be obtained for many years to come.

"There appears to be great firmness and no little religion among the people of Scotland; but in the chiefs of that nation one can see little else than cruelty and ignorance, for they resist and oppose the truth in every possible way. As to the Commonalty, however, it is the general opinion that greater numbers of them are rightly persuaded as to true religion than here among us in England. This seems to be a strange state of things, that among the English the ruling powers are virtuous and godly, but the people have for a long time been most contumacious; while in Scotland, on the contrary, the rulers are most ferocious, but the nation at large is virtuous, and exceedingly well disposed towards our most holy religion. I have no hesitation in writing this to you, for both what I say is true, and I perceive that this circumstance is frequently and seriously deplored by the English themselves.

"I saw, moreover, an island which they commonly call Holy Island. The land is of small extent, and surrounded by the sea, which they call the [German] ocean. It is not far from the town of Berwick, and abounds in all kinds of fish, and also in much gold. The inhabitants there are rightly instructed in religion, and obedient to all the laws and ordinances of the English. May the Almighty God, the Chief Governor of all things, grant that our life and actions may sometime correspond to the word and doctrine of his Son, which is at this time gloriously proclaimed both by land and sea. All persons are beginning to speak well about Christ; but there are yet very few who live agreeably to Christian principle. Farewell, most learned sir.*

"Bradgate, *May* 29, 1551."

* "Original Letters relative to the English Reformation," p. 434. (Parker Society.)—Bradgate, near Leicester, was the Seat of the Marquis of Dorset, and the home of Lady Jane Grey. It is interesting to think of John Willock, Knox's friend, as having been for several years the pastor and teacher of that pious, accomplished, and unfortunate lady. It was, no doubt, he who taught her in the first instance to think so highly of Bullinger, whose correspondent she became; for Willock too, like Knox, was a reformer of the Helvetic type. The only letter of his found among the Zurich collection was drawn from him by a kind reference made to him by Bullinger, in the dedication of the Fifth Decade to the Marquis of Dorset. "Your piety," said Bullinger to the Marquis, "needs none of my teaching, seeing that it is well enough instructed in true religion, and is surrounded with most learned and godly men on all sides, of whom Master Robert Skinner and Master John Willock, very excellent individuals, are none of the least." Whereupon Willock, in a letter of May 12, 1552, from Oxford, thus expresses his gratified feelings: " Health in Christ. I came over to Oxford on the 11th of May, which as soon as John ab Ulmis knew, he has never ceased asking me, most excellent sir, to send you a letter. I wrote you soon after Christmas, but knew not whether my letter ever reached you; I will, therefore, only at present briefly touch upon the heads of what I then wrote. First of all, everlasting thanks for the kindness by which you were induced to make such affectionate mention of me in your dedicatory preface to our Prince [The Marquis of Dorset, now Duke of Suffolk]. I have ever admired your universally acknowledged learning and erudition. The Prince certainly received that little present of yours with a most grateful and well-disposed mind; and you must know that you have not acted more honourably than usefully and piously; for, as Socrates says, the exhortations of great men are as a whip and spur to happy perseverance in a praiseworthy course of life. Every night, when we were employed on the Scottish borders, after the book had been received there from John ab Ulmis, with great difficulty on his part, his Highness was not satisfied with having a large portion of your book merely read to him, but would have it diligently examined, by which I perceived him, endued as he was with a most excellent disposition, greatly to improve; and, indeed, he very often expressed himself greatly obliged to you for it."

It is curious to read the above notice, coming to us from so unexpected a quarter, of the religious condition of so interesting a spot as Holy Island, where St. Aidan, nearly a thousand years before, had fixed the head-quarters of his renowned mission to the Saxon kingdom of Northumbria, and from which, as a holy centre, the Gospel of Jesus Christ, as it was understood and loved in the monastery of Iona, was radiated all round to the heathen subjects of good King Oswald.

If, as early as 1551, the Gospel had been restored to the island of St. Aidan and St. Cuthbert, it cannot be doubted that this was the work of John Knox. There was no other preacher in that remote corner of the kingdom to do it at so early a date but himself. Though located in Berwick, we know that he was an Evangelist to all the country round. He resumed and repeated, after many centuries of darkness and superstition, the work of the Columban missionaries; and if Aidan has been justly called the Apostle of Northumbria, the four years of incessant and devoted labour which Knox spent in carrying back the lost Gospel to the same interesting region, may well entitle him to the gratitude of all Protestant Northumbrians, as the second apostle of the English border.

Before the scene of our narrative changes to Newcastle, the following interesting paragraph must be added here from the pages of Knox's learned biographer:—

"Before he left Berwick, Knox had paid his addresses to Marjory Bowes, and met with a favourable reception. Her mother, also, was friendly to the match; but, owing to some reason, most probably the presumed aversion of her father, it was deemed prudent to delay solemnizing the union. But, having come under a formal promise to her ("faithful promise before witness," as he wrote himself), he considered himself from that time as sacredly bound, and, in his letters to Mrs. Bowes, always addressed that lady by the name of 'Mother.'"*

* M'Crie's "Knox," i. p. 89.

NOTE.—*On the Influence of Bullinger upon Archbishop Cranmer.*

In 1849, Mr. Gorham published "Extracts from the Writings of Martyr and Bullinger on the Effects of Baptism; in Illustration of the Doctrine held by the Church of England," in which pamphlet, at p. 5, he makes the following statement:—

"Henry Bullinger's views on the Sacraments produced a powerful influence on the mind of Cranmer, as well as of other English divines. It is a very remarkable and a most important fact (though unknown, with any distinctness, till my advocate, Dr. Bayford, produced the evidence in the Court of Arches), that, in 1551, Cranmer expressed his unqualified approbation of Bullinger's 'Tract on the Sacraments,' which was, by the Archbishop's earnest desire, published in England in a separate form by John-A-Lasco, contemporaneously with its appearance in the Fifth Decade of the eminent Zurich divine, although neither Cranmer nor John-A-Lasco was aware of the fact of its foreign publication till the tract had issued from the English press. The conclusion is inevitable that Cranmer's views on Baptism were not opposed to, but in principle consentient with, those of Bullinger."

In the preface to Dr. Cardwell's "Liturgies of Edward VI.," it is stated that when John-A-Lasco presented to Cranmer Bullinger's treatise, "De Sacramentis," the Archbishop desired it might be printed immediately, observing that "Nothing of Bullinger's required to be read and examined previously."

The authority upon which Mr. Gorham's and Dr. Cardwell's statements rest is a letter from John-A-Lasco to Bullinger, written from London on the 10th of April, 1551, which is included in the collection of A-Lasco's letters published by Gerdesius in his "Scrinium Antiquarium," vol. iv., part 2. The following is the passage referred to:—

"Libellus tuus de Sacramentis ante triennium ad me missus jam tandem sub prelo est. Ubi ad me cum reliqua bibliothecæ meae parte nuper advectus est, exhibui illum D Cantuariensi. Is vero ubi audisset nondum esse editum, voluit ut ederetur, etiamsi eum non legisset, hoc addens, Tua nulla egere inspectione. Itaque propediem exibit. Dicabo illum Sorori Regiæ, virgini et doctissimæ et pientissimæ, Elizabethæ. Mississem tibi aliquot exemplaria, si absolutus fuisset, sed hac hebdomade futura absolvetur."

The title of Bullinger's tract referred to was "Absoluta de Christi Domini et Catholicæ ejus Ecclesiæ Sacramentis Tractatio." The editor of the Parker Society's edition of the Decades (Rev. Thomas Harding) states that it was composed in the year 1546, and sent first to Calvin, who approved of it, and then to John-A-Lasco, and by him published at London, in April, 1551. The substance of this treatise was embodied by Bullinger in his Fifth Decade. It is remarkable that Cranmer should have expressed a desire for its publication in England before having read it. That could only have been because he was already acquainted with Bullinger's views of the Sacraments, and approved of them. It is to be remembered that the "Consensus Tigurinus," containing the Sacramental doctrine held equally by Bullinger and Calvin, had been published as early as 1549, of which Cranmer could not be ignorant; and, in fact, he had openly declared himself a convert to that doctrine in 1548-49, while the First Prayer-book of Edward was in preparation. This is clear from a letter of Traheron to Bullinger, dated London, December, 1548, in which he informs him that a disputation had been held at London concerning the Eucharist in the presence of almost all the nobility of England. "The argument was sharply contested by the bishops. The Archbishop of Canterbury, contrary to general expectation, most openly, firmly, and learnedly maintained your opinion on this subject. His arguments were as follows :—' The body of Christ was taken up from us into heaven. Christ has left the world. Ye have the poor always with you, but me ye have not always.' . . . The truth never obtained a more brilliant victory among us. I perceive it is all over with heathenism, now that those who were considered its principal and almost only supporters have altogether come over to our side." John ab Ulmis adds a postscript to Traheron's letter, in which he says : "The foolish bishops have made a marvellous recantation"—plainly referring to Cranmer and Ridley, who had hitherto been attached to the Lutheran doctrine of Consubstantiation and the ubiquity of the body of Christ. The influence of Bullinger, therefore, upon Cranmer and Ridley was of an earlier date than the publication of the Fifth Decade in 1551. But the wish of Cranmer, that the earlier tract, which was incorporated with that work, should be published in England without delay, was a proof not only of his own cordial acceptance of its Sacramental teaching, but also of his opinion that the work was well fitted to prepare the minds of English theologians for a more unequivocal confession of that doctrine in the Second Prayer-book of Edward VI., which was already in hand in 1551–52, than he had been able to obtain from the rest of the bishops and doctors of the Church in 1548–49.

CHAPTER II.

KNOX IN NEWCASTLE, 1551-53.

IN the early summer of 1551, Knox was transferred, no doubt by authority of the Privy Council, from Berwick to Newcastle-upon-Tyne, where he remained, with occasional absences in London and other parts of the kingdom, till the spring of 1553.

But this was not the first of his connection with Newcastle. In the spring of 1550 an incident had occurred to him there which was of great importance, not only to his personal status and usefulness, but to the interest of the Reformation throughout the whole northern province; and to this incident we must go back before proceeding to speak of his Newcastle ministry in 1551-52.

"The 4th of April, in the year 1550, was appointed to John Knox to give his Confession why he affirmed the Mass idolatry; which day, in presence of the Council and Congregation, amongst whom was also present the Bishop of Durham and his doctors, in this manner he beginneth."[*]

In explanation of this incident, Dr. M'Crie remarks that "although the town of Berwick was Knox's principal station during the years 1549 and 1550, it is probable that he was appointed to preach occasionally in the adjacent country. Whether in the course of his itinerancy he had preached in Newcastle, or whether he was called up to it in consequence of complaints against the sermons which he had delivered at Berwick, it is difficult to ascertain. It is, however, certain that a charge was exhibited against him before the Bishop (Tunstall), for teaching that the Sacrifice of the Mass was idolatrous, and that a day was appointed for him publicly to assign his reasons for this opinion." In a note the author adds that "Knox might owe to the Council of the North, and not to the Bishop, the liberty of this public

[*] Knox's Works, vol. iii. p. 33.—"A Vindication of the Doctrine that the Sacrifice of the Mass is Idolatry."

defence," and we quite concur with him in that opinion. However "disposed Tunstall might be to listen to the informations which were lodged against Knox by the clergy, he durst not inhibit him from preaching, as he was acting under the authority of the Protector and Privy Council;" and if the Bishop durst not inhibit him, as little would he have dared to summon him either before his own tribunal at Durham or before the Council at Newcastle. But it is every way probable that Tunstall had complained to the Council, of which he was a member, of the Reformer's proceedings, and that it was by command of the Council that Knox now appeared before them "to give his confession why he affirmed the Mass idolatry." The Council of the North was no ecclesiastical tribunal; it did not sit at Newcastle to pronounce judgment upon a charge of heresy, and in all probability it took action upon Tunstall's information and complaint in a very different sense and direction from what he wished and hoped. To summon the preacher before him merely "to give his *confession why*," without laying against him any charge or even complaint, was not the act of men who wanted to shut his mouth and put a stop to his ministry. It looks much more like the action of men who were not sorry to embrace such an opportunity of preparing the way for introducing into the northern counties the Reformed Liturgy, which was already in use in the rest of the kingdom. For as long as the popular belief in the high sanctity of the Mass remained unshaken throughout the border counties, no decided step could be taken in that direction; and, as the representatives and administrators of the King's Government they were bound, and would not be reluctant, to avail themselves of every fair opportunity of promoting the reforming policy of the State, such as that which was now, by the mistaken action of "dreaming Durham," laid to their hand.

The Council, besides, could not have been ignorant of the change of opinion on the subject of the doctrine of the Mass which was now rapidly advancing in the highest quarters both of the Church and the State. Bishop Ridley had openly declared against Transubstantiation, and Cranmer, under his influence and that of Bucer, Martyr, John-A-Lasco and Bullinger, had recently gone over to the same Protestant view. At a disputation held at Cambridge in the preceding year, 1549, before the King's Commissioners, the questions moved were, "That Transubstantiation could not be proved by Scripture nor be confirmed by the consent of ancient Fathers for a thousand years past; and that the Lord's Supper is no oblation or sacrifice, otherwise than a remembrance of Christ's death;" and after "three solemn disputations, the Bishop of Rochester had determined the truth of these questions *ad placitum suum*," *i.e.*, in the anti-Roman sense.* In these circumstances, the Council of the North, in calling Knox before them, could have meant nothing else than that he should have the best possible opportunity of "confessing" in the North the same doctrines which so many men in the highest place had been confessing in the South; and it was no doubt with this view that Knox was not called to answer for himself at the Council board, but was sent into the pulpit of the great church of St. Nicolas to preach before the congregation as well as the Council—an "honourable audience," the greatest and most august before which he had ever stood up to defend what he took to be the truth of God.†

In this manner he beginneth :—

"This day I do appear in your presence, honourable audience, to give a reason why so constantly I do affirm the Mass to be, and

---

* "Strype's Memorials of Archbishop Cranmer," vol. i. pp. 292-3. Routledge's edition, 1853.

† The chief names of the King's Council in the North were the following (Strype's "Ecclesiastical Memorials," vol. ii., part 2, p. 161):—

Francis Earl of Shrewsbury, Lord President.
Henry Earl of Westmoreland.
Henry Earl of Cumberland.
Cuthbert Bishop of Durham.
William Lord Dacres, of the North.
John Lord Conyers.
Thomas Lord Wharton.
John Hind, Knight, one of his Majesty's Justices of the Common Pleas.
Edmund Molineux, Knight, Serjeant-at-law.
Henry Savile, Knight.
Robert Bowes, Knight, &c., &c.

The following members "were bound not to depart without the President's leave":—

Robert Bowes, Knight.
Leonard Beckwith, Knight.
William Babthorpe, Knight.
Thomas Gargrave, Knight.
Robert Chalyner, Esq.
Secretary Thomas Eynns, Esq.

at all times to have been, idolatry and abomination before God. And because men of great erudition in your audience affirmed the contrary, most gladly would I that here they were present, either in proper person or else by their learned men, to ponder and weigh the causes moving me thereto; for unless I evidently prove mine intent by God's holy Scriptures, I will recant it as wicked doctrine, and confess myself most worthy of grievous punishment.

"How difficult it is to pull forth of the hearts of the people the thing wherein opinion of holiness standeth, declareth the great tumult and uproar moved against Paul by Demetrius and his fellows, who by idolatry gat great vantage, as our priests have done by the Mass in time past. The people, I say, hearing that the honour of their great goddess Diana stood in jeopardy, with furious voices cried, 'Great is Diana of the Ephesians;' as if they would say, 'We will not have the magnificence of our great goddess Diana, whom not only Asia, but the whole world worshippeth, called in doubt, come in question or controversy; away with all men intending that impiety;' and hereunto were they moved by long custom and false opinion. I know that in the Mass hath not only been esteemed great holiness and honouring of God, but also the ground and foundation of our religion, so that, in the opinion of many, the Mass taken away, there resteth [remaineth] no true worshipping nor honouring of God in the earth. The deeper hath it pierced the hearts of men, that it occupieth the place of the last and mystical Supper of our Lord Jesus. But if I shall, by plain and evident Scriptures, prove the Mass in her most honest garment to have been idolatry before God, and blasphemous to the death and passion of Christ, and contrary to the Supper of Jesus Christ, then good hope have I, honourable audience and beloved brethren, that the fear, love, and obedience of God, who in his Scriptures hath spoken all verity necessary for our salvation, will have you to give place to the same.

"O Lord Eternal, move and govern my tongue to speak the verity, and the hearts of thy people to understand and obey the same."

Addressing himself to his theme, after this remarkable prologue, he announced the plan of his discourse as follows :—

"That ye may the better perceive and understand the manner of my doctrine in this my confession, *first*, will I collect and gather the sum thereof in a brief and short *syllogismus*, and hereafter explain the same more largely. *The Mass is idolatry.* All worshipping, honouring or service invented by the brain of man in the religion of God, without his own express commandment, is idolatry; the Mass is invented by the brain of man without any commandment from God. Therefore it is idolatry."

The *syllogismus* was meant for the bishop and his doctors and other learned men present. The "more large explanation" which followed, and which was of the most plain and popular kind, was meant for the congregation as well as the council, and needs to be compared with the terms of the *syllogismus* in order that these may be rightly understood.

It would have been well if the preacher had explained at starting the sense in which he used the term "idolatry," which would have guarded his syllogism from the objection that he had unduly extended the scope of his "major proposition." For it must at once have struck his hearers, as it now strikes his readers, that if he intended to use the word "idolatry" in its strict literal sense of idol-worship, or "the worshipping of the thing which is not God," that proposition was greatly too extensive, and the "probation" which he brings from Scripture to establish it very far from adequate. Ceremonies without number might manifestly be introduced by the brain of man into "the religion of God" without any one of them involving idolatry in its strict sense, or substituting a false god for the true God; such, *e.g.*, as the use of the cross, or of oil and salt in baptism, or the use of kneeling, and of wafer-bread instead of common bread in the Lord's Supper.

But we have only to compare the explanations of the syllogism which follow it, to see that he uses idolatry in a much larger and looser sense than its strict technical signification. All the examples which he adduces from Scripture of "Idolatry" are of another nature than that of "worshipping the thing which is not God." They are all examples of what can at most be called "constructive idolatry;" for "idolatry" as he remarks, "is not only to worship the thing which is not God, but also to trust or lean unto that thing which is not God, and hath not in itself all sufficiency; and therefore Paul calleth covetous men idolaters, because their confidence and trust is in their riches; much more would he call him an idolater whose heart believeth in remission of sins by a vain work done by himself, or by any other in his name." And we find the same large and inexact use of the term in other parts of his writings, as in the following passage of his "Godly Letter to the Faithful in London "*:—

"It shall nothing excuse us to say we trust not in idols, for so will every idolater allege; but if either you or they, in God's honour, do anything contrary to God's word, you shew yourself to put your trust in somewhat else besides God, and so are you idolaters. Mark, brethren, that many maketh an idol of their own wisdom and fancy, more trusting to that which they think good, than unto God, who plainly saith, " Not those things which seem good in thine eyes do unto thy God, but what thy Lord God hath commanded thee."

We have here the key to the meaning and drift of the whole of Knox's reasonings, in his "Vindication of the Doctrine that the Mass is Idolatry." He used the term idolatry in the widest sense, as including all virtual or constructive "worshipping of the mind or brain of man in the religion of God," such as he took to be involved in the invention of all "strange worshippings of God," introduced without any warrant from his Word.

It is singular that Knox should have omitted to define the terms of his syllogism before proceeding to probation, in the instance before us, because he was well aware of the necessity of this preliminary care in all disputation. "Ye are not ignorant, my Lord," said he, twenty years later, when the interesting "Reasoning" took place at Maybole, in Ayrshire, between him and Quintine Kennedy, the Abbot of Crossragwell, on the same subject of the Mass, "Ye are not ignorant that, in every disputation, the ground ought so to be laid that the matter disputable, or the question, either come under a perfect definition, or else under a sufficient description, and especially when the question is *De Voce simplici*, as is ' Missa.' If it please your Lordship to define the Mass, or yet sufficiently do describe it, I will take occasion of that which I think wrong, and if not, then must I explain my mind what Mass it is that I intend to impugn, and have called 'idolatry;' not the blessed institution of the Lord Jesus, which he hath commanded to be used in his Kirk, to his again coming, but that which is crept into the Kirk visible without all approbation of the Word of God."

But it was as necessary for a disputant to define what was meant by "Idolatry" as by "Missa;" all the more because, as Knox himself again reminded the Abbot a little further on in the

* Knox's Works, vol. iii. p. 196.

discussion, the same term might have both generic and specific senses, as, for instance, the term "sacrifice:" "Your Lordship is not ignorant that in every definition there ought to be *genus*, which I take your Lordship here maketh this term Sacrifice; but because the term is general, and in the Scriptures of God is diversely taken, therefore it must be brought to a certain *kind*. For in the Scriptures there be sacrifices called *Eucharistica*—that is, of thanksgiving. The mortification of our bodies, and the obedience that we give to God in the same, is also called "sacrifice." Prayer and invocation of the name of God hath also the same name within the Scriptures. Liberality to the poor is also so termed. But there is one sacrifice which is greatest and most of all, called *Propiciatorium*, which is that sacrifice whereby satisfaction is made to the justice of God being offended at the sins of man, &c. Now, I desire of my Lord that he appoint unto the Mass which of these sacrifices best pleaseth him."

The term "Idolatry," upon Knox's own showing, admits of a variety of *kinds* of meaning; and it would have been well if he had been as mindful of the necessity of "definition" of terms when he was framing a syllogism of his own, as when his business was to "impugn" the propositions defended on the other side of the question.*

After stating his syllogism, Knox proceeds to "probation of the first part," or the major proposition; and "forth of God's Scriptures," says he, "I will bring the witnesses of my words. And first let us hear Samuel speaking unto Saul, after he had sacrificed unto the Lord upon Mount Gilgal, what time his enemies approached against him: 'Thou art become foolish, thou hast not observed the precepts of the Lord which he commanded thee. Truly the Lord had prepared to have established thy kingdom above Israel for ever. But now thy kingdom shall not be sure.'† Here is the ground of all his iniquity, and of this proceedeth the cause of his dejection from the kingdom, that he would honour God otherwise than was commanded by His express word. For he, being none of the tribe of Levi appointed by God's commandment to make sacrifice, usurpeth that office not due to him; which was most high abomination before God, as by the punish-

* *Vide* "The Reasoning betwixt Knox and the Abbot of Crossragwell," at the end of this chapter.
† 1. Sam. xiii. 8-14.

ment appeareth. Consider well that no excusations are admitted by God, as that his enemies approached and his own people departed from him; he could not have a lawful minister, and gladly would he have been reconciled to God, and consulted with Him of the end and chance of that journey; and therefore he, the King anointed by God's commandment, maketh sacrifice. But none of all these were admitted by God, but Saul was pronounced foolish and vain. For no honouring knoweth God, nor will accept, without it have the express commandment of his own word to be done in all points. And no commandment was given unto the King to make or offer unto God any manner of sacrifice."

His second argument is taken from I. Sam. xv. 13-23, where Saul brought upon himself a second rebuke from the Prophet for sparing the best of the sheep and oxen of the Amalekites, in the face of the Lord's commandment to destroy the whole, under the pretext of reserving them for the sacrifice to the Lord in Gilgal:—"'Hath the Lord,' demanded Samuel, 'as great delight in burnt offerings and sacrifices as in obeying the voice of the Lord? Behold, to obey is better than sacrifice, and to hearken than the fat of lambs. For rebellion is the sin of witchcraft, and stubbornness is iniquity and idolatry. Because thou hast rejected the word of the Lord, He hath also rejected thee from being King.'

"As if Samuel would say 'There is nothing that God more requireth of man than obedience to his commandment; yea, He preferreth obedience to the self-same sacrifice ordained by Himself, for that esteemeth God so odious that He doth compare it to the two sins most abominable—Incantation and Idolatry.' So that disobedience to his voice is very idolatry.

"Disobedience to God's voice is not only when man doeth wickedly contrary to the precepts of God, but also when, of good zeal, or good intent, as we commonly speak, man doeth anything to the honour or service of God not commanded by the express word of God; as in this matter plainly may be espied. For Saul transgressed not wickedly in murder, adultery, or like external sins, but saved an aged and impotent King (which thing who would not call a good deed of mercy?), and permitted the people to save certain cattle to be offered unto the Lord, thinking that God should therewith stand content and well pleased, because he and the people did it of good intent.

CH. II.] *PROOFS FROM OLD TESTAMENT.* 59

"But both these called Samuel idolatry; first, because they were done without any commandment of God; and secondly, because in doing thereof he thought himself not to have offended. And that is principal idolatry when our own inventions we defend to be righteous in the sight of God, because we think them good, laudable, and pleasant. We may not think us so free nor wise, that we may do unto God and unto his honour what we think expedient. No! the contrary is commanded by God, saying, 'Unto my word shall ye add nothing, nothing shall ye diminish therefrom; that ye might observe the precepts of your Lord God,'* which words are not to be understood of the decalogue and law moral only, but of statutes, rites, and ceremonies; for equal obedience of all his laws requireth God; and in witness thereof, Nadab and Abihu, offering strange fire, whereof God had given to them no charge, were instantly, as they offered, punished to death by fire. Strange fire which they offered unto God was a common fire, and not of that fire which God had commanded to burn day and night upon the altar of burnt sacrifice, which only ought to have been offered unto God.

"In the punishment of these two is to be observed that Nadab and Abihu were the principal priests, next to Aaron their father, and that they were comprehended [taken] neither in adultery, covetousness, nor desire of wordly honour, but of a good zeal and simple intent were making sacrifices, desiring no profit of the people thereby, but to honour God and to mitigate his wrath. And yet in the doing of this self-same act and sacrifice were they consumed away with fire, whereof it is plain that neither the pre-eminence of the person or man that maketh or setteth up any religion without the express commandment of God, nor yet the intent whereof he doth the same is accepted before God; for nothing in his religion will He admit without his own word, but all that is added thereunto doth He abhor, and punisheth the inventors and doers thereof. . . . Of these precedents it is plain that no man on earth hath power nor authority to statute anything to the honour of God not commanded by his own word."

We add the Reformer's characteristic reply to the objection commonly taken to the stringent doctrine here maintained by him from the alleged power of the Church "to set up, devise, or invent honouring of God as it thinketh most expedient for the glory of God."

* Deut. iv. 2.

"This is the continual crying of the Papists. The Church, the Church hath all power; it cannot err, for Christ saith, 'I will be with you to the end of the world. Wheresoever two or three are gathered in my name, there am I in the midst of them.' Of this falsely conclude they, the Church may do all that seemeth good to the glory of God, and whatsoever the Church doeth, that accepteth and approveth God. I could evidently prove that which they call the Church not to be the Church and immaculate spouse of Jesus Christ, which doth not err; but, presently, I ask if the Church of God be bound to this perpetual precept, 'Not that thing which appeareth righteous in thine own eyes, that shalt thou do, but what God hath commanded, that observe and keep; and if they will deny [this], I desire to be certified who hath abrogated and made the same of none effect? In my judgment Jesus Christ confirmeth the same, saying, 'My sheep hear my voice. And a stranger's they will not hear, but fly from him.' To hear his voice (which is also the voice of God the Father) is to understand and obey the same; and to fly from a stranger is to admit none other doctrine, worshipping, or honouring of God than hath proceeded forth of his own mouth, as he himself testifieth, saying, 'All that are of the verity hear my voice.' And Paul saith, 'The Church is founded upon the foundation of the Prophets and Apostles,' which foundation, no doubt, is the Law and the Evangel. So that it may command nothing that is not contained in any of the two, for if so it doth it is removed from the only foundation, and so ceaseth to be the true Church of Christ.'

"Secondly, I would ask if that Jesus Christ be not King and Head of his Church? This will no man deny. If He be King, then must He do the office of a king, which is not only to guide, rule, and defend his subjects, but also to make and statute laws, which laws only are his subjects bound to obey, and not the laws of any foreign princes. Then it becometh the Church of Jesus Christ to advert what He speaketh, to receive and embrace his laws, and where He maketh end of speaking or lawgiving [here to rest]. So that all the power of the Church is subject to God's word; and that is most evident by the commandment given of God to Joshua, his chosen captain and leader of the people, in these words: ' Be strong and valiant, that they may do according to the holy law which my servant Moses commanded unto thee. Decline not from it, neither to the right hand nor to the left; let not the book of the law depart from thy mouth, but meditate in it both day and night, that you may keep and do in all things according to that which is written therein.'

"Here was it not permitted to Joshua to alter one jot, ceremony, or statute, in all the law of God, nor yet to add thereunto, but diligently to observe that which was commanded. No less obedience requireth God of us than He did of Joshua his servant, for He will have the religion ordained by his only Son Jesus Christ most straitly observed, and not to be violated in any part. . . . O God Eternal, hast thou laid none other burden upon our backs than Jesus Christ laid by his word? Then who hath burdened us with all these ceremonies, prescribed fasting, compelled chastity, unlawful vows, invocation of saints, and with the idolatry of the Mass? The devil, the devil, brethren, invented all these burdens to press down imprudent men to perdition. . . .

"Greatly it is to be marvelled that men do not advert that the Book of God's law, that is, of all his ordinances, testament, promises, and exhibition thereof, was sealed and confirmed in the days of the Apostles, the effects and contents thereof promulgated and published; so that most extreme impiety it is to make any alteration therein; yea, and the wrath and fearful malediction of God is denounced to fall upon all them that dare attempt to add or diminish anything in his religion, confirmed and proclaimed by his own voice. O Papists! where shall ye hide you from the presence of the Lord? Ye have perverted his law; ye have taken away his ordinances; ye have placed up your own statutes instead of his. Woe and damnation abideth you. Albeit that the Apostles had made laws other than the express Word commanded, what appertaineth that to you? Have ye the spirit of truth and knowledge in abundance as they had? Was the Church of Christ left imperfect after the Apostles' days? Bring yourselves to mind, and be ashamed of your vanity. For all men whose eyes Satan hath not blinded may espy that neither wisdom nor authority of man may change or set up anything in the religion of God, without his own express commandment or Word. . . . And thus I think the first part of my argument sufficiently proved."

He then proceeds to the second part of his syllogism—or the minor premiss—or "to prove the Mass to be the mere invention of man set up without all commandment of God." Into this argument, however, we cannot follow him, nor into his second syllogism, in which he boldly—his hearers must have thought audaciously—undertakes to prove that even if "the whole *action of the Mass* were the institution and very ordinance of God, and never one jot of man's invention therein," still the present practice of the Church of Rome therein was an abomination before God; the syllogism being thrown into this form, "All honouring or service of God *whereunto is added a wicked opinion* is abomination. Unto the Mass is added a wicked opinion —viz., that the Mass is a sacrifice and oblation for the sins of the quick and the dead. Therefore it is an abomination."

The logic of Bible proof and common sense, and the battery of sarcasm and irony which the preacher brought to bear upon this second argument were irresistible, and must have had a stunning effect upon his auditory. We can only quote a specimen of the grim irony of one of his appeals to the Papists, before giving the emphatic terms in which he winds up the whole argument of this second part of his discourse.

"Consider now, brethren, if the opinion of the Mass—viz., that it is a sacrifice and oblation for the sins of the quick and the dead —be not vain, false, and deceivable. Caused they not you to believe it was a sacrifice whereby remission of sins was obtained? And ye may plainly perceive that no sacrifice there is nor at any time was for sins but the death of Jesus Christ only. For the sacrifices of the Old Law were only figures of that very and true sacrifice once offered by Jesus Christ. And in them was commemoration of sins made, but neither was remission of sins obtained nor purgation made by any such sacrifice. What will ye do, Papist priests? There resteth no sacrifice to be offered for sin by you nor by any mortal man.

"These are dolorous tidings to your hearts, and no marvel; for by that vain opinion that the Mass was a sacrifice for sin have ye so quietly rested in that flood of Euphrates (*i.e.*, the waters of Babylon), that is, in all worldly felicity, which flowed unto you as a continual flood. But the Mass known not only to be no sacrifice, but also to be idolatry, the waters appear to dry up; and it is like that ye lack some liquor to refresh your tongues, being cruciat (tormented) with drought and heat intolerable. Would ye hear glad tidings? What if that I should allow unto you (as one willing to play the good fellow and not to be stiff-necked) that the Mass were a sacrifice for sin, would ye be content that this were allowed unto you? I think ye would, for therefore have ye long contended.

"Then let us consider what should subsequently follow thereupon. A sacrifice for sin was never perfect until that the beast offered was slain. If in your Mass ye offer Jesus Christ for sin, then necessarily in your Mass must ye needs kill Jesus Christ. Do not esteem, beloved brethren, these words shortly spoken to be vain or of small effect. They are collected of the very grounds of Scriptures, for these plainly testify that Christ to be offered, Christ to suffer, and Christ to shed his blood to die, are all one thing. . . . . Consider diligently that remission of sins is attributed sometime to the shedding of Christ's blood, sometime to his death, and sometime to the whole sacrifice which He made in suffering all pain. . . . . And so, Papists, if ye offer Christ in sacrifice for sin, ye shed his blood, and thus newly slay Him. Advert to what end your own desire shall bring you, even to be slayers of Jesus Christ. Ye will say, ye never intended such abomination. I dispute not what ye intended, but I only show what absurdity doth follow upon your own doctrine. . . . . But now will I relieve you of this anguish. Dolorous it were daily to commit manslaughter, and oftentimes to crucify the Lord of glory. Be not afraid, ye do it not; for Jesus Christ may suffer no more, shed his blood no more, nor die no more. For that He hath died, He so died for sin, and that once; and now He liveth, and death may not prevail against Him. And so do ye not slay Christ, for no power ye have to do the same. Only ye have deceived the people, causing them to believe that ye offered Jesus Christ in sacrifice for sin in your Mass, which is frivolous and false, for Jesus Christ may not be offered, because He may not die."

He winds up the whole of this part of his argument in these earnest words:—

"I most gently exhort all desiring to object against these precedents [foregoing statements] ripely to consider the ground thereof, which standeth not upon the opinion of man, but upon the infallible word of God; and to resume [reconsider] every part of their arguments, and lay them to the whole body of God's Scriptures; and then I doubt not that all men whose senses the Prince of Darkness and of this world hath not execated [blinded] shall confess with me that in the Mass can be no sacrifice for sin. And so, I think, the Mass to be abominable and idolatry I think no man of indifferent [impartial] judgment will deny."

The Reformer next proceeded to draw a contrast between the Mass and the Lord's Supper in its original Divine institution; but this part of the "Vindication" has been already brought into view in the preceding chapter.

He ended this "Notable Sermon" with several references of a personal kind which are interesting and suggestive :—

"Let no man think," cried the preacher, "because I am in the realm of England that therefore so boldly I speak against this abomination. Nay, God hath taken that suspicion from me, for—this body lying in most painful bonds among the midst of cruel tyrants—his mercy and goodness provided that the hand should write, and bear witness to the confession of the heart more abundantly than ever yet the tongue spoke.*

"And here I call my God to record that neither profit to myself, hatred of any person or persons, nor affection or favour that I bear towards any private man, causeth me this day to speak as ye have heard, but only the obedience which I owe unto God in ministration, showing of his word, and the common love which I bear to the salvation of all men.

"Such doctrine as was taught in your audience upon Sunday before noon, I will prove, as opportunity shall permit, by God's Scriptures, not only unprofitable, but also erroneous and deceivable. But first, according to my promise, I will send unto the teacher the extract thereof, to add or diminish as by his wisdom shall be thought most expedient. For God knoweth my mind is not captiously to trap men in words, but my only desire being that ye, my audience, be instructed in the verity wherefrom dissenteth some doctrine taught you (if truly I have collected) moveth me to speak against all that may have appearance of lies and superstition.

"And pray with me, brethren, that the spirit may be ministered unto me in abundance, to speak at all times as becometh a true messenger. And I will likewise pray that ye may hear, understand, and obey with all reverence the good will of God, declared

---

* Referring to a confession addressed to the congregation of the Castle of St. Andrew's, in 1548—possibly, or even probably, the same confession referred to in the preceding chapter under the title of "Justification and Good Works."

unto the world by Jesus Christ, whose omnipotent spirit remain with you for ever. Amen.*

Knox speaks in these paragraphs not at all in the tone and manner of a man labouring under any dangerous accusation—he is evidently void of any apprehensions of personal risk or danger; he rather speaks as if he had the prospect of continuing for some time to preach to the same audience. The hostility of Tunstall and his learned doctors had not only proved harmless to him—it had been of positive advantage to his influence and fame. It had procured for him the use of one of the most influential pulpits of the province—the pulpit which commanded at the time† the audience of the members of the Council of the North. It had drawn around him in the church of St. Nicholas a congregation including much of the wealth and station and intelligence of the two chief towns of the counties of Durham and Northumberland. Bishop Tunstall himself had been compelled to listen to the preacher of whom he had complained, with ears which must have tingled under such a "blast of the trumpet." From that memorable day John Knox stepped to the front; his name became known over England as the hammer of the Popish bishops and divines, and it was not long before he was singled out for the distinction of being named one of the royal chaplains, and of having the offer of a rich bishopric.

It is very remarkable that, while these thunderings and lightnings of denunciation of the Mass of Rome were issuing from the pulpit of St. Nicholas's in Newcastle, others quite as loud and vivid had begun to issue for the first time from the Palace of Lambeth. In the same year—1550—appeared from the press Archbishop Cranmer's "Defence of the true and Catholic Doctrine of the Sacrament," wherein "he took upon himself to refute and throw down—first, the corporal presence; secondly, the phantastical transubstantiation; thirdly, the idolatrous adoration; fourthly, the false error of the Papists, that wicked men do eat the natural body

---

* At the end of the printed sermon is added the signature "Johne Knox," with the doxology "Give the glory to God alone." It was first printed in Geneva, in 1556, after his return from his first visit to Scotland, and afterwards, with additions, in 1558.

† The Council had its headquarters in York, but held sessions of a month's continuance each in Hull, Durham, and Newcastle. Apparently, it was during its annual session in Newcastle that Knox preached before it, and probably he was appointed preacher for the whole month of its session.

of Christ; and, lastly, the blasphemous Sacrifice of the Mass. Whereupon, in conclusion (*i.e.*, in 1551, when he published his answer to Gardiner's crafty and sophistical 'Cavillation'), he wrote five books for the public instruction of the Church of England, which instruction yet to this day standeth and is received in this Church of England."*

The subject of both these memorable manifestoes was precisely the same. The Primate, though slowly, had at last come to be "thoroughly persuaded in the right knowledge of the Sacrament, and fully ripened in the same." Knox had been fully ripe four years before in St. Andrew's, as we have seen above; but, vehement as the language of his "Vindication" had been, it was not a whit more so than that of the newly-converted Primate. It is a grave mistake to suppose that the strong language of Knox upon the Mass and the other abuses and corruptions of the Church of Rome, was exceptionally strong. Cranmer himself, who was usually mild and moderate in speech, and who was master of a style to which a living historian has applied the appropriate term "silvery," makes use of language in both his treatises on the Lord's Supper which does not admit of quotation at the present day; and the later writings of Thomas Becon, who was one of Cranmer's chaplains, contain passages upon Romish corruptions much more violent than any either of Cranmer or Knox. Polemical vehemence, in short, was the style of the age, and equally so on both sides of the great ecclesiastical question of that age; and historical justice demands that no exceptional reproach should rest upon the name and memory of Knox in that respect. Equally to Knox and to Cranmer, the "Mass" of the Church of Rome revealed itself at last—though in both cases very slowly, and after long resistance to the reformed doctrine—as a "heinous abomination and idolatry, wherein the priests have taken upon them the office of Christ to make a propitiatory sacrifice for the sins of the people;"† and they were both equally plain and outspoken in denouncing it as such to the world, when once their eyes were fully opened to its true nature and qualities.

But the manner in which these two Reformers lay out and con-

---

* "Life, State, and Story of Thomas Cranmer;" prefixed to the Parker Society's edition of his works.

† This is the language of Cranmer at p. 350 of his "Writings and Disputations on the Lord's Supper." Parker Society edition.

struct their reasonings upon the subject is very different. Knox sets out to prove the Mass an idolatry on Puritan principles. Cranmer's argument to the same effect is what was to be expected from an Anglican Churchman, and from the man whose pen drew up the First Prayer-book of King Edward, and the Declaration touching "Ceremonies" which has formed a part of every prayer-book of the Church of England, published by authority, down to the present day. Knox's first syllogism in the "Vindication" came as appropriately from one who had already carried into effect at Berwick, in his conduct of public worship, and his administration of the Sacraments, the same comprehensive and sweeping principles which he lays down in its major proposition. But that form of argument was not the only mode, it was not even the best mode, of establishing the affirmation that the adoration of the Mass was idolatrous. Properly taken, and as commonly understood, to call it idolatrous meant something much more serious than that it was an act of worship not warranted by the express sanction or appointment of the word of God. To the general sense of the reformed churches, idolatry meant the worshipping of an idol, of that which was not God, whatever form the idol might assume, whether the form of a living saint or angel in heaven, or of an image of saint or angel on earth, or the form of the consecrated Host upon the altar—that object which, above all others, the reformed churches abhorred, abominating it as the "bread-god," the "wafer-idol" of the Church of Rome. But as before remarked, the argumentation of Knox was not directed to prove that the Host was an idol in this strict and proper sense, as Cranmer's reasonings were directed to establish, and succeeded in establishing to the admiration of none more than the Scottish Reformer himself. In truth, the argument had been conducted in the same way as Cranmer put it, by all the great teachers of the Reformation from the beginning. All the more remarkable was it that Knox for the first time adopted another method.

So far as we know he was the first to construct the argument upon lines so broad, or upon principles so comprehensive, as would admit of its being brought to bear upon all the corruptions of "the religion of God" in one heap, and at one blow. His very first proposition was a *universal* one on the subjects to which it referred, and these were not only all *worshipping*, but all *honouring*, and even all *service*, "invented by the brain of man in the religion of God without his own express commandment." That formula comprehended a multitude of particulars connected with divine worship and service, beyond what was called "the service of the altar." What his mode of reasoning lost in point of intensity and weight, as directed against all the forms of idolatry proper, was compensated by the sweep and effectiveness of its bearing upon all liturgical corruptions and superstitions of other kinds and in other forms, as well as upon the idolatry of the Mass in particular. But the word of God which condemned those other corruptions, much more of course condemned this properly idolatrous corruption as immensely more heinous, so heinous that, along with all other false gods and idols, it was expressly prohibited and condemned by the first two commandments of the decalogue.

But Knox's argumentation had the advantage over Crammer's of being a universal test of liturgical purity. It was a theological weapon, as able to do trenchant execution upon a thousand corruptions as upon one. It was a *generalization* of Puritan sense, and wide reformatory scope, such as we suppose had not been brought forward and put to use before upon the English soil; and hence the praise for boldness and thorough-goingness which his able biographer bestows upon the "Vindication." "The propositions," he justly observes, "on which he rested his defence are very descriptive of his characteristic boldness of thinking and acting. A more cautious and timid disputant would have satisfied himself with attacking the grosser notions which were generally entertained by the people upon this subject, and exposing the glaring abuses of which the priests were guilty in the lucrative sale of Masses. Knox scorned to occupy himself in demolishing these feeble and falling outworks, and proceeded directly to establish a principle which overthrew the whole fabric of superstition. He engaged to prove that the Mass, "even in her most high degree, and when stripped of the meretricious dress in which she now appeared, was an idol struck from the inventive brain of superstition which had supplanted the Sacrament of the Supper, and engrossed the honour due to the person and sacrifice of Jesus Christ."*

After having given in Newcastle so notable a specimen of his powers as a preacher of Reformation doctrine, it is not surprising that Knox should have been ere long transferred to that influential

* M'Crie's "Life of Knox," vol. i. p. 84, fifth edition, 1831.

post, as the centre of his stated ministry. The Vicar of St. Nicholas in 1551-53 was William Purye, A.M., of whose opinions on the great controversy of the time nothing has been recorded, and by what arrangement, made no doubt by authority of the Council, the appointment of Knox to preach in his pulpit was conciliated with Purye's vicarial rights, we are left in ignorance. In all probability Purye seldom or never preached himself, as his name does not occur among the divines who were specially licensed to preach in Edward's reign. Very probably, too, the service which Knox conducted in his own Puritan manner was carried on at hours reserved for himself.

It fortunately happens that his "Epistle to the congregation of Berwick," referred to in the last chapter, which was written late in 1552, while he was still preacher in Newcastle, helps us to form a very distinct and lively conception of his Newcastle ministry. This document contains an explicit and formal statement of what " he understood under the Gospel," that "holy Evangel" to which he refers so often and so lovingly, and in whose "high puissance and virtue" for the saving of souls he had so intense a faith. The following paragraphs of the Epistle bring before us a valuable analysis of the Gospel as he was wont to preach it in Newcastle as well as Berwick :—

"God I take to witness and the Lord Jesus, before whom at once shall all flesh appear, that I never teached unto you, nor unto any others my auditory, that doctrine as necessary to be believed which I did not find written in God's holy law and testament; and therefore in that case with Paul will I say, " If an angel from heaven shall teach unto you another Gospel than ye have heard and externally received, let him be accursed. Under the Gospel I understand,—

"1. The infinite goodness of God, whose merciful providence hath placed our life and salvation in his only Son, Jesus Christ, who of God is made to us justice, sanctification, wisdom, and redemption.

"2. And our Lord Jesus, together with all such gifts as by Him are given to the elect Church of God, as remission of sins, resurrection of the flesh, and life everlasting, is the second thing I understand by the Gospel.

"3. And the third thing is true faith, which, as it alone apprehendeth and understandeth all these precedents, so doth it alone justify before God, without all respect of works by-past, present, or to come; which good works hath God our Father prepared, that we, his children adopted and chosen in Christ Jesus, before the foundation of the world was laid, to life everlasting, should walk in them.

"4. Which is the fourth thing I conclude within the Gospel—to wit, a holy and godly conversation, wherein we should obey our God all the days of our life, to the praise and glory of his holy name, who hath appointed us to be his heirs when yet we were not.

"5. And last, under the Gospel I understand invocation unto God alone by Jesus Christ, and thanksgiving unto Him for his great benefits received; which sometimes are private, while man alone in any tribulation, necessity, or action, incalls the aid and help of his God for Christ his Son's sake; but are commanded openly to be done in participation of Christ's sacraments, left and commanded to be used in his Church, for sealing up and better memory to be had of those benefits that we have received by the communion that we have with Christ Jesus in his body and blood."

Such, under his own hand, were "the chief and principal points" of the Gospel which he preached in England. But what of all errors and corruptions of doctrine antagonistic to these chief points?

Immediately after the passage just given, he writes in the following unfaltering strain:—

"If in any of these chief and principal points any man vary from that doctrine which ye have professed, let him be accursed.

"As, if any man teach any other cause moving God to elect and choose us than his own infinite goodness and mere mercy.

"Any other name in heaven or under the heaven wherein salvation stands but only the name of Jesus Christ.

"Any other means whereby we are justified and absolved from wrath and damnation that our sins deserve, than by faith only.

"Any other cause or end of good works than that first we are made good trees, and thereafter bring forth fruits accordingly, to witness that we are lively members of Christ's holy and most sanctified body, prepared vessels to the honour and praise of our Father's glory.

"If any teach prayers to be made to others than to God alone.

"If any mediator betwixt God and man but only our Lord Jesus.

"If more or other Sacraments be affirmed or required to be used than Jesus Christ left ordinary in his Church, to wit, Baptism and the Lord's Table or Mystical Supper.

"If any deny remission of sins, resurrection of the flesh, and life everlasting to appertain to us in Christ's blood, which, sprinkled in our hearts by faith, doth purge us from all sin, so that we need no more nor other sacrifices than that oblation once offered for all, by the which God's elect be fully sanctified and made perfect. If any, I say, require any other sacrifice to be made for sins than Christ's death, which once He suffered, or any other manner whereby Christ's death may be applied to man than by faith only, which also is the gift of God, so that man hath no cause to glory in works; and yet if any deny good works to be profitable as not necessary to a true Christian profession, let the affirmers, teachers, or maintainers of such doctrine be accursed of you, as they are of God, unless they repent."

Equally plain-spoken and fearless in what he affirmed and in what he denied upon the authority of God's Word, Knox's Protestantism was in the first instance positive—setting out comprehensively all the "chief and principal points" of Gospel truth; but it was negative as well—protesting loudly and boldly against all Popish, semi-Popish, and Antinomian errors and corruptions. His summary of essential truth is as large and inclusive as apostolic doctrine demands; and if he does not shrink from denouncing anathema upon all antagonistic teachings and practice, this mandefying courage was no doubt an important element of his impressiveness and power—it was this prophet-like fearlessness and apostle-like authority of speech which bowed down the souls of men under the weight of God's Word proclaimed by him, and without which he would probably have proved unequal to the arduous work committed to his hands. The fervid intensity of his convictions of Divine truth was the very life and soul of his ministry, and men could hardly fail to be deeply moved and shaken under his appeals, when this intensity of faith and feeling was brought to bear upon them in the double form of burning love to God's truth, and burning wrath and indignation against the Devil's lie.

What was the personal quality and spirit of his ministry in Newcastle, as distinguished from the doctrinal substance of his teaching—what was the very heart and soul of the preacher himself in his work—is revealed to us with startling vividness in his "Epistle to the Inhabitants of Newcastle and Berwick," addressed to them in print from Geneva in 1558. In that year he had come to understand that the Protestants of these towns, as well as many others "who sometime in the realm of England professed Christ Jesus," were "now returned to the bondage of Idolatry," and he wrote to them in great anguish of heart, as his "dear brethren, of whose boldness I once rejoiced, and for whose fall, God knoweth, I now mourn." Hence the deep pathos of the writing—so full of moving recollections of what they had once been in the days of his labours among them, compared with the state of apostacy into which they had lapsed under the terrors of the Marian persecution; and hence also much plain and earnest speaking, both of "what manner of man" he had been among them "at all times," which so forcibly recalls to us the example of St. Paul in dealing with his Corinthian and Galatian converts— to which Apostle, in truth, in the intense glow of his feelings both of joy and grief, under the opposite and everchanging conditions of ministerial labour, the per-fervid Reformer bears a striking resemblance.

"John Knox, to the Inhabitants of Newcastle and Barwike, and unto all other who sometyme in the Realm of England professed Christ Jesus, and now be returned to the bondage of Idolatry, wisheth true and earnest repentance by the power and operation of that same Spirit who called from death Jesus, the only Pastor of our Souls.

"God is witness, and I refuse not your own judgments, how simply and uprightly I conversed and walked amongst you, though in his presence I was and am nothing but a mass of corruption, rebellion, and hypocrisy; yet, as concerning you and the doctrine taught amongst you, as then I walked so now do I write in the presence of Him who only knoweth and shall reveal the secrets of all hearts, that neither for fear did I spare to speak the simple truth unto you, neither for hope of worldly promotion, dignity, or honour did I willingly adulterate any part of God's Scriptures, whether it were in exposition, in preaching, contention, or writing; but that simply and plainly, as it pleased the merciful goodness of my God to give unto me the utterance, understanding, and spirit, I did distribute the bread of life (I mean God's most holy Word) as of Christ Jesus I had received it. I sought neither pre-eminence, glory, nor riches. My honour was that Christ Jesus should reign; my glory that the light of his truth should shine in you; and my greatest riches that in the same ye should be constant. Let him amongst you that is furthest declined, convict me if he can, if that ever he did perceive me, by crafty or unlawful means, to seek the substance or riches of any; yea, if I have not refused that which by diverse hath been offered, and that also, by the common opinion, might lawfully have been received.

"But to what purpose is this recited? Is it to brag of mine own justice, or yet to defend mine own innocency? Not so, dear brethren, not so (for what I acknowledge myself to be before God I have already confessed), but to let you understand, that if I have this testimony of conscience as concerning my office, ministry, and doctrine, and am notwithstanding wounded almost to the death for that my labours have not better succeeded, what ought to be your fear, lamentation, and trembling? . . . My conscience doth neither accuse me that amongst you was I a false prophet, mercenary, nor idle person, and yet I quake, I fear and tremble, remembering your horrible fall; and ought ye to rest, be quiet, and rejoice, against whom God's vengeance is so plainly declared?"

Another remarkable passage of the "Epistle" brings out the high degree of success which had attended the Reformer's labours in the North of England, though, under the conditions in which the Epistle was written, we are not allowed to contemplate only the bright side of the picture, but in every fervid sentence are in presence of the painful contrast between the past and the present:—

"Consider with me, dear brethren (I speak to you of Newcastle and Barwick), your miserable estate and most dolorous condition. Your profession did once declare before men that ye were branches planted and engrafted in Christ Jesus, whose holy Gospel (which is the power of God to the salvation of all that believe it) ye appeared to have received with all reverence and gladness. The displeasure of your natural and carnal friends, who then were enemies to Christ Jesus and to his eternal verity, some of you did patiently bear. Ye feared not to go before statutes and laws; yea, openly and solemnly ye did profess, by receiving the Sacraments not as man had appointed, but as Christ Jesus, the wisdom of God the Father, had instituted, to be subject in all things concerning religion to his yoke alone, to acknowledge and avouch him before the world to be your only Lawgiver, Sovereign, Prince, and only Saviour. Thus, I say, ye appeared at that time to have been the delicate plants of the Eternal, the workmanship of his own hands, and the trees that, in season and time, should have produced good fruit in abundance.

"But oh, alas! how are ye changed! How are ye corrupted! Whitherunto are ye fallen! And how have ye deceived the expectation of those that then did labour in planting and watering you, and now do sob unto God for your ingratitude, calling with tears unto his mercy for your conversion, and that unfeigned repentance may suddenly [quickly] appear in you. O miserable change, that ye who were once fervent professors of Christ Jesus and of his Gospel should now be subjects to Antichrist, giving obedience to his false and deceavable doctrine. O grievous fall, and more than grievous, that from the dignity of the Sons of God (which prerogative ye had by grace and not by nature) ye are become slaves to Satan, justifying by your presence most abominable idolatry! . . . God did not call you from darkness to light, He did not send his Son Christ Jesus unto you, contemning and refusing so many thousands more noble, more wise, more ancient, and more puissant than ye are or ever were—God, I say, did not so familiarly communicate himself with you, in his only beloved Son Christ Jesus, to the end that ye at your pleasure and appetite, or for the fear of worldly men, for losing of goods or corporal life, should return to darkness and should refuse to serve that Sovereign Prince in the day of his battle, before whom all knees shall bow : but contrarywise, that according as ye were called to the participation of light, that so constantly ye should walk in the same; that as ye were appointed soldiers to fight against Satan, the Prince of this world, and against his progeny, enemies to Christ Jesus, so should ye boldly abide in the rank in which God had placed you. . . . Which things I thought once had been so deeply grafted in your hearts, that albeit angels from heaven should have persuaded you to the contrary, that ye should have holden them accursed, and so in that behalf have rejected their persuasion and doctrine as a poison most pestilent, which is death and damnation to all that receive it. For so did ye once profess, and such was my hope of you that so in heart you had determined; for Christ Jesus was not preached amongst you without his cross.

"How oft hath it been beat in your ears that 'the servant cannot be above the Lord;' that 'the members must be conformed to the Head;' that 'by many tribulations we must enter into the kingdom of God;' that 'all that will live godly in Christ Jesus must suffer persecution;' and that, partly, because Satan the Prince of this world can never be so bridled during this battle but that he will strive to recover strength, and, partly, because that sin remaineth in us, he is permitted to sting with his venomous tail when his head is bruised. Was not this doctrine common unto you? Yea, have ye not heard oftener than once that your eyes should see Christ Jesus persecuted in his poor members? that his verity should be oppugned? that superstition, lies, and idolatry should prevail and have the upper hand? that the kingdom of heaven, the true preaching of his Evangel, should be taken from you for the ingratitude and stubbornness of men who more delighted in darkness than in light. None of these things at that time did appear strange unto you, neither did they discourage you; but ye seemed, being admonished what danger it was to refuse Christ Jesus, most steadfastly to cleave to the verity, notwithstanding that the whole world should have refused the same.

"How oft have ye assisted to Baptism! How oft have ye been partakers of the Lord's Table, prepared, used, and ministered in all simplicity, not as man had devised, neither as the King's proceedings did allow, but as Christ Jesus did institute, and as it is evident that St. Paul did practise! These two Sacraments, seals of Christ's Evangel, ye commonly used, Baptism for your children, and the Table of the Lord to your own comfort, and for the open confession of your religion. And so oft, I say, dear brethren, did ye witness before men and swear before God, that ye would die with Christ Jesus, to the end that ye might live by Him—that ye would refuse the doctrine of men, and the participation of all idolatry, and would constantly stand and stick fast to that religion which then ye confessed and approved.

"But O, alas! what miserable ruins hath this sudden and short storm made of that building which was begun amongst you! The winds have blown, and the floods are come, and the walls are fallen in one heap (God grant that the foundation abide!). The fire is come, but in you, alas! is neither found gold, silver, nor precious stones, but all is brent, and all is consumed; so that if I shall judge the fruit of my poor labours amongst you by mine own judgment, reason, or apprehension, I should judge myself and my labours accursed of God, for that I see no better success. O consider, dear brethren, what grief it is that in such a multitude none shall be found faithful, none constant, none bold in the course of the Lord Jesus, whom so boldly before they had professed."

Though himself a hero in the faith of Christ, all his converts in England had not proved themselves to be heroes in his own image. When he wrote in this strain of intense love and sorrow, expostulation and reproof, he was himself in bitter exile for the truth, and he mourned that his converts at home, who were still his "dear brethren," had not preferred to share that bitter exile with him rather than to turn back, even in appearance though it might not in heart, to the corrupt worship which he had taught them to forsake. Still, though "troubled" about their case, it is manifest that he is not "in despair." He has still hope that "the foundation" which as a master-builder he had been instrumental in laying broad and deep among them will, by God's grace, "abyde;" and he does not forget, even in moments of deepest discouragement, that only to the wisdom of God, who "looketh not on the outward appearance, and not to "the reason of man"—who cannot "look upon the heart"—it belongeth "to judge what fruit ensueth the painful travail of God's most faithful servants, who at his commandment study to repair his city and to purge his temple." If "man's reason enterprise such judgment," "not only shall their labours be esteemed for a time to be vainly spent, but scarcely shall the wisdom of God through man's rash judgment escape condemnation, neither shall the verity of his promises be free from suspicion of falsehood and vanity."*

The reader will not have failed to notice in these quotations from Knox's Epistle of 1558 abundant evidence to show that, during all his stay in Newcastle, he was still left as much at liberty as he had been before in Berwick to conduct the public services of religion according to his own views of the requirements of God's Word. This may well seem surprising, considering that Newcastle was from time to time the seat of administration for "the Council of the North," and considering also that the Council had received from the King's Government such "Instructions" as will be found in the note below.† But the fact is

---

* "Knox's Works," vol. v. pp. 475-494.

† In "State Papers" (Domestic), Edward VI., Addenda, vol. iii., is found a "Draft of Instructions to the Council of the North, on occasion of Lord Shrewsbury being made President of the Council in 1549-50." Among many others the following Instructions occur:—"And his Grace's pleasure further is: that in every such sittynge [referring to Sessions of the Council in York, Hull, Durham, and Newcastle], and in all other places where the said Lord

unquestionable, although evidence is not wanting, on the other hand, to show that this posture of Nonconformity was maintained in opposition to the wishes and the only half-concealed dislike, of several members of the administration, and of at least one leading member of the municipality of the town, Sir Robert Brandling, the mayor.

In 1552 the most powerful statesman of the kingdom, John Dudley, now Duke of Northumberland, was made Warden General of the border counties, and was for some time resident in Newcastle, when he must have been one of Knox's hearers in the great church of St. Nicholas; and in a letter written to Secretary Cecil from Chelsea, on the 27th of October in that year, he gives as one of his reasons for wishing to see Knox promoted to a bishopric, that "he should not continue the ministration in the north contrary to this set forth here;" meaning the order set forth in King Edward's First Prayer-book; where it is worth noticing that the Duke speaks of "the north" at large, not of

President and Counsaill shall have any notable assemblies before them, they shall give straight charge and commandment to the people to conform themselves in all things to the observation of such lawes, ordennances, and determynacions as be made, passed, and agreed upon by his Grace's Parliament, touchinge religion and the most godlie service set furth [in their mother tongue for their comfort, and likewise to the laws for the abolishing of the usurped and pretended power of the Bishop of Rome, whose abuses they shall so beat into their heads by continual inculcation, as they may smell and understand the same to be declared with their hearts, not with their tongues onlie for form. And likewise they shall declare the order and determination taken and agreed upon for the abrogation of certain vain holidays, being appointed by the Bishop of Rome to blind the world, and to persuade the same that they might make saints at their pleasures, and thereby through idleness do give occasion to the increase of many vices and inconvenients ; which points his Majesty doth earnestly require and straitly command the said Lord President to set forth with all dexterity, and to punish extremely for example all offenders in the same. And his Majesty willeth the said Counsaill, as he nothing doubteth but they will most earnestly, to set furth all such other things and matters, as for the confirmation of the people in these matters, and other the King's matters, proceedings, and things to be remembered, be, or shall be, set furth, or devised, or sent unto them for that purpose"]. It is remarkable that the whole of what is included between brackets in the above is scored out in the original. This scoring out, of course, must have been done after the document left the hands of the Privy Council in London. The name of Thomas Eynns, who was Secretary to the Council of the North, appears upon the document, from which we may infer that it had come into the hands of the Council in York, and that the scoring was theirs.

Newcastle only, implying, it would seem, that Knox, more than any other man, was the upholder of this state of Nonconformity in the border counties, and that, upon his removal to the south, a different state of matters might be expected to ensue—a singular tribute to the weight of influence and authority which he had then acquired, not only with the northern community, but with the King and Privy Council, whose commission he held and so energetically carried out.

Another reason assigned by the Warden General is very curious and suggestive. It is " that the family of Scots now inhabiting in Newcastle, chiefly for his fellowship, would," in the event of Knox's removal, " not continue there, whereon many resort to him out of Scotland, which is not requisite." And he returns to the same subject in a subsequent letter, 23rd November of the same year, in which he writes: " And further I have thought good to putt you and so my Lords (of the Privy Council) in memory that some order be taken for Knokks, otherwise you shall not avoyd the Scottes from out of Newcastell, which, all things considered, methink should not be forgotten." What harm the Duke feared to ensue from allowing "the family of Scots" to continue and to grow in Newcastle in what was now a time of peace between the two kingdoms, it is not easy to see; but the notice is an interesting one, revealing the fact that they were there "chiefly for Knox's fellowship," and that the same powerful magnet was expected to draw more and more to join them. And these "Scottes" must have been chiefly people of some rank and condition in life, to be able to afford such a gratification of their religious desires and sympathies. Knox's name was evidently already in high repute in his own country. The fame of his ministry in Berwick had spread into the south of Scotland, and had been published in Haddington and other districts by the English soldiers who had listened to his oratory on their way to the field of war. Perhaps some of his eager admirers in Newcastle were members of his former flock at St. Andrews. Perhaps some of them had seen and read his " Confession of the Article of Justification," which he had sent from the galley of 'Notre Dame,' in the Seine, "to all professors of Christ's true Evangell."* Putting together what good was thus

---

* In the "State Papers," Scotland, vol. i., under the years 1550–51, occur numerous letters of Regent Arran to Edward VI. requesting letters of safe

done to the "Scottes," either upon English ground by Knox, or under English protection in counties of Scotland which were occupied for a long time by those English arms, by Willock and other preachers in the train of the good Marquis of Dorset, we have, in these incidents, a very curious passage in the history of the Scottish as well as of the English Reformation.

In these last references, however, in connection with the name of the Duke of Northumberland, we have anticipated by some months the progress of events in the history of Knox's Newcastle ministry.

"In the month of December, 1551, it was thought fit," says Strype, "that the King should retain six chaplains in ordinary, who should not only wait upon him, but be itineraries, and preach the Gospel all the nation over—two of these six to be ever present at Court, and four absent abroad in preaching; one year, two in Wales, two in Lanchashire and Derby; the next year two in the marches of Scotland, two in Yorkshire; the third year, two in Devonshire, two in Hampshire; the fourth year, two in Norfolk and Essex, and two in Kent and Sussex. And these six to be Bill, Harley, Perne, Grindal, Bradford, and the sixth dashed out in the King's journal, but probably Knox, for he was one of the preachers in the north, at Newcastle and elsewhere, and had a salary paid him out of the Exchequer. But the number was reduced to four (Bradford also being left out), who were styled the King's Ordinary Chaplains."*

This suggestion of Strype that the dashed name in King Edward's journal was that of Knox has been recently set aside by conclusive ocular proof, as the editor of Strype's work for the "Ecclesiastical History Society" discovered, with the assistance of Sir Frederick Madden, that the name so erased was Eastwick, not Knox.† But admitting this to be the true state of matters, as regards the entry in the journal, it is certain that Knox must have taken the place of Eastwick, or whoever else was first named to be the sixth of the royal chaplains, very shortly afterwards, for in the register of the

conduct for merchants of Edinburgh, Leith, Preston, and Dysart to pass into England "to do their lawful errands and business." These were, no doubt, the "Scottes" whom the Duke found "in family" at Newcastle.

* "Ecclesiastical Memorials," vol. ii. p. 521
† This statement is made by Mr. Barnes, editor of Strype's "Memorials of Cranmer." Routledge's edition, 1853, vol. i. p. 423.

Privy Council there appears, under date the 27th day of October, 1552, the following entry :—

"A warrant to the foure gentlemen of the privie chamber to pay to Mr. Knokes, preacher in the north, in way of the King's Majesty's reward, the sum of XL*l*."

From which entry it is not only certain that he was one of the King's chaplains at that date, but also highly probable that he had been so for at least the better part of a year before, if not for a whole year, unless it were allowable to suppose that he was paid the amount of his salary in advance. But such a supposition is set aside by another piece of evidence of the most authentic kind, viz., his own statement in a letter to Mrs. Bowes, written in January, 1553-54, that "Either the Queen's Majesty (Mary) or some THESAURER will be XL. pounds the richer by me for sa mekall (so much) lack of dewtie of my patentis," *i.e.*, of what was due to him of stipend, as one of the King's chaplains. This makes it certain that his stipend was not paid in advance, and reckoning back one year, from the beginning of 1553-54, to that of 1552-53, we must infer that the amount of stipend paid to him in October, 1552, could not have been in advance, but had reference to the preceding twelvemonth, which of course carries back his appointment to the last quarter of 1551.

From this well-ascertained date, then, we are to think of Knox as occupying at Newcastle the high and influential position of one of the six chaplains of the King, all of them men selected on account of their distinction as preachers—"accounted," says Burnet, "the most zealous and ready preachers of that time, who were thus sent about as itinerants to supply the defects of the greatest part of the clergy, who were generally very faulty." Of the six names of King's chaplains given above, that of Bradford disappears in the year 1552, and the name of Robert Horn, Dean of Durham, is substituted ; and of the list thus modified, no fewer than three— Harely, Grindal, and Horn—were afterwards raised to the bench of Bishops.

This dignified and well-remunerated appointment was a signal mark of the confidence and favour of the pious young King and his honourable Council, and must have added much to Knox's consideration and weight in the social scale, however little it could add to his now fully-developed powers as a pulpit orator. It also very materially enlarged the field of his mission. Hitherto

CH. II.] *HIS VIEW OF DUTY AS A ROYAL CHAPLAIN.* 81

his labours, for aught that appears, had been confined to Berwick and Newcastle and their immediate neighbourhood; but now, his commission extended to the whole along with one of his colleagues—we know not which of them—of the border counties east and west, and notices begin to appear in his letters of his labours as a preacher in more places than one in districts even as distant from Newcastle as Carlisle.

It would seem, also, that his royal chaplaincy was interpreted by him as imposing upon him a special pulpit responsibility in relation to public affairs. He had always, indeed, used the liberty and fulfilled the duties of his office in testifying against national as well as individual sins, and in calling the nation to repentance and amendment by the dread of coming judgments; but as yet we have met with no instance of his administering public rebuke to men in power, or to any of the great parties or factions of the Court and the kingdom. But it is worth noticing how soon after his royal appointment he began to extend the range of his pulpit animadversions and rebukes in this delicate and dangerous direction; and we cannot help inferring that this was no accidental coincidence, but the effect of a deliberate deduction of his enlarged warrant and duty from the heightened dignity and station to which he had been advanced. A few incidents of this exciting kind are preserved in the following passages of his own writings, which are all extremely characteristic of the Reformer's spirit and manner as a public man and minister of God.

In his "Godly Letter to the Faithful in London, Newcastle, and Berwick," of the year 1554,* written at Dieppe, on hearing of the relapse of many of his former converts to the Popish worship, he is forewarning them of the national punishment and plagues which must certainly ensue from such an apostacy, "except repentance prevent;" and he continues his faithful discourse as follows :—

"This my affirmation shall displease many and shall content few. God, who knoweth the secrets of all hearts, knoweth that it also displeases myself; and yet, like as of before I have been obliged to speak in your audience and in audience of others such things as were not plausible to the ears of men, whereof, alas! a great part is this day come to pass, so I am compelled to wryte, with the tears of my eyes, I know to your displeasure.

* "Knox's Works," vol. iii. p. 167.

G

My pen, I trust, shall now be no more vehement than my tongue has been oftener than once, not only before you but also before the chief of the realm. What was said in Neweastle and Berwick before 'the sweating sickness' I trust some in those parts yet bear in mind," alluding to the prevalence of that fatal disease in England in the summer and autumn of 1551. "And upon the day of All Saints (as they call it), in the year that the Duke of Somerset was last apprehended, let Newcastle witness." This event occurred 16th October, 1551. "What before him, that then was Duke of Northumberland, in the town of Newcastle, and in other places more . . . If men will not speak, yet shall the stones and timber of those places cry in fire, and shall bear record that the truth was spoken, and shall absolve me in that behalf in the day of the Lord."

What the prophet-like preacher had given note of warning of on these occasions, he does not distinctly record; but we can gather, from the connection in which these allusions occur, that the promotions he had given his hearers in all these instances had been of plagues and public calamities, which, he foresaw, were about to ensue, as judgments from Heaven upon the iniquity which he saw abounding among both people and rulers. For here is the context in which they stand: "Suspect not, brethren, that I delight in your calamities, or in the plagues that shall fall upon that unthankful nation. No; God I take to record that my heart mourneth within me, and that I am cruciate with remembrance of your troubles; but if I should cease, then should I do against my conscience, as also against my knowledge, and so should I be guilty of the blood of them that perish for lack of admonition, and the plague not a moment the longer be delayed. For the Lord has appointed the day of his vengeance, before the which he sends his trumpets and messengers, that his elect, watching and praying with all sobriety, may, by his mercy, escape the vengeance that shall come."

The incident which gave rise to the most remarkable of these pulpit manifestoes was the "lamentable execution of the Duke of Somerset, ex-Protector of the Kingdom, on Tower Hill, on the 22nd of January, 1552, brought about," as Strype records, " by a faction headed by the proud Duke of Northumberland. It was then reported that the chief assisters of Northumberland in bringing the Duke to his end were the Earl of Arundel, the Lord Wriothesley, and Sir

Richard Southwell, all great Papists, and the two former then under a cloud, and therefore very enemies to the Duke. These Northumberland useth, soon after bringeth again into the Court, and who in such favour now with the King as they? By this means, it is said, many false rumours and forged letters were sent about, to the defamation of the Duke of Somerset, and to make him criminal."*
Somerset, whatever had been the errors of his administration in some matters, and however chargeable he might have been with designs of monopolizing power, during the King's minority, at the expense of his political rivals, had been a sincere friend of the Reformation, and had done much to sustain and promote it, in the face of its numerous and powerful adversaries both in the Church and the State. Knox was one of many in England who lamented his fall and death as a public calamity, and as soon as the news reached Newcastle, the pulpit of St. Nicholas rang with the mingled explosions of his grief and indignation :—

"What the Devil and his members, the pestilent Papists, meant by his away-taking, God compelled my tongue to speak in more places than one; and especially before you, the professors of God's truth, and in the Newcastle, as Sir Robert Brandling did not forget of long time after. God grant that he may understand all other matters spoken before him then as at other times, as rightly as he did that mine interpretation of the vineyard whose hedges, ditches, towers, and winepress God destroyed because it would bring forth no good fruit; and that he may remember that whatever was spoken by my mouth that day is now complete and come to pass; except that the final destruction and vengeance of God is not yet fallen upon the greatest offenders, as assuredly shortly it shall, unless that he and such other of his sort that then were enemies to God's truth, will speedily repent, and that earnestly, of their stubborn disobedience. God compelled my tongue, I say, openly to declare that the Devil and his ministers intended only the subversion of God's true religion by that mortal hatred amongst those which ought to have been knit together by Christian charity and by benefits received (referring to Northumberland and Somerset), and especially that the wicked and envious Papists, by that ungodly breach of charity, diligently minded the overthrow of him that, to his own destruction, procured the death of his innocent friend. Thus, I say, I was compelled of conscience, oftener than

* Strype's "Ecclesiastical Memorials," vol. ii. p. 535.

once, to affirm that such as saw and invented the mean how the one should be taken away, saw and should find the means also to take away the other; and that all that trouble was devised by the Devil and his instruments to stop and hinder Christ's disciples and their poor boat."

In the margin of this characteristic passage the author printed the note: "This was affirmed, both before the King, and also before Northumberland, oftener than once," which could only have been some time later in this year, 1552, when Northumberland visited the border as Warden General of the Marches, and when Knox preached in his course before the King at Court.*

The good opinion which Knox so early published from his pulpit of Somerset, the victim of an unscrupulous rival and a Popish cabal, has been confirmed by the incisive research of the latest historian of those troubled times.

"In revolutions the most excellent things are found ever in connection with the most base. The enthusiast for the improvement of mankind works side by side with the adventurer to whom change is welcome, that he may better his fortune in the scramble; and thus it is that patriots and religious reformers show in fairest colours when their cause is ungained, when they are a struggling minority, chiefly called upon to suffer. . . . Too often, as the Devil loves most to mar the fairest works, the good, when success is gained, are pushed aside as dreamers, or used only as a shield for the bad deeds of their confederates. . . . The historian, who in Somerset's life sees much to censure, can find but good words only for the victim of the treachery of Northumberland."

The warning note of the preacher, too, was only an echo of one of the "good Duke's" last words upon the scaffold. "I have been always, being in authority, a furtherer of religion, to the glory of God, to the uttermost of my power, whereof I am nothing sorry, but rather have cause and do rejoice most gladly that I have so done, for the greatest benefit of God that ever I had, or any man might have in this world; beseeching you all to take it so, and to follow it on still; for, if not, there will follow and come a worse and great plague."†

* The passage occurs in "A Faithful Admonition to the Professors of God's Truth in England," printed abroad in 1554, which was the first year of Knox's exile after the accession of Mary. "Works," vol. iii. pp. 277-78.
† Froude's "History of England," ch. 28.

It was a salient feature of Knox's ministry in England, as afterwards in Scotland (though he was far from standing alone in this respect, for it was the practice of all the greatest preachers of the age), that he was so often constrained by an irresistible pressure of conscience, to utter such plain-spoken warnings of coming retribution for national sins, or for the crimes of parties or high-placed individuals in Church or State. It is impossible to doubt the perfect sincerity of his convictions on all these occasions; or the thorough purity of the motives which impelled him to hold that kind of language in which his admonitions so often passed into the prophetic style, and his warnings into seer-like sentences of doom. How, then, did he come by such forecastings of the future, near or remote? Does he throw any light himself upon this interesting question? Not seldom he does so—as, for example, in immediate sequence to the passage which we have just now cited, where he continues his discourse in the following remarkable terms: "But ye would know the grounds of my certitude. God grant that, hearing them, ye may understand and steadfastly believe the same. My assurances are not the marvels of Merlin, nor yet the dark sentences of profane prophecies; but (1) the plain truth of God's word, (2) the invincible justice of the everlasting God, and (3) the ordinary course of his punishments and plagues from the beginning, are my assurance and grounds.

"God's word threateneth destruction to all inobedient; his immutable justice must require the same. The ordinary punishments and plagues show examples. What man, then, can cease to prophesy? The word of God plainly speaks, that if a man shall hear the curses of God's law, and yet, in his heart, shall promise to himself felicity and good luck, thinking that he shall have peace, albeit he walk after the imaginations of his own will and heart; to such a man the Lord will not be merciful, but his wrath shall be kindled against him, and He shall destroy his name from under heaven. How the Lord threateneth plague after plague, and even the last to be sorest, until finally He will consume realms and nations, if they repent not, read the 26th chapter of Leviticus, which chapter oft have I willed you to mark, and yet I do unfeignedly. And think not it appertaineth to the Jews only. No, brethren, the Prophets are the interpreters of the law, and they make the plagues of God common to all offenders. The punishment ever beginneth at the household of God."

This passage of the Reformer's writings is of primary authority as a standard of interpretation for all those places—and they are numerous—where he speaks in what, in an accommodated sense, may be called a prophetic tone and manner; and in which it has sometimes been thought that he spoke not without some endowment of supernatural insight and foreknowledge. We have indeed, for our part, no $à\ priori$ difficulties or objections to urge against even such a mode of explanation. But we behove to guard carefully against the danger that such a freedom from undue preoccupation of mind on one side of the question may insensibly slide into a too great facility of belief on the other; and to guard us on this side such an explanation of the "grounds of his certitude," deliberately volunteered by the Reformer himself, ought surely to be sufficient. Now among these grounds there is no place whatever assigned to any supernatural communication, save "the plain truth of God's word." All the bases of Knox's "assurance," in such cases, were the same which are open and accessible to every believing man as much as to him, viz. : "God's word threatening destruction to all inobedient; his immutable justice requiring the same, as it must; and the ordinary punishments and plagues showing examples before the eyes of all; what man, then, can cease to prophesy?"

Such a power and manner of prophecy was no marvel or puzzle in any man. It called for no special explanation in Knox. It was simply the utterance of his strong faith in the immutable word of the Eternal—a faith however of the very strongest that mortal man ever possessed—a faith of the miracle-making kind, that can remove mountains. As Thomas Carlyle expresses it, "In heartfelt instinctive adherence to truth, in sincerity, as we say, he has no superior. Nay, we might ask, what equal he has? The heart of him is of the true prophet cast. He resembles more than any of the moderns an old Hebrew prophet—the same inflexibility, intolerance, rigid, narrow-looking adherence to God's truth; stern rebuke in the name of God to all that forsake truth—an old Hebrew prophet in the guise of an Edinburgh minister of the sixteenth century—we are to take him for that, nor require him to be other."*

The visit before referred to which the Duke of Northumberland made to the border counties in the summer of 1552, in his capacity

* "Lectures on Heroes, Hero-worship, and the Heroic in History," p. 137, 1872.

as "General Warden of all the Marches towards Scotland," was not without important influence upon the chapter of Knox's life which we shall have next to narrate. He came accompanied by the Earls of Huntingdon and Pembroke and a brilliant retinue, and spent several weeks in the province, inspecting the fortifications of Berwick and other border strengths, giving orders for new military works, and making new dispositions of the March-wardenries, including the appointment of Lord Wharton to be his Deputy Warden General. Knox tells us that he preached before him "in Newcastle, and in other places moe," from which we may probably gather that he accompanied him as the representative of the King (for the Duke was Lord Lieutenant, as well as Lord Warden) in the capacity of royal chaplain throughout the province. The powerful statesman and the great preacher had thus an opportunity of observing and studying one another, which would appear to have been not unimproved on either side. Dudley would seem to have been deeply impressed with Knox's character and powers, and with the value of his services in the cause of the Reformation; for from that time he became his good friend and patron. What Knox thought of Dudley, as the result of his observations made at this time and soon after at Court, we shall see by-and-by. But, meanwhile, they would appear to have been so closely associated together in their movements through the country for several months, that Knox began to be spoken of in London as the chaplain of the great and all-powerful Duke.

SUPPLEMENT TO CHAPTER II.

"The Reasoning betwixt Knox and the Abbott of Crossragwell."

In 1563 Knox published in Edinburgh an extremely curious and interesting tract, entitled "Heir followeth the coppie of the ressoning which was betwix the Abbote of Crossragwell and John Knox, in Mayboill, concerning the Masse, in the yeare of God, a thousand five hundredth thre scoir and two yeares." It will be found in the sixth volume of Dr. Laing's edition of "Knox's Works." A considerable extract from it, containing the argument of the Abbot against Knox's syllogism against the Mass, was included by Dr. M'Crie among the many curious articles of his Appendix to the Reformer's "Life."

In 1561 an Oration by Master Quintine Kennedy, Commendator of Crossragwell, had been published, in which he exhorted "all thais of the Congregation* to espy how wonderfully they are abusit by their dissaitful preachers," and Knox had been singled out to bear almost the whole brunt of this clever but by no means successful attack.

A copy of the Reformer's "Vindication of the Doctrine that the Mass is Idolatry," had come into the Abbot's hand, along with his letter to the Queen Regent of Scotland, both of which had been published in 1556; and Kennedy had quickness enough to perceive what advantage Knox had given to his opponents by that ambiguity in the use of the term idolatry in his first syllogism, on which we have commented above. He resolved therefore to make this very syllogism the starting point of his Oration, and he introduced his critique upon it in the following extremely well-put exordium :—

* "The Congregation," and "the Lords of the Congregation," were the names assumed by the Scottish Protestants and those of the nobility who joined them.

"Movit and constrainit, not only by natural affection through tenderness of blood whilk is betwix me and divers noblemen of the Congregation, but rather compellit in my conscience, I have thought expedient to bestow and apply the talent and grace whilk God has given me (if there be ony) in such manner as may be to the glory of God, true setting forth of his word to those whilkis are abusit with false, wicked, and ungodly doctrine; specially in this maist dangerous time, whereinto all heresies appear to be assembled and gathered together as an arrayed host to invade, oppress, and utterly downthrow the true faith and religion of Christian men, so dearly coft [bought] with the precious blood and death of Jesus Christ our Saviour. And to the effect that we may, by God's grace and favour, fulfil this our godly pretence [proposal] and purpose, shortly will we call to remembrance ane notable syllogism or argument set forth by ane famous preacher, callit John Knox, in his sermon against the Mess, in manner as after follows :—

" All worshipping, honouring, or service invented by the brain of man in the religion of God," &c., &c.

" Have patience, beloved brethren in Jesus Christ, and suffer me to decipher and declare this disguisit syllogism, and, God willing, I shall make you clearly to understand if the same be godly, properly, and learnedly applied for confirmation of his purpose to prove the Mess idolatry."

The clever Abbot shuts his eyes, of course, to all the evidence which Knox himself supplies of his use of the word idolatry in its widest sense, ethical as well as theological. He takes care to understand him as referring only to idolatry in its narrowest sense, as the worship of an idol instead of God, and has no difficulty therefore in showing that one at least of the examples adduced by Knox from the Old Testament (for he is careful also to refer to no more than one of them), that of Saul's offering sacrifice to the Lord without a divine warrant, is inadequate to prove that this invention of Saul's own brain was an act of idolatry. "For why," says he, "idolatry is to ascribe God's glory to any other save to God himself, or to worship any other as God, which Saul did not, because he made his sacrifice and oblation to the living God, wherethrough he committed no idolatry; wherefore it is manifest that this testimony of Scripture is improperly applied for probation of idolatry.". . " And to be assured of the same, ye shall mark the words of Samuel the prophet, speaking unto Saul: 'Thou art become a fool that hast not observed the precepts of the Lord, which he hath commanded thee.' Mark how Samuel found fault with Saul because that Saul broke the commandment of God, and not that he committed idolatry; for all breaking of the commandment of God is not idolatry, but all idolatry is the breaking of the commandment of God; whilk difference this subtile reasoner apparently has not diligently markit; and albeit the Scripture does affirm that stubbornness is as the wickedness of idolatry, nevertheless, stubbornness is not idolatry. Likewise the Scripture does call disobedience as the sin of witchcraft, yet disobedience is not witchcraft. Thus may we perceive how men unlearnit are oft times deceaved by the Scripture falsely interpreted. Now do I appeal the conscience of all those of the Congregation to be equal judges, and decern [decide] if this syllogism above rehearsed be godly, properly, and learnedly applied for confirmation of Knox's wicked opinion against the blessed sacrifice of the Mess. For Christ's sake take heed how miserably ye are deceaved by the deceitful doctrine of your devote doctor, of whom some of you have intolerable vain persuasion, thinking him to have the Spirit of God, as had Peter or Paul."

All this artful handling of Knox's argument was of course exceedingly unfair and uncandid, as he had plainly enough indicated the wider sense in which he had employed the term idolatry, in the syllogism which was thus dexterously impugned. But Knox had laid himself open to this attack from his clever antagonist by omitting to define the term in form, before he proceeded to make use of it; and he would even seem to have become sensible of his miscarriage in this particular, from the show of advantage which Kennedy had derived from it; for it is remarkable that though the Abbot sent him a copy of his "Oration" before the disputation at Maybole began, with the taunting remark, "Please to receive a confutation of your syllogism whilk I have sent you, and if ye defend the same weill, ye are mair able to make impugnation of mine," Knox never once returned to the defence of his syllogism, nor even once alluded to it; though he makes ample amends for this, both to his cause and to himself, in the form of a "Prologue unto the reader," in which he makes such an assault upon "the great idol presented by the Papists to be worshipped in their Mass" as is not to be paralleled for withering rebuke and sarcastic mockery in any of his other writings. Here, at least, he uses the word "idolatry" in as literal, strict, and gross a sense as anywhere it is used in the writings of the ancient prophets —those stern and grand old image-breakers—justifying his language by theirs, and, if possible, even exceeding theirs in severity, in the vehemency of his resolve, "by all means possible to let the blind world see the vanity of that idol, considering that by it hath the glory of God been more obscured than ever it was by any idol on the earth; for to none was never absolutely given the name, nature, power, and honour of God, but to that idol alone."

The reader who has not access to the "Prologue" in the "Works" (vol vi. pp. 171-75), will probably value the following extracts from it, which are well worth perusal. It begins thus :—

"John Knox unto the reader wisheth grace, mercie, and peace, from God the Father, and from our Lorde Jesus Christe, with the spirit of righteous judgement.

"After that the Prophet Isayas in great vehemencie had rebuked the vanitie of idolles and idolaters, as in the 40 and 41 chapters of his prophecie doth appear, at last he burseth forth in these wordes: 'Let them bring forth their gods,' saith he, 'that they may show unto us things that are to come, that we may understand you to be gods; let you do either good or evill that we may declare it.' Be [by] which wordes the Prophet doeth, as it were, in mockage provoke idolaters and the idoles to produce for themselves some evident testimonies by the which men might be assured that in them was power, and that there religion had approbation of God; which when they could not do, he is bold to pronounce this sentence, 'Behold ye are of nothing, and your making is of nothing; abomination hath chosen you.' In which wordes the Prophet damneth both the idoles and the idolaters—the idoles, because they can declare nothing to prove any power or vertue to be in them why they should be worshipped as gods; and the idolaters, because from God's mouth they could bring no assurance of their addulterat and usurped religion.

"If this reasoning of the Prophet had sufficient strength in his age to show the vanitie of the idoles, and the phrenetic foolishness of such as worshipped them, then may the godlie this day most assuredly conclude against the great idole presented by the Papists to be worshipped in their Masse, and against the patrons of the same, that it and they are vane, foolish, odious, and abominable before God; it, because it hath mo [more] makers than ever had the idoles amongst the Gentiles, and yet hath no greater power that they had, albeit it hath been worshipped as God Himself; and they, because they worshipped their own imagination, and the workmanship of their own hands, without any assurance of God and his word.

"If any think that I speak more liberally than I am able to prove, let him consider what makers the idoles of the Gentiles had and what makers the god of bread [the host or wafer] hath; and then let the power of both be compared, and let me be rebuked if I speak not the treuth. The Prophet in description of their vanities maketh these gries [steps]: 'The earth bringeth forth the tree, it groweth by moistour and natural wakness (humidity), it is cutted down by the hand of the hewar. A parte thereof is burnt, a parte spent in uses necessarie to man, another parte chosen to be made an idole. This is formed to the licknes of man or woman, and then set up, and worshipped as a god.' All these and some mo shall we find to assist and concurre in the making of this great god of bread. The wheaten is sowen and nourished in the earth; rain, dew, and heat bring it to maturitie; the reaper or scherer cutteth it downe; the carte or sled drawen by hors, or some other beast, draweth it to the barne or to the barnyaird; the tasker or the foot of the ox tredeth it out; the fan delivereth it from the chaff; the millar and the millstones, by the help of wind or watter, maketh it to be meall; the smith maketh the yrnes that gives to that god his lenth and breaid, lickness and form; the fyne substance of that god is nether wood, gold, or silver, but watter and meal made in manner of a drammock; and then must the workmen take good heed to their hand; for, if the fyre be too hote, that god's skin must be burnt, if the yrnes be evill dight [ill-wiped] his face will be blecked [blackened], if in making the roundness the ring be broken, then must another of his fellowes receive that honour to be made a god, and the crased or craked miserable caik, that once was in hope to be made a god, must be given to a babby to play him withal. And yet is not all the danger past; for if there be not an anoynted preist to play his parte aright, all the former artificers have lost their labours, for without him that god cannot be made; yea, if he have not intention to consecrate, the fashioned god remaneth bread, and so the blind people commit idolatrie.

"These are the artificers and workmen that travell in making of this god. I think as many in number as the Prophet reciteth to have travelled in making of the idoles; and if the power of bothe shal be compared, I think they shal be found in all thinges equall, except that the god of bread is subject unto mo dangers then were the idoles of the Gentiles. Men made them; men make it. They were deaf and dum; it cannot speak, hear, nor see. Brieflie, in infirmitie they wholie aggre, except that (as I have said) the poore god of bread is most miserable of all other idoles. For according to their matter whereof they are made, they will remaine without corruption many years; but within one year that god will putrifie, and then he must be burnt. They can abyde the vehemencie of the wind, frost, rain, or snow. But the wind will blow that god to the sea; the rain or the snow will make it daigh [dough] again— yea, which is most of all to be feared, that god is a pray (if he be not wel kept) to rattes and mise, for they will desyre no better denner then white, round gods ynew [enough]. But O, then, what becometh of Christes natural bodie? By myrackle, it flies to the heaven againe, if the Papists teach treullie; for how sone soever the mouse takes hold, so sone flieth Christ away and letteth her gnaw the bread—a bold and puissant mouse, but a feble and miserable god. Yet wold I ask a question—Whether hath the preist or the mouse greater power? By his wordes he made a god; by her teith it ceaseth to be a god; 'let them arise, and then answer.'

"If any think that I oght not to mock that which the world so long hath holden, and great princes yet holde, in so great veneratioun, I answer that not onelie I, but also all godlie, ought not onelie to mock, but also to curse and detest whatsoer is not God, and yet usurpeth the name, power, and honour of God; and also that we oght to mock, gainsay, and abhor all religion obtruded to the people without assurance of God and his word; having nether respect to antiquitie, to multitude, to authoritie, nor estimatioun of them that mantean the same. The idoles of the Gentiles were more ancient than is the idole in the Mass. Their worshippers, manteners and patrons were mo in multitude, greater in authoritie, and more excellent before the world, then ever was any that bowed to that idole; and yet feared not the Prophet Isayas to mock and jest them (Is. xlii.)—yea, sharplie to rebuke them in these wordes: 'They are dung [driven] backward with shame, they shal be ashamed whosoever truseth in a graven ymage, and that say to the molten ymage "Ye are our gods." All the makers of graven ymages are vaine, their pleasing thinges shall not proffet them (Is. xliv.), for they themselves are witnesses to their idoles, that they nether see nor understand anything, and therefore they shal be ashamed.' 'Who then,' sayeth he, 'shall forge a god or a molten ymage that profiteth nothing? Behold! all those that are of the fellowship thereof shal be confounded, for the workmen themselves are men; let them all be gathered together and stand up, yet they shall feare and be confounded together.'

"And when he hath fully painted forth their vanitie he concludeth, 'They have not understand [understood], for God hath shut up their eyes that they cannot see, and harts that they cannot understand; none considereth in his hart, I have burnt half of it, even in the fyre, and have baken bread also upon the coalles thereof; I have rosted fleshe and eaten it, and shall I make the residew therof an abomination? shall I bow to the stock of a tree?' etc. Thus, I say, we see how the Prophet doeth triumph against the idolaters in mocking of their madnes, and painting forth of their vanitie. Who, then, can justlie be offendit against me or any other, albeit by all meanes possible we make the blind world see the vanitie of that idole, considering that by it hath the glorie of God bene more obscured then ever it was by any idole in the earth? for to none was never absolutelie given the name, nature, power, and honour of God but to that idole alone.

"If any think that the Scriptures of God give unto them patrocinie [patronage or favour], ether to believe Christis naturall body to be there after the wordes of consecration (as they cal them), ether yet to beleve that Christ Jesus in his Last Supper did offer unto God his Father his body and blood under the formes of bread and wine, he is miserablie deceaved; for the Scripture maketh no mention of conversion or transubstanciation of bread in [into] Christes naturall bodie, but witnesseth that bread remaneth bread, yea even when the faithfull receave the same, as the Apostle affirmeth in these wordes: 'The bread which we break is it not the communication of Christes body? The cup of blessing which we blesse, is it not the communion of the blood of Christ? We many are one bread and one bodie, because we are all partakers of one bread.' And after, he sayeth, 'As oft as ye shall eat of this bread and drink of this cup,' &c. By these wordes we may clearlie understand what judgment the Apostle had of the substance of that Sacrament, even in the very action of the same.

"And as touching that foolish opinion that Christ Jesus did offer his body unto God his Father under the formes of bread and wine, &c. (which the Papists make the ground of their Masse), what suffrage that ever it hath by man, of God nor his word it hath none. The Scripture doeth witness that God the Father gave his Sone unto the world that the world might be saved by Him, and that Jesus Christ did offer Himself once unto God for the destruction of sinne, and for to take away the sinnes of many; but that ever He did offer Himself under the formes of bread and wine (as the Papists allege) the Holy Ghost doeth nowhere make mention; and therefore the faithfull may not onlie reject it as the dreame and invention of man, but also are bound to abhor and detest it as a doctrine brought in by Satan to deceave such as delight not in the veritie of God, to whose mouth and voice are the faithfull onely bound. . . .

"If Mr. Quintyne will not be reputed ane false prophet, and one that teacheth lies in the name of God, and so expose himself to God's hote displeasure, he may propose no doctrine to the Church of God the assurance whereof he bringeth not from the mouth of God. If Mr. Quintyne were bawling in the scooles, or bragging of knowledge amongest the philosophers, I wold pacientlie abyde that he should affirm as many paradoxes as pleaseth him; but in the Church of God to affirme that God hath spoken or done that which he is not able to prove by his plain word that he hath done, so to do (I say) is altogether intollerable; and therefore let Mr. Quintyne searche the Scriptures for the probation of his affirmative, or els I will cry als loud as I can that he hath lost his cause, and is convicted ane manifest lear, in that he hath affirmed Jesus to have done that which no Scripture doeth witness that he hath done. Let all men, therefore, that will not follow lies, detest the Mass till that it find a ground within the Booke of God, as I am assured it never shall."

We add from Abbot Kennedy's Oration the closing paragraph, in which he gives a summary of its contents, and which will serve as a specimen of the style in which he was pleased to throw down the glove to Knox and his colleagues, from which it will be seen that all the "rude vehemency" of speech which is so alien to the usage and taste of modern controversy, was not confined to the Reformer's side of the question :—

"Now will we brevelie collect the effect and substance of our oration, contenit in thre heidis. In the first heid is abundantlie and sufficiantlie confutit Knox's disagysit syllogisme, quhilk is his fundament quharupon he gadderis and biggis [gathers and builds] all his furie, mokerie, and dispite aganis the Mess, quhilk being subvertit (as it is indeed be [by] Scripturis propirlie appliit), the rest (be rasone) biggit upon this ruinouss fundament gois to the grounde. In the secunde heid is maid manifest quhat calamite, miserie, and hurt hes the commoun wele of this realme daly sustenit and sufferit be Knox and utheris factious prechouris to the congregatioun, thrawand [wresting] the Scripture of Almycti God by [past] the godlie menyng of the samyne, to be scheilde and buklar to thair lustis and hereseis. Into the third, we testify our affectioune and grete gude will to all thaise of the congregatioune, specialy sick [such] as ar unleirnit, gevande thaim cleirlie to understande how Knox, thair mischeant minister, and the rest, plays the jugleour in ministratione of the blissit Sacrament of the altare, contrare to the ordinance and institutione of Jhesus Christ our Salviour, according to the doctrine and interpretatione of all men of gudlie leirnyng and gude lyfe; quhilk is ane of the cheif Sacramentis quharby Jhesus Christ our Salviour hes appointit, for salvatione of manne, the frutt of his deith and passione to be daly renewit and appliit. And thus we conclude, nocht deuttande [doubting] bot the congregatioune (specialie thais of leirning and sober judgment) will tak this our godlie doctrine to hart, or at the least suspend thair opinioune and jugement unto the time thair ministeris and preacheouris mak sufficient answere and confutatioun to this our oratioune. Quharfor, with all my hart, exhortis, prays, and but [without] mercie, appellis thar pestilent precheouris, puffit up with vane glore, quhilkis rackinnis thaimselfis of gretar knawlege nor [than] Christis haill Kirk, cumand but [without] authorite, subvertand, subornande, and circumvenande the simple peple, cersande [seeking] thair pray like the Devillis rachis [bloodhounds], barkand baldly like bardis, aganis the blissit Sacrament of the altare, the sacrifice of the Mess, and all uther godlie ordinance of Jhesus Christ and his Kirk, to preiss [press] thair wittes and ingines [genius], and to streik [stretch] all thair pennis in my contrar;

makande the congregatioune and all utheris to understande, gif [if] I do propirly, treuly, and godlie or nocht, invey aganis thair devillische doctrine and doyings ; failyeande tharof, recant, for shame, recant (ye famouse precheouris*), and cum in obedience to the Kirk of God, quhilk ye have stubbornlie misknaun this lang tyme bipast (and that nocht without grete dangere to your aune saulis and mony utheris), thairfor recant, in tyme recant, as ye lufe your salvatioun, and cry God mercie; to quham, with the Sone and Holye Gaist, be prayse, honour, and glore, for ever ande ever. Amen.

"Progenies viperarum fugite a ventura ira ; nam securis ad radicem arboris posita est ; penitentiam agite" (Math. iii.).

---

* On the margin of the Auchinleck MS., from which the Oration was first printed by Sir Alexander Boswell in 1812, are written the names of the "famouse preacheouris" whom Kennedy had in his eye—"Knox, Willock, Winrame, Gudmane, Dowglase, Heriot, Spottiswode, and all the rest."

CHAPTER III.

KNOX AS ROYAL CHAPLAIN AT THE COURT OF EDWARD VI.—HIS IN-
FLUENCE UPON THE LITURGY AND ARTICLES OF THE CHURCH.

NOTHING further is recorded of Knox's movements and work till his visit to Court, in his capacity as one of the King's chaplains, in the autumn of 1552, which would appear to have been the first occasion of his preaching in his turn before the young King and his Court and Council.

The Court had returned to Windsor from a progress through several of the western counties towards the end of September, and a remarkable sermon was delivered at that time before the young King by a preacher, who is described but not named, by the only writer who has given any account of or made the most remote allusion to the incident. In a letter of John Utenhovius, to Henry Bullinger, dated London, October 12, 1552, occurs the following piece of ecclesiastical news :—

"Some disputes have arisen within these few days among the bishops in consequence of a sermon by a pious preacher, chaplain to the Duke of Northumberland, preached by him before the King and Council, in which he inveighed with great freedom against kneeling at the Lord's Supper, which is still retained here in England. This good man, however, a Scotsman by nation, has so wrought upon the minds of many, that we may hope some good to the Church will at length arise from it, which I earnestly implore the Lord to grant.*

* " Original Letters relative to the English Reformation" (Parker Society), p. 591. The passage in the original letter runs thus :—

" Hic nunc a paucis saltem diebus subortæ sunt turbae quaedam inter episcopos ex concione pii cujusdam viri, concionatoris ducis Northumbriae, quam habuit coram rege ac consiliariis ejus, in qua vere libere invectus est in geniculationem coenae Dominicae, quae hic etiamnum inter Anglos adhuc servatur. Ille tamen vir bonus, Scotus natione, ita affecit multorum animos ut speremus

The learned editor of the "Original Letters Relative to the English Reformation," from which the above extract is taken, Dr. Hastings Robinson, appends to the passage the following note (p. 591): "The preacher referred to was probably Knox, though it does not appear that he was chaplain to the Duke of Northumberland, but possibly this statement may have been a mistake of the writer. There is also some difficulty about the date, as, though Knox was questioned before the Council on his objections to kneeling at the Lord's Supper, this did not take place till April, 1553."

But these difficulties are of no force against Dr. Robinson's conjecture that Knox was the Scotsman referred to, which was as historically correct as it was sagacious, when first made a quarter of a century ago. The difficulty arising from his being spoken of as the chaplain of the Duke of Northumberland disappears when it is known that this nobleman had been engaged that very year in the execution of his office as Warden General of the Border counties, and had came into close contact with Knox as King's chaplain in Newcastle, and other parts of the Northern province. The difficulty, again, connected with the date of Utenhovius's letter comes to nothing as soon as we know, from ample evidence now brought to light, that Knox was undoubtedly in London in the very month of October when the letter was written.

A later writer, Mr. Perry,* commenting upon Utenhovius's letter,

aliquid boni inde tandem ad ecclesiam rediturum esse. Quod ut faxit Dominus etiam atque etiam rogo. Londini, 12 Octobris, 1552. Jo. Utenhovius."

John Utenhovius, a Flemish gentleman of rank, and a fervent Protestant, was at this time a Senior or Elder of the Protestant Church of Foreigners established in London in 1550, by John A-Lasco, the celebrated Polish Reformer, and to which was granted, by Edward VI., the church of Austin Friars, for the conduct of its worship. The more than ordinary interest which Utenhovius took in the incident at Court is accounted for by the curious fact that at this very time A-Lasco was pleading hard with Cranmer and Ridley to be allowed to introduce the practice of sitting in the Communion. In the Royal Deed of Gift of Austin Friars church it had been conceded to the Foreigners that they should have entire freedom of worship and sacramental ritual, but hitherto Cranmer, and, still more tenaciously, Ridley, now Bishop of London, had refused to sanction that innovation in the use of the Lord's Supper, as a dangerous precedent. Hence the natural aspiration of Utenhovius that some good might accrue to the Church from the discussions which had sprung up at Court upon the same subject. Some further illustrations of this point will be found in a note at the end of this chapter.

* *Vide* "Some Historical Considerations relating to the Declaration on was able to express himself more confidently than Dr. Robinson. "Though Knox," says he, "is not here mentioned by name, there can be little doubt that the passage refers to him; for (1) his office of royal chaplain would account for his preaching before this congregation; (2) the writer (who does not seem to have known much of the preacher) may, likely enough, have been ignorant of his recent promotion." Mr. Perry also founds upon the fact, mentioned by Knox himself in his "Admonition to the Professors of God's truth in England," etc., that he had preached before Edward VI. But these reasons of course are inconclusive as to the fact of his having been the preacher at Court upon the particular occasion referred to by Utenhovius, though they are of sufficient weight to make it probable; nor will any evidence be enough to convert this probability into certainty, except such as would establish beyond a doubt that Knox, at that very time of the year 1552, was in London.

This evidence will come out clearly in the course of this chapter; and meanwhile the reader has been prepared, by some of Knox's antecedents in Berwick and Newcastle, to understand why *he* should have chosen such a subject as kneeling at the Lord's Supper to preach upon before the King and his Court. It was a subject, as we have seen, which had been much upon his mind and his tongue during the three preceding years. It was one of the points that further Reformation of the Church's worship which he had actually carried into effect in two of the principal towns of the North; and it was only what might have been expected, that he should have seized the earliest opportunity of preaching before the King on the right administration of the Lord's Supper. Nor was he the first Protestant preacher who had called the attention of the King and his Council to the subject. John Hooper, now Bishop of Gloucester, only two years before had set the example, and pressed for reform in the very same particular and upon the same general grounds.

In his sermons on the Book of Jonas, preached in Lent, 1550, Hooper, in speaking of the Lord's Supper, observed that "the outward behaviour and gesture of the receiver should want all kind of suspicion, shew, or inclination of idolatry. Wherefore, seeing kneeling is a shew and external sign of honouring and

Kneeling appended to the Communion Office of the English Book of Common Prayer," by the Rev. Thomas Walter Perry. London: Masters, 1863.

worshipping, and heretofore hath grievous and damnable idolatry been committed by the honouring of the Sacrament, I would wish it were commanded by the magistrates that the communicators and receivers should do it standing or sitting. But sitting, in mine opinion, were best, for many considerations. The Paschal lamb was eaten standing, which signified Christ yet not to be come, that should give rest, peace, and quietness. Christ and his Apostles used this Sacrament, at the first, sitting; declaring that He was come that should quiet and put at rest both body and soul; and that the figure of the Passover from thenceforth should be no more necessary; nor that men should travel no more to Jerusalem once in the year, to seek and use a Sacrament of the Lamb to come, that should take away the sins of the world. Let us submit ourselves, all our wisdom and learning, unto his Word, and think what Christ and his Apostles have instituted and used, it can in no ways be bettered by us. And you, my gracious Lord and King, restore the right use of the Supper of the Lord, as Josias did the right use of the Paschal lamb, after the Word of God."*

The question, then, of Kneeling in the Sacrament was no new one to the King and his Court, and Edward, though still a boy-King, must have been able to estimate the force of Knox's arguments and appeals better than he had been, two years before, to appreciate those of Hooper. The sermon of the fervid Scottish Reformer made quite a stir at Court. What his reasonings were on the occasion we are nowhere told; nor has he anywhere alluded to the sermon himself; but we shall see in the sequel, from a newly-discovered source, what his thoughts were upon the subject, and, no doubt, these were the same in substance as those which produced upon the audience of the Chapel Royal so marked an effect. His discourse, we are told, was a vehement one, and " wrought " with so much effect upon the minds of many of the nobles and great men who heard it, that something was expected to come out of it for the further reform of the Church. It had kindled a dispute among several of the Bishops themselves. If Hooper, which is probable, was of the number in attendance at Court at the time, it cannot be doubted that he sided with Knox; and a curious and valuable letter has recently come to light, which lets us know that Cranmer took side against him.

* " Early Writings of Bishop Hooper," pp. 536–7. (Parker Society.)

In order to understand clearly the situation of all parties in relation to the point now brought into dispute, it is necessary to bear in mind that in the Second Prayer-book of Edward VI., which was then in the press, and had been appointed by the Parliament of that year to come into use in the churches on the first day of November, All Saints' Day, a Rubric had for the first time been inserted, appointing the Lord's Supper to be administered to the communicants in a kneeling posture. That had for ages been the accustomed posture, and no rubric ordaining it to be used had appeared in the First Prayer-book, on that account. But in the interval between the two books opinion had begun to grow in favour of substituting what was called the "Table Gesture" in the room of kneeling, and had even found expression, as we have just seen, in the preaching of Hooper at Court. As Cranmer, Ridley, and the most of the other Reforming Bishops did not approve of the proposed innovation, they had thought it seasonable to check the tendency towards it by the addition of the new Rubric; and hence the warmth of the debate which arose among them from the vehemence of Knox's attack upon the old usage, and the agitation produced by the stirring up again of a question which had been so recently deliberated upon and settled.

But it was equally natural that Knox, considering what his preaching and sacramental practice had been for several years, should feel strongly on the subject of the new Rubric, and should do what he could to bring about a fresh consideration of the point in dispute. We have seen that both in Berwick and Newcastle he had been under no liturgical restrictions at all; and his surprise must have been great when he found, probably on his arrival in London, that the new Prayer-book was to enjoin a practice which had never been enjoined before, and which he had never hitherto followed. He foresaw at once all the inconvenience and trouble which this change would entail upon his congregations in the North. He would necessarily feel, from his own point of view, that the insertion of such a Rubric was a retrograde step; and it may even have occurred to him that as the new Book had not yet issued from the press, the Rubric might yet be withdrawn by the authority of the King and Council, if he might hope to gain them over to his own views. Hence his choice of the right administration of the Lord's Supper as his subject of discourse in the Chapel Royal; and hence also the earnestness and vehemence with which he handled it before his august audience.

On the 7th of October, 1552, the Archbishop of Canterbury addressed to the Privy Council the letter before referred to, which is of great importance for the light which it throws upon the situation which Knox had so suddenly originated:—

"After my right humble commendations unto your good Lordships, whereas I understand by your Lordships' letters, that the King's Majesty's pleasure is that the Book of Common Service should be diligently perused, and therein the printers' errors to be amended, I shall travail therein to the uttermost of my power, albeit I had need first to have had the book written which was passed by Act of Parliament sealed with the great seal, which remaineth in the hands of Mr. Spilman, clerk of the Parliament, who is not in London, nor I cannot learn where he is. Nevertheless I have gotten the copy which Mr. Spilman delivered to the printers to print by, which I think shall serve well enough.

"And whereas I understand farther, by your Lordships' letters, that some be offended with kneeling at the time of the receiving of the Sacrament, and would that I, calling to me the Bishop of London, and some other learned men, as Mr. Peter Martyr or such like, should with them expend and weigh the said prescription of kneeling, whether it be fit to remain as a commandment, or to be left out of the Book, I shall accomplish the King's Majesty his commandment, albeit I trust that we with just balance weighed this at the making of the Book, and not only we but a great many bishops, and other of the best learned within this realm, and appointed for that purpose.* And now, the Book being read and approved by the whole state of the realm in the High Court of Parliament, with the King's Majesty his royal assent, that this should be now altered again without Parliament, of what importance this matter is I refer to your

---

* Alluding to the meeting for revising the First Book of Common Prayer held at Windsor, referred to in the following passage of Strype's "Ecclesiastical Memorials," vol. ii. part ii. p. 20: "The revising, perusing, explaining, and finishing the Book of Common Prayer and administration of the Sacraments had been committed to the Archbishop and certain other learned divines, whereof Dr. Cox was one, who, being met together at Windsor, diligently, as their scope was, reformed the Book according to the word of God."

Lordships' wisdom to consider. I know your Lordships wisdom to be such that I trust ye will not be moved by these glorious and unquiet spirits, which can like nothing but that is after their own fancy, and cease not to make trouble and disquietness when things be most quiet and in good order. If such men should be heard, although the Book were made every year anew, yet should it not lack faults in their opinion.

"But, say they, it is not commanded in the Scripture to kneel, and whatsoever is not commanded in the Scripture is against the Scripture, and utterly unlawful and ungodly. But this saying is the chief foundation of the error of the Anabaptists and of divers other sects. This saying is a subversion of all order as well in religion as in common policy. If this saying be true, take away the whole Book of Service. For what should men travail to set an order in the form of service, if no order can be set but that [which] is already prescribed by the Scripture. And because I will not trouble your Lordships with reciting of many Scriptures or proofs in this matter, whosoever teacheth any such doctrine (if your Lordships will give me leave) I will set my foot by his to be tried by fire, that his doctrine is untrue, and not only untrue, but also seditious, and perilous to be heard of any subjects, as a thing breaking the bridle of obedience and loosing them from the bond of all princes' laws.

"My good Lordships, I pray you to consider that there be two prayers which go before the receiving of the Sacrament, and two immediately follow, all which time the people, praying and giving thanks, do kneel, and what inconvenience there is, that it may not be thus ordered, I know not. If the kneeling of the people should be discontinued for the time of the receiving of the Sacrament, so that at the receipt thereof, they should rise up and stand or sit, and then immediately kneel down again, it should rather import a contemptuous than a reverent receiving of the Sacrament. But it is not expressly contained in the Scripture, say they, that Christ ministered the Sacrament to his Apostles kneeling. Nor they find it not expressly in Scripture that he ministered it standing or sitting; but if we will follow the plain words of Scripture, we shall rather receive it lying down on the ground, as the custom of the world at that time [was] almost everywhere, and as the Tartars and Turks use yet at this day to eat their meat lying upon the ground. And the words of the Evangelist import the same, which be ἀνάκειμαι and ἀναπίπτω, which signify properly to lie down upon the floor or ground, and not to sit upon a form or stool. And the same speech use the Evangelists where they shew that Christ fed five thousand with five loaves, where it is plainly expressed that they sat down upon the ground and not upon stools.

"I beseech your Lordships to take in good part this my long babbling, which I write as of myself only, because the Bishop of London is not yet come, and your Lordships required answer with speed; and therefore am I constrained to make some answer to your Lordships afore his coming. And thus I pray God long to preserve your Lordships, and to increase the same in all prosperity and godliness. At Lambeth this viith of October, 1552.

"Your Lordships' to command,

"T. CANTR."

Addressed "To my very good Lords of the King's most honourable Council."*

Here, then, we see the situation distinctly revealed. Five days earlier than the date of Utenhovius's letter to Bullinger, the effect which he speaks of as having followed the Scotsman's sermon had already made itself felt in the proceedings of the Privy Council. There had been meetings of Council at Hampton Court both on the 4th and the 6th of October, as we know from its Registers, and it was, no doubt, at either the one or the other of these that the letter to which Cranmer's was a reply had been ordered to be sent. On the 7th the Council met again— the same day on which the Archbishop penned his reply—on

---

* This letter is preserved in the Public Records Office, Fetter Lane, and is included in the Calendar of State Papers, of the reign of Edward VI. When I first came across it, and discovered its importance, I was surprised to find that it was not included either in the Parker Society's collection of "Cranmer's Letters," or in that of Jenkyns in his edition of "Cranmer's Remains." It is not even noticed in the recent "Life of Cranmer," by Dean Hook, nor in the works of Archdeacon Hardwick on the Reformation, and on the Articles of the Church of England. I was under the impression, therefore, for some time, that it had never been printed nor referred to by any of our writers. At last, however, I came upon a printed copy of it in Mr. Perry's work before mentioned, and by him I find it was first given to the public.

which day they "sent to him," says Strype, "to stay his going into Kent till Tuesday, because the Lords would confer with him," that is till October 11, when he was again present at Council. "The Archbishop now retired into his diocese, and was at his house at Ford, whither several messages and letters were sent to him from the Council."* There was plainly a party in the Council favourable to Knox's proposal that the Rubric ordaining kneeling should be removed before the Prayer-book was issued to the Church, and pressing it so strongly that the King and Council went so far as to consent that the subject should be reconsidered, and the bishops instructed to hold a fresh consultation upon it. Ridley, Bishop of London, and the learned Peter Martyr, at Oxford, are again to be called in to give their advice in the new circumstances which have emerged; and what is to be done must be done quickly. The Council request from the Archbishop an immediate reply, and they receive from him the assurance that he has already sent for Ridley. Meanwhile the publication of the new Service Book is stopped, not only till certain errors of the press, detected in the copies already issued, have been corrected by Cranmer's care, but also for this new reason—that it is possible some Rubrical change may have to be introduced; and the matter is urgent, for it is now the second week of October, and, by Act of Parliament, the use of the new book is appointed to commence on the day of "All Saints." We hear no more, however, of Cranmer's consultations with Ridley and their result; though, no doubt, the Archbishop, as soon as possible, communicated that result to the Council. Probably he made the communication at the meeting of the 11th October, at which he conferred with the Lords, or he might send it from Ford, to the meeting of the 20th, of the business to be done, of which a memorandum, in the hand of Secretary Cecil, has been preserved. This paper includes the following brief entry:—

"Mr. Knocks—b. of Cat^{rb} | ye book in ye B. of Durh^m"—

a very significant conjunction of names and things, showing that at that meeting some subject was to come up in which both Knox and the Archbishop were concerned, and along with which was to be taken up some question connected with the use of the book in the bishopric of Durham, in which Knox, the preacher of

* Strype's "Cranmer," vol. i. p. 435. Routledge's edition.

Newcastle, had a special interest.* But, unhappily, no record exists either of the communications made by the Archbishop to the Council at that meeting, or of the decisions which were arrived at on either of the subjects so obscurely hinted at in Cecil's memoranda. No further evidence of any kind is available for this stage of the business. We are left entirely to our own conjectural inferences from what has already come before us in regard to the dispositions both of Cranmer and Ridley upon the question; and it need not be doubted for a moment that the Archbishop's report was opposed to the omission of the Rubric. If nothing, therefore, had taken place subsequently to that meeting to alter the situation, there is no reason to think that the Council would have seen their way to take any new course, or to interpose any farther delay in the publication of the new Prayer-book. In other words, when the Council rose on the 20th of October, it did not seem probable that anything practical would result from the bold procedure of Knox in intervening at so late a stage on the subject of the Communion office. All the agitation which had taken place in Court and Council for the last four weeks seemed likely to end in nothing. For the majority of the Council had evidently not been gained over to the side of change. It was only a minority of the Council, perhaps only the young King himself, who was more bent on a thorough reform than any of his Councillors, that sided with the reasonings of Knox against those of Cranmer and Ridley. But, curious to relate, an incident of business took place at this same meeting of the 20th of October, which, without being imagined at first to have any connection with the question of the Rubric on Kneeling, was immediately afterwards brought into close contact with it, and so as to exercise an important influence upon the form in which the question was finally settled.

* I had observed this significant memorandum in one of the State Papers of Cecil, before I knew that it had been noticed by Mr. Perry, and I quite agree with him in his "conjecture" that the "former part of the note looks very much indeed like an allusion to Knox's alleged complaint of the Rubric on kneeling, and the Archbishop's defence of it." But I put a different interpretation from his on the latter part of the memorandum; and, instead of thinking that it refers to the subject of appointing a Bishop of Durham, I have no doubt that it refers to a proposal to introduce the new Book of Common Prayer into the diocese of Durham, where no Reformed Prayer-book, as we have seen above, had ever been as yet used.

This incident is recorded in the following Record of Council, dated October 20, 1552:—

"A letter was directed to Mess. Harley, Bill, Horn, Grindal, Pern, and Knox, to consider certain Articles exhibited to the King's Majesty, to be subscribed by all such as shall be admitted to be preachers or ministers in any part of the realm, and to make report of their opinions touching the same."

These "Articles of Religion," the original draft of the Thirty-nine Articles, had been in preparation by the Archbishop and the other reforming Bishops since 1551, and had recently been submitted by Cranmer in person to the King, who had laid them before the Council apparently at this meeting. They were forty-five in number as they came from the hands of Cranmer to the King, though afterwards reduced to forty-two, and a copy of them, signed by all the six royal chaplains to whose judgment they were now referred, is still preserved among the State Papers of this reign.[*]

The Article numbered 38 in this authenticated copy had for its subject "The Book of Common Prayer," recently sanctioned by Parliament, and appointed to come into use on the first day of the month of November, now close at hand. It ran in these terms: "Liber qui nuperrime authoritate Regis et Parlamenti ecclesiae Anglicanae traditus est, continens modum et formam orandi et sacramenta administrandi in Ecclesia Anglicana, similiter et libellus ille eadem authoritate editus de ordinatione ministrorum Ecclesiae, quoad doctrinae veritatem pii sunt, et quoad ceremoniarium rationem salutari evangelii libertati, si ex sua natura

---

[*] The date assigned to this document in the Calenders of State Papers by Mr. Lemon, is the 21st of October, which was suggested to him by the late Archdeacon Hardwick, in the following note, which is prefixed to the document:—

"*St. Catharine's Hall, Cambridge,*
"*8th March*, 1851.

"MY DEAR SIR,

"I am now able to inform you, with respect to the Articles of Religion which you were kind enough to assist me in collating, that they were sent to the royal chaplains, whose signatures they bear, on the 21st of October, 1552, and were again in the hands of Archbishop Cranmer on the 20th of November following. "Believe me to remain, dear Sir,

"Very faithfully yours,

"R. Lemon, Esq. "C. HARDWICKE."

ceremoniae illae estimentur, in nullo repugnant sed probe congruunt, et eandem in complurimis imprimis promovent, atque ideo ab omnibus Ecclesiæ Anglicanae fidelibus membris, et maxime a ministris verbi cum omni promptitudine animarum et gratiarum actione recipiendi, approbandi et populo Dei sunt commendandi."

Knox, on perusing this Article, must have immediately felt that it was impossible for him to approve of that portion of it which referred to the ceremonies still retained in the revised Prayer-book, such as the use of the cross in baptism, and the practice of kneeling in the Sacrament now for the first time enjoined by Rubric.

The publication of the Prayer-book by Grafton had commenced in the preceding month of September, and Knox and the other chaplains had doubtless copies of it in their hands.* He saw much to approve of and give God thanks for, in the numerous alterations which had been made upon the Book of 1549; but in view of what he deemed the impurities and corruptions of the primitive worship of the Church of Christ, which were still unremoved, it was impossible for him to give a favourable judgment of the 38th Article in its present form. How could he consistently do so after his recent attack upon the practice of kneeling in the Sacrament as a remnant of Popish superstition? How could he approve an Article which asserted that this and several other ceremonies which he condemned, were worthy to be received with all readiness and thanksgiving, and to be approved and commended to the people of God? And then the thought would seem to have flashed upon him that he had now another and quite an unexpected opportunity of making a fresh appeal to the King

---

* The Register of the Privy Council has the following entry, dated 26th September, 1552 :—

" A letter to Grafton, the printer, to stay in any wise from uttering any of the books of the new Service, and if he have distributed any of them amongst his company (his fellow-printers or publishers), that then to give strait commandment to every of them not to put any of them abroad until certain faults therein be corrected."

This implies that the sale of copies had already commenced, and none would be more eager purchasers than those ministers of the Church who were most zealous for reform.

and Council on that very question of the Rubric on kneeling, which was still apparently in dependence.

There was still time to make one more attempt. In addition to his judgment upon the Articles at large, which need not go before the Council so quickly, what if he should single out this 38th Article on the Prayer-book and make it the subject of a separate representation; and, distinguishing between the ceremony of kneeling and all the rest, what if he should confine the bulk of his representations to this single point, which was now the only one on which it was feasible to look for any immediate alteration?

Such appears to have been the genesis of a remarkable document which is now for the first time brought forward to clear up the history of "The Declaration on Kneeling," which, on the 20th of October, 1552, had not yet been added to the Communion Office of the Prayer-book, but which, on the 27th day of the same month, was ordered by the King in Council to be appended to it. The document referred to is not an original paper, bearing the signatures of its writers; it is only a cotemporary transcript of the original. But it carries in its contents ample intrinsic evidence of having come from the pen of Knox.

Referring the reader to the second part of this volume for the document itself and the evidence of its authorship, attention is invited here to a single remarkable and very convincing proof that it is a writing which formed a real part of the history which is now before us, which grew out of the incidents and affairs of that very time and place, and could not have belonged to or grown out of any other—in a word, a proof of its historical genuineness.

The Article which the document singles out for comment is referred to more than once as No. 38, bearing the title "De Libro Ceremoniarum Ecclesiae Anglicanae." Now when the Articles handed to the chaplains, forty-five in number, were soon afterwards reduced to forty-two, they were also thrown, to a considerable extent, into a new arrangement, and the Article which came to be numbered 38 had now for its subject the lawfulness of oaths, while the Article which was numbered 38 before was numbered 35 in the new arrangement. If, therefore, the document before us had been of any date later than this year 1552, or even any month of this year later than November, on the 24th of which it is certain that Cranmer returned the Articles in their altered and definitive order to the Privy Council, it would have referred to the Article on the Ceremonies as the 35th instead of the 38th.

After the Articles, in their reduced number and revised order, had been settled in November, 1552, and published in 1553, no representation could have been made to the Privy Council against an Article as 38 in number which was no longer such but 35. In truth, any such representation would have been too late and out of date, which was later in being laid before the Council than the 20th of November, 1552, when the Council "despatched the Articles to Ford to be reviewed by the Archbishop, and for his last hand;"* for they were never again taken into consideration by the Council. The drawing up of the document is thus clearly limited to the short interval of time between October 20 and November 20 of the same year.

Nor is this all. The contents of the document are such as to make it manifest and indubitable that it must have been drawn up within the brief interval of a week, between the 20th of October and the 27th. These contents almost exclusively refer to the subject of kneeling in the Lord's Supper, setting out at considerable length the arguments against it, and in support of the sitting posture. But such a representation to the Council would have been too late after the meeting of the 27th of October, when the question which had agitated the Council for a month was finally disposed of by the adoption of the Rubric called the Declaration on Kneeling. On that day an order of the King in Council was sent to Grafton for the insertion of that Rubric, and on All Saints' Day the new Book of Service began to be used in St. Paul's and other churches. Within the limits of a single week, the document was possible and relevant, and might be of use. Before the week began it was not possible, for Knox and the other chaplains were not consulted upon the the Articles till October 21, and after the week was over, the document could have no relevancy or effect, because the question to which it referred had then been finally disposed of.

In the absence of all names from the transcript of the document which has come to light, it is impossible to determine by how many of the King's chaplains the original was signed. But there must have been more signatures attached to it than that of John Knox, as the wording of it implies a plurality of sub-

* Strype's "Cranmer," vol. i. p. 394.

scribers; and if it should be thought improbable that Knox would be joined in such a representation by any of the other five chaplains, having regard to their known or probable opinions on its subject, it is not at all unlikely that he may have been joined in it by one or more of certain other learned men who are referred to in a subsequent Minute of Council as having been consulted about the Articles. For the Minutes of Council dated November 20, 1552, prove that the Articles had been considered by *certain* of his Highness's chaplains and *others*. One or more of these *others*, therefore, may have been associated with Knox in the preparation of the document; and we shall even be able to indicate, in the sequel, with a high degree of probability, two at least of these learned referees.

The document itself, which its authors call a "Confession," begins in this form:—

"Commanded by your letters, most honourable, in writing to report our judgments and opinions on such Articles as, exhibited to the King's Majesty, were directed to certain learned preachers, and among whom we most unworthy were accounted, that, the same by them and us advisedly considered, report might be made of our opinions to your honours again. We therefore, besides that our weak and base [poor] judgment, which we have committed to writing in the Latin tongue, most humbly do offer unto your honours this our confession upon the 38th Article, whereon we think shall stand most doubts and contention; protesting first unto your honours, taking to record in our conscience the Lord Jesus, in presence of whose tribunal seat all flesh shall once appear, where shall be disclosed the secrets of hearts, that neither of arrogance nor vain curiosity, as some may suspect, nor yet of mind to have any innovation in things that be well ordered (for we are not altogether ignorant what inconveniences may ensue the frequent alteration of religion, [but] do most abhor the same; God we take therefore to witness in our conscience, that none of the precedents do move us to offer unto you, most Honourable, and to affirm this our subsequent confession, but only convicted by manifest verity, we are compelled, with all soberness, to offer and confess that which the Scripture of God teacheth unto us, what we trust is persuaded to us to be most true; lest that, commanded to speak and yet keeping silence on so weighty a matter, we shall be accused for betrayers of the truth; and yet in this assertion we desire the honours and authority of all men to be saved, in so far as Christian charity and obedience to God's most sacred truth shall permit and suffer."

After this prologue, which in these last words manifestly alludes to the opposite judgment in the matter on hand of Cranmer and other bishops, and in disowning the influence of arrogance and a restless love of innovation, not obscurely hints at the broad accusations of the Archbishop's letter given above, the writers proceed to set out the subject of their Confession as follows:—

"In the 38th Article the Book of Common Prayer, now last published by the King's Majesty, and confirmed by consent and Act of Parliament, is confirmed to be holy, godly, and not only, by God's Scriptures, probable in every rite and ceremony, but also in no point repugnant thereto, as well concerning common prayers and ministration of the Sacraments, as the ordering and admission of priests, deacons, bishops, and archbishops.

"This Article and assertion in all points not to be tolerable and true, moveth us these three reasons subsequent."

Referring the reader to the full text of the document in Part II., only the heads of the subsequent reasoning can be exhibited in this place.

First, "No man, as we suppose, of holy judgment will deny but kneeling in the action of the Lord's Table proceeded from a false and erroneous opinion, to wit: that there was Christ's natural body contained, either by way of transubstantiation, or else by conjunction, real or corporal, of his body and blood with the visible elements. Then, if by a law may be confirmed, without offence to God's Majesty, that ceremony which has sprung forth from a false opinion, and that feedeth the same in the hearts of men, and that permitteth the idolater to continue in his idolatry, we desire the censure [the judgment] of God's Holy Scriptures." . . .

Secondarily, "By kneeling in the Lord's Supper, the consciences of weak brethren are not a little offended; for by violence of a law, are they compelled to honour God (their conscience reclaiming thereto) in such sort as in that action neither the example of Christ, nor yet any express commandment of his Sacred Word assured them of well-doing."

Thirdly, "The Church of God that be strong and grown to some perfection, is greatly injured; for it is permitted to idolaters to triumph over the Church of God, saying that after so long contention between the professors of the truth and maintainers of idolatry, the worst part, that is idolaters, have vanquished the best [part] by reason of this law aforesaid."

In the following passage the writers plainly have in view the objection raised by Cranmer to the abolition of kneeling, viz., that the adoption of the sitting posture pleaded for would lead to irreverence and disorder in the Communion Service:—

"The contempt of Christ's institution, and dangers that may ensue if men should sit in the Lord's Table, Jesus Christ, our Lord and Master, in whom all treasures of wisdom and knowledge be hid, did never see nor suspect; for no mention is made in his Holy Scriptures that sitting at the Table should bring contempt of his Institution. Wonder it is that men are become more circumspect and wise than God himself. Alas! are we not afraid of that terrible sentence pronounced in the prophet Isaiah, saying, 'The wisdom of the wise shall perish, and the understanding of the prudent vanish?' If the case be not alike let God's Scriptures it pronounce."

We only add here the following remarkable paragraph, in which the writers foresee and predict the evil consequences which would result from retaining this sacramental gesture in a Reformed Church, and what fatal advantage might be taken of it by Romanists and Romanizers in after times:—

"It is greatly to be feared that our wisdom build such strongholds for our enemies in this case, that hereafter they repair the walls of Jericho to our own displeasure, and yet shall he be cursed of God that shall lay the foundation thereof. To be plain: If Papists hereafter, when this generation shall pass, who lack no eyes to espy their advantage how they may repair the decay of their kingdom, shall inquire of our posterity why were the ceremonies devised by the Church abolished and taken away now of late days; and if it shall be answered, 'Because they were Popish plants, never planted by the Heavenly Father, whereby the rude and ignorant people were deceived;' and if they further shall require, 'Why, then, was kneeling left in the action of the Lord's Supper?' and if they answer (as we assign the cause), that by that decent ceremony the Sacrament should be kept in estimation, and that the people by kneeling shall avoid the profanation and disorder which about the Holy Communion might else have ensued ; in this answer, most strong to our judgments, which we teach our posterity to give to their adversaries, have we not ministered a weapon to wound—yea, utterly to kill—ourselves and posterity? For these shall be their darts : 'Your kneeling, which you have of us,' shall the Papists say, 'hath no more firmament [foundation] in God's word than our ceremonies that ye have abolished. The profit that cometh of your kneeling is nowhere in God's Word expressed, but only in the imagination of your own brains. Like damages, and more, are annexed with your kneeling in that action than with the rest of our ceremonies. Wherefore our ceremonies ought equally to remain with your kneeling." Affections laid aside, let indifferent [impartial] men judge how these darts can be avoided. By God's Scriptures assuredly we are not able to decline them. But if our Religion were builded upon that only which Jesus Christ did and commanded to be done in his remembrance, then might not the gates of hell prevail against the same."

The rest of the "Confession" is occupied with the question, " Why the sitting in the action of the Lord's Table is preferred to kneeling?" and will well repay perusal, by the rich and high sacramental doctrine which it contains ; "high," that is to say, not in the Romish, but the Protestant and Evangelical sense of the word. It is enough to read this single effusion of Knox's pen to see that he was no Zwinglian in the sense (an incorrect one) in which that epithet is often understood, *i.e.*, as a Sacramentarian of the lowest type—in the sense in which the Sacramental elements are regarded as signs and nothing more or higher—*nuda signa*. He was in truth a theologian of the Helvetic School, without being a Zwinglian, in so far as Zwingli was supposed (though erroneously) to be an imperfect example of the Helvetic type. He was already a Calvinist, before having made the personal acquaintance of Calvin. His doctrine of the Eucharist was the doctrine of the *Zurich Consensus*, which expressed not more the doctrine of Calvin than the judgment of Zwingli as understood and exhibited by Bullinger, Zwingli's successor and true interpreter.

This portion of the Confession opens with the following remarkable paragraphs : " As kneeling is no gesture meet at the Table, so doth it obscure the joyful significations of that holy mystery. Kneeling is the gesture most commonly of suppliants, of beggars, or such men as, greatly troubled by knowledge of misery or offence committed, seek help or remission, doubting whether they shall obtain the same or not. But in the Lord's Supper, chiefly in the action of eating and drinking, neither should appear in dolour, poverty, nor sign of any misery. But, commanded to eat and drink by the Lord Jesus, in remembrance of Him, with glad countenance we ought to obey ; and so, calling to our mind things that be past, present, and to come, all sign and fear of servitude and thraldom ought to be removed ; to wit, that we sometimes by nature were the sons of God's wrath, but [are] now by grace recounted and chosen in the number of the sons of God through the faith which is in Jesus our Lord—heirs of God and fellow-heirs with Jesus Christ our Lord, in whom we rest, and by whom the Father of Mercy hath caused us to *sit* amongst heavenly things, and with whom at the end we shall eat and drink at his own Table prepared for us in the Kingdom of that Everlasting Father. Of which things the Lord's Table is, as it were, our assurance and seal, in using whereof all signs of dolour ought to be removed. . . . .

"Dejected in our own sight, and yet erected and raised up through God's free promise, and so commanded by his Son to eat and drink, not as beggars (for by grace we are made rich in Christ), but as sons and inheritors whom that victorious King hath placed at his Table,—ought we not most gladly to receive the honour and dignity that is offered to us, seeing that we cannot do more honour to God than to obey his voice, and so to prepare ourselves to that holy action that we appear not betrayers of our own faith and hope, which is, that thraldom and servitude is taken away, and that we are the children of God—yea, priests and kings united by Christ's blood? And therefore, without doubting or wavering, at Christ's commandment pass we to the Table not as slaves or servants, but as children of the King and the redeemed people, praising the goodness of Him that hath called us to that honour and estate ; and therefore, taught by Christ's example at his holy Table, we *sit*, as men placed in quietness and in full possession of our Kingdom."

After further argument of a very ingenious and interesting if not very convincing kind, founded upon the resemblances and differences between the Passover and the Eucharist, and which has all the appearance of having been traced by a different pen from that of Knox—the pen, it seems highly probable, of the excellent Thomas Becon, then minister of St. Stephen's, Walbrook—the

Confession closes with the following strong appeal to the Lords of the Council*:—

"Thus have we given unto your Honours, most Honourable, our plain confession why, in the Lord's Table, we cannot admit kneeling. Yet again taking God to record in our conscience . . . that in this case we only seek the glory of God and the advancement of Christ's truth; and albeit some withstand us, of zeal also, as we suppose, towards the truth, yet when they shall consider the necessity that kneeling be avoided at the Lord's Table in these perilous days, we doubt not that then shall they, according to their excellent gifts and solid judgment, more earnestly and more profoundly persuade unto the King's Majesty's Highness, and to your Honours, that in Christ's religion, and chiefly in so high a mystery, ye bind not that thing under a law whereof you neither have commandment nor example of Jesus Christ nor of his Apostles, but is the mere invention of man, proceeding from a false opinion, which also hath been the gesture of idolaters, of whom, alas! no small number remaineth unto this day. . . . These and more causes deeply considered, we doubt not but their fervent desire to Christ's glory shall move them boldly to speak. So shall your Honours' careful diligence provide that Christ's religion in this realm—all praise and honour be unto God—now tending to perfection and maturity—so surely be founded upon Christ and upon his express Word, that not only it may abide the stormy wars of men's judgment, but also the warfare, the trial of God's secret Word we mean, which when it cometh, as it must needs consume and burn away the stubble, hay and wood, without respect of persons, so must it try and declare to be fine the gold, silver, and precious stones, how contemned [soever] that other builder appeared that builded such fine stuff upon the sure fundament!

"Our weak judgment touching the reformation of other ceremonies contained in the foresaid book, we have committed to writing in the Latin tongue, being ready upon commandment to put the same also in English. Unfeignedly beseeching the Father of all mercies that so your hearts may be ruled by the Holy Ghost, that in all the actions of your life, you may prefer the will

---

* For evidence in support of this suggestion see notes appended to the "Confession" in Part II., where also the name of Roger Hutchinson, of Eton College, is conjectured, with some degree of probability, to have been associated with that of Knox.

and pleasure of God, contained within his sacred Word, to long process of time [and] consuetude of man's authority; and so, no doubt but when that great Bishop and only Pastor of our souls, Jesus Christ our Saviour, shall appear, at whose presence shall tremble and ever be confounded all tyrannous oppressors of his truth; He shall acknowledge you his true professors, purged with his blood, clad with justice and grace, with Him made inheritors of life everlasting. So be it."

Let it be noticed in the paragraph last quoted that this "Confession" was sent in to the Privy Council by itself. Other judgments of the writers upon the Articles submitted to them, and upon other ceremonies of the Prayer-book, were for the present withheld, and would be sent in by-and-by, and in an English form if the Council desired it. Why, then, this haste to send in at once this English confession upon the 38th Article, and upon the single ceremony of kneeling in the Sacrament? Evidently for some special reason, and one involving urgency for immediate action. There was plainly some particular object to be gained by this proceeding, and which there would have been no chance of gaining if instant action had not been taken. But this again implies that the final decision upon the question argued in the "Confession" had not yet been arrived at. If it had been already decided where would have been the use of sending in an earnest representation upon this single point? The withholding of their judgment on other ceremonies which they objected to, was due to there being no prospect at the moment of those other ceremonies being taken into consideration at the Council table. The expediting of their confession on this single point of kneeling as plainly implied that this question was still *sub judice*, and that what Knox and his coadjutors deemed a right decision might still be hoped for.

And the hope thus cherished was not entirely disappointed. The "Confession" was in time for the meeting of the 27th of October, and was no doubt maturely considered. We know nothing of the discussion which ensued, except that the councillors who assisted at the decision arrived at were the Lord Chancellor (Bishop Goodrich of Ely), the Lord Treasurer (Marquis of Winchester), the Duke of Suffolk, the Lord Chamberlain (Marquis of Northampton), Mr. Comptroller (Sir Anthony Wyngfield), Mr. Vice-Chamberlain (Sir John Gates), Mr. Secretary Cecil, and Sir Robert Bowes. The decision itself was thus recorded in the Register of Council:—

"*At Westminster*, the xxvii. *day of October*, 1552.

" A letter to the Lord Chancellor, to cause to be joined unto the Book of Common Prayer lately set forth a certain declaration signed by the King's Majesty, and sent unto his Lordship touching the kneeling at the receiving of the Communion."

The "declaration" appeared accordingly in all copies of the new Prayer-book, which had not been issued before the injunction sent to the publisher on the 26th September preceding. The publication of the Service had been suspended for a whole month, awaiting the issue of the deliberations of the Council. The printing and the correction of the press had been finished for weeks, and all that could now be done was to insert the "declaration" on a separate leaf at the end of the Communion office. It interrupted the pagination. All readers could see at once that it was an extra leaf, and that the insertion of it had been an afterthought carried into effect at the last moment. There are still preserved in the great libraries of the kingdom a considerable number of copies of this first edition of Edward VI.'s Second Prayer-book which exhibit this intercalated leaf, though there are other copies also extant which do not contain it—the two classes of copies thus remaining a palpable memorial of the whole curious and important transaction of which Knox had been the sudden and sole originator, and which both by pulpit and pen he had powerfully contributed to bring to a conclusion—a conclusion which, though not realizing all he wished, was something upon which he congratulated himself and others who shared his views, and which continues, even to our own time, a highly important feature of the English liturgy. The "Declaration on Kneeling" is not, indeed, an object of equal admiration to all Anglicans; to many of them, we fear, it is a "black Rubric," a *bête noire;* but to all except the un-Protestant section of the Church of England it is a truly valuable element of her liturgy, and a standing monument of the Reformation-truth and Reformation-life from which she sprang.

"The Declaration on Kneeling," and the Rubric which it explains, stand thus in the Second Prayer-book of Edward VI.:—

The Rubric.—"Then shall the minister first receive the Communion in both kinds himself, and next deliver it to other ministers, if any be there present (that they may help the chief minister), and after to the people in their hands *kneeling*. And when he delivereth the bread, he shall say:—

"'Take and eat this in remembrance that Christ died for thee, and feed on Him in thy heart by faith, with thanksgiving.'

"And the minister that delivereth the cup shall say:—

"'Drink this in remembrance that Christ's blood was shed for thee, and be thankful.'"

The "Declaration" added at the end of the Communion office is as follows:—

"Although no order can be so perfectly devised, but it may be of some, either for their ignorance and infirmity, or else of malice and obstinacy, misconstrued, depraved, and interpreted in a wrong part: and yet, because brotherly charity willeth that, so much as conveniently may be, offences should be taken away: therefore we, willing to do the same; whereas it is ordained in the Book of Common Prayer, in the administration of the Lord's Supper, that the communicants kneeling should receive the Holy Communion, which thing being well meant for a signification of the humble and grateful acknowledging of the benefits of Christ given unto the worthy receiver, and to avoid the profanation and disorder which about the Holy Communion might else ensue; lest yet the same kneeling might be thought or taken otherwise, we do declare that it is not meant thereby that any adoration is done, or ought to be done, either unto the sacramental bread and wine there bodily received, or to any real and essential presence there being of Christ's natural flesh and blood. For as concerning the sacramental bread and wine, they remain still in their very natural substances, and therefore may not be adored, for that were idolatry to be abhorred of all faithful Christians; and as concerning the natural body and blood of our Saviour Christ, they are in heaven, and not here; for it is against the truth of Christ's true natural body to be in more places than in one at one time."[*]

The "Declaration" has all the appearance of having come from the hand of Cranmer. Its spirit and style are the same as those

---

[*] *Vide* "The Two Liturgies, with other Documents set forth by authority in the reign of King Edward the Sixth." Parker Society, 1844. The editor adds in a note that in one of two copies of the Grafton editions of 1552, used in printing the Parker Society's edition, the extra leaf was pasted in after the copy was bound, while several copies are without it.

of the preface of "Ceremonies; why some be abolished and some retained," prefixed for the first time to the same Prayer-book. If his conjecture be sustained, the suggestion at once occurs, that as Cranmer was not at any meeting of Council in October, 1552, later than that of the 11th, and could not therefore have framed the declaration at the Council Board, either on the 20th or the 27th; it had been written by him at Ford, and communicated to the Council at one or other of these latter meetings. But if it was communicated to the Council on the 20th of October, and discussed at that meeting, it is certain that no action arose out of the deliberations of that day—in the direction of giving effect to it—for the final order to insert "the declaration" was not agreed to till the 27th, although if a majority could have been obtained for it on the 20th, there was the strongest reason for hastening the order for its insertion in the copies of the new Prayer-book, the publication of which had now been arrested for several weeks. If, therefore, the Council saw their way to adopt and publish "the declaration" on the 27th, it is reasonable to conclude that this decision could only have been due to some new element having been imported into the question.

The "Confession" of Knox and his coadjutors, presented on that day, was, we are convinced, this new element. When the Council resumed the subject on that day, the question before them lay between Knox's proposal to abolish kneeling as urged anew in the "Confession," and the Archbishop's plan to retain the practice and the new Rubric enjoining it, but to add the new and supplementary Declaration. The compromise prevailed; but, apparently, there would not have been so much as a compromise obtained if the "Confession" had not been thrown into the scale at the very last moment. Knox's promptitude and energy therefore, in preparing this last contribution to the controversy, had not been thrown away. His last blow had the effect of overcoming the resistance to all further change which a majority of the Council had hitherto maintained.

It would have been interesting to have known with certainty and in detail what part in these proceedings of the Council was taken by the young King. That he signed the Declaration is expressly stated, which he would not have consented to do if he had not in his conscience approved of it; but neither would he at the earliest stage of the discussion have concurred in sending an instruction to Cranmer to reconsider the question, and to stay in the meanwhile the progress of the press, if he had not been shaken in his previous opinion by the earnest preaching of Knox. In truth, there would be no great hazard in surmising that the proposal, which Knox had broached, found favour with no one at the Council-Table more than with the King himself. In Cecil's "Memorandum" for the meeting of the 20th of October, there occurs the following suggestive entry :—

"A Brief of the Dispute at Windsor, for the King."

This "Dispute at Windsor" was, no doubt, the same "dispute among the Bishops" to which Utenhovius refers as occasioned by Knox's Sermon at Court. Apparently it had not taken place in the presence of the King, but he had heard of it, and had expressed his pleasure that a "Brief" of the arguments used on both sides should be drawn up for his perusal. That Brief had been prepared, perhaps by Cecil himself, for the approval of Council, before it was handed to Edward. He must have time to weigh the arguments which had been used on both sides. Hence, probably the delay of the Council in coming to a decision on that day. But at the meeting of the 27th, the same day when Knox's "Confession" was put in, the King was prepared to declare his mature opinion, and that opinion plainly did not side with those of the Bishops who had argued at Windsor against all change in the Prayer-book as about to issue to the Church. Up to that meeting there is nothing to indicate that more than a minority of the Council had been convinced of the necessity of annexing the "Declaration." What, then, were the new elements introduced into the case at that meeting? We already know that one of these was "the Confession of Knox." We may now add, with some degree of probability, upon the evidence of Cecil's "Memorandum," that a second element was contributed to the solution arrived at by the now ripened conviction of the young King. It was in all likelihood the combined pressure of the King's influence, and of the seasonable support to it which his zealous chaplain brought into the field at the last moment, which at length prevailed with the Council to accept the "Declaration."

We do not of course claim for this representation of the young King's part in this important business more than the weight of a probable conjecture, for it may well seem precarious to hang upon the peg of Cecil's "Memorandum," a more confident conclusion. But, on the other hand, it is not to be forgotten that the forwardness of Edward's zeal in the work of Church-Reformation was much in advance of that of most of his councillors. His piety was sincere and deep, and his allegiance to the Word of the King of kings profound. There was no man at the Council-Table more likely than he to feel the solemn force of the appeals which Knox had made in support of his views, both in the pulpit and by the pen, to the Institution and the example of Christ. But of course, in his yet tender age, he could not prudently disregard the advice and the wishes of his wisest councillors; and as Knox had failed to convince a majority of the Council of the duty of abolishing kneeling in the Sacrament, though possibly he may have convinced the King himself, he was content to obtain their assent to the explanatory "Declaration on Kneeling," to which at the Council-Table he put his royal hand.*

The unjust reflections to which Knox had been subjected for his energetic intervention in this weighty business produced no diminution whatever in the esteem entertained for him by his Royal Master. Knox kept a high place in Edward's favour and grace to the end. He continued to preach at Court in 1552, till the middle of December. He preached again in his turn in the following spring, and the repeated offers of preferment which he had during the next six months either came directly from the King, or must have received his sanction. And on Knox's side, this excellent young Prince's name was never named by him in his writings, to the end of his life, without the warmest demonstrations of admiration and love.

The discussions of the Council upon the new Rubric of kneeling in the Prayer-book, could not fail to have some effect upon the important question of the new Articles submitted by Cranmer and the other reforming bishops. Nothing is known of the reports sent in by those of the royal chaplains and other learned men who did not join with Knox and one or more who drew up the Confession on kneeling. Several of the chaplains, we know, sent in

---

* For John-A-Lasco's testimony to the advanced ecclesiastical views of the King, *vide* Extracts from his writings, at the end of the chapter.

such reports of their judgments, but no record of them has been preserved. Nor is anything further known of Knox's judgment than what is contained in the Confession, which refers to his "judgment touching the reformation of other ceremonies contained in the foresaid Book." This judgment, when sent in to the Council, must evidently have been directed against several other points of the Prayer-book besides the Rubric on kneeling, and must therefore have pressed for the omission or modification of the 38th Article, which expressed an entire approbation not only of the doctrine of the Book, but also of all the rites and ceremonies which it had either continued or added. Whether any similar suggestion had come from any of the other chaplains, it is of course impossible to say, but the issue of the whole matter was very remarkable:—

"AT WESTMINSTER, the 20th *November*, 1552.

"A letter was ordered to be sent to the Archbishop of Canterbury, with the Articles heretofore drawn and delivered by him to the King's Majesty, which being since that time considered by certain of his Highness's chaplains and others, are in some part altered; and therefore returned to him to be considered, so as, after the perfecting of them, order may be given for the putting the same in due execution."*

On the 23rd Nov. the amended Articles reached Cranmer at Ford, and on the following day he returned them to the Council, with a letter, which has been preserved:—

"After my very humble recommendations unto your good Lordships, I have sent unto the same the Book of Articles which yesterday I received from your Lordships. I have sent also a schedule inclosed, declaring briefly my mind upon the said Book, beseeching your Lordships to be means unto the King's Majesty, that all the bishops may have authority from him to cause all their preachers, archdeacons, deans, prebendaries, parsons, vicars, curates, with all their clergy, to subscribe to the said Articles. And then I trust that such a concord and quietness in religion

* Council Book, vol. iii. p. 645.

shall shortly follow thereof, as else is not to be looked for many years. God shall thereby be glorified, his truth shall be advanced, and your Lordships shall be rewarded of Him as the setters forward of his true Word and Gospel, unto whom is my daily prayer, without ceasing, to preserve the King's Majesty with all your honourable Lordships. From my house at Ford, the 24th of this present month of November.

"Your Lordships' ever to command,

"T. CANT.

" To my very good Lords of the King's Majesty his most honourable Council."

The Archbishop does not appear to have made any change in the text of the Book of Articles as returned to him by the Council, but to have limited himself to a "brief schedule" of notes upon it, which no doubt had reference to the alterations which the Council had made by advice of the divines whom they had consulted upon the original Draft. But whatever his "mind" in these notes may have been, it is plain that he was well satisfied with the Articles, even in their altered form, and anticipated the best results, to "the glory of God, and the advancement of the truth," to follow from their public authorization and use.

Now what was the character of these alterations of Cranmer's original draft? The authentic copy of that draft, still preserved among the State papers of 1552, and signed by the royal chaplains, has happily supplied the means of a collation with the Articles as finally authorized and published in June of the following year; and the late Archdeacon Hardwicke executed for the first time such a collation with the utmost care, with the assistance of the late Mr. Lemon, of the State Paper Office. The results are to be seen in full detail in the appendix to his "History of the Articles of Religion," where he collates the Articles of 1552-3 (in Latin and English) with the thirty-nine Articles of 1562 and 1571 (both the Latin and English editions); and further, notes very carefully the differences of the forty-two Articles of 1552-53 from the Draft of forty-five Articles submitted to the judgment of the King's chaplains and others. Of these variations, which are by no means so numerous as might have been expected, considering the of the Articles, and the largeness of some of them, it will be sufficient to present here the following :—

The reduction of the number of Articles from forty-five to forty-two arose simply from making one long Article, *De Coena Domini* (Of the Lord's Supper), out of four short ones in the Draft, which followed consecutively.

The only other differences of a formal character were simply either of a verbal kind, or alterations of the numerical arrangement of the Articles.

The differences of substance in every case are not without some importance, either in a doctrinal or ecclesiastical point of view, and they almost always consist of things omitted in the final draft, which had appeared in the original draft. They consist, in other words, almost always of *retrenchments* of the first draft—of instances in which, either from conscientious conviction, or from views of policy and expediency, the King and his Council considered that the Primate had put things too strongly, or had exceeded due limits. And of all these omissions, the most remarkable was that which appeared in the 38th Article, on which Knox had commented so severely, now numbered the 35th Article; from which literally everything was omitted to which he had taken objection in his "confession." All that had appeared in the first draft on the subject of the "Ceremonies" of the Prayer-book was cancelled, and nothing retained save what referred to the *doctrine* of the Book, to which Knox, it will be remembered, had taken no exception. The following important clause of the Article was withdrawn by the Council, and not insisted upon by the Archbishop : "Et quoad ceremoniarum rationem, salutari evangelii libertati, si ex sua natura ceremoniae illae estimentur, in nullo repugnant sed probe congruunt, et eandem in compluribus imprimis promovent."

"And as to the character of the ceremonies, they are repugnant in nothing to the wholesome liberty of the Gospel, if they are judged from their own nature, but very well agree with it, and in very many respects further the same in a high degree."

The Article on the Book of Common Prayer and Ceremonies, &c., stood in the end thus, as authorized and published by King and Council, with the consent, it is believed, of the Convocation of 1553, or a delegation of its most important members :—

"Art. 35. Of the Book of Prayers and Ceremonies of the Church of England.

"The Book which of very late time was given to the Church of England by the King's authority and the Parliament containing the manner and form of praying and ministering the Sacraments in the Church of England, likewise also the Book of Ordering Ministers of the Church, set forth by the foresaid authority, are godly, and in no point repugnant to the wholesome doctrine of the Gospel, but agreeable thereunto, furthering and beautifying the same not a little; and, therefore, of all faithful members of the Church of England, and chiefly of the ministers of the Word, they ought to be received, and allowed with all readiness of mind and thanksgiving, and to be commended to the people of God."*

The reader will mark here the curious fact that, while all mention of the ceremonies is omitted from the last form of the Article, the most of the language which had been in the first instance applied to the "ceremonies," in their relation to the wholesome "liberty" of the Gospel, is now applied to the Book in its single relation to the "wholesome doctrine" of the Gospel. The Article has not been so much cut down in bulk as restricted in scope, and, by a singular economy, almost parsimony, of speech, the language which was before used of a subject now dropped from the Article is applied to a totally different subject, the only one now retained and insisted upon.

The influence of Knox upon this curious and really important issue is again conspicuous and undeniable. It is impossible to compare his "Confession," laid before the Council, with this result, without seeing that the one must have led, at least in part, to the other, and that, in all probability, the upshot would have been different but for his intervention. It is not meant to imply that Cranmer was brought over to Knox's judgment as regards the merits of the question. It is very unlikely, indeed, that he was, considering the disparaging opinion which he had so shortly before expressed of the preacher's spirit and tendencies. But the majority of the Council apparently had been gained over to Knox's view, or, at the very least, had come to see that, as a matter of policy, it would be wiser not to adhere to the Article in its original extent, but to retrench altogether its assertions touching the ceremonies. And the Council judged very wisely, for such retrenchment was now evidently necessary to secure the end for which the King and

* Cardwell's "Synodalia," vol. i. p. 31.

his Council had determined to prepare the Book of Articles. This end was expressed and set out in the very title which the Articles bore when they at length appeared: "Articles agreed on by the Bishops and other learned men in the Synod at London, in the year of our Lord God MDLII., for the avoiding of controversy in opinions, and the establishment of a godly concord in certain matters of Religion." But it had now become manifest to the Council, and, doubtless, to Cranmer himself, that it was necessary for the Articles to be silent on some points not of vital importance, if controversy was to be avoided and a godly concord to be established, even among the best friends and promoters of the Reformation themselves. They never had proposed to do more in the Book of Articles than to handle "certain matters of religion;" they never designed to put it forward as a complete and exhaustive Church symbol or confession of faith; and they came in the end to see that, along with many other subjects omitted, it would be prudent and politic to omit all reference to "the Ceremonies" of the Prayer-book.

But if these remarkable differences between the first and the final drafts of the Articles of Edward VI. are strongly suggestive of the influence of Knox upon their ultimate authoritative form, it must not be omitted to call attention also to their remarkable resemblance, and, indeed, almost perfect identity, in matters of doctrine. Whatever efforts Knox had made, and whatever influence he had put forth in the matter of rites and ceremonies, it does not appear, at least by the results, that he had sought to make any changes in the first draft, in the matter of doctrine. And let this remark be specially applied to two great doctrinal topics of the Articles—the doctrine of the Sacraments, and the doctrine of Predestination—on both of which it is no unusual thing, among Church of England writers, to represent him as of "a different spirit from the fathers and founders of that reformed branch of the Catholic Church of Christ."

Avoiding all discursive remark upon this theme, we confine ourselves strictly to the evidence which emerges from Archdeacon Hardwicke's collation of the two authentic documents before us: What is the outcome, the whole outcome, of that collation on the two subjects in question? Nothing more than a few very unimportant variations, which leave the substance, and even the form, of the doctrines precisely the same in both the documents, although the Articles occupied with these two subjects are much the longest and most comprehensive of the whole body of Articles. We have thus a very palpable proof that Knox and the other divines who reported their judgments to the Council upon Cranmer's draft were entirely of Cranmer's mind upon these two capital heads of doctrine. Knox was neither more nor less of a " Sacramentarian " and a " Predestinarian " than the Primate himself, and the other fathers and founders of the Reformed Church of England who had been associated with him in preparing these Articles. He accepted their dogmatic definitions, and wished nothing more or better. If he was a Predestinarian, so were they. If they were Sacramentarians, in the highest and richest Helvetic sense, he was the same, and nothing less nor more. He and they all alike held the Sacramental theory of Bullinger and Calvin, as distinguished from the Lutheran theory of Consubstantiation on the one hand, and that of Carlstadt and other rationalizing extremists on the other.

But this matter has often been represented—and still is occasionally—very differently, viz., that Knox and the whole party who pressed for the abolition of kneeling in the Lord's Supper, and obtained the insertion of the "Declaration on Kneeling," were men who took a much lower view of Sacramental efficacy than Cranmer and Ridley, and were much more in sympathy with the extreme views of the continental ultra-Protestants. An impression to this effect is evidently conveyed, for example, in the following passage of Archdeacon Hardwicke*:—

"The Reformers (of Edward VI.'s reign) must be carefully subdivided. Laying out of the question a multitude of revolutionary spirits, Anabaptists and other sectaries, who started up afresh at the beginning of the new reign, the party in the Church that favoured progress was composed of elements in some degree at variance with each other. One active section of the Church Reformers, constituting what may be entitled the first race of Puritans, embraced opinions such as we have sketched in those parts of Switzerland in which the principles of Zwingli and Œcolampadius had taken root. They bore the general name of Sacramentaries, and some of their brother Reformers, both here and on the Conti-

---

* *Vide* " History of the Christian Church during the Reformation," 1856, p. 208.

nent, did not scruple to place them in the same class with Anabaptists."

There is a mixture of historical truth and error in such statements as these, which is very misleading. It is true that Knox and other eminent divines of Edward VI.'s reign differed from Cranmer, and almost all the other reforming bishops, on many points of ritual and Church order, so much so as to justify their being called "the first race of Puritans;" and it is also true, as we have seen above, that the fundamental principle upon which they reasoned *upon such subjects* appeared to Cranmer, and no doubt to other Churchmen, to resemble one of the principles maintained by the Anabaptists, viz., that nothing was lawful in religious worship or order except what rested upon the prescription and warrant of the word of God. But it is, on the other hand, contrary to the truth of history to represent the difference between the "first race of Puritans" and the bishops to have extended to matters of doctrine —and especially on the subject of the Lord's Supper. If they were called Sacramentaries, they were such in no other sense nor degree than those in which the same name might have been given, and no doubt by Lutherans and Romanists was given, to Cranmer, Ridley, and Latimer, or to Bullinger, Calvin, and Peter Martyr; and in all these cases alike the name meant no more than that they who were so called rejected both the theories of Rome and of Wittemberg. The truth is that Knox and his coadjutors were as strongly opposed to the "bare signs," the "nuda signa" of Carlstadt, as Cranmer himself.

Mr. Perry does our Reformer no more than historical justice when he remarks that "some of the language used by Knox upon this subject exceeds what probably would be used by many who disclaim all sympathy with Knox, and would be sorry to be under the least suspicion of not being greatly in advance of his Sacramental views." And we cannot do better than quote the language of Knox upon which this just observation is based. It is that of the "Confession" of the Reformed Church of Scotland of 1560, drawn up by Knox's own hand:—

"In the Supper, rightly used, Christ Jesus is so joined with us that he becomes the very nourishment and food of our souls. Not that we imagine any transubstantiation of bread into Christ's natural body, and of wine into his natural blood (as the Papists have perniciously taught and damnably believed); but this union and communion which we have with the body and blood of Christ Jesus in the right use of the Sacrament is wrought by the operation of the Holy Ghost, who, by true faith, carries us above all things that are visible, carnal, and earthly, and makes us to feed upon the body and blood of Christ Jesus, which was once broken and shed for us, which now is in the heaven, and appeareth in the presence of God for us. And yet, notwithstanding the far distance of place which is betwixt his body now glorified in the heaven, and us now mortal in this earth, yet we most assuredly believe that the bread which we break is the Communion of Christ's body, and the cup which we bless is the Communion of his blood. . . . But all this, we say, comes by true faith, which apprehendeth Christ Jesus, who only makes his Sacraments effectual unto us ; and therefore whosoever slandereth us, as that we affirmed or believed Sacraments to be only naked and bare signs, do injury unto us, and speak against a manifest truth. But this liberally and frankly we must confess, that we make a distinction betwixt Christ Jesus in his natural substance, and betwixt the elements in the Sacramental signs, so that we will neither worship the signs in place of that which is signified by them ; neither yet do we despise and interpret them as unprofitable and vain."*

When Knox penned these remarkable statements of the Scottish Confession, his views of the Lord's Supper had been matured and deepened by his intercourse of several years with Calvin in Geneva. But he had held substantially the same views nearly ten years before he and Calvin met, and while he was still the disciple and attendant of George Wishart. And Wishart had learned these views, be it remembered, from the First Helvetic Confession of 1536, which he translated into his mother tongue, and from his intercourse with the Divines of the Helvetic Church in 1540. In 1549 was drawn up and published the " Consensus " of Zurich, in which Bullinger and Calvin, and the other Divines of German and French Switzerland arrived at a clear and full understanding on the subject of the Lord's Supper; and that not in any low sense, such as is usually but unfairly understood by the epithet, Zwinglian or Œcolampadian, but in a sense so high and rich that it made a convert of Melancthon from the Lutheran theory of Consubstantiation, and for some time seemed to have wrought out

---

* " Knox's Works," vol. ii. pp. 114-115.

a *consensus* between Calvin and Luther himself. Nor was the date of the "Consensus" of Zurich the earliest date of this sense of the Eucharist in the convictions and thought-habit of the Helvetic Churches. The same sense of it is expressed in the clearest manner in the confession of Bâle, drawn up in the year 1532, shortly after the death of Œcolampadius, and in a treatise of Vadian, the reformer of St. Gall, the intimate friend and correspondent of Zwingli, published in 1536 by Bullinger, and introduced by a Preface from his pen, in which he expresses, in the warmest terms, his approval of the work. For documentary proofs of these statements, the reader is referred to a note at the end of the chapter; and these proofs are of high historical importance in their bearing upon the question of the Sacramental teaching of the brother Reformers of Zurich and Basel—Zwingli and Œcolampadius—respecting which it is surely only right and reasonable that we should accept the interpretation rather of their own disciples and successors in the churches which they reformed and ruled, than the one-sided and suspicious representations of Lutherans and Anabaptists.

At the close of this section of Knox's life and work in England, we are naturally led to estimate the importance of the effects which he obtained by his influence in the King's Court and Council. The 'Declaration on Kneeling' may not at first appear to have been a matter of much importance. It may seem to have no higher degree of significance than the question of Sacramental gesture to which it refers. If that point could only have become a question of gravity from adventitious circumstances, and the special exigencies of the time and the Church's situation, it may not unreasonably be asked, how could a 'declaration' on such a subject become a greater and more weighty affair for the Church of England than the subject itself? But the answer to this inquiry is, that the real importance of the Declaration consists, not in the subject of which it speaks, but in the language which it uses in speaking of it. That language had a vastly larger scope and effect than the question of gesture which gave occasion to its use, and amounted to a protest against the whole Eucharistic theory both of Rome and Wittemberg. In fact, there is nothing in the whole English liturgy which is, to say the least, more Protestant than the "Declaration," a quality of it which has sometimes obtained for it the name of "the Black Rubric." "As concerning the Sacramental bread and wine, they remain still in their very natural substances, and therefore may not be adored, for that were idolatry to be abhorred of all faithful Christians." Even Knox's trumpet could not have blown a louder blast against the Roman Mass than that. "And as concerning the natural body and blood of our Saviour Christ, they are in heaven, and not here. For it is against the truth of Christ's true natural body to be in more places than in one at one time." Was not this a second blast of the trumpet against the ubiquitarianism of Luther and the Lutherans?

And thus it strangely came to pass that upon a peg so small as a point of ceremony or religious posture there was hung a declaration against the Sacramental theory of the whole unreformed Church of the West, and, almost in the same breath, against the favourite theory of the Mother Church of the Continental Reformation itself.

It was impossible that such a Rubric should not have a powerful influence on Church life and Church administration, not only at the time when it was added to the Liturgy, but also in such periods and ecclesiastical situations as the succeeding centuries brought forth. So important in its bearing upon the peace and strength of the Reformed Church of England was it seen to be, at the time it was adopted, that the King and Council dangerously stretched the prerogative of the Crown, in adding it to the Prayer-book without the consent either of Parliament or Convocation; and Cranmer himself finally acquiesced in the step, although he had put before the Council so plainly, only a few weeks before, the seriousness of altering the text of the Book without that consent. So the leaders of the nation interpreted its importance for the Protestant Church—for the "concord and quietness in religion" which it was expected to promote. And the estimate of the gravity of its significance formed by the leaders of the Catholic party was equally earnest and pronounced. Only eighteen months later, April 18, 1554, at Oxford, in what is called "Latimer's Disputation," Dr. Weston, one of his opponents, and in his place as Prolocutor, made use of the remarkable words, "A runagate Scot did take away the adoration or worshipping of Christ in the Sacrament (*i.e.*, in Romish usage, the consecrated Host), by whose procurement that heresy was put into the last Communion Book; so much prevailed that one man's authority at that time."* In which words he could only have alluded to the terms of the Declaration; for kneeling, the attitude of worship, had not been taken away, but retained. It was this added Rubric which contained the sting of the whole Reformed Communion-Office, in the feeling and judgment of the Oxford Catholics.

That this "runagate Scot" of Dr. Weston was Knox, and could only be Knox, need not be proved at this advanced stage of our narrative. But there have been respectable authorities for referring the allusion to Alexander Alesius Scotus, a disciple of Luther and Melancthon, who was for some years in England, and was appointed by Henry VIII. King's Scholar and Reader of Theology in the University of Cambridge. But this was as far back as 1537, before the Statute of the Six Articles, under which, as a married priest, he was obliged for his life to return to Wittemberg, and it is certain that he was never afterwards again in England. It is preposterous, therefore, to apply Weston's language to him, though this is done by such writers as Dr. Wordsworth,† Dr. Townsend, editor of Fox, and the Parker editor of "Latimer's Remains." Mr. Perry's reasonings on this point are quite conclusive. ‡

So much for the insertion of the Declaration in Edward's time; but that was only the beginning of its fortunes. It was so weighty an affair at first, that it has had a long history of its own. At the accession of Elizabeth the "Declaration" was dropped out of the Prayer-book, along with that portion of the 35th Article—"De Coena Domini"—upon which it rested; and it remained outside the Liturgy for a hundred years. And why? Simply because its omission was judged as important by the Church's leaders now as its insertion had been at first. Elizabeth's Church policy was a comprehension policy, and neither James I. nor Charles I. had any wish to depart from it. She wished, and so did her Council and first Parliament, to make it as easy as possible for the Roman party to continue in the National Church, but she and they knew that such a comprehension was impossible as long as the "Declaration on Kneeling" remained in the Prayer-book. Its insertion had taken place in

* Fox, "Acts and Monuments," vol. vi. p. 510.
† "Eccles. Biog." vol. v. p. 250.
‡ "Historical Considerations," &c., pp. 99–102.

order to "comprehend" the Puritan party, to the exclusion of the Romanists; and now its omission took place in order to comprehend the Romanists, at the risk of driving out the Puritans.

But why do we now find the "Declaration" restored to its old place? What was the motive of so remarkable a rehabilitation in 1662? It is easy to discern it. The circle of Church evolution and change had then returned into itself. In 1662 the old policy of conciliating and comprehending the Puritans instead of the Catholics was again in season—was again the key of the situation. To this policy the "Declaration on Kneeling" was again indispensable, and again, therefore, this most remarkable Rubric was restored, in substantially the same form, to its vacant place. Nor has its history yet exhausted itself. It has retained its recovered place through all the changes of the last two centuries, only to come forward into new significance and importance in our own day. The last chapter of its history was written only the other day in the long discussions, and the fateful decision of the Bennett case. Its simple but trenchant language was often quoted in the pleadings, and passed into the body of the judgment itself: "As concerning the natural body and blood of our Saviour Christ, they are in heaven, not here. For it is against the truth of Christ's true natural body to be in more places than in one at one time."

Nor is the history of "The Black Rubric," we may be sure, yet ended. We cannot, indeed, be so bold as to predict what the last chapters of its long, eventful story are likely to be, and whether it is its destiny to suffer a second ejectment, to be followed by a second restoration. But of one thing we may be quite sure—that as long as the Protestant evangelical character of the Church of England is to be maintained, the "Declaration on Kneeling" can never again be cast out of the Liturgy; and that as long as it retains its long-recovered place, it will never be possible to deny that the written doctrine and ritual of the Church of England are those of a truly Reformed Church, through whatever phases of doctrinal decay and liturgical corruption the inside non-conformity of some of its many parties may have yet to pass. If it is true that the members of a Church may often be better than the written teachings and the authorized practice of the Church itself, the converse is no less true—that a Church may often be purer in both respects than some of its parties and many of its members.

We do not write here polemically—we refer only to facts of history, past, present, and no doubt also future. In judging of all churches alike in Christendom, this palpable distinction between the written and the unwritten factors of their history, condition, and prospects, must be kept in view; and, though in all churches alike, present and growing corruption and declension are ill compensated by the purity of their standards, still it is the inestimable value of such pure standards that so long as these are preserved to a Church, though, to use the beautiful figure of Isaiah, there may be "a great forsaking" of these for a time, " yet in it there shall be a tenth, and it shall return : as a teil tree, and as an oak, whose substance is in them, when they cast their leaves."

ADDITIONAL NOTES TO CHAPTER III.

1. *Note on the "Register of the Privy Council," or the "Council Book."*

IN view of the use which is made in the narrative of this chapter of the "Register of the Privy Council," it is important to notice that though it is often referred to by historians under the name of the "Minutes of Council," it is not really a book of Minutes in the ordinary sense of that term, and was not intended to be a record of that character when the use of it was revived by Henry VIII. and his Council, after long discontinuance. "On the 10th of August, 1540," writes Sir Harris Nicolas, editor of "Proceedings and Ordinances of the Privy Council of England," vol. vii., preface, pp. 1–13, "an order was taken and determined by his Majesty, with the advice of his Highness's Privy Council, that there should be a clerk attendant upon the said Council to write, enter, and register all such decrees, determinations, letters, and other such things as he should be appointed to enter in a book, to remain always as a ledger," &c. . . . . "The Register of the Council of Henry VIII. therefore resembles the Book of the Council of the times of Henry V. and VI., in which the decrees rather than the deliberations of the Privy Council are entered, and it consequently differs materially from the original Minutes of the same period, which often contained the individual opinions of the members upon the business which happened to be discussed." In the reign of Edward VI. the "Register" or "Council Book" continued to be drawn up in the same way as during the reign of Henry VIII. It contains no Minutes of the deliberations, or "of the individual opinions of the members," only the "orders," "warrants," "letters" of instructions, or other executive documents, in which the deliberations of Council issued. A Book of Minutes was also kept, and is very often referred to in the "Register" as a distinct record; but unfortunately these Minutes appear to be hopelessly lost. It is no proof therefore that any particular subject of business was not brought before the Council, *e.g.*, the Memorial or Confession of Knox and others on the subject of kneeling in the Sacrament, that no mention is made of the incident in the "Register" or Council Book. All that is to be looked for there is what is actually found—the "Order" for the publication of the "Declaration on Kneeling" in the Prayer-book about to issue to the Church. The "Minutes of Council," containing all the deliberations which preceded the "Order," were a distinct and additional record, the loss of which can only be regretted, not repaired.

2. *On certain Writings of John A'Lasco which have a bearing upon the English Reforma'ion.*

The earliest in date of these writings is a letter or memorial addressed by John A'Lasco, as superintendent of the three foreign Protestant congregations in London to Archbishop Cranmer, in which he earnestly presses for his consent and sanction to the introduction among these congregations of the administration of the Lord's Supper to communicants in a *sitting* posture, and without the use of the vestments common in England. It was first published, without Cranmer's name, in Gabbema's "Epistolae Illustrium Virorum," A.D. 1669, and was reprinted by Gerdesius in his "Scrinium Antiquarium," tom. ii. pars. ii., who had no difficulty in perceiving that it was to Cranmer that it must have been addressed, and in the year 1551. "Neque autem est dubium," he writes, "quin, licet Gabbema eum non nominet, Thomas Cranmerus sit idem ille ad quem haec epistola est data, quippe quod ex universo ejus argumento satis conficitur." The reasonings of this long and interesting paper bear a strong resemblance to those of Knox in the Confession presented to the Privy Council. The following sentences may suffice as a specimen of the whole :—

" Si negari non potest Christum Dominum mensae accumbentem accumbentibus etiam suis apostolis coenam suam administrasse, sic ut accubitus ille a parte totius actionis illius mysticae excludi non possit, Quae Ratio nos movet ut eam actionis Dominicae partem ab ipsius institutionis in mandato illo (Hoc facite) excludere quam includere malimus? Equidem rectius fecerimus si id mandato huic includamus, quod Evangelistae ipsi in parte actionis memorant, quam si id nulla authoritate nullaque justa ratione innixi excludamus.

"Cum sciamus horribilem esse in Papae Ecclesia Coenae Dominicae profanationem, atque ipsius doctrinam ali confirmarique genuum ista in coenae usu flexione, quam adhuc plerisque locis observatam fuisse videmus; et nostri officii sit publice testari modis omnibus nos ab ea idolatria abhorrere, adeoque et illi adversari quantum omnino possumus; nulla vero esse possit aptior testificatio alieni animi nostri ab illa idolatria quam publicus in Coena Ecclesiae Consessus, ab ipso praesertim Christi exemplo apostolicaque observatione petitus, merito illum sane instaurare observareque deberemus."

We gather from this paper that A'Lasco had hitherto been unsuccessful in bringing over Cranmer to these views, and that the latter had made use of the same answers to his arguments as those which we find in Cranmer's letter to the Privy Council in reply to Knox; so that the subject was no new one to the Archbishop at the date of that letter, and he had already fully made up his mind upon it in 1551, although he appears, on other grounds, to have at length acceded to the earnest and repeated requests of A'Lasco and his numerous flock, which in truth they were entitled to claim under the terms of the King's grant of the church of Austin Friars.

In the following year, 1552, John A'Lasco published an important work, entitled "Brevis et dilucida de Sacramentis Ecclesiae Christi Tractatio," to which was appended a reprint of the "Consensus Tigurinus" of 1549—the sacramental doctrine of which the Polish reformer cordially approved. The work was addressed to Edward VI. in a dedication, of which a considerable portion will be found translated in Strype's "Ecclesiastical Memorials of King Edward VI.," vol. ii. part ii. pp. 34-36. The book is now very rare, but a copy of it exists in the Grenville Library, British Museum. It appeared at the critical time when the first Prayer-book of Edward was undergoing revision, and it must have contributed much to prepare the minds of the Church's rulers for the changes which were soon after introduced into the Communion office. Its influence also is very palpably seen in some parts of

Knox's "Confession." We can only find space for the following specimen of its reasonings:—

"At vero cum Dominus ipse, tradito mundato illo (Hoc facite) omnem nostram prudentiam, omnemque auctoritatem concludat sub exempli sui obedientiam; Cum Paulus item non aliud sit ausus tradere suis Corinthiis quum quod a Domino accepisset, subjiciamus et nos hic nostrum omnem prudentiam omnemque nostram auctoritatem divini hujus mandati obedientiae, valereque omnino faciamus papisticam illam indulgentiam qua se illi divina omnia laxare astringereque (pro bona sua intentione) posse putant. Et ea ipsa tantum esse signa sacramentorum statuamus, eaque duntaxat etiam in ministerio nostro observemus, quae exemplo Christi nobis proposita mandatoque ipsius nobis imperata habemus."

In 1555 A'Lasco published at Frankfort a work of great interest and of much historical importance in relation to the earliest organization of Presbyterian Puritanism in England, with the following title: "Forma ac Ratio Tota Ecclesiastici Ministerii, in peregrinorum, potissimum vero Germanorum Ecclesia instituta Londini in Anglia per pientissimum Angliae, &c. Regem Eduardum ejus nominis Sexti, Anno post Christum natum 1550."

The date 1550, commonly given to this very rare volume, is not correct. That was the date of the formation of John A'Lasco's Church. In 1556 appeared a French translation of the work, which was used by Dr. McCrie in the extracts given in his Notes and Illustrations to the life of Knox. Some extracts from this work, bearing upon the right order of the administration of the Lord's Supper, will be hereafter given in Part II. of this volume. It was published too late to have any influence upon Church matters in England in Edward's time; but it is a very full and authoritative representation of the constitution, worship, and discipline of the Church of the Foreign Protestants in London, which, though dispersed in the reign of Popish Mary, was restored at the accession of Elizabeth, and continues down to the present day under the name of the Dutch Church, Austin Friars.

The work is preceded by a lengthened address to Sigismund Augustus, king of Poland, from which we subjoin the following interesting and important reference to the religious zeal and large Reformation views of Edward VI.:—

"Cupiebat Rex ille sanctissimus ita restitutam (quoad ejus fieri posset) in universo regno suo, omnem plane religionem, ut nulla fere alia de re (pro aetate sua) solicitus magis esset. Adhibebat in ejus rei consilium, quos pietate, eruditione ac judicio, aliis antecellere intelligebat, inter quos praecipuum habebat Thomam Cranmerum, Cantuariensem Episcopum. . . . . . Hujus igitur hortatu, cum ego quoque, per Regem illum vocatus essem, et leges quaedam patriae obstarent quominus publici potissimum cultus divini ritus sub Papismo usurpati (pro eo ac Rex ipse cupiebat) repurgari protinus possent; Ego vero pro Peregrinorum ecclesiis sedulo instarem; ita demum placuit ut ritus publici in Anglicis Ecclesiis per gradus quosdam (quantum per leges patrias omnino liceret) repurgarentur, Peregrinis vero hominibus (qui patriis hac alioqui in parte legilus non usque adeo tenerentur) ecclesiae concederentur, in quibus omnia libere, et nulla rituum patriorum habita ratione (juxta doctrinam duntaxat atque observationem apostolicam) instituerentur. Ita enim fore ut Anglicae quoque ecclesiae ad puritatem Apostolicam amplectendam unanimi omnium regni ordinum consensu excitarentur. Ejus vero consilii Rex ipsemet (pro sua pietate), praecipuus non autor tantum, sed etiam propugnator fuit, Etsi enim id in Senatu Regio omnibus propemodum placeret, ipseque Cantuariensis Archiepiscopus rem modis omnibus promoveret, non deerant tamen qui id moleste ferrent, adeoque et reluctaturi fuerint huic instituto Regio, nisi Rex ipse, non tantum auctoritate sua restitisset, sed productis etiam instituti hujus rationibus conatus eorum repressisset."

3. *Note on the Eucharistical Doctrine of the Earliest Helvetic Confessions.*

The earliest of these Confessions was that of Basel, published in 1534, soon after the death of Œcolampadius, and the first draft of which is said to have been drawn by his hand. It was a local confession—being confined in the first instance to the ministers of that city, though soon after accepted by the city of Mühlhausen. Its language on the Lord's Supper need not be given, as the same divines who prepared it, only two years later joined in accepting the more important First Helvetic Confession, which expressed the Faith of all the Reformed German-speaking Cantons. Its 22nd Article defined the Eucharist as follows :—" Coenam mysticam esse, in qua Dominus corpus et sanguinem suam, *i.e.*, se ipsum suis vere ad hoc offerat ut magis magisque in illis vivat, et illi in ipso; non quod pani et vino corpus Domini et sanguis vel naturaliter uniantur, vel hic localiter includantur, vel ulla huc carnali praesentia statuantur, sed quod panis et vinum ex institutione Domini symbola sint, quibus ab ipso Domino, per ecclesiae ministerium, vera corporis et sanguinis ejus communicatio, non in periturum ventris cibum, sed in eternae vitae alimoniam exhibeatur." This teaching surely was not justly chargeable with reducing the signs of the Sacrament to *nuda signa*; it acknowledged them to be the divinely appointed media or instruments of the true communication of Christ's body and blood; and we are able to produce a very weighty proof, dating from the same year 1536, that the divines of Zurich and St. Gall repudiated such a charge when it was laid against them. This proof comes from Vadian, the Reformer of St. Gall, who wrote in that year an "Epistola qua hanc explicat quaestionem; An Corpus Christi propter conjunctionem cum Verbo inseparabilem alienas a corpore conditiones sibi sumat." It was drawn up by Vadian, at the suggestion of Bullinger, and was published by the latter at Zurich in 1539, with the title, "Orthodoxa et erudita D. Joachimi Vadiani Epistola—nostro seculo perquam utilis et necessaria." A copy of this extremely rare work is to be seen in the city library of St. Gall, from which, a few years ago, we took the following extract, which will now serve a useful purpose : " Boni autem consulimus horum suspicionem, qui, cum viderent nos cum Augustino et veteribus Corpus Domini certo aliquo in loco esse asseverare, veriti ne quid praefractius circa Eucharistiam committeremus, vere adesse illi Corpus Domini et vere sumi in coetu docuerunt—et simul vacuum usum signorem damnarunt. *Non enim aliud nostri senserunt* carnem, videlicet, et sanguinem Domini in coena vere edi et potari, nec nudis signis mysterium perfici, aut nudis symbolis fideles participare, etiamsi aliis atque aliis sermonum formulis variavimus. Edimus quidem vere panem, et vinum vere bibimus, Caeterum non hoc fine ut tam aestimemus signorum evidentiam quam rerum veritatem spectamus et sumimus. Harum enim symbola consecrata per verbum et a Domino sanctificata, externo et visibili usu rituque in coetu recipimus."

This is a weighty and conclusive testimony to the sacramental teaching of the divines of Zurich and St. Gall. The following passage taken from Vadian's "Aphorismorum Libri sex de Consideratione Eucharistiae," published at Zurich, in 1535, gives his own personal view of the "genuinus sensus Coenae Domini":—

"Proinde sensum istum ut pium et consonum cum instituto tum verbo et doctrinae Christi accipio.—Dominum nostrum Jesum, in institutione sacramenti redemptionis nostrae, panem et vinum consecrando, apostolis verum suum et mox cruci affigendum corpus edendum exhibuisse, et sanguinem verum qui crastino lancea et clavis haustus est, eisdem praebuisse potandum. Nec minus hoc modo et posteris ordinasse quod dedit discipulis, quippe qui hoc idem facere discipulis jussit quod ipse fecesset—hoc est ut pane fracto et propinato coelice, verum corpus Jesu et ejus sanguinem verum in hoc mysterio a se instituto ecclesiis exhiberent, morte ejus annunciata donec ipse ad judicium ingloria esset venturus. Excessurus enim ex hoc mundo et coelestem conditionem induturus, Christus memoriam sui sacramento nobis panis et calicis instituit, claris verbis admonens suum se nobis corpus dare ut eo vesceremur, et sanguinem suum offerre quem potaremus. Hic enim cibus et hic potus tam certe relictus est ecclesiae credentium in Eucharistia quam certe Christus vita nostra pro nobis crucifixus et mortuus est. Et recte est a Gregorio dictum quod calix quem sacerdos consecrat non est alius ab illo quem Apostolis Dominus ipse tradidit.

"Vere igitur in coetu, ex ejus instituto peracto, corpus Christi verum credentibus exhibetur, in illo enim vere et reipsa fideles communicant, nec abest enim a sacro illo Christus ipse et corporis Christi veritas; alioqui signa illa inutiliter interpretaremur, et vere non vesceremur carne ejus, quem verumtamen esse cibum nostrum dicimus—nec vere potaremur sanguine, qui verus tamen potus est; sed ludus potius et fabula esset, quod jejunis nobis in vacua illa symbolorum nuditate porrigeretur. Capio autem et intelligo verbo Christi potissimum effici, quod carne et sanguine ejus satiamur; ante enim est dictum, quod fides nostra per illud excitatur, neque non alimoniæ nostrae pars illi debetur, juxta illud—'Non in solo pane,' etc. Non est autem aliud in hoc esu mystico certius aut aptius verbum quam quod institutionis sacramenti, praeterea mortis ejus et redemptionis, in suo nomine congregatos admonet.

"Cum Augustino autem dico, miserabilem esse servitutem signa pro rebus accipere, et supra creaturum corpoream oculum mentis ad hauriendum lumen eternum non levare."

If now we compare with these statements of the First Helvetic Confession, as illustrated by those of Vadian, the language of the Consensus of Zurich, we shall not be sensible, I think, of any material *development* of doctrine in the latter, in the direction of making the *signa* of the Sacrament less *nuda* than they are still in some quarters supposed to have been in the view of the Zurich divines before Calvin induced them to accept the "Consensus." The 21st paragraph of the Consensus runs thus: "Tollenda est quaelibet localis praesentiae imaginatio. Nam quum signa hic in mundo sint, oculis cernantur, palpentur manibus; Christus, quatenus homo est, non alibi quam in Coelo, nec aliter quam mente et fidei intelligentia quaerendus est. Quare perversa et impia superstitio est, ipsum cum elementis hujus mundi includere.—No. 23. Quod autem carnis suae esu et sanguinis potione, quae hic figurantur, Christus animas nostras per fidem, spiritus sancti virtute pascit, id non perinde accipiendum quasi fiat aliqua substantiae vel commixtio vel transfusio, sed quoniam ex carne semel in sacrificium oblata et sanguine in expiationem effuso vitam hauriamus."

It is manifest, on a careful comparison of these documents with one another, that the idea entertained by many that the "Consensus of Zurich" was a victory gained by Calvin over Zwinglianism is quite a misconception of the real historical situation. Calvin and the Zurich divines were all along of substantially the same mind—but explanations on both sides were necessary before they came to understand that this was the case—and the correspondence which passed on that occasion between Calvin and Bullinger shows that the chief difficulty of arriving at the desired "Consensus" was not felt on the side of the former but the latter; that is to say, it was rather Bullinger who feared that Calvin was too much of Luther's way of thinking about Consubstantiation, or the doctrine of the Real Presence, than it was Calvin who feared that Bullinger had too much of the opinion of Carlstadt and other extremists as to the *nuda signa*. But the effect of the friendly correspondence on both sides was to satisfy Bullinger and his brethren that they were mistaken in regard to Calvin's views and tendencies; and when this point was reached, the "Consensus" was reached. If Bullinger and the Zurichers had been "Zwinglians," in the sense in which that name is now often understood, Calvin could never have had any hope of drawing them into a joint confession of Eucharistic faith, and as little would they have listened to any overtures proceeding from Calvin with that design.

The conclusion which we deduce from all these premises is, that as it is impossible to draw any doctrinal distinction between Cranmer and Knox in their definitions of the Eucharist—as these stand in the Articles of the Church of England and the National Confession of the Church of Scotland, it is equally hopeless to set up any distinction in their relations to the Theologies of Zurich and Geneva—inasmuch as in the Doctrine of the Sacraments these schools declared themselves to be at one, and had always been so from the first, though not always fully and clearly conscious of their agreement.

CHAPTER IV.

OFFER AND DECLINATURE OF THE SEE OF ROCHESTER—EPISTLE TO THE CONGREGATION OF BERWICK.

KNOX continued in London till nearly the end of 1552, and was, no doubt, closely engaged all that time in preaching, either at Court or in the City, or both, although no memorials remain of his ministry during that time.

To a man of so much shrewdness of observation, and so much faithfulness in judging and correcting his own mental habits of thought and feeling, of hope and fear, of forecast and reflection, a sojourn of several months in the Court and capital could not fail to be highly instructive and suggestive, and to originate currents of sentiment and feeling which were as various and contending as they were fresh and unaccustomed. He had then a nearer view of men and things in England than ever he had had before, and a view of them, besides, in the highest places, and on the broadest surface.

On every occasion of his preaching alternately with his colleague chaplain before the King, he had opportunity to read with his own eyes the great men who crowded the Court, and filled the Council chamber; and every day in the great city he mixed with all classes of society, and noted their fashions and ways of speech and life. And it was, no doubt, anything but an accidental coincidence that, from this time forward, we can discern in his preachings and writings a prevailing tendency to forecast the near future which was awaiting the English Church and nation, and can see that, along with an open eye to all that was encouraging and worthy of thankfulness in the state of religion and morals, both among high and low, rich and poor, he was often found in a less buoyant and more presaging mood; often ready to fear and foretell that evil days were at hand, and that a short sunshiny day, such as had succeeded the long night of Henry VIII.'s despotic reign, would soon set again in a night of still darker gloom, and still crueller oppression to the friends of truth and reformation.

It was probably during this visit to London that he first made the acquaintance of two religious families of high standing in the city—the Lockes and the Hickmans—of the class of wealthy merchants.

Among his "Familiar Epistles" are found several addressed, a few years later, from Dieppe and Geneva, to Mrs. Locke and Mrs. Hickman, "merchandis wyffis in Londoun," and from these we can gather what was the tone and mood of his early intercourse with them in matters of religion and the Church:—

"When I consider and call to mind how God, I doubt not, brought us into such familiar acquaintance that your hearts were incensed and kindled with a special care over me, as the mother useth to be over her natural child, and how my heart was opened and compelled, in your presence, to be more plain in such matters as after have come to pass, than ever I was to any—for, ye remember, as I suppose, how, after great anguish and sorrow of heart, which many days I sustained, at last I was compelled with weeping tears to open unto you that which almost no man could have believed. Ye remember my judgment, and what communication we had upon the same. God grant that ye remain in the same mind that then I found you, which was that ye little regarded the rest of the world, or yet the law of your country, in respect of that life to come, and that ye rather would leave possessions and friends, nor that ye should admit idolatry. When all these things I call to mind, and how often I have exhorted you to take example of me, who was a stranger [foreigner], and yet, by God's grace, had found favour, not only in your eyes, but also before many (howbeit with none I was so familiar); and when I remember that commonly I used to admonish you to be of good comfort, albeit ye should be compelled, for Christ's sake, to leave your native country, for God should never leave you comfortless, but should always provide for you, even as He had done for other, his elect, before you, and as ye presently saw his mercy shewed unto me. And when I remember that all such admonitions I used when no appearance there was of such troubles as after have ensued, and more abundantly shall ensue—

when all these things I call to mind, I can no otherwise judge but that God used our familiarity and communication for that present as a preparative for a sharper medicine."

The letter is signed,—

"Your brother, that shewed this vision unto you when no such thing was suspected,

"JOHNE KNOX."

So, then, even in those days of apparent high promise and hope, immediately after his own successful exertions at Court and with the Privy Council, Knox had his "visioun" of "years drawing nigh," when "he and many more should say they had no pleasure in them." There was something in the aspect and feeling of the time which sunk his strong spirits in spite of himself, and in spite even of his own joyful acknowledgment, when addressing the Privy Council in his "Confession," that "Christ's religion in this realm, all praise and honour be unto God, was now tending to perfection and maturity." And that "something" must have been somewhat that he had never seen anywhere else before—something, therefore, most probably, that he had discovered in the highest places of the land, and in the characters and lives of the men in highest office, who stood nearest to the Throne.

No man knew better than Knox how much the prosperity of religion and the Church depended upon the wise counsels and the godly example of the nation's heads and rulers; and his first visit to the young King's Court would seem to have brought home to him a foreboding impression, which we know that his second visit in the following spring did a great deal to deepen and confirm, that there was "something rotten in the state of England," even under her pious and gifted young King; that, in short, the Prince was ill served by his most trusted servants; that not a few of his most influential councillors were not men honestly "fearing God and hating covetousness;" that, ever since the judicial murder of Somerset, the Popish leaven which had all along been left in the King's Council, had been working and steadily gathering force; and that nothing but the life of a Prince of delicate constitution, and without promise of long life, stood between the Kingdom and the succession of a bigoted Romish Princess.

Public incidents bearing this sinister significancy were of frequent occurrence during the ensuing months, and gradually grew deeper in portent, till at last the worst—and more than the worst—of all his forecastings were realized in the condition of an oppressed kingdom and a recaptured and re-enslaved Church.

Since the fall and execution of the Duke of Somerset, the most powerful statesman of the kingdom was Somerset's relative and rival, John Dudley, Duke of Northumberland. His recent appointment to the Wardenry of the Borders had brought him into closer relations than before with the King's chaplain at Newcastle. He had resided there, as we have seen, for some time in the summer of that year, 1552; had heard Knox preach at St. Nicholas' and elsewhere, and though not approving in all points of his mode of conducting public worship, had formed a high opinion of his character and pulpit power, and, indeed, of his fitness to hold high place and office in the Church.

During his stay in the North, he had had it in his power either materially to strengthen or weaken Knox's influence and authority in the province, and the Reformer had had no reason to complain of the line he had taken in that respect. In fact, the relations between the statesman and the preacher had been so close and cordial in public estimation, that when Knox came up to London to preach at Court, he passed as the Duke's chaplain with many who had not previously heard of him as one of the King's chaplains.

It is not surprising, then, to find that a proposal to make Knox a bishop, which dates from this period of his chaplaincy, should have originated with Northumberland; a fact which, along with several other curious particulars of this remarkable incident of Knox's life, was discovered by the late Mr. Tytler, who was the first to publish to the world the following letters from the Duke to Cecil. These letters, preserved among the State papers of this reign, were not known to Dr. M'Crie, and may be fitly introduced here in full, on account of the important light which they throw not only upon this particular affair, but also upon a change which began to take place about this time in the relations of this powerful and unprincipled nobleman to Knox and other Reformers.

The first letter is dated 27 October, 1552:—

"I would to God it might please the King's Majesty to appoint Mr. Knox to the office of Rochester bishoprick; which, for three purposes, should do very well. The first, he would not only be a whetstone to quicken and sharp the Bishop of Canterbury, whereof he hath need; but also he would be a great confounder of the Anabaptists lately sprung up in Kent. Secondly, he should not continue the ministration in the North, contrary to this set forth here. Thirdly, the family of the Scots, now inhabiting in Newcastle, chiefly for his fellowship, would not continue there, wherein many resort to them out of Scotland, which is not requisite. Herein, I pray you, desire my Lord Chamberlain and Mr. Vice-Chamberlain to help towards this good act, both for God's service and the King's. And then for the North, if his Majesty make the Dean of Durham [Robert Horne] Bishop of that See, and appoint him one thousand marks more to that which he hath in his Deanery, and the same houses which he now hath, as well in the city as in the country, will serve him right honourably; so may his Majesty receive both the castle, which hath a princely site, and the other stately houses which the Bishop had in the country, to his Highness; and the Chancellor's living to be converted to the Deanery, and an honest man to be placed in it; the Vice-Chancellor to be turned into the Chancellor; and the Suffragan, who is placed without the King's Majesty's authority, and also hath a great living, not worthy of it, may be removed, being neither preacher, learned, nor honest man; and the same living, with a little more to the value of it—a hundred marks—will serve to the erection of a Bishop within Newcastle. The said Suffragan is so pernicious a man, and of so evil qualities, that the country abhors him. He is most meet to be removed from that office and from those parts.

"Thus may his Majesty place godly ministers in these offices as is aforesaid, and receive to his Crown 2,000 lib. a year of the best lands within the north parts of his realm. Yea, I doubt not it will be four thousand marks a year, of as good revenue as any is within the realm; and all places better and more godly furnished than ever it was from the beginning to this day.

"Scribbled in my bed, as ill at ease as I have been much in all my life.

"Your assured friend,
"NORTHUMBERLAND."

Here, then, was a whole budget of ecclesiastical proposals, which had all evidently sprung out of the Duke's late visit to the North, and the shrewd observation of men and things which his practised eye had made in the course of his visitation—Knox to be made Bishop of Rochester, both for God's service and the King's, *i.e.*, both for religious and political reasons, which the Duke would have Cecil and the Council to believe are both of equal weight with him—and a complete upturn to be made of the great Palatine See of Durham, now finally rid of Tunstall; the Dean to be made Bishop, but without the Bishop's castles and palaces, and Palatine rights and dignities; the See to be cut down to ordinary dimensions, and a new See made out of it for Newcastle and Northumberland, and the present Suffragan Bishop to be removed from his office and from the province as a man of evil qualities, and his "great living" to go, with an addition of a hundred marks, to support the new Bishop of Newcastle. The scheme would have been, at least, respectable in its aims, though not a little drastic, if it had come from a man as godly and King-loving as he pretended to be. But in a short time Northumberland laid bare, with his own hand, the selfish motives from which the whole scheme had sprung; for, when his proposals were entertained and agreed to by the King and Council, he was not ashamed to sue to his Majesty for a grant, to himself and his heirs, of the Palatine rights and revenues of the despoiled bishopric.

Nothing had been done in the matter of the vacant See of Rochester on the 23rd of November, when Northumberland wrote a second letter to Cecil, referred to in last chapter, "to put him and the Lords in memory that some order be taken for Knokks." But on the 7th of December a third letter, one of those published by Mr. Tytler, was written to the secretary of the Council, from which it appears that the affair had at length begun to take shape. Knox had been sent for by Cecil to be informed of what was in contemplation, and had been desired by him to wait upon Northumberland to communicate to him his views and wishes; and here was the singular and unexpected result:—

"Master Knoxs being here to speak with me, saying that he was so willed by you, I do return him again, because I love not to have to do with men which be neither grateful nor pleasable. I assure you I mind to have no more to do with him but to wish him well. Neither also with the Dean of Durham, because, under the colour of a false conscience, he can prettily malign and judge others against good charity, upon a froward judgment. And this manner you might see in his letter, that he cannot tell whether I be a dissembler in religion or not; but I have for twenty years stand [stood] to one kind of religion, in the same which I do now profess, and have, I thank the Lord, past no small dangers for it."

So then the all-powerful statesman found our Reformer neither "grateful nor pleasable" in the matter of the bishopric, and the offer which he had been the prime mover in obtaining for him came to nothing by default of Knox himself. But why was he not even grateful to the Duke for his kind intentions? Why had the Duke found that he was not even pleased with his good offices in his behalf? Knox was by no means a man of morose and uncourteous manners, and if he expressed on this occasion no gratitude nor pleasure to his powerful patron, it could only have proceeded from some deep suspicion which he had been led to conceive of his entire want of sincerity in his religious professions, and of the plotting selfishness that ere long revealed itself to the world at large in the most wicked and portentous schemes of self-aggrandisement.*

But, perhaps, the charge of ingratitude and "unpleasableness" was only the construction which Northumberland put upon Knox's declinature of the promotion which he put within his reach. Perhaps it did not mean that Knox had been deficient in politeness and good manners. Very likely, to a man like Northumberland, so thoroughly selfish and unprincipled, the high conscientiousness and pure-minded disinterestedness of a man like Knox would be so distasteful, especially when crossing some pet schemes of his own, that he chose to call them by very different names, and to stamp the man who was so much above the level of ordinary goodness with epithets which, if justly applied to him, would have sunk him quite as far beneath it.

But not often in history has a more conscientious and disinterested declinature of proffered wealth and dignity been recorded. Not often has the *nolo episcopari* been more sincerely pronounced than in the present instance. The bishoprics of the Reformed Church of England were as yet unreformed in the sense which Knox held to be imperative. Without mooting the question of

* The Duke's own letter discovers to us that Dean Horne, of Durham, had indicated the same suspicion in a letter addressed apparently to Cecil. So that Knox did not stand alone in this early prognostication of what was to follow in Northumberland's career.

the Scriptural warrant of diocesan episcopacy, he had concurred a few years before with Balnaves in laying down the requirement that the bishop should "not meddle with secular affairs or business, for that is not his vocation. If ye will remember duty upon the office ye are called to who are bishops, ye shall find you to have a great charge and work to do, and not a great dignity or lordship. But alas! now ye take thought of the lordship, dignity, rent, and profit, and look never to the work ye should do, the cause whereof is the neglecting of your vocation." And he continued of the same mind in the latest exhortation which he addressed to the people of England, that of 1559 from Geneva; for in the remarkable programme of reformation there sketched, one of the demands made was that "your bishopricks be so divided that of every one as they be now (for the most part) be made ten;" for "your proud prelates' great dominions and charge," he added, "impossible by one man to be discharged, are no part of Christ's ministerie, but are the maintenance of the tyranny first invented and yet retained by the Roman Antichrist.*

Long afterwards, in Scotland, a few months before his death, Knox reverted to this singular incident in his career—the offer of one of the oldest sees in England. It was upon occasion of the consecration of John Douglas, Rector of the University of St. Andrews, to be archbishop of that see. Knox, being then resident in St. Andrews, was asked by the Regent Morton to inaugurate Douglas, but declined, on public grounds, to give any sanction or countenance to the transaction, and even pronounced an anathema against both the donor and the receiver of the bishopric. He regarded the proceeding as an invasion of the constitution of the Reformed Church of Scotland, but was unjustly accused of being actuated in his declinature by the meanness of envy and personal disappointment. He rebutted the accusation with high disdain: "whereunto Mr. Knox made answer the next Sunday in the pulpit that he had refused a greater bishoprick than ever that was, which he might have had, with the favour of greater men than ever the other had this bishoprick, and yet did refuse. But only that he spake (referring to the anathema) for discharge of his conscience, and that the Kirke of Scotland should not be subject to that order, which then was used [the episcopate], considering the lords of Scotland had subscribed and also confirmed in Parlia-

* "Knox's Works," vol. v. p. 518.

ment the order already and long ago appointed by the Book of Discipline." "In the General Assembly held at St. Andrews in the following month—1572," as Mr. McCrie informs us, he not only entered a protest against the election of Douglas, but also "opposed himself directly to the making of bishops." For "though Knox," he remarks, "was of opinion that in certain circumstances of the Church a power might be delegated to some ministers to inspect the congregations within a particular district, and accordingly recommended the appointment of superintendents at the first establishment of the Reformation in Scotland, yet he did not allow of any class of office-bearers in the Church, under whatever name, who were superior in office or in order to ministers or presbyters." His sentiments were not more favourable to diocesan episcopacy in his latter than they had been in his earlier days. Writing to a correspondent in England in the year 1568, he says, "I would most gladly pass through the course that God hath appointed to my labour, giving thanks to his holy name for that it hath pleased his mercy to make me not a lord bishop, but a painful preacher of his blessed Evangel."

It was not long time after his memorable interview with Northumberland at Chelsea that Knox returned to his charge in Newcastle, where we find him preaching on Christmas Day. But before leaving London he would seem to have prepared and sent off to Berwick that remarkable "Epistle to the Congregation of Berwick," from which several fresh contributions to the history of his life in England have already been drawn in the preceding chapters. It is not dated, in the only existing copy, either as to time or place; but the reader will find in the second part of this volume reasons derived from the epistle itself, as compared with what we now know of the historical matters to which it refers, in support of the approximate date which is here assigned to it. The evidence of its genuineness will also be found stated there; upon which we only remark here that the contents of the epistle are so perfectly in keeping with the incidents and situations of Knox's recent life, that these, as now clearly known to us, are easily recognized in its allusions or implications; while these latter, in return, serve to reveal the state of thought and feeling which his recent observation and experience in high places had called forth; and this reciprocal light and help is itself a strong proof of the genuineness of the epistle, and of its authentic historical character, even if it were possible for a moment not to recognize in it Knox's unmistakable vigorous but "rude hand."

"I have thought it my duty," he thus begins after the apostolic form of salutation, "most dearly beloved brethren, not only to signify unto you my present estate, but also, in the bowels of Jesus Christ, to require of you bold continuance in that truth which once ye professed. For ignorant am I not what arts our adversary, the Devil, most commonly useth to draw back such as would go forward in the happy journey of life everlasting."

Taking up the latter topic first, viz., the duty of "bold continuance in the faith" which they had professed, he pursues it at great length through many pages, all full of his accustomed vigour and fervour, and thickly strewn with examples and illustrations drawn from the Old Testament histories and prophecies, his favourite storehouse and armoury, but having no farther historical interest than as they serve to throw light upon his present mood of mind touching the near future, and as indicating some of the signs and tokens of approaching judgments "which be not observed and marked of all men, but only of such as have their eyes opened by the Holy Ghost to understand and see that the immutable judgments of God in no age long delayed to take vengeance upon manifest transgressors, when iniquity is come to ripeness and maturity, albeit a mean number did look for the same."

The historical and biographical interest and value of the Epistle lies in its latter portion, where he speaks freely of his own "present estate," and applies himself to the question of liturgical conformity, which he expected would very soon be forced upon the attention of his former flock:—

"Here must I speak of my present estate, and what I would ye esteemed of me, nothwithstanding rumours and fame which soundeth and bloweth most commonly to the worst of God's messengers, especially in their absence.

"First, as touching my life and conversation, I am even yet such in heart as I was in your presence, when I walked before you, not as an hypocrite, counterfeiting, and preferring [putting forward] gravity before men and yet lacking God's fear in heart, but contrariwise, trembling for my sins before the face of God, I accompanied with you as your common brother, like the common sort of

God's elect children that continually lament and groan for sin that remaineth in this our corrupt nature during the days of this transitory life—which my frailty I never concealed from you, nor from the knowledge of the common congregation. Nor yet never pretended I, by policy or craft, to advance myself otherwise than God hath appointed, by preaching of his truth unto men. By which truth if God hath wrought in the hearts of any such favours unto me as displeased some men (alluding here, no doubt, to his adversaries in Newcastle), I will crave of you, beloved brethren, in the bowels of Christ's mercies not to suspect craft or deceit in me, which God knoweth neither was nor is in me concerning that matter. . . .

"These things do I signify unto you that ye be not slandered nor offended, as that some spirit of pride were late creppin into me. Not so, dear brethren. I unfeignedly praise God of his free gift, and with tears I pray for continuance of the same. This day I am more vile and of less reputation in my own eyes than I was either that day that my feet were chained in the prison of dolour (the Galleys, I mean), or yet that day that I was delivered by his only providence from the same. For better now I am taught of my own infirmity, which, as it compelleth me frequently to groan, so, God be praised, it is a scourge and bridle that admonisheth me never to glory in flesh. And thus for my life and present purpose.

"And as touching my doctrine, God beareth record at this hour to my conscience that I have spoken the truth amongst you, and have laboured to instruct you in the same. And therefore, as touching the chief points of religion, I neither will give place (God assisting my infirmity) to man or angel teaching the contrair to that which ye have heard. But as for ceremonies or rites, things of smaller weight, I am not minded to move contention, so that, with conscience, and without reproach of my former doctrine, I may avoid the same."

Then follows the passage, before quoted, against kneeling in the Lord's Supper, and assuring his old congregation that he has never either repented or recanted his former doctrine; after which he proceeds in the following remarkable paragraphs:—

"But because I am but one, having in my contrair magistrates, common order, and judgments of many learned, I am not minded, for maintenance of that one thing, to gainstand the magistrates in all other and chief points of religion agreeing with Christ and his true doctrine; nor yet to break nor trouble common order thought meet to be kept for unity and peace in the congregation for a time; and least of all intend I to damn or lightly regard the grave judgments of such men as unfeignedly I fear, love, and will obey in all things by them judged expedient to promote God's glory; these subsequents granted unto me, viz.:

"First, That the magistrates make known (as that they have done if ministers were willing to do their duty) that kneeling is not retained in the Lord's Supper for maintenance of any superstition, much less that any adoration appertaineth to any real presence of Christ's body natural there contained or joyned with those elements of bread and wine; but only for uniform order to be kept, and that for a time, in this Church of England.

"Secondly, That common order claim not kneeling in the Lord's Supper as either necessary or decent to Christ's action, but only as a ceremony thought good by man and not by Christ himself; for otherwise shall common order accuse Christ and his action of indecency or lacking some gesture necessary.

"And lastly, That my fathers whom I fear and honour, and my brethren in labours and profession whom I unfeignedly love, do not trouble my conscience, imputing upon me any foolish enterprise, for that I have, in ministration of Christ's Sacraments, more regarded attempting to follow what Christ himself did in his own perfect action than what any man after hath commanded to be done.

"These things granted unto me, I neither will gainstand godly magistrates, neither break common order, nor yet contend with my superiors or fellow-preachers, but with patience will I bear that one thing, daily thirsting and calling unto God for reformation of that and others. And this I do bear, brethren, not for fear of any trouble (as knoweth God) that can apprehend me in my own person; for I know who hath the cup that I must drink in his own hand, even God our heavenly Father, whose merciful providence so ruleth and guideth all creatures that neither man nor devil can trouble nor molest me nor the least of his elect, but as He will and hath before determined them and me to be tried in the furnace of tribulation, for consuming and burning away of vanity and dross that remaineth in this our corrupt nature. And therefore, brethren, it is not fear of corporal punishment, but the only fear that Christian charity be violated and broken, that suadeth and moves me to give place in this behalf. Albeit I could, with soberness and obedience, shew causes reasonable why sitting at the Lord's Table is to be preferred unto kneeling, yet if the upper powers, not admitting the same, would execute upon me the penalty of their law (because they may not suffer a common order to be violated), assuredly Christian charity were broken and dissolved upon the one part, either by me, that, for so small a matter, obstinately would gainstand such magistrates as profess themselves earnest promoters of Christ's Gospel; or else by them, that, persuaded by some manlye [human] reasons of certain dangers to follow if common order should not universally be kept in the realm, should trouble the body or stop the mouth of him that, to his knowledge, hath spoken nothing but Christ's plain verity."

Not many, perhaps, of the readers of these remarkable paragraphs were prepared before reading them for such a tone of moderation and modesty on the part of their author, especially on a subject on which he had shortly before expended so much zeal and energy in the highest places of the kingdom. It is plain now that Cranmer had mistaken and misrepresented the character of the man whom he had spoken of in his letter to the Privy Council as a "glorious and unquiet spirit," who "could like nothing but what was after his own fancy, and could not cease to make trouble and disquietness when things were most quiet and in good order." What a magnanimous return does Knox here make, in the shape of reverence and deferential consideration, for the reproaches which had been cast upon him! Nor is there any inconsistency between his previous vehemence in counselling the abrogation of kneeling and his present submission in the interest of charity to its continuance, in the hope of further reformation at a future time. Most men of energy, indeed, who are vehement in speech are also intemperate in action. But Knox was an instance, not only on this occasion, but on not a few others of his life, of a man of great original force, who could be as moderate in action as he could be vehement, even to occasional intemperance, in language. Like all wise men, he knew and remembered that there is a time to speak, and a time to be silent—a time when it is a duty, in the interest of truth, to oppose, and a time when it is equally a duty, in the interest of peace and charity, to cease from opposing, and to set an example of submission under protest.

Not only was he content to conform to the practice of Sacramental kneeling in his own person, but one of the chief purposes of this epistle was to give counsel to the congregation of Berwick to adopt the same course, when required by "the upper powers" to conform to all the rubrics of the new Prayer-book. Of that compulsory enforcement there was now, it is plain, a near prospect, and the reader cannot fail to notice, with deep interest, the following paragraphs in which their former teacher, and much trusted guide expounds to them his views of what would be their duty, in an emergency which could not fail to be very unwelcome and trying:—

"If now, by especial commandment of your upper powers, ye shall be compelled to observe the common order, God forbid that ye shall be damned or judged as shrinking from Christ; if, firstly, ye rejoice not that ye are called back again to a gesture that is joined with dangers in that action. Secondly, if openly ye profess that that which ye do now, as it proceedeth neither of your will, pleasure, nor election, so do ye not approve nor allow the same, but only do bear and suffer it for obedience unto magistrates, and peace to be kept amongst the congregation; thirsting and praying in the mean season that God of his great mercy, for Christ his Son's sake, please so to move and illuminate the hearts and eyes of magistrates and rulers, that they might understand and see Christ's institution to be most perfect, and men's devices and wisdom in matters of religion ever to have displeased God; that by contemplation thereof they may study to eradicate and pull out all such plants as the Heavenly Father hath not planted: and, lastly, if, hating in your hearts all superstition and idolatry, ye likewise openly protest that ye communicate with such as in that action adore any corporal or real presence of Christ's natural body, which is not there but in heaven, which behoveth to receive Him till all be complete that is spoken by the mouths of God's holy prophets—if these things by you be righteously observed, understood, and believed, God forbid that of any ye shall be suspected as that your fervency towards the truth began to abate and wax cold, albeit (contrary to your heart's desire) your order be altered; which unto my heart is so dolorous, that if any corporal pain that my wicked carcase is able to sustain might confirm and establish that order which God's truth hath planted among you without trouble or danger of you, rather I should suffer the death, than your quietness and consciences should be molested.

But seeing that my resistance should rather stir the magistrates against you than establish you in quietness, the counsel of all godly, as also the testimony of my own conscience, is that less offence it is to bear this one thing (with dolour of your hearts, daily calling unto God for reformation of the same), than to provoke the magistrates to displeasure, seeing that in principals we all agree. This for your order, which ye shall not alter nor change until ye be especially commanded by such as have authority."

Such was the moderate course which Knox advised his former flock at Berwick to follow, when the moment should arrive which they all wished to be deferred as long as possible. And he sent them this advice, it will be noticed, as "the counsel of all godly." He had brought the subject beforehand, we hence gather, under the notice of his pious friends in London, as soon as he had become aware that the Prayer-book was to be introduced into the northern counties. For it will be remembered that at the meeting of Council on October 20th, one of the items of business set down for consideration, in the same line with mention of Knox and the Archbishop, was "The Book in the bishopric of Durham," and that we have also come upon traces of a desire on the part of the powerful Warden-General of the Borders, to see the same conformity enforced in the northern province as in the rest of the Kingdom. The course of duty, therefore, in anticipation of the coming change, had to be well weighed, and we are now aware of what had been the result of these deliberations in Knox's own mind, and in the judgment of "all godly," the duty of present and provisional conformity, with unabated desires and prayers for future reformation of what was still amiss.

At what precise date the expected orders from the higher powers arrived, there is no record to show. But it must have been in the course of the spring of 1553, probably not till Knox himself had been removed from Newcastle to the south, which took place near Easter that year. We are now, then, fully in presence of the very remarkable fact that, for four years after the issue of the First Prayer-book of Edward VI.—*i.e.*, from 1549 to 1553 —the border counties of England were exempted from the obligation of conformity to the authorized liturgy of the National Church, and that the Puritan forms of worship and sacramental administration were in use in several, at least, of their most important parish churches. John Knox preached and prayed and dispensed the Sacraments during all these years, entirely according to his own views of Scripture warrant and prescription, not only statedly for two years in Berwick, and for two years more in Newcastle, but also occasionally in Carlisle, and in many other places of the two most northern counties. And he used this Puritan franchise not only with the full cognizance of the King and the Privy Council, but with their cordial recognition and support, manifested on more than one occasion, when the enemies of his ministry endeavoured to discredit him, and to bring his work among them to a close.

These facts are curious and important in the history both of the Anglican Church and of the Puritan party. They form the first chapter of the history of English Puritanism—a history which has now run on for upwards of three centuries—which has been most intimately interwoven at many points with the history and progress and development of the nation itself—and which has still, no doubt, many more chapters of history awaiting it in the nation's future. As an applied and embodied mode of religious thought and belief, it took its rise in England at its extreme northern boundary, and in the course of the next Protestant reign it spread itself from new centres in London and the two universities over the whole kingdom ; and, most curious fact of all, it was a Scottish Reformer who was the father of Anglican as well as Scottish Puritanism, and who rocked its cradle.

CHAPTER V.

The Last Year of Knox's Work in England, 1553.

IN anticipation of Knox's return to Newcastle for a time, a letter was sent from the Privy Council on the 9th of December, 1552, to Lord Wharton, now Deputy Lord Warden of the Northern Borders, commending him to his favour and support.* In the course of that month he had returned to his important post, and we hear of him in the pulpit again on Christmas Day.

"It cometh to my mind," says he, in his Admonition to the professors of God's truth in England,† "upon Christmas Day, in the year of our Lord 1552, preaching in Newcastle-upon-Tyne, and speaking against the obstinacy of the Papists, I made this affirmation, that whosoever in his heart was enemy to Christ's Gospel and doctrine, which then was preached within the realm of England, was enemy also to God, and secret traitor to the Crown and commonwealth of England. For as they thirsted nothing more than the King's death, which their iniquity would procure, so they regarded not who should reign over them so that their idolatry might be erected again. How these my words at that time pleased men, the crimes [accusations] and action intended against me did declare. Against me were written articles, and I compelled to answer, as unto an action of treason. But let my very enemies now say, from their conscience, if those my words are not proved true."

In the absence of any record of the proceedings immediately commenced against Knox by Sir Robert Brandling, it is fortunate that a long letter of the Duke of Northumberland upon the subject has been preserved, and was given to the world by the late Mr. Tytler.‡ It is addressed to Cecil, and runs thus:—

* Strype's "Memorials of Cranmer, book ii. cap. 33.
† "Knox's Works," vol. iii. p. 297.
‡ Tytler's "England under the Reigns of Edward and Mary," vol. ii. p. 158.

"After my right hearty commendations herewith I do return unto you, as well Mr. Morrison's letters as also the Lord Wharton's, and do also send with the same such letters as I have received from the said Lord Wharton, of the 2nd and 3rd of this instant, with also one letter from poor Knox, by the which you may perceive what perplexity the poor soul remaineth in at this present; the which, in my poor opinion, should not do amiss to be remembered to the rest of my Lords, that some order might be taken by their wisdom for his recomfort. And as I would not wish his abode should be of great continuance in those parts, but to come and to go as shall please the King's Majesty and my Lords to appoint him, so do I think it very expedient that his Highness's pleasure should be known as well to the Lord Wharton as to those of Newcastle, that his Highness hath the poor man and his doings in gracious favour; otherwise some hindrance in the matters of religion may rise and grow among the people, being inclined of nature to great inconstancy and mutations. And the rather do I think this meet to be done, for that it seemeth to me that the Lord Wharton himself is not altogether without suspicion how the said Knox's doings hath been here taken; wherefore I pray you that something may be done wherby the King's Majesty's pleasure to my Lords may be indelayedly certified to the said Lord Wharton, of the King's Majesty's good contentation towards the poor man and his proceedings, with commandment that no man shall be so hardy to vex him or trouble him for setting forth the King's Majesty's most godly proceedings, or [what he] hereafter by his Majesty's commandment shall do; for that his Majesty mindeth to employ the man and his talent from time to time, in those parts and elsewhere, as shall seem good to his Highness, for the edifying of his people in the fear of God. And that something might be written to the Mayor for his greedy accusation of the poor man, wherein he hath, in my poor opinion, uttered his malicious stomach towards the King's proceedings, if he might see a time to serve his purpose, as knoweth God, to whose infinite goodness let us pray that all things may prosper to his glory, and to the honour and surety of the King's Majesty.

"From Chelsey, this 9th of January, 1552–3.

"Your assured loving friend,

"NORTHUMBERLAND."

The powerful statesman had been as good as his word to Cecil a month before—that he would still wish the zealous preacher well, though as a patron he would have nothing more to do with seeking his promotion. He proved himself his well-wisher in this emergency, to good purpose. Instructions were sent down to Wharton and the Council of the North. The storm passed away as quickly as it had gathered, and the sky once more was clear. Sir Robert Brandling, the "greedy accuser," was baulked of his revenge; Lord Wharton was made to understand how highly the King and Council approved of Knox's proceedings, and that it was his duty as Warden General to protect the preacher from all who, like Brandling, had "a malicious stomach" towards the King's godly proceedings, and Knox was left at leisure to proceed without molestation in the work of his ministry and pastoral care.

Of this pastoral care it was now a constant and considerable part to keep up his religious correspondence with Mrs. Bowes.

"At Newcastle, in great haste, the 26th of February, 1553," he closes a letter with the following paragraph, which preserves the memory of a personal peculiarity of manner which was characteristic of him, besides other particulars not without interest :—

"After the writing of these preceding, your brother and mine, Harie Wickleif,* did advertise me by writing that your adversary took occasion to trouble you, because that I did start back from you rehearsing your infirmities. I remember myself so to have done, and that is my common consuetude when anything pearceth or toucheth my heart. Call to your mind what I did standing at the cupboard in Alnwick. In very deed I thought that no creature had been tempted as I was; and when that I heard proceed from your mouth the very same words that he troubles me with, I did wonder, and fra my heart lament your sair trouble, knawing in myself the dolour thereof. And na other thing, dear sister, meant I, and therefore think not that I either flatter you, or yet that I conceal anything fra you; na, for if I had been sa minded, I had not been sa plain in other cases. My other great

---

* This Harie Wickleif would seem to have been the brother-in-law of Mrs. Bowes, married to her only sister, joint heiress with herself of their father, Sir Richard Aske, of Aske, near Richmond. There had been frequent marriages between the Askes, Wickleiffs, and Bowes', owing to the contiguity of their estates on either side of the Tees; so that Knox's connection by marriage with the house of Bowes linked him also to that of the Wickliffes of Wickliffe, the family of the illustrious English Reformer of the 14th century.

labours permit me not to write as I would. I will pray for your continuance in Christ."

In another interesting letter, written about the same time, we see the great preacher "sitting at his book," with a folio of Chrysostom lying open on his study table beside his English Bible.

"Dearly beloved sister in Jesus our Lord, in the instant moment that your messenger delivered to me your letter, was I sitting at my book, and in contemplating Matthew's Gospel, in this place wherein the parable of good seed is sawin, the Enemy also sawing wicked cokill among the same, I revolved some maist godly expositions, and, amangis the rest, Chrysostome, wha notes upon thir [these] words: 'The Enemy did this, that we may knaw that whasoever is beloved of God has the Devil to his enemy, and therefore ought we maist rejoice when we find the Devil maist rage against us, for that is an evident sign that we are not under his bondage, but are free servants to Jesus Christ, to whom because the Devil is enemy he must also declare himself enemy to us.' In reading of this his holy judgment, your battle and dolour was before my eyes, and as I prayed God that ye might be assisted to the end, so wished I that ye had been present with me; and even at the same instant called your servant, whereof I praised my God, and addressed me to write, after the reading of your letter, as I might. The place of Luke's Gospel touching them that shall seek and shall not find, ought not to discourage you, for it doth not mean that any thirsting for salvation by Jesus Christ shall be deceived, but of such as seek to enter into the kingdom of God by other ways than by Christ only, as ye do knaw there is a great number doth. And where Christ says, 'There is few that are chosen,' that is true in respect of the reprobate. For all England this day is called, but ye knaw how mean is the number that obeys the voice of the Caller; and therefore ought ye greatly to rejoice, knawing yourself to be ane of the small and contemned flock to whom it has pleased God to give the kingdom.

"The pain of my head and stomach troubles me greatly; daily I find my body decay, but the providence of God shall not be frustrate. I am charged to be at Widdrington upon Sunday, where I think I shall also remain Monday. The Spirit of the Lord Jesus rest with you. Desire such faithful as with whom ye communicate your mind, to pray that, at the pleasure of our good God, my dolour, both of body and spirit, may be relieved somewhat; for presently

... ... Spirit, I praise my God, so
... ... be declared; and therefore
... ... yet we see not.
... ... brother in Christ."
... ... graphically interesting, are
... ... of his letters to the same
... ... —
... ... morrow, and so shall we
... ... ye knaw to be the day
... ... if your trouble be intoler-
... ... your pain, do as the
... ... I will be offended with
... ... how glad should I
... ... the sick! Your mes-
... ... and maist dolorous
... ... when we twa meet.
... ... the petitions
... ... free us from
... ... place thereof shall
... ...
... ... Job, yet maist
... ... in this life. The
... ... of my heart, alter
... ... unto Job; but
... ... And this is
... ... have ane fellow
... ... Christ: for the head
... ... he is stinging us

... ...
... ... me strongly, by
... ... of the Pagan

... ... and behold!
... ... making many
... ... Scarcely
... ... life from one
... ... most opposite kind;
... ... and dishonour, of good
... ...

The scene shifts immediately. He had his forebodings, as we see above, of "something abiding or awaiting that yet we see not"— some new crisis or extremity for which the Spirit of God was preparing him; and here it is, recorded by his own hand in one of his letters to Mrs. Bowes:—

"Urgent necessity will not suffer that I satisfy [fully explain] my mind unto you. My Lord of Westmoreland has written unto me this Wednesday, at six of the clock at night, immediately thereafter to repair unto him, as I will answer at my peril. I could not obtain license to remain the time of the sermon upon the morrow. . . . As for myself, albeit the extremity should now apprehend me, it is not come unlooked for. But allace! I fear that yet I be not ripe, nor able to glorify Christ by my death; but what lacketh now, God shall perform in his own time."

A new storm had burst upon him, apparently quite suddenly, though not without some forebodings of coming distress. What it meant we can gather somewhat from his words addressed to the same friend on the 23rd of March, after it had passed away. Alluding to the letter just quoted, he remarks that "it was written at such time as many thought I never should write after to man. Heinous were the delations laid against me, and many are the lies that are made to the Council. But God one day shall destroy all lying tongues, and shall deliver his servants from calamity. I look but one day or other to fall in their hands, for mair and mair rageth the members of the Devil against me. This assault of Satan has been to his confusion, and to the glory of God; and therefore, sister, cease not to praise God and to call for my comfort, for great is the multitude of enemies, whom every one the Lord will confound."

The Council referred to was the Privy Council in London; for there is a letter of his to Mrs. Bowes, dated "London, the 1st of March, 1553," in answer to letters from her, and "his dearest spouse" her daughter, which had reached him "the last of Februar." Apparently his old adversaries in Newcastle had again attempted to ruin his credit with the King and Council, which they had been foiled in, two months earlier, by the intervention of Northumberland. But the snake had only been scotched, not killed. The biter bit again, and planted afresh his poisoned fang. What the "heinous delations laid against him" were, we do not know. It is enough to be certified by himself that they were all "the untruths of lying tongues," and to know that the upshot of this new assault was confusion to his enemies, and glory to God as the Defender of the right, and the Helper of his servants in the time of trouble.

But let the reader mark again, in the very midst of this other "strong battle," how tender-hearted and gentle is this "hero of a hundred fights." Wrestling with giants in the high places of the field, how striking the contrast presented by the following scene in an apartment of one of the friendly families of London with whom he was wont to reside on his visits to the South, perhaps in the house of Mr. and Mrs. Locke, in Bow Church-yard, Cheapside :—

"Fear not, mother, that the care of you passes from my heart—Na! He to whom nothing is secret knaweth that I never present myself, by Jesus Christ, before the throne of my Father's mercy, but there also I commend you; and seldom it is that otherwise ye pass from my remembrance. The very instant hour that your letters were presented unto me was I talking of you, by reason that three honest poor women were come to me, and were compleaning their great infirmity, and were shewing unto me the great assaults of the Enemy, and I was opening the cause and commodities thereof, whereby all our eyes weeped at anis [at one time], and I was praying unto God that ye and some others had been there with me for the space of twa hours; and even at that instant came your letters to my hands, whereof ane part I read unto them, and ane of them said 'O would to God I might speak with that person, for I perceive there be more tempted than I.' I write na lie unto you, but the very truth of our communication what time I received your letters.—Your Son, &c."

John Knox, the wrestler, the strong battler, in tears, with "three poor honest weeping women," whom he is doing his best to comfort by his skilful teaching, and by the sympathy of his congenial prayers! and remembering tenderly his yearning mother, three hundred miles away, and writing to her by return of post to say, "Fear not, mother, that the care of you passes from my heart!"

On the 23rd of the same month of March, as we have seen, he was again in Newcastle, strong as ever, victorious over calumny and hatred, and looking forward to the future with a good courage. "Great is the multitude of enemies, whom every ane the Lord will confound. I intend not to depart fra Newcastle before Easter, my daily labours must now increase, and therefore spare me sa mekkill [much] as ye may. My auld malady troubles me sair, and na thing is more contrarious to my health than writing. Think not that I weary to visit you, but unless my pain shall cease, I will altogether become unprofitable. Work, O Lord, even as pleaseth thy infinite goodness, and relax the troubles, at thy own pleasure, of such as seeketh thy glory to shine. Amen. I bid you heartily farewell in Christ our Sovereign."

In a few weeks more, every day full of labours, and bearing up manfully against bodily pain, which as we see was chiefly a trouble to him because it threatened to make him unprofitable to the Church of God, his ministry at Newcastle came to a close, and he turned his face once more to the south.

He was to preach in his course a second time before the Court, and a scene was now to open upon him which would put his heroic uprightness to a severer proof than any which it had ever yet sustained. At his first appearance in the Chapel Royal he had spoken his mind with a fearless frankness on outstanding questions of Church Reform, and these were testing enough to a royal chaplain's integrity and courage. But on the present occasion his discourse was to be of living men—the greatest of the great—the mightiest of the mighty in the King's counsels and in the government of the realm. God had said to him, in the open ear of his pure conscience, as He said once to Jeremiah, "Gird up thy loins, and arise, and speak unto them all that I command thee. Be not dismayed at their faces, lest I confound thee before them. For behold, I have made thee this day a defenced city, and an iron pillar, and brazen walls against the whole land."

It was in the month of April, after Easter, that it fell to Knox to appear again in the pulpit of the Chapel Royal. The Court was then at Westminster, and a new Parliament, convened by Northumberland, was still sitting, or had just risen. A very recent scene in the Upper House, between Northumberland and Cranmer, may be mentioned, to show how difficult and perilous a duty it had now become to speak God's truth in the hearing of the King's Councillors and Ministers of State. It is thus given by Mr. Froude:—

"At the end of March Cranmer produced in the House of Lords

his reformed Code of Canon Law. Northumberland rose, and turning fiercely on the Archbishop, bade him attend to the duties of his office. The clergy were going beyond their province, presuming in their sermons to touch the doings of their superiors. 'You bishops,' he said, 'look to it at your peril. Take heed that the like happen not again, or you and your preachers will suffer for it together.' The Archbishop ventured a mild protest. He had heard no complaints of the preachers, he said; they might have spoken of vices and abuses, he did not know. There were vices enough, Northumberland answered violently, no doubt of that; the fruits of the Gospel in this life were sufficiently meagre."*

What plain speaking of the preachers, without respect of persons, the enraged Duke alluded to in this violent outbreak, we best learn from a remarkable account of Knox himself, given in his "Godly Letter sent to the Faithful in London, Newcastle, Berwick, &c."† He is describing, from his own observation, the religious and moral state of the kingdom during the last years of King Edward, "a King of so godly disposition towards virtue and the truth of God, that none, from the beginning, passed him, and to my knowledge none of his years did ever match him, in that behalf, if he might have been lord of his own will. Allace! I eschame to rehearse it. Universal contempt of all God's admonitions; hatred of them that rebuked vice; authorising of them that could invent most villany against the preachers of God's Word. In this matter I may be admitted for a sufficient witness; for I heard and saw, I understood and knew, with the sorrow of my heart, the manifest contempt and crafty devices of the Devil against those most godly and learned preachers that this last Lent, anno MDLIII., were appointed to preach before the King's Majesty; as also against all others whose tongues were not tempered with the holy water of the Court—plainly to speak, who, flattering against their own consciences, could not say all was well and nothing needed reformation. What reverence and audience, I say, was given to the preachers this last Lent, by such as then were in authority, their own consciences declared; assuredly even such as by the wicked Princes of Judah was given to Jeremiah. They hated such as rebuked vice, and stubbornly they said, We will nocht amend. And yet how boldly their sins were rebuked, even in their faces, such as

* "History of England," Edward VI. chap. 29.
† "Knox's Works," vol. iii. pp. 175-177.

were present can witness with me. Almost there was none that occupied the place but he did prophesy and plainly speak the plagues that are begun and assuredly shall end. Maister Grindall plainly spake the death of the King's Majesty, complaining on his household servants and officers, who neither eschamed nor feared to rail against God's true Word and against the preachers of the same. The godly and fervent man, Maister Lever, plainly spake the desolation of the common weal, and the plagues which should follow shortly. Maister Bradford spared not the proudest, but boldly declared that God's vengeance strike them that then were in authority, because they abhorred and loathed the true Word of the everlasting God. And, amongst many others, willed them to take example by the late Duke of Somerset, who became so cold in hearing God's Word that the year before his last apprehension, he would go visit his masons, and would not deign himself to go from his gallery to his hall for hearing of a sermon. 'God punished him (said the godly preacher), and that suddenly, and shall He spare you that be double more wicked? No, He shall not. Will ye, or will ye not, ye shall drink the cup of the Lord's wrath—Judicium Domini, Judicium Domini—the judgment of the Lord, the judgment of the Lord!' lamentably cried he, with weeping tears. Maister Haddon most learnedly opened the causes of the bypast plagues, affirming that the worse were to follow unless repentance should shortly be found. Much more I heard of these four, and of others, which now I may not rehearse, and that (which is to be noted) after that the whole Council had said, they would hear no more of their sermons; they were undiscreet fellows—yea, and prating knaves." Such was the temper of the Court and Council, with the single exception of the godly young King, when Knox stood up again to preach before them. Never had preacher an audience less well affected to his person and order, and yet never was preacher less likely to quail before their hostility, or to keep back from them any whit of what he conceived to be the counsel of God, the Word in season, or present truth.

All we know of his preaching on this occasion is from his own pen, writing within a year later, his "Admonition to the Professors of God's Truth in England," July, 1554* :—

"Let no man wonder though I say that the crafty policies of pestilent Papists wrought all mischief, for who could better work

* "Knox's Works," vol. iii. pp. 280–82.

mischief than such as bore authority and rule? And who, I pray you, ruled the roast in the Court all this time by stout courage and proudness of stomach but Northumberland? But who, I pray you, under King Edward, ruled all by counsel and wit? Shall I name the man? I will write no more plainly now than my tongue spake the last sermon that it pleased God that I should make before that innocent and godly King, Edward the Sixth, and before his Council at Westminster, and even to the faces of such as of whom I meant. Entreating this place of Scripture: 'Qui edit mecum panem sustulit adversus me calcaneum suum'—*i.e.*, 'He that eateth bread with me hath lifted up his heel against me,' I made this affirmation that commonly it was seen that the most godly princes had officers and chief councillors most ungodly, conjured enemies to God's true religion, and traitors to their princes. Not that their wickedness and ungodliness was speedily perceived and espied out of the said princes and godly men, but that for a time those crafty colourers could so cloak their malice against God and his truth, and their hollow hearts towards their loving masters, that, by worldly wisdom and policy, at length they attained to high promotions. And for the proof of this mine affirmation, I recited the histories of Achitophel, Shebna, and Judas, of whom the two former had high offices and promotions, with great authority, under the most godly princes, David and Hezekias, and Judas was purse-maister with Christ Jesus. And when I had made some discourse in that matter, I moved this question: 'Why permitted so godly princes so wicked men to be upon their council, and to bear office and authority under them?' To the which I answered: 'That either they so abounded in worldly wisdom, foresight, and experience, touching the government of a commonwealth, that their counsel appeared to be so necessary that the commonwealth could not lack them; and so, by the colour to preserve the tranquillity and quietness in realms, they were maintained in authority: or else they kept their malice, which they bare towards their masters and God's true religion, so secret in their hearts that no man could espy it, till, by God's permission, they waited for such occasion and opportunity that they uttered all their mischief so plainly that all the world might perceive it.' And that was most evident by Achitophel and Shebna, for of Achitophel it is written that he was David's most secret councillor, and that because his counsel in those days was like the oracle of God. And Shebna was unto good King Hezekias sometime comptroller, sometime secretary, and, last of all, treasurer; to the which offices he had never been promoted under so godly a prince, if the treason and malice which he bare against the King and against God's true religion had been manifestly known. 'No!' quoth I, 'Shebna was a crafty fox, and could shew such a fair countenance to the King, that neither he nor his council could espy his malicious treason; but the prophet Esaias was commanded by God to go to his presence, and to declare his traitorous heart and miserable end.'

"'Was David,' said I, 'and Hezekias, princes of great and godly gifts and experience, abused by crafty councillors and dissembling hypocrites? What wonder is it, then, that a young and innocent King be deceived by crafty, covetous, wicked, and ungodly councillors! I am greatly afraid that Achitophel be councillor, that Judas bear the purse, and that Shebna be scribe, comptroller, and treasurer.' This and somewhat more I spake that day, not in a corner (as many yet can witness), but even before those whom my conscience judged worthy of accusation. And this day no more do I write (albeit I may justly, because they have declared themselves more manifestly), but yet do I affirm that under that innocent King pestilent Papists had greatest authority."

These were hot bolts to be shot from the pulpit against men like the proud and plotting Duke of Northumberland, and Paulet, Marquis of Winchester; and it may readily be thought by many that nothing but a Prophet's direct commission from God, like that of Esaias referred to by the bold preacher, could have warranted Knox to go thus into their presence to declare their traitorous hearts. And this judgment would be just if their traitorous designs had been known only to God, or only surmised by the preacher, instead of having "manifestly declared themselves" to the eyes of men who had a near view of them, and who watched them narrowly. Knox was one of those, perhaps only a few, who already discerned in these dissembling politicians all the malice and treason against the truth which, only a few months later, became manifest to all. He had not misread them in the least—he had not dared to carry his own mere suspicions of them into so sacred a place as the pulpit; he had both a deep insight and foresight of these crafty and unprincipled plotters;

and, if his words about them were bold enough—too bold, belike, to be approved by modern taste, their own open and shameless deeds soon fulfilled them too well, and vindicated the sagacity, if not the prudence and moderation, of the preacher. Let public necessity also plead for the intrepid freedom of the King's chaplain, and the public benefit resulting from a criticism of public men so honest and plain-spoken.

Mr. Froude looks at the incident in this sensible light: "The power of passing censures on the conduct of public men, in the name of right and wrong, is one which, in some form or other, has existed, and ought to exist, in every well-ordered community. The most effective and least objectionable instrument of such criticism is the public Press as it is conducted at the present day in this country." If the Pulpit had not done the work of moral criticism upon dangerous statesmen in Edward's days, this useful work would not have been done outside the walls of Parliament at all; and, as Northumberland would not hear of Cranmer's new book of discipline, or reformed code of Canon Law, it was not amiss that the Court preachers, "who felt the enormity of the times," should "establish by their own authority this second form of excommunication."*

This was Knox's last sermon before the young King. Soon after its date, the Court removed to Greenwich. Edward was confined to the chamber of his last illness, and though his chaplain was soon afterwards summoned to appear before the Privy Council, there is no reason to think that he was ever again in a presence which he so much honoured and loved.

It was on the 14th of April, 1553, that he appeared for the second time before the Council within two months. His first appearance had had so honourable an issue, that on the 2nd of February a letter was addressed "to the Archbishop of Canterbury in favour of Mr. Knokes to be presented to the vicarage or parsonage of Allhallows, in Bredstrete, in his Lordship's disposition, by the preferment of Thomas Sampson, to the Deanry of Chichester." At what date the presentation had been issued by Cranmer in his favour we do not know, but Knox had declined it, as he had before declined the See of Rochester; and apparently this repeated declinature of preferment on the part of one of the King's chaplains had given offence, or at least had excited

* "History of England," Edward VI. chap. 29.

surprise. Hence the desire of the Council to confer with him, not, as they explained to him, "of any evil mind," or with a view to any proceedings against him, but to obtain satisfaction from him as to the reasons of his declinature. Why, he was asked, did he refuse the benefice offered to him? to which he replied that "his conscience did witness to him that he might profit more in some other place than in London; and farther, that Northumberland had given a contrary command." Then suspecting, with good reason, that these were not his only, nor perhaps his chief reasons, the Council demanded, "whether he thought that no Christian might serve in the Ministry of England according to the rules and laws of the realm?" To which he frankly answered that, unless many things were reformed, no minister could discharge his office before God in England, for no minister in England had authority to divide and separate the lepers from the whole, which was a chief point of his office. Yet did he not refuse such office as might appear to promote God's glory in utterance of Christ's Gospel in a mean (small) degree. A third query followed, Why he kneeled not at the Lord's Supper? which is significant, showing that, as yet, he had not conformed in that respect to the Prayerbook, though he had made up his mind to do so when required by the "upper powers;" and that as yet the upper powers, who were now interrogating him, somewhat superfluously, as to his reasons for abstaining from this point of conformity, had not yet proceeded to that act of authority. To the which interrogation he replied, as might have been anticipated, that "Christ's action in the Sacrament was most perfect; that it was most sure to follow his example; that kneeling was man's addition or imagination." "In this last question there was great contention between the whole table and him. There were present there the Bishops of Canterbury and Ely, the Lord Treasurer, the Earls of Bedford, Northampton, Shrewsbury, the Chamberlain, both the Secretaries, and others. After long reasoning, it was said to him that they were sorry to know him of a contrary mind to the common order. He answered that he was more sorry that the common order should be contrary to Christ's institution. He was dismissed with some gentle speeches, and willed to advise with himself if he would communicate according to that order."* The "gentle speeches," following the

* Calderwood's "History of the Kirk of Scotland" (Wodrow Society), vol. i. pp. 280-1.

"great contention between the whole table and him," were very creditable to the tolerant spirit of the Council, and still more so was their willingness to continue him in his King's chaplaincy after his declinature to accept, for conscientious reasons with which they appear to have felt little sympathy, any preferment in the Church; the effect of which moderation was, that a door of usefulness still remained open to him as an itinerant preacher, and the Council could still give him, as such, the countenance and support of their official authority. Accordingly, when his term of duty at Court, of which no farther details have been preserved, was completed, he received a fresh commission to go upon a preaching tour in the county of Buckingham, probably at the suggestion of the Earl of Bedford, of which the following notice appears in the Council Register:—

"At Grenewich, the 2nd of June, 1553.

"A letter to the Lord Russell, Lord Windesour, the Justices of the Peace, and the rest of the gentlemen within the Countie of Buckingham, in favour of Mr. Knockes, the preacher, according to the minute."

Though, no doubt, glad to remove from the precincts of a Court where there were so many evil councillors, and where he saw more and more clearly every day that mischief was in preparation for the Church and kingdom, it must still have been with a heavy heart and many gloomy forebodings that he entered upon his fresh task. Here is the political situation, as sketched by the latest and best historian of the time:—

"No sooner was Edward known to have been removed to Greenwich, in consequence of illness, than his death was instinctively anticipated. Only once after his arrival there, he was seen in the garden; after that he was confined entirely to his room. The country was felt to be on the eve of a new reign. Vast as, at such a prospect, the excitement must have been, the accession of Mary, should the King die, was looked forward to as a matter of course. The long agitation of the subject, the anxieties and scandals which the uncertainty had occasioned in the last reign, and the deliberate settlement of the Crown by Act of Parliament, as well as by her father's will, in Mary's favour, had familiarized the minds of all men with the name of the Princess as their future sovereign, should Edward leave no children. The question had been mooted, had been discussed, had been decided; and, on grounds of public safety, there was no disposition to raise further doubt on a subject of so much magnitude. Although a Queen was a novelty in the constitution, the people would rather submit to a Queen, and to a Queen of ambiguous legitimacy, than risk the chance of another war of the Roses."*

"Northumberland's Conspiracy" to put Lady Jane Grey, the new married bride of his son, Lord Guilford Dudley, on the throne, settled upon Princess Mary, was already formed and on foot. On the 25th of May, a week before Knox left for Buckinghamshire, " London was startled with three extraordinary marriages—extraordinary, and, considering the King's illness, and the rank of the ladies concerned, in the highest degree indecent. Lady Catherine Dudley was married to Lord Hastings. The two elder daughters of the Duke of Suffolk, princesses of the blood, and possible heirs of the Crown, were disposed of together; Lady Jane Grey to Lord Guilford Dudley, and Lady Catherine to Pembroke's son, Lord Herbert.... Yet what the project was continued a mystery. On the 30th of May, Scheyfne (the ambassador of Charles V. at the English Court), wrote again that the King was sinking, slowly but surely. His head and legs were swelling, and he could only sleep with the assistance of opiates. He might, perhaps, live two months, but that was the longest; while an attempt, it was now certain, would be made to exclude Mary from the throne. Religion would be one pretext, and others could be made or found." The ambassador might know as much, but there is no reason to suppose that Knox knew more than that the Gospel-loving King was dying, and that his Gospel-hating sister would be his successor.

It is easy to imagine what must have been the colour of his thoughts at such a woeful prospect. Plainly the dark days which he had been so long anticipating and predicting were at hand— "days of rebuke and blasphemy"—of God's rebuke upon an unthankful and ungodly people, who "knew not the time of their visitation," and of man's "blasphemy" against the Gospel of Jesus Christ, now so happily recovered to the nation, but again to be persecuted and cast out as an unclean and accursed thing. He saw all the perils, or rather all the dark certainties, of the crisis, and his feelings in proceeding to the field of his new mission could

---

* "History of England," Edward VI., chap. 29.

only be those of a preacher of coming doom rather than those of a messenger of good tidings, publishing peace ; rather those of a Jonah crying, " Yet forty days and Nineveh shall be overthrown," than those of the Evangelical Prophet exclaiming, " Comfort ye, comfort ye, my people, saith your God."

Till the King's death, on the evening of the 6th of July, and the troubles that instantly ensued, we hear nothing of Knox's preaching in Buckinghamshire; that is to say, nothing which is expressly recorded of his sayings and doings there.

But it is not difficult to detect in his writings of that and the two following years several passages which contain reminiscences of that period of his ministry, or which at least may be assigned to that period with higher probability than to any other; for, fortunately, it was much his habit when in exile to cast back his thoughts to his remarkable labours in England, and to recall trains of thought and feeling which he could remember to have pursued in discourses which he had preached in many parts of the land. Not that he had usually kept by him any written copies of his sermons and expositions. It was his habit to preach his sermons before he wrote them, and, for aught that appears, it was seldom that he wrote them out afterwards. But sometimes his recurrence in after years to a text which he had preached upon before would recall to his recollection the thoughts and sentiments which it had then suggested and called up; and sometimes a note which he had made on the margin of his Bible would serve to bring back again to his memory the train of reflections which had passed through his mind and found expression in the pulpit at the time when the note had been written down.

One of these suggestive notes mentioned by him may with great probability be referred to his Buckinghamshire ministry. The passage where it is referred to is the commencement of his " Faithful Admonition to the Professors of God's Truth in England, anno 1554 :—

" Having no less desire to comfort such as now be in trouble within the realm of England (and specially you for many causes most dear to me) than hath the natural father to ease the grief and pain of his dearest child, I have considered with myself what argument or parcel of God's Scriptures was most convenient and meet to be entreated for your consolation, in these most dark and dolorous days. And so, as for the same purpose I was turning my book, I chanced to see a note in the margin written thus in Latin, 'Videat Anglia'—let England beware; which note, when I had considered, I found that the matter written in my book in Latin was this: 'Seldom it is that God worketh any notable work to the comfort of his Church, but that trouble, fear, and labour cometh upon such as God hath used for his servants and workmen; and also tribulation most commonly followeth that Church where Christ Jesus is most truly preached.'

"This note was made upon a place of Scripture written in the 14th chapter of St. Matthew's Gospel, which place declareth that after Christ Jesus had used the Apostles as ministers and servants to feed (as it had been by their hands) five thousand men, beside women and children, with five barley loaves and two fishes, He sent them to the sea, commanding them to pass over before Him to the other side; which thing as they attempted to obey, and for the same purpose did travail and row forth in the sea, the night approached, the wind was contrary, the vehement and raging storm arose, and was like to overthrow their poor boat and them. When I had considered (as dolour and my simplicity would suffer) the circumstances of the text, I began to reckon and ask account of myself (and, as God knoweth, not without sorrow and sobs) whether at any time I had been so plain by my tongue as God had opened his holy will and wisdom in the matter unto me, as mine own pen and note did bear witness to my conscience. And shortly it came to my mind that the same place of Scripture I had entreated in your presences, what time God gave opportunity and space that you should hear, and God's messenger should speak the words of eternal life; wherefore I thought nothing more expedient than shortly to call to mind again such things as then I trust were touched—albeit, peradventure, neither of me so plainly uttered, neither of you so plainly perceived, as these most dolorous days declare the same to us."

There can be no doubt, then, that we have in the "Faithful Admonition" an expansion of what he had frequently preached during the sad and threatening weeks when Edward was approaching his early death, and when all men began to see plainly that a grave crisis was at hand, and a heavy storm about to break upon the Church and nation. It would not be very difficult, therefore, to take out of that celebrated tract, which was the cause of so much trouble to its author, an outline of one of the Bible-expositions which he was in the habit of using in Buckinghamshire, to prepare his hearers for the evil days which were approaching.

In after years, as he tells us in his "Godly Letter to the Faithful,"* he was "oft revolving how God had used his tongue plainly to speak the troubles" which soon after came; and "oft occurs to my mind," he continues, "a certain admonition that God would I commonly should use in all congregations. The admonition was this: 'That the last trumpet was then in blowing within the realm of England, and therefore ought every man to prepare himself for battle. For if the trumpet should altogether cease and be put to silence, then should it never blow again with the like force within the said realm till the coming of the Lord Jesus.' O, dear brethren, how sore these threatenings pierce my own heart this day, only God knoweth. I sob and groan, I call and pray that in that point I may be deceived. But I am commanded to stand content, for it is God Himself that performs the word of his own true messengers —his justice and order cannot be perverted."

But was he a prophet only of evils? Did he see nothing in the future but a horror of great darkness? No, he did not so understand God and his dealings with his Church. "God will suffer tribulation and dolour to abound, that no manner of comfort shall be seen in man, to the intent that, when deliverance cometh, the glory may be his whose only word may pacify the tempests most vehement. He drowned Pharaoh and his army. He scattered the great multitude of Benhadad; by his angel He killed the host of Sennacherib, and so delivered his afflicted, when nothing appeared to them but utter destruction. So shall He do to you, beloved brethren, if patiently ye will abide his consolation and counsel. God open your eyes that rightly ye may understand the meaning of my words. Amen."

Knox was back in London on the 23rd of June, 1553, which is the date of the first of his printed letters, which throws no light, however, upon his recent labours; but we find him in Buckinghamshire again in the month of July. He was still there when Edward died, on the 7th of July, and he preached in the ancient burgh of Amersham on Sunday, the 16th of July, when that county, like the rest of the kingdom, was in alarm and confusion with the troubles of a disputed succession. "Sir Edward Hastings, Lord Huntingdon's brother, had called out the musters

---

* "Knox's Works," iii. p. 205.

of Buckinghamshire in Mary's name, and Sir Edmund Peckham, Cofferer of the Household, who had gone off from Court with the treasure under his charge, had joined him." The country, Catholic and Protestant, "was arming to the teeth," and Knox spoke in the old church, "at the peril of his life, among the troopers of Sir Edward Hastings."* Two years later he recalled the agitated scene, and some of his own remarkable words, in the following passage of "The Admonition":—" In writing hereof it came to mind that, after the death of that innocent and most godly King Edward the Sixth, while that great tumult was in England, for the establishing of that most unhappy and wicked woman's authority (I mean of her that now reigneth in God's wrath), entreating the same argument in a town of Buckinghamshire, named Amersham, before a great congregation, with sorrowful heart and weeping eyes I fell into this exclamation:—

"'O, England, now is God's wrath kindled against thee. Now hath He begun to punish as He hath threatened a long while by his true prophets and messengers. He hath taken from thee the crown of thy glory, and hath left thee without honour, as a body without a head. And this appeareth to be only the beginning of sorrows, which appeareth to increase. For I perceive that the heart, the tongue, and the hand of one Englishman is bent against another, and division to be in the whole realm, which is an assured sign of desolation to come.

"'O, England! England! dost thou not consider that thy commonwealth is like a ship sailing on the sea; if thy mariners and governors shall each consume another, shalt thou not suffer shipwreck in short process of time!

"'O, England! England! alas, these plagues are poured upon thee, for that thou wouldest not know the most happy time of thy gentle visitation. But wilt thou yet obey the voice of thy God and submit thyself to his holy words? Truly, if thou wilt, thou shalt find mercy in his sight, and the estate of thy commonwealth shall be preserved.

"'But, O, England, England! if thou obstinately wilt return into Egypt, that is, if thou contract marriage, confederacy, and league with such Princes as do maintain and advance idolatry (such as the Emperor, which is no less enemy unto Christ than ever was Nero); if for the pleasure and friendship (I say) of such princes,

* Froude's "History of England," chap. 30.

then return to thine old abominations, before used under the Papistry, then assuredly, O, England, thou shalt be plagued and brought to desolation, by the means of those whose favour thou seekest, and by whom thou art procured to fall from Christ and to serve Antichrist. This, and much more, in the dolour of mine heart, that day, in audience of such as yet may bear record, God would that I should pronounce. The thing that I then most feared, and which also my tongue spake (that is the subversion of the true religion and bringing in of strangers to reign over that realm), this day I see come to pass in men's counsels and determinations.'"

When Knox stood in the pulpit of Amersham that day, it was no time to recall the local memories of a century, the instant hours were so full of anxiety and of doom. But whether he thought of it or not, he was then speaking in one of the old centres of Lollardy. In the preceding century Amersham had given up not a few martyrs to the doctrine of John Wycliff, and never had her people heard again till now a preacher so much " in the spirit and power" of that old English prophet of truth and of liberty. Nor was the old Wycliffite spirit among the Amersham men even yet dead. It was only slumbering. The voice of Wycliff's successor roused it up again into fresh life. For it is a remarkable fact that, in two or three years after Knox's visit, Amersham again figured in the lists of Protestant martyrdom.

On the 19th of July Knox was in London, when the short reign of Lady Jane Grey, "the twelfth-day Queen, as she was termed in scornful pity," collapsed, and Mary, her too powerful rival, was proclaimed. "'God save the Queen!' 'God save the Queen!' rung out from tens of thousands of throats. The Lords of the Council, with the Mayor and heralds, surrounded by the shouting multitude, walked in state to St. Paul's. As they came out again the apprentices were heaping piles of wood for bonfires at the crossways. The citizens were spreading tables in the streets; there was free feasting for all comers, and social jealousies, religious hatreds, were forgotten for the moment in the ecstasy of the common delight" (Froude). There was, at least, one far-seeing man in the crowd who did not share in the ecstasy. To him it was a pitiful sight to see the people intoxicated with a blind and mad joy, which was so soon to be exchanged for the horrors of the confessor's prison, and the martyrs' flaming pile. "They know not what they do." He saw clearly what was coming, and "in London, in more places than one, when the fever of joy and riotous banquetting were, at the proclamation of Mary," he declared from the pulpit his sad forebodings of the coming apostasy and the gathering storm.* Still he hoped against hope for a time, and was careful to set an example of loyalty to the Queen's authority by offering up public prayers in behalf of herself and her Council, and for the repression of all rebellion in the realm. For several months he was in the habit of using in the pulpit the following touching and most characteristic prayer :—

"Omnipotent and everlasting God, Father of our Lord Jesus Christ, who, by Thy eternal providence disposes kingdoms as best seemeth to Thy wisdom, we acknowledge and confess Thy judgments to be righteous in that Thou hast taken from us, for our ingratitude, and for our abusing of Thy most Holy Word, our native King and earthly comforter.

"Justly mayest Thou pour forth upon us the uttermost of Thy plagues, for that we have not known the days and times of our merciful visitation. We have contemned Thy word and despised Thy mercies; we have transgressed Thy laws, for deceitfully have we wrought every man with our neighbours ; oppression and violence we have not abhorred ; charity hath not appeared among us, as our profession requireth. We have little regarded the voice of Thy prophets ; Thy threatenings we have esteemed vanity and wind, so that in us, as of ourselves, rests nothing worthy of Thy mercies, for all are found fruitless ; even the princes with the prophets, as withered trees, apt and meet to be burnt in the fire of Thy eternal displeasure.

"But, O Lord, behold Thy own mercy and goodness, that Thou mayest purge and remove the most filthy burden of our most horrible offences. Let Thy love overcome the severity of Thy judgments, even as it did in giving to the world Thy only Son Jesus, when all mankind was lost, and no obedience was left in Adam nor in his seed. Regenerate our hearts, O Lord, by the strength of Thy Holy Ghost. Convert Thou us, and we shall be converted. Work Thou in us unfeigned repentance, and move Thou our hearts to obey Thy holy laws.

"Behold our troubles and apparent destruction, and stay the

---

* "Knox's Works," v. iii. p. 168.

sword of Thy vengeance before it devour us. Place above us, O Lord, for Thy great mercies, such a head with such rulers and magistrates as feareth Thy name, and willeth the glory of Christ Jesus to spread. Take not from us the light of Thy evangely, and suffer Thou no Papistry to prevail in this realm. Illuminate the heart of our Sovereign Lady Queen Mary with pregnant gifts of Thy Holy Ghost, and influence the hearts of her Council with Thy true fear and love. Reform Thou the pride of those that would rebel, and remove from all hearts the contempt of the Word. Let not our enemies rejoice at our destruction, but look Thou to the honour of Thy own name, O Lord, and let the Gospel be preached with boldness in this realm. If Thy justice must punish them, punish our bodies with the rod of Thy mercy. But, O Lord, let us never revolt nor turn back to idolatry again. Mitigate the hearts of those that persecute us, and let us not faint under the cross of our Saviour, but visit us with the Holy Ghost, even to the end."

On the 26th July he is again in the North in the execution of his office as King's Preacher, as we learn from a letter to Mrs. Bowes of that date. There is a second letter to her, probably written about the same time, dated "Carlisle, this Friday, after sermon ;" but we have no other memorials of this journey, which was probably undertaken by him on his own responsibility, without instructions from the Council, and as a prudent precaution against personal danger in the event of the Queen taking immediate steps to apprehend the Protestant bishops, and other leading Reformers. For she had lost no time in revealing her zeal against the Protestant leaders. As soon as she reached the capital to assume the Government she ejected Ridley from London, Ponet from Winchester, and Scory from Chichester, while Bishops Tunstal, Day, and Heath were set at liberty and restored to their dioceses. Gardiner was again Chancellor, and Bonner again Bishop of London, and all these incidents were of evil omen to a man so prominent and bold as Knox.

For a season, however, the Queen withheld her hand from any deeds of great severity. On the 16th of August she published, by advice, a proclamation granting toleration to all until further orders, "forbidding her Protestant and Catholic subjects to interrupt each others' services, and prohibiting at the same time all preaching on either side without license from herself." Knox probably interpreted this last prohibition not to apply to those, like himself, who held a Royal Patent, and he soon exchanged again the Northern province for the county of Kent.

On the 25th of September, as appears from a letter to Mrs. Bowes of that date, he had just returned to London from Kent, where he says he had been labouring before receiving her last letter, and for some weeks apparently, as he mentions having a long time kept other letters which he had written to her beside him for want of a bearer. He was again in the capital, and speaks of his "great labours" there, without, however, going into any details of his recent and present work.

But this letter contains some allusions, of a personal and painful kind, to his matrimonial engagement, from which we may gather that the recent great change of public affairs had exercised a sinister influence upon his happiness in that respect. Sir Richard Bowes, the father of his affianced wife, was a trimmer in religion, and was now quite prepared to fall back, if expedient, to the Romish worship; and, foreseeing nothing but exile or death for his resolute and devoted son-in-law, he had manifested a stronger dislike than ever to his daughter's match. His wife, however, and daughter remained as steadfast as ever both in their religion and their attachment to Knox, while Knox himself expresses in this letter his determination to remain true to his engagement, and to follow it out, at whatever cost, even at the jeopardy of his life.

"My great labours, wherein I desire your daily prayers, will not suffer me to satisfy my mind (*i.e.*, fully to express it) touching all the process between your husband and you touching my matter concerning your daughter. I praise God heartily both for your boldness and constancy. But I beseech you, mother, trouble not yourself too much therewith. It becomes me now to jeopard my life for the comfort and deliverance of my own flesh (meaning his wife), as that I will do, by God's grace, both fear and friendship of all earthly creatures laid aside. I have written to your husband, the contents whereof I trust your brother Harie will declare to you and to my wife. If I escape sickness and imprisonment, be sure to see me soon. Yet, mother, depend not upon me too much, for what am I but a wretched sinner? If ye receive any comfort it comes from above, from God the Father, who shall provide for you abundantly. Whatever becomes of me, remember, mother, the gifts of God are not bound to any one man, but are common to every man in his measure that incalls [calls upon] the Lord Jesus, whose omnipotent Spirit rest with you for ever.

"YOUR SON."

His mind, it is plain, has now become familiar with the thought that bonds and even death may ere long abide him; and hence his "great labours" in the great city—he is "redeeming the time, because the days are evil."

It was expected that things would come to a crisis in the new Parliament which was to assemble on the 5th of October. The reaction in the public mind against the Reformation of King Edward was violent; three-fourths of the population, it is estimated by historians, were still attached to the old religion, and the Parliament reflected in fair proportions the state of Church parties. In November a bill passed the Commons, by a majority of 350 against 80, restoring the Mass and the celibacy of the clergy, and enacting that from the 20th of December next "there should be no other form of service but what had been used in the last year of Henry the 8th, leaving it free to all till that day to use either the books appointed by King Edward or the old ones at their pleasure" (Burnet). In these circumstances Knox was still at liberty, under prudent limitations, to continue his labours in London for some time longer. A letter to Mrs. Bowes of "this sixth of November" must have been written in London, and refers to a painful interview which he had on that day with her brother-in-law, Sir Robert Bowes, whose residence, as Master of the Rolls, was now in the capital, on the subject of his marriage. Sir Robert's "disdainful, yea despiteful words had so pierced his heart that his life was bitter unto him;" and were it not that "no man's unthankfulness should move him, God supporting his infirmity, to cease to do profit unto Christ's congregation, the days should be few that England should give him bread; I regard not what country consume this my wicked carcase."

During these autumn months in London, he was probably a guest successively with the families of the Lockes and the Hickmans, and it was also, doubtless, at this time that he began to draw up two of his shorter pieces, afterwards published, his Exposition of the 6th Psalm for the private use of Mrs. Bowes, and his "Godly letter to the faithful in London, Newcastle, Berwick, and all others within the realm of England, that love the coming of our Lord Jesus

Christ." These works were both unfinished when he was compelled to leave the kingdom, at the beginning of 1554.

It would have been dangerous for so conspicuous an enemy of Rome to have remained in London beyond the 20th of December. After that date Protestant worshippers "were thrown out of the protection of the law, and were exposed to the pains decreed against heretics." Many, indeed, of the reformed bishops and ministers were already committed to prison, and many others had escaped beyond sea. He might be less exposed to danger among his friends in Newcastle; and might still hope to be useful to "Christ's congregation" in that old field. We find him there about the middle of December, and on the 22nd he writes to his mother-in-law "with troubled heart and weak body," adding the significant postscript, "I may not answer the places of Scripture, nor yet write the exposition of the 6th Psalm, for every day of this week must I preach, if this wicked carcase will permit." He had had a return of his old complaint—the gravel—and "had not been nor yet was in good case to have travelled." It will not be till after the 12th of January that he can be at Berwick, and "almaist," he sadly adds, "I am determined not to come at all. Ye know the cause (alluding to her husband's unkindness). God be mair merciful to some than they are equitable to me in judgment. The testimony of my own conscience absolves me before his face who looks not upon the person of man."

To these private family griefs the persistent and vigilant hostility of his old Newcastle enemies were soon able to add a crowning sorrow, which defeated all expectation of seeing the two friends whom best he loved on earth at the time he had specified, and compelled him to save his life by flight to a foreign shore. This closing passage of his life in England may be given in the words of his biographer: "The enemies who had been defeated in their attempts to ruin him under the former government, had now access to rulers sufficiently disposed to listen to their information." They were not dilatory in improving the opportunity. In the end of December, 1553, or beginning of January, 1554, his servant was seized as he carried letters from him to his wife and mother-in-law, and the letters were taken from him in the hopes of finding in them matters of accusation against the writer. As they contained merely religious advices and exhortations to constancy in the

Protestant faith, which he was prepared to avow before any Court to which he might be called, he was not alarmed at their interception. But being aware of the uneasiness which the report would give to his friends at Berwick, he set out immediately with the design of visiting them. Notwithstanding the secrecy with which he conducted this journey, the rumour of it quickly spread; and some of his wife's relations, who had joined him, perceiving that he was in imminent danger, prevailed on him, greatly against his own inclination, to relinquish the design of proceeding to Berwick, and retire to a place of safety on the coast, from which he might escape by sea, provided the search for him was continued. From this retreat he wrote to his wife and her mother, acquainting them with the reasons of his absconding, and the small prospect which he had of being able at that time to see them. "His brethren," he said, "had, partly by admonition, partly by tears, compelled him to obey, somewhat contrary to his own mind, for never could he die in a more honest quarrel than by suffering as a witness for that truth of which God had made him a messenger." Notwithstanding this state of his mind, he promised, if "providence prepared the way, to obey the voices of his brethren, and give place to the fury and rage of Satan for a time." Having ascertained that his friends were not mistaken in the apprehensions which they felt for his safety, and that he could not hope to elude the pursuit of his enemies if he remained in England, he procured a vessel, which landed him safely at Dieppe, on the 20th of January, 1554.

A few extracts from his two last letters before embarking will reveal the feelings with which he brought his life and work in England to a close, and will also supply a few interesting personal details.

"Shortness of time and multitude of cares will not let me write at this present as plentifully as I would. Ye will me to charge you in such things as I mister [need]. God grant that ye may be able to relieve the needy. Ye may be sure that I would be bold upon you, for of your good heart I am persuaded, but of your power and ability I greatly doubt. I will not mak you privy how rich I am, but off London I departed with less money than ten groats; but God has since provided, and will provide, I doubt not, hereafter, abundantly for this life. Either the Queen's Majesty or some Thesaurer will be Forty Pounds richer by me, for sa mekill lack

I of duty of my patents [as Royal Chaplain]. But that little troubles me. Rest in Christ Jesus."

In forwarding to Mrs. Bowes the first part of his "Exposition upon the Sixth Psalm of David," immediately before his embarkation, he wrote to her the following letter of Christian farewell:—

"Presently I may write no more unto you in this matter, beloved mother; but as God shall grant unto me more opportunity by his grace who giveth all, you shall receive from my hands the rest of David's mind on this Psalm. Most earnestly beseeching you in the bowels of Christ Jesus patiently to bear your present cross and dolours, which shortly shall vanish, and after shall never appear. I cannot express the pain which I think I might suffer to have the presence of you, and of others that be like troubled, for a few days. But God shall gather us at his good pleasure, if not in this wretched and miserable life, yet in that state where death may not dissever us. My daily prayer is for the sore afflicted in those quarters. Some time I have thought that impossible it had been so to have removed my affection from the realm of Scotland, that any realm or nation could have been equal dear unto me. But God I take to record in my conscience that the troubles present and appearing to be in the realm of England, are double more dolorous unto my heart than ever were the troubles of Scotland.

"But hereof to speak I now supersede; beseeching God of his infinite mercy so to strengthen you that in the weaker vessels Christ's power may appear. My hearty commendation to all whom effeires, I mean unto such as now boldly abideth with Christ. I bid you so heartily farewell as can any wicked and corrupt man do to the maist especial friends. In great haste and troubled heart, this 6th day of January" [1553-4].

On his arrival at Dieppe his first care was to prepare for Mrs. Bowes a second portion of his Exposition of the Sixth Psalm. Ever mindful of what he terms "the spiritual cross" under which she suffered, not even the deep depression into which his own spirits must have sunk, when he found himself alone, forlorn—an unknown stranger and exile on a foreign shore—could prevent him from rousing himself to this new effort of sympathy and affection.

The name long afterwards given to the little book by its London editor, Abraham Fleming, "A Fort for the Afflicted," might have been justly applied to the author himself. What a marvellous mixture of strength and of sweetness—of the spirit of power and the spirit of love—is to be seen in "the most effectual medicine" which he never wearies in administering to that sorely tried and tempted soul! The title he gave to the tract himself is full of expression: "An Exposition, wherein is declarit David's Cross, Complaints, and Prayers, necessary to be read of all them, for their singular comfort, that under the Banner of Christ are by Satan assaulted, and feel the heavy burden of sin with whilk they are oppressed."

"To his belovit Mother John Knox sendeth greeting in the Lord.

"The desire that I have to hear of your continuance with Christ Jesus in the day of this his battle, whilk shortly shall end to the confusion of his proud enemies, neither by tongue nor by pen can I express, beloved mother. Assuredly it is such that it vanquisheth and overcometh all vain remembrance and solicitude whilk the flesh useth to take for feeding and defence of herself. For in every realm and nation God will stir up some one or other to minister those things that appertain to this wretchit life. And if men will cease to do their office, yet will He send his ravens, so that in every place, perchance, I may find some feathers to my body [raiment]. But alas! where I shall find children to be begotten unto God by the word of life, that can I not presently consider. And therefore the spiritual life of such as sometime professit Christ (God knoweth) is to my heart more dear than all the glory, riches, and honour in earth. And the falling back of such men as I hear daily do turn back to that idol again (the Mass), is to me more dolorous than, I trust, the corporal death shall be whenever it shall come at God's appointment. Some will ask, then why did I fly? Assuredly, I cannot tell; but of one thing I am sure, the fear of death was not the chief cause of my flying. I trust that one cause hath been to let me see with my corporal eyes, that all had not a true heart to Christ Jesus that in the day of rest and peace bare a fair face. But my flying is no matter. By God's grace I may come to battle before that all the conflict be endit. And haste the time, O Lord, at thy good pleasure, that once again my tongue may yet praise thy holy name before the congregation, if it were but in the very hour of death.

"Here must I put you in mind, dearly beloved, how oft have you and I talked of these present days, till neither of us both could refrain tears, when no such appearance there was seen by man. How oft have I said unto you that I looked daily for trouble, and that I wondered at it that so long I did escape it. What moved me to refuse, and that with displeasure of all men (even of those that best loved me), those high promotions that were offered by him whom God hath taken for our offences? [King Edward]. Assuredly the foresight of trouble to come. How oft have I said unto you that the time would not be long that England would give me bread. Advise with [refer to] the last letter that I wrote unto your brother-in-law, and consider what is therein contained. While I had this trouble, you had the greater; sent, I doubt not, to us both of God, that in that great rest, as we may call it, when the Gospel triumphed, we should not be so careless and so insolent as others were; who, albeit they professed Christ in mouth, yet sought they nothing but the world, with hand, with foot, with counsel and wisdom. And albeit at this present our comfort appeareth not, yet before that all the plagues be poured forth it shall be known that there is a God who taketh care of his own.

"The merciful providence of our God, willing our salvation, will not suffer us to come to that unthankfulness and oblivion, and therefore He permitteth us to our enemies, with his Apostle Paul, to be buffeted, to the end that we may mourn for sin, and hate the same; that we may know the only Mediator and the dignity of his office; that we may unfeignedly thirst the coming of the Lord Jesus; and that we neither be presumptuous, lightly esteeming Christ's death, neither yet unmindful of our former estate and miseries. And so this cup is as it were a medicine prepared by the wisdom of an Eternal Physician, who only knoweth the remedies of our corrupt nature.

"Advert and mark, dear mother, that all cometh to us for our most singular profit. It is a medicine, and therefore presently it cannot be pleasing. But how gladly would we use and receive, when the bodies were sick (how unpleasant and bitter that ever it were to drink), that medicine which would remove sickness and restore health. But O, how much more ought we, with patience and thanksgiving, to receive this medicine of our Father's hands, that from our souls removeth so many mortal diseases (his Holy Ghost so working by the same), such as pride, presumption, contempt of grace, and unthankfulness, which be the very mortal diseases that by unbelief killeth the soul, and doth restore unto us lowliness, fear, invocation of God's name, remembering of our own weakness and of God's infinite benefits by Christ received, which be the very evident signs that Jesus Christ liveth in us.

"Dearly belovit, accept this cup from the hands of our Heavenly Father; and albeit your pains be almost intolerable, yet cast yourself, because you have no other refuge, before the throne of God's mercy, and with the Prophet David, being in like trouble, say unto Him—'Have mercy upon me, O Lord, for I am weak. O Lord, heal me, for all my bones are vexit.'

"Now seeing it is uncertain, belovit mother, if ever we shall meet in this corporal life; whilk words I will ye take not in any displeasure, for if God continue you in life and me in corporal health I shall attempt and assay to speak with you, face to face, within less time than is passed since the one of us last saw the other. And be ye assured, belovit mother, that neither shall it be the fear of death nor the rage of the Devil that shall impede or hinder me; and therefore, I beseech you, take not my words in that part, as although I were not minded to visit you again. No, I assure you that only God's hand shall withhold me. But because our life doth vanish like as the smoke before the blast of wind, my conscience moveth me to write unto you as though I should take from you my last good night in earth. The sum whereof is this, to exhort and admonish you, even as that ye will have part with Christ Jesus, to continue in the doctrine to the end, whilk before the world ye have professit. For before God, before Christ Jesus his Son, and before his Holy Angels, neither ashame I to confess, nor doubt I to affirm, that the doctrine which ye and others have heard, not only of my mouth, but also faithfully taught by the mouths of many others (of whom some are exilit, some cruelly cast in prison, and the rest commandit to silence), is the only word of life, and that all doctrine repugnant to the same is diabolical and erroneous, whilk assuredly shall bring death and perpetual condemnation to all those whilk thereto shall condescend and agree. And therefore, mother, be not moved with any wind, but stick to Christ Jesus in the day of this his battle; also I admonish you to avoid that abomination whilk oft ye have heard by me affirmed to be damnable idolatry. And God I take to record in my conscience, that neither then nor now I spake, neither do speak, for pleasure or hatred of any living creature in earth, whatsoever that it be; but as my conscience was certified by the infallible and plain Word of God, from whilk, I praise my most merciful Father, I am not this day one jot removed. Neither repent I of that my blessed and maist happy society with the truth of Christ's Gospel, unto whilk it hath pleasit God to call me, the maist wretchit of others. Neither forthink I [do I regret] that God hath made me an open and manifest enemy to Papistrie, to superstition, and to all that filthy idolatry whilk newly is erectit, in God's hot displeasure; neither yet would I recant (as they term it) one sentence of my former doctrine, for all the glory, riches, and rest that is on earth.

"And, in conclusion, I would not bow my knee before that most abominable idol for all the torments that earthly tyrants can devise, God so assisting me, as his Holy Spirit presently moveth me to write unfeignedly. And albeit, I have in the beginning of this battle appeared to play the faint-hearted and feeble soldier (the cause I remit to God), yet my prayer is that I may be restored to the battle again; and blessed be God, the Father of our Lord Jesus Christ, I am not left so bare without comfort, but my hope is to obtain such mercy that, if a short end is not made of all my miseries by final death (whilk to me were no small advantage), that yet by Him who never despiseth the sobs of the sore afflicted, I shall be so encouraged to fight that England and Scotland shall both know that I am ready to suffer more than either poverty or exile for the profession of that doctrine, and that heavenly religion whereof it hath pleased his merciful providence to make me, among others, a simple soldier and witness-bearer unto men. And therefore, mother, let no fear enter into your heart as that I, escaping the furious rage of those ravening wolves that for our unthankfulness are lately loosed from their bonds, do repent anything of my former fervency. No, mother, for a few sermons to be made by me within England my heart, at this hour, could be content to suffer more than nature were able to sustene, as by the grace of the most mighty and most merciful God, who only is God of comfort and consolation, through Christ Jesus, one day shall be known.

"In the mean season, yet once again, and, as it were, my final Gudnycht and last testament in this earth, in the bowels of Christ Jesus I exhort and admonish you constantly to continue with the verity, whilk yet shall triumph and obtain victory, in despite of Satan and his malice; and avoid idolatry, the maintainers and obeyers whereof shall not escape the sudden vengeance of God, whilk shall be poured forth upon them according to the ripeness of their iniquity; and when they shall cry quietness and peace (whilk never remainit of any continuance with the ungodly), then shall their sudden destruction come upon them without provision. The God of peace and consolation, who of his power infinite and invincible hath called from death the only true and great Bishop of our souls, and in Him hath placed our flesh above principalities and powers of what pre-eminence that ever they be in heaven or on earth, assist you with his Holy Spirit in such constancy and strength that Satan and his assaults be confounded now and ever in you, and in the congregation, by Christ Jesus our Lord, to whom with the Father and with the Holy Ghost be all praise and honour eternally. Amen.

"Upon the very point of my journey, the last of February, 1553-54.

"Yours with sorrowfull heart,
"JOHNE KNOX.

"Watch and pray."

Equally fervent in faith and zeal, equally exalted above all fear and mistrust, was the "Godly Letter" sent from the same spot at the same date, "to the Faithful in London, Newcastle, and Berwick, and to all others within the realm of England that love the coming of our Lord Jesus Christ." It was a "Letter of Warning or Admonition," addressed to all Englishmen that "unfeignedly mourned for the great shipwreck of God's true religion," which had so lamentably come to pass in the "realm of England, to which God's true word had been offered;" to whom, said the author, "I purpose to communicate such counsel and admonitions now by my rude pen as sometime it pleasit God I should proclaim to your ears. The end of whilk my admonition is: That even as ye purpose and intend to avoid God's vengeance, baith in this life and in the life to come, that so ye avoid and fly, as well in body as in spirit, all fellowship and society with idolaters in their idolatry."

"The reader of this letter," says Dr. McCrie, "cannot fail to be struck with its animated strain, when he reflects that it proceeded from a forlorn exile in a strange country, without a single acquaintance, and ignorant where he would find a place of abode or the means of subsistence;" and " as a specimen of elevated piety and the most fervid eloquence," he cannot refrain from quoting the conclusion of the letter, " in which he addresses their consciences, their hopes, their fears, and adjures them by all that is sacred, and all that is dear to them as men, as parents, and as Christians, not to start back from their good profession and plunge themselves and their 'posterity' into the gulf of ignorance and idolatry." But Dr. McCrie could only quote a small portion of a composition which abounds with passages all aglow with fervour and intensity. We add here a few quotations more:

" O, dear brethren, remember the dignity of our vocation. You have followed Christ; you have proclaimed war against idolatry; you have laid hand upon the truth, and have communicate with the Lord's table. Will ye now suddenly slide back? Will ye refuse Christ and his truth, and make paction with the Devil and his deceivable doctrine? Will ye tread the maist precious blood of Christ's testament under your feet, and set up an idol before the people? Whilk things assuredly ye do, as oft as ever ye present your bodies amongst idolaters before that blasphemous idol. God, the Father of all mercies, for Christ his Son's sake, preserve you from that sore temptation, whose dolours and dangers very sorrow will not suffer me to express. . . . And therefore avoid it as that ye will be partakers with Christ, with whom ye have sworn to die and to live, in baptism and in his Holy Supper. Shame it were to break promise to men, but is it not mair shame to break it unto God? Foolishness it were to leave that king whose victory ye saw present, and to take part with him whom ye understood and perceived to be so vanquished that neither might he ganestand [withstand], neither yet abide the coming of his adversary. O brethren, is not the Devil, the prince of this world, vanquished and casten out? Hath not Christ Jesus, for whom we suffer, made conquest of him? Hath He not, in spite of Satan's malice, carried our flesh up to glory? And shall not our champion return? We know that He shall, and that with expedition. . . . The battle shall appear strong which ye are to suffer, but the Lord Himself shall be your comfort. Flie from idolatry and stand with Christ Jesus in this day of his battle, whilk shall be short and the victory everlasting, for the Lord Himself shall come in our defence with his mightie power. He shall give us the victory when the battle is maist strong; and He shall turn our tears into everlasting joy. He shall consume our enemies with the breath of his mouth, and He shall let us see the destruction of them that are now maist proud, and that maist pretendeth to molest us. From God alone we abide redemption.

"The God of all comfort and consolation, for Christ Jesus his Son's sake, grant that this my simple and plain admonition (yea, rather the warning of the Holy Ghost) may be received and accepted of you with no less fear and obedience than I have written it unto you with unfeigned love and sorrowful heart. And then I doubt not that baith you and I shall be comforted when all such as now molest us shall tremble and shake by the coming of our Lord Jesus, whose omnipotent Spirit preserve and keep you undefiled, body and soul, to the end. Amen.

"The peace of God rest with you all. From ane sore troubillit heart upon my departure from Deipe, whither God knoweth. In God is my trust, through Jesus Christ his Son, and therefore I fear not the tyranny of man, neither yet what the Devil can invent against me. Rejoice, ye faithful, for in joy shall we meet, where Death may not dissever us.

"Your brother in the Lord,

"JOHN KNOX."

To the "Godly Letter" is added the following godly prayer, which matches well with it, and reveals the supreme source from which this Hero of the Faith drew, by profound humility before the face of God, the grand courage, and the incorruptible uprightness with which he spoke God's truth before the face of all men :—

"Ah, Lorde! most strong and mighty God, which destroyest the counsayles of the ungodly, and ryddest away the tyrauntes of this worlde out of the earth at thy pleasure, so that no counsaille or force can resiste thyne eternal counsaill and everlasting determination, we, thyne poor creatures and humble servants, do most instantly desyre Thee, for the love that Thou hast to thyne well-beloved and only-begotten Sonne our Lorde and Saviour Jesus Chryst, that Thou wilt loke upon thyne cause, for it is tyme, O Lorde, and bring to naught all those thinges that are or should be apoynted, determined, and fully agreed agaynste Thee and thy Holy Worde. Let not the enemyes of thy truth too miserablye oppresse thy Word and thy servantes which seke thy glorie, tender the advancement of thy pure religion, and above all things wishe in their hartes that thy holy name may onely be glorified amonge all nations. Geve unto thy servantes the mouth of thy truthe and wysedom, which no man maye resiste. And although we have moste justlye deserved thys plague and famyne of thyne hande, yet upon our trew repentance, grante, we beseke Thee, we may be thereof released; and here we promise, before thy Devyne Majestie, better to use thy gifts than we have done, and more strayghtlye to order our lyves according to thy holye will and pleasure; and we will synge perpetual prayses to thy moste blessed name, worldes without ende, through Jesus Christe our Lorde. Amen."

There is a remarkable passage in "The Admonition," written in 1554, about eight months after his departure from England, which will form a most appropriate close to the account which has been given above, of his pulpit work during his five years' sojourn in the country:*

"The ministers, who were the distributors of this bread—the true Worde of God, wherewith the multitude within England was fed—lacked not their offences, which also moved God to send us to the sea; and because the offences of no man are so manifest unto me as mine own, only of myself will I be the accuser.

"It is not unknown to many that I (the most wretched) was one of that number whom God appointed to receive that bread (as it was broken by Christ Jesus), to distribute and give the same to such as He had called to the banquet, in that part of his table where He appointed me to serve. It is not in my knowledge nor judgment to define nor determine what portion or quantity every man received of this bread, neither yet how that which they received agreed with their stomachs. But of this I am assured, that the benediction of Christ Jesus so multiplied the portion that I received at his hands, that during that banquet (this I write to the praise of his name, and to the accusation of mine own unthankfulness) this bread never failed when the hungry soul craved or cried for food; and at the end of this banquet, mine own conscience beareth witness that my hands gathered up the crumbs that were left in such abundance that my basket was full among the rest.

* "Knox's Works," vol. iii. pp. 268-272.

"To be plain, mine own conscience beareth record to myself how small was my learning, and how weak I was of judgment when Christ Jesus called me to be his steward; and how mightily, day by day, and time by time, He multiplied his graces with me, if I should conceal, I were most wicked and unthankful.

"But, alas! how blinded was my heart, and how little I did consider the dignity of that office, and the power of God that then multiplied and blessed this bread which the people received of my hands, this day mine own conscience beareth witness to myself. God I take to record in my conscience that I delivered the same bread that I received of Christ's hands; and that I mixed no poison with the same; that is, I teached Christ's Gospel without any mixture of men's dreams, devises, and phantasies. But, alas! I did it not with such fervency, with such indifferency (impartiality) and with such diligence as this day I know my duty was to have done. Some complained in those days that the preachers were indiscreet persons; yea, and some called them railers, and worse, because they spake against the manifest iniquity of men, and especially of those that then were placed in authority, as well in the Court as in other offices universally throughout the realm, both in cities, towns, and villages.

"And, among others, peradventure my rude plainness displeased some who did complain that rashly I did speak of men's faults, so that all men might know and perceive of whom I meant. But, alas! this day my conscience accuseth me that I spake not so plainly as my duty was to have done; for I ought to have said to the wicked man, expressly by his name, 'Thou shalt die the death.' For I find Jeremy the Prophet so to have done to Pashur the High Priest, and to Zedekias the king. And not only him, but also Elias, Eliseus, Micha, Amos, Daniel, Christ Jesus Himself, and after Him his Apostles expressly to have named the blood-thirsty tyrants, abominable idolaters, and dissembling hypocrites of their days. If that we, the preachers within the realm of England, were appointed by God to be the salt of the earth (as his other martyrs were before us), alas! why held we back the salt, where manifest corruption did appear? (I accuse none but myself.) The blind love that I did bear to this wicked carcase was the chief cause that I was not fervent and faithful enough in that behalf; for I had no will to provoke the hatred of all men against me, and therefore so touched I the vices of men in the presence of the greatest, that they might see themselves to be offenders; I dare not say that I was the greatest flatterer, but yet, nevertheless, I would not be seen to proclaim manifest war against the manifest wicked; whereof unfeignedly I ask my God mercy.

"As I was not so fervent in rebuking manifest iniquity, as it became me to have been, so was I not so indifferent (impartial) a feeder as is required of Christ's steward; for in preaching Christ's Gospel, albeit mine eye (as knoweth God) was not much upon worldly promotion, yet the love of friends and carnal affections of some men with whom I was most familiar, allowed me to make more residence in one place than in another, having more respect to the pleasure of a few, than to the necessity of many. That day I thought I had not sinned if I had not been idle; but this day I know it was my duty to have had consideration how long I had remained in one place, and how many hungry souls were in other places to whom, alas! none took pains to break and distribute the Word of life.

"Moreover, remaining in one place, I was not so diligent as mine office required, but sometime, by counsel of carnal friends, I spared the body. Sometime I spent in worldly business of particular friends, and sometime in taking recreation and pastime by exercise of the body.

"And, albeit men may judge these to be light and small offences, yet I knowledge and confess that, unless pardon should to me be granted in Christ's blood, every one of these three offences aforenamed, that is to say, the lack of fervency in reproving sin, the lack of indifferency in feeding those who were hungry, and the lack of diligence in the execution of mine office, deserved damnation.

"And, beside these, I was assaulted, yea, infected and corrupted, with more gross sins, that is, my wicked nature desired the favours, the estimation, and praise of men, against which, albeit that sometime the Spirit of God did move me to fight, and earnestly did stir me (God knoweth I lie not) to sob and lament for these imperfections, yet never ceased they to trouble me, when any occasion was offered; and so privily and craftily did they enter into my heart, that I could not perceive myself to be wounded till vain-glory had almost gotten the upper hand.

"O Lord, be merciful to my great offence, and deal not with me according to my great iniquity, but according to the multitude of thy mercies; remove from me the burden of my sin; for of purpose and mind to have avoided the vain displeasure of man, I spared little to offend thy Godly Majesty.

"Think not, beloved of the Lord, that thus I accuse myself without just cause, as though, in so doing, I might appear more holy; or that yet I do it of purpose and intent, by occasion thereof, to accuse other of my brethren, the true preachers of Christ, of like or of greater offences. No! God is judge to my conscience, that I do it even from an unfeigned and sore troubled heart; as I know myself previously to have offended the majesty of my God, during the time that Christ's Gospel had free passage in England. And this I do to let you understand that the taking away of the heavenly bread, and this great tempest that now bloweth against the poor disciples of Christ within the realm of England (as touching our part), cometh from the great mercy of our Heavenly Father, to provoke us to unfeigned repentance, for that neither preacher nor professor did rightly consider the time of our merciful visitation; but, altogether, so we spent the time as though God's Word had been preached rather to satisfy our phantasies than to reform our evil manners; which thing, if we earnestly repent, then shall Jesus Christ appear to our comfort, be the storm never so great. Haste, O Lord, for Thy name's sake."

CHAPTER VI.

KNOX IN FRANKFORT AND GENEVA. HIS INFLUENCE UPON THE PURITAN PARTY OF THE CHURCH OF ENGLAND, 1554-1559.

KNOX had spent five of the best and most vigorous years of his life in England, and the five years which followed—from January, 1554, to January, 1559—were chiefly spent in the service and society of the English Protestant exiles who sought refuge from the Marian persecution in the hospitable cities of evangelical Germany and Switzerland. These five years proved a period of great importance in the history of the English Reformation. They saw the rise of the Puritan party in the Church of England. There had been single Puritans in the Church before not a few, and some of them in high places—John Hooper, a bishop, William Turner, a dean, and Thomas Lever, the head of a great college in Cambridge—but it was not till now that Puritan churchmen began to be organized into a party, holding distinctive principles, pursuing a special well-defined line of its own, and aiming at ends with which other churchmen had little or no sympathy, or to which they were zealously opposed.

The rise of this party in the Church was an event pregnant with consequences, which the lapse of three centuries has not yet exhausted. Immensely more than any other single event in England's annals, with the single exception of Henry the Eighth's rupture with Rome, it has given colour and character to the ecclesiastical history not only of these kingdoms, but of the whole English-speaking world down to the present day.

As Fuller quaintly observed when, at a distance of only one century from the event, he recorded it as "the saddest difference that ever happened in the Church of England, if we consider either the time, how long it continued, the eminent persons therein engaged, or the doleful effects thereby produced. It was about matters of Conformity. Alas, that men should have less wisdom than locusts, which, when sent on God's errand, did not 'thrust one another;'* whereas here such shoving and shouldering, and hoisting and heaving, and jostling and thronging, betwixt clergymen of the highest parts and places. For now Nonconformity, in the days of King Edward was conceived; which afterwards, in the reign of Queen Mary (but beyond sea, at Frankfort), was born; which, in the reign of Queen Elizabeth, was nursed and weaned; which, under King James, grew up a young youth or tall stripling; but, towards the end of King Charles's reign shot up to the full strength and stature of a man, able not only to cope with, but conquer the hierarchy, its adversary."†

In following Knox into the five years' history of the English exiles, I have no intention to write over again a chapter of his life, which has already been adequately penned by his able biographer. No fresh materials of importance have become available for such a purpose, even from the publication of the Zurich letters by the Parker Society, and none of the Knox papers now published for the first time have any bearing upon this section of the Reformer's life. All that I propose to do is to make use of the history of the exiles, as already well known and easily accessible, for the single purpose of showing the place which Knox took in the Puritan movement in Frankfort and Geneva; what influence he exercised upon it; what contributions he made to its organization; what share he had in stimulating and assuring its subsequent development; and what justification his conduct, in these affairs, afforded for the opposite views which have been taken by historians of his violence or his moderation.

With regard to his *place* in the Puritan movement, he was plainly its foremost and most conspicuous man, both at Frankfort and Geneva; and this not by his own seeking, but by the unanimous and cordial invitation, in both cases, of his like-minded brethren. In the autumn of 1554 he was quietly and contentedly pursuing his studies in Geneva, under the eye of Calvin, when he received an urgent call from the English congregation at Frankfort to become one of their ministers. He would gladly have declined the call, in order to continue his studies in Hebrew and other branches of learning, but "at the commandment of Mr. Calvin, that notable

* Joel ii. 8.   † "Church History of Britain," book vii. cent. xvi. 23.

servant of God," as he himself writes, "albeit unwillingly, he obeyed the vocation." Two learned and godly English divines had been called at the same time—James Haddon and Thomas Lever—but Haddon, who was studying in Strasburg, at once declined the invitation; and though Lever proceeded from Zurich to Frankfort, after Knox had been there several weeks, he entered upon his office only tentatively, "for so much," he pleaded, "as that office was of so great importance, and that he had not been in the like before," it being his desire "that between that and Easter they might have a trial of him and he of them, and so at the end of that time either take or refuse." And "let none account it incongruous," says Fuller, that among "so many and able English divines" as were then abroad, "a Scotchman should be made pastor of the English church at Frankfort, the most visible and conspicuous beyond the seas; seeing Mr. Knox's reputed merit did naturalize him, though a foreigner, for any Protestant congregation."

The first place was thus conceded to Knox at Frankfort, even by such men as Bishop Bale, John Fox the Martyrologist, George Whitehead, Anthony Gilby, and Christopher Goodman, all of whom, without exception, were afterwards men of high rank among the Puritans. And it was the same at Geneva, after he was compelled, by "the troubles of Frankfort," to withdraw from that difficult and disturbed charge. As soon as the English congregation of Geneva was formed, in the autumn of 1555, Knox was made choice of in his absence to be joint-pastor along with Goodman; and it was in obedience to their earnest request that he left Scotland, which he visited in 1555–1556, to enter upon that charge in the autumn of the latter year; from which date, till his final return to Scotland, in January 1559, he remained at his post there, the foremost man of a church which was destined to become famous in history as the first purely Puritan congregation of English Protestants that was ever successfully organized. The previous attempt to carry out Puritan principles at Frankfort proved confessedly a failure; but the reiterated attempt made by the same hands at Geneva was confessedly as complete a success.

Knox's *influence* in maintaining and advancing the Puritan cause amidst the "troubles at Frankfort" was conspicuous and paramount, as long as the battle between parties was contested with fair and honourable weapons. Without entering into narrative, it was he, along with William Whittingham, afterwards Dean of Durham, who obtained the learned judgment of Calvin upon the Liturgy of King Edward, which had an instant effect in adding to the numbers of the Puritan party at Frankfort,* and continued, long afterwards, to be appealed to as a testimony of high authority on the side of further reform in the Anglican Prayer-book. It was Knox also who "set his face like a flint" to resist the bold attempt of Dr. Cox and others, who came to Frankfort for the purpose of upsetting the agreement which had been arrived at, by compromise, as to the Order of Service, and immediately began to "break the Order," insisting, in reply to the remonstrance of "the seniors and others, that the Church should have an English face, and roundly declaring that they would do there as they had done in England." No wonder that such arrogance roused a man like Knox, and called forth from him such a sermon as neither he nor any other man had ever preached from an English pulpit before on the subject of that great Puritan question which was now rapidly growing to ripeness in many religious and energetic souls. He gives his own outline of it as follows :—

"At the time appointed for the sermon I began to declare what opinion I had sometime of the English book, what moved me from the same, and what was my opinion presently. I had once a good opinion of the book, I said; but even so, I added, like as yours is at the present, that it ought not in all points to be observed. Then afterwards, by the stubbornness of such men as would defend the whole, and the deeper consideration of the damage that might ensue thereof, and by contemplation of our estate which requireth all our doings to have open defence of the Scriptures (especially in God's service to admit nothing without God's Word), I was driven away from my first opinion; and now do I tell them plainly, that as by God's Book they must seek our warrant for religion, and without that we must thrust nothing into any Christian congregation; so, because I do find in the English book (which they so highly prize and advance above all other Orders) things superstitious, impure, unclean, and unperfect (the which I offered myself ready to prove and to justify before any man),

* "It so wrought in the hearts of many that they were not before so stout to maintain all the parts of the Book of England, as afterwards they were bent against it."—"The Troubles at Frankfort," p. 36.

therefore I could not agree that their book should be of our Church received.

"And furthermore I told them, that it became not the proudest of them all to enterprise the breach of any Order within that Church gathered in the name of Christ, because He was head amongst them, and this I would also justify. At which time also I put them in remembrance of the Order taken; and added, moreover, that though we had changed countries, God had not changed his nature. Wherefore, if we from England brought the same vices that we had in England, and obstinately did continue in the same, his justice must needs punish us here in Germany also, and translate us beyond the places of our expectation, as were sometimes the Israelites beyond Babylon.

"Among many sins that moved God to plague England, I affirmed that slackness to reform religion, when time and place was granted, was one; and therefore that it did become us to be circumspect how we did now lay our foundations, and how we went forward. And because that some men nothing ashamed to say and affirm openly that there had been no impediment nor stop in England, but that religion might go forth and grow to the purity, and that it was already brought to perfection, I reproved this opinion as feigned and untrue, by the lack of discipline, which is not in the Book, neither could in England be obtained; and by the trouble that Mr. Hooper sustained for the rochet and such trifles, in the Book allowed; as also by that which appeared in all men's eyes, that one man was permitted to have power of five benefices, to the slander of the Gospel and defraudation of Christ's flock of their lively food and sustenance."*

Thus boldly and faithfully spoke out the intrepid Puritan. The time to speak out had come. He and the majority of his flock had tried conciliation, and it had failed. They had agreed to a compromise, and the compromise had been violated and exploded, not by them but by the other party. "Dr. Cox and his Company" had tried to browbeat the Pastor and his flock by acts of arrogant assumption and aggression, and it was in the above manly and undaunted style that Knox rebuked and repelled the aggression. Puritanism was only then in its cradle, but already this infant

* "Knox's Works," vol. iv. p. 43. "A Narrative of the Proceedings of the English Congregation at Frankfort in March, 1555."

Hercules was summoned by his enemies to begin his long career of labours and exploits.

This sermon of Knox, in Frankfort, was probably the very earliest pulpit manifesto of ripened Puritanism. It expressly refers to the development of Puritan principles and views which had been recently going on in his own mind, and it distinctly foreshadows the ground which came to be taken up, in after years, in the Elizabethan Church. In significant terms, the preacher warned his brethren to be circumspect how they now laid their foundations, and how they went forward. Did not that mean that they had taken in hand to press for the rebuilding of the Church of England, from the very foundations?—to plead by word and deed for the great and all-including principle of going back to the foundations of the Apostles and Prophets, Jesus Christ himself being the chief corner-stone.

His own account of this Sermon is also very interesting as revealing the causes which had led to that change of opinion and feeling with regard to the Liturgy of Edward VI., which he then so frankly avowed. When he referred to the stubbornness of some men, in defending the whole "Book," his allusion probably went farther back than to his recent experience in Frankfort, and glanced at the opposition of Cranmer and others which had persistently encountered him in the Privy Council. But "he had been driven away from his first opinion" of the Book by considerations of a kind with which nothing of the nature of personal feeling, arising from past conflict, had anything to do. He had been led of late to "deeper consideration of the damage" to the cause of the Reformation, which would ensue from the want of thoroughness in carrying out the principle of the supreme authority of the Word of God, in everything connected with the worship and order of God's house. He had come to see clearly, upon a closer and deeper "contemplation of the estate" of the Reformed Churches, and of the powerful Popish reaction which was now in full movement against them, that their only safety was in having the manifest defence of the Scriptures to show *for all their doings*. This was what the present situation of the whole Protestant Church imperatively "required." These thoughts had evidently been growing upon him in his exile, upon a nearer view of the exigencies of the contest still raging on the Continent, as well as in England, between the Reformation and its enemies; and they had at length gathered such power over him, as to carry him completely over to the side of Puritanism in practice as well as in theory, as the only logical, consistent, and impregnable form of the fundamental principle of all true Church-reform, viz., the alone, undivided, and supreme authority of the Word of God.

It was a part of Knox's precedence and prominence, as a Puritan, that he was the first man called to suffer in the service of Puritanism, and to suffer for it at the hands, not of strangers, but of his own fellow-churchmen and fellow-Protestants—the first, alas! of a long train of victims, reaching down through many generations. The story of his expulsion from Frankfort, at the instance of Dr. Cox and his party, is a melancholy one; and it would be no pleasant task to narrate it once more. The version of it given two centuries ago by Fuller, that most candid of churchmen, will suffice for the ends of historical justice. "The wringing of the nose," saith wise Agur, "bringeth forth blood, so the forcing of wrath bringeth forth strife."* See here the Coxian party depressed, embrace a strange way to raise themselves, and accuse Knox to the State for no less than high treason against the Emperor, in an English book of his, entitled "An Admonition to Christians," first privately preached in Buckinghamshire, and now publicly printed to the world. Eight places therein were laid to his charge; the seven last may well be omitted, the first was so effectual to the purpose, wherein he called the Emperor "no less an enemy to Christ than was Nero." Strange that words spoken some years since, in another land and language, against the Emperor, to whom Knox then owed no natural allegiance (though since a casual and accidental one, by his removal into an imperial city), should, in this unhappy juncture of time, be urged against him by exiles of his own religion, even to no less than the endangering of his life. But what said Rachel of Leah?—"With great wrestlings have I wrestled with my sister, and I have prevailed."† With *great* rather than *good* wrestlings. Such, too often, is the badness of good people, that in the heat of passion they account any play to be fair play which tends to the overturning of those with whom they contend. Hereupon, the State of Frankfort (as an imperial town, highly concerned to be tender of the Emperor's

* Prov. xxx. 33. † Gen. xxx. 8.

honour) willed Knox to depart the city; who, on March 25, 1556, to the great grief of his friends and followers, left the congregation.*

The contributions which Knox made to the organization of English Puritanism on the Continent were of great importance. The first step taken in this direction by the Frankfort congregation, after Knox's entrance upon his pastorate there, in November, 1554, was to come to an agreement that "the Order of Geneva," *i.e.*, the Order drawn up by Calvin for the Reformed Church of that city, "which then was already printed in English, and some copies there among them, should take place as an Order most godly, and farthest off from superstition. But, Maister Knox being spoken unto, as well to put that Order in practice, as to minister the Communion, refused to do either the one or the other, affirming that for many considerations he could not consent that the same Order should be practised till the learned men of Strasburg, Zurich, Emden, &c., were made privy; neither yet would he minister the Communion by the book of England, for that there were things in it placed (as he said) only by warrant of man's authority, and no ground in God's Word for the same; and had also a long time, very superstitiously in the Mass, been wickedly abused. But if he might not be suffered to minister the Sacraments according to his conscience, he then requested that some other might minister the Sacraments, and he would only preach. If neither could be admitted, he besought them that he might be discharged. But to that the congregation would in no wise consent."†

It was honourable to the moderation and the brotherly courtesy of Knox that he declined to introduce the English translation of the Order of Geneva, without previous communication with the leading exiles scattered in other cities; especially as there was nothing in that famous Order which was not perfectly agreeable to his own ideas of what was "most godly and farthest off from superstition." And it was the less to be regretted that he took that course, that it led immediately to the drawing up of a "Book of Common Order" which was better adapted to English use than

---

* "Church History of Britain," book viii. cent. xvi. 3-5.
† "A Brief Discourse of the Troubles begun at Frankford in Germany, A.D. 1554," p. xxvii. Reprinted, London, 1846.

any foreign book could be, and which bore upon it the stamp of English nationality.

This interesting and important incident is briefly recorded in the following passage of the " Troubles at Frankfort :"—

" The congregation could not agree upon any certain Order, till after long debating to and fro it was concluded that Maister Knox, Maister Whittingham, Maister Gilby, Maister Fox, and Maister T. Cole should draw forth some Order meet for their state and time; which thing was by them accomplished and offered to the congregation (being the same Order of Geneva, which is now in print)."*

If this new " Order" had been accepted and brought into use by the Church of Frankfort, it would not have come to be known in history as the " Order of Geneva." But its authors were disappointed in this respect. It was indeed " very well liked of many," but "such as were bent to the book of England," whose numbers were always increasing by the arrival of fresh exiles, "could not abide it; yea, contention grew at length so hot, and the one party, which sought sincerity [purity], so far charged with new-fangledness and singularity, and to be the stirrers of contention and unquietness, that Maister Gilby, with a godly grief (as well appeared), kneeled down before them and besought them, with tears, to reform their judgments, solemnly protesting that in this matter they sought not themselves but only the glory of God, as he was verily persuaded; wishing, farther, that that hand, which he then held up, were stricken off, if by that a godly peace and unity might ensue and follow."†

* Not, of course, the "Order of Geneva" before referred to (which was the work of Calvin), but "The Forme of Prayers and Ministrations of the Sacraments, etc., used in the English Congregation of Geneva," as printed and published there in 1556.

† "Knox's Works," vol vi. pp. 279, 280. It may be useful, here, to add the following particulars of the title and contents of this historically important work. The first Geneva edition bore the following title: "The Forme of Prayers and Ministrations of the Sacraments, &c., used in the English Congregation at Geneva, and approved by the famous and godly learned man, John Calvyn. Imprinted at Geneva by John Crespin, MDLV." The contents of the book were the following:—

1. The Confession of the Christian Faith.
2. The order of electing Ministers, Elders, and Deacons.
3. The Assembly of the Ministry every Thursdaye.
4. An order for the interpretation of the Scriptures and answering of dowtes, observed every Mondaye.

P

All that could, for the present, be gained in this divided state of opinion and feeling, was a compromise—an "Order" which could be accepted equally by Knox and his colleague, Thomas Lever, who had by this time arrived in Frankfort, and who, though a Puritan as well as Knox, did not go the same length as he in his repugnance to King Edward's liturgy. The account handed down to us of this compromise is honourable to the moderation of all parties.

"In the end another way was taken by the congregation, which was that Maister Knox and Maister Whittingham, Maister Parry and Maister Leaver, should devise some order, if it might be, to end all strife and contention. These four assembled for that purpose. And first Maister Knox spake to the rest on this wise: 'For so much,' saith he, 'as I perceive that no end of contention is to be hoped for, unless the one part something relent, this will I do, for my part, that quietness may ensue. I will shew my judgment how (as I think) it may be best for the edification of this poor flock; which, if ye will not accept nor follow, after that I have discharged my conscience, I will cease and commit the whole matter to be ordered by you, as you will answer before Christ Jesus at the last day, and to this his congregation in this life,' etc. Whereupon, after some conference, an Order was agreed upon, some part taken forth of the English book, and other things put to, as the state of that Church required; and this Order, by the consent of the congregation, should continue to the last of April following. If any contention should arise in the meantime, the matter then to be

5. A Confession of our Synnes, used before the sermon, and framede to our state and tyme.
6. Another Confession, for all states and tymes.
7. A General Prayer, after the sermon, for the whole estate of Christ's Churche.
8. The Ministration of Baptism and the Lord's Supper.
9. The forme of Marriage, the Visitation of the Sycke, and the Maner of Buryall.
10. An Order of Ecclesiastical Discipline.
11. One-and-fifty Psalms of David, in metre.
12. The Catechism of Mr. Calvyn. Et cet.

In the same year, 1556, was published, in Geneva, a Latin translation of the same book, usually attributed to Whittingham:—"Ratio et Forma publice orandi Deum atque Administrandi Sacramenta, et caet. In Anglorum Ecclesia quae Genevae colligitur, recepta cum judicio et comprobatione D. Iohannis Calvini."

determined by these five notable learned men, to wit: Calvin, Musculus, Martyr, Bullinger, and Viret. This agreement was put in writing; to that all gave their consents. This Order was taken the 6th of February. This day was joyful; thanks were given to God; brotherly reconciliation followed; great familiarity used; the former grudges seemed to be forgotten. Yea, the holy communion was, upon this happy agreement, also ministered; and this friendship continued till the 13th of March following, at which time Dr. Cox, and others with him, came to Frankfort, out of England, who began to break the Order which was agreed upon."*

The part taken by Knox on this trying occasion is characterized in the margin of the old narrative as "the modestie of Knox;" and this commendation of his moderation and temper will be acknowledged to be just. Nor would it be fair to leave it unsaid that Lever and Perry met Knox and Whittingham in the same spirit, though to Knox belongs the credit of having set the first example.

In the "troubles" which followed the arrival of Dr. Cox, nothing more was heard of the earlier "Order" drawn up by Knox, Whittingham, Gilby, Fox, and Cole. As the full embodiment of the principles and wishes of the party of which these eminent men were the leaders, that work could not be brought forward again till the party found themselves in circumstances to act freely upon their own views; and this situation was not reached till they had left Frankfort, and had obtained leave, through the exertions of Whittingham, to form themselves into a congregation, in Geneva. They reassembled there in the autumn of 1555, where "they were received with great favour and much courtesy both by the magistrates, ministers, and people;" and they lost no time in organizing themselves into a church, in strict accordance with the principles they held touching all that was essential to the good order of the Church of Christ as to doctrine, worship, and discipline.

The "Order," which they had drafted at Frankfort the year before, was taken in hand again and revised, and after being submitted to the judgment of Calvin, was published, with a Preface, probably from the pen of Whittingham, which bears date 10th of February, 1556. Knox was not then in Geneva; he was on a visit

* "Discourse of the Troubles," xxxvii. xxxiii.

to Scotland, to which he had set off in the preceding August. But he was no doubt consulted before the work was finally adopted and committed to the press, because as soon as " the church was erected, on the 1st of November, 1555," he was chosen, in his absence, to be one of its two pastors. But he was none the less one of the principal authors of the work. In its published form it was substantially, probably all but verbally, the same (excepting the Preface) which had been prepared at Frankfort; and in determining the substance and arrangement of that draft, it cannot be doubted that his influence was paramount, as he was the recognized leader of the party whose views the document embodied. The style, however, we do not claim to be his; it is much smoother and fluenter than his English style ever became, and was, in all probability, from the accomplished pen of Whittingham, to whom the Preface is usually ascribed.*

The importance of this " Order of Geneva," for the subsequent history of British Puritanism, was very signal and memorable. Though it never received any sanction in England from any public authority, civil or ecclesiastical, it continued throughout the whole of the long reign of Elizabeth to be regarded by the English Presbyterian Puritans as a book of standard authority in doctrine, worship, and discipline, and was even used and brought into application as such by the Presbyterians who seceded from the National Church in the first decade of Elizabeth's reign, and in subsequent years. But it took a much more distinguished place in the Reformed Church of Scotland. Knox had carried it with him from Geneva, and had the gratification of seeing it

---

* Dr. McCrie and Dr. Laing both express doubt regarding the date, 10th of February, 1556, attached to the Preface, whether it may not possibly indicate, after the old style of reckoning, the year 1557; in which case Knox would have been again residing in Geneva when the work was published, and the Order must have issued from the press under his own eye. But we have been able to satisfy ourselves that the new style of dating the commencement of the year had been introduced in Geneva a considerable time before the year 1555. In the curious and valuable reprint of Anthoine Fromment's " Les Actes et Gestes Merveilleux de la Cité de Geneve," published in Geneva in 1854, there is an Appendix of " Extracts from the Public Registers of the City for the years 1532–1536," and in these the years all begin with the 1st of January. And in the " History of the Troubles at Frankfort" there is a letter of Calvin to Knox and Whittingham, dated from Geneva, the 20th of January, 1555, which we are certain, from its contents, does not belong to the year 1555–56; but, if dated in the old style, would have fallen under the years 1554–55.

cordially and unanimously embraced by the National Church of his native country in the very year—we might almost say, in the very moment—of its new ecclesiastical birth. For several years before that event the "congregation" had made occasional use of King Edward's Liturgy to some extent, but "We hear no more," says Dr. Laing, "of the English Prayer-book in 1560." In the "Book of Discipline," prepared in December of that year, the only formulary mentioned is "our Book of Common Order," called the Order of Geneva; and at the meeting of the General Assembly, held on the last day of December, 1562, "It was concludit," in the form of an Act, "that ane uniform ordour salbe takin and keipit in the administration of the Sacraments and Solemnization of Marriages, and Burial of the Dead, according to the Book of Geneva." The same forms, with various additions, including Calvin's Catechism, and the Psalms in English metre, were approved and received by the Church of Scotland in 1564, and the copies usually pass under the name of Knox's Psalms and Liturgy. A more suitable title is that by which it is generally known in early times, The Book of Common Order. This "Liturgy," as it is usually but inexactly called, with various omissions or alterations, continued to be republished at Edinburgh and Aberdeen till the years 1640 and 1643. In England some attempt was apparently on foot to introduce the Geneva form as late as the meeting of the Long Parliament, as it was reprinted and "Humbly presented to the Most High Court of Parliament, London, 1641." And other two editions appeared in 1643.*

Throughout the five years which Knox spent chiefly on the continent, his pen was incessantly at work to promote and defend the cause of gospel truth both in England and Scotland during the dark and miserable days of the two Marys—Queen Mary of England, and Mary of Lorraine, the Queen Regent of Scotland. The writings which he composed and procured to be printed abroad in this service, were the earliest of his publications, and along with his private epistles, addressed chiefly to English correspondents, make up the largest part of three volumes of his collected Works; and the most of these writings have the remarkable peculiarity, that, though not thrown into the technical

* "Knox's Works," vol. vi. "The Book of Common Order." Introductory Notes by the Editor.

form of pulpit addresses and appeals, they are intensely personal, spoken quite as much from heart to heart, from conscience to conscience, with quite as much glow of feeling, and fire of affection, and fervour of enthusiasm as if he had still been preaching at Newcastle or Amersham, or before the King and Council. Usually, in almost all these pieces, which even at this distance of time still feel to the touch like live coals, it is not doctrines he handles but persons—either the "faithful Christians in London, Newcastle, Berwick, and others," or their cruel persecutors; either "his afflicted brethren in England" or "the blood-thirsty wretches who devour Christ's small flock;" dispensing to the one class either "Comfortable Epistles," full of loving words, or "Faithful Admonitions" and "Warnings," no less instinct with the very soul of love, though more roughly spoken, as they could not miss to be; and dealing out to the other class, like a prophet of God and herald of coming Judgment, such messages of holy wrath and what he calls "perfect, *i.e.*, sinless hatred," as must have made their ears to tingle. And it need scarcely be said in a single word, how powerfully all these fervid discharges of the electricity of this heroic soul must have helped to keep alive in many English hearts the spirit of Puritan Protestantism in the worst times; and to preserve a remnant of true-heartedness and manly courage of faith and patience in the sorely bestead and afflicted kingdom, against the coming day of deliverance never meant by England's God to be long-distant.

But we must confine ourselves to the last and the briefest of all these most characteristic missives of the Reformer's fiery and yet most generous and beneficent zeal—a piece long lost and forgotten, not known even to the erudite and far-searching Dr. McCrie, and which was reprinted for the first time by Dr. Laing, less than twenty years ago. We refer to his "Brief Exhortation to England for the speedy embracing of Christ's Gospel, heretofore by the tyranny of Mary suppressed and banished." It bears date "At Geneva, 1559."

The tyranny of Mary against the Gospel and the Gospellers was now come to an end. Elizabeth, the Protestant Queen, was upon the throne of her devout brother, King Edward, and England and all the world expected to see Edward's Reformation-work restored. But Knox expected as well as wished for more. He hoped and prayed to see Edward's Reformation itself reformed; and his "Brief Exhortation" possesses the remarkable interest of containing a programme of what this Reformation reformed should be—a programme which was honourable alike to his zeal and his moderation; to his insight and to his foresight; to the equal boldness and sagacity of his reforming and constructive genius.

This remarkable piece is addressed thus: "To the Realm of England and to all Estates within the same, John Knox wisheth true repentance to be given from God, the Father of Our Lord Jesus Christ, with the Spirit of wisdom, discretion, and true understanding."

After referring, at the commencement, to an Epistle addressed to the inhabitants of Newcastle and Berwick, dated the 10th of November, 1558, which was printed along with the present Exhortation to England at large, "I thought it my duty," he continues, "in few words, to require of thee, and that in God's name, O England in general, the same repentance and true conversion unto God that I have required of those to whom before particularly I wrote. For in very deed, when in dolour of heart I wrote this former letter, I neither looked nor could believe that the Lord Jesus would so suddenly knock at thy gate (alluding to the unexpected death of Mary and the happy accession of Elizabeth, which had taken place only seven days after the above date, and the tidings of which had only recently reached Geneva), or call upon thee in thy open streets, offering Himself to pardon thy iniquity, yea to enter into thy house, and so to abide and make his habitation with thee, who so inobediently had rejected his yoke, so disdainfully had trodden under foot the blood of his Testament, and so cruelly had murdered those that were sent to call thee to repentance. This thy horrible ingratitude considered, I did rather look for punishments and plagues universally to have been poured forth than for mercy, by the sound of his trumpet, so suddenly to have been offered to any within that miserable isle.

"But when I did more deeply weigh that such is the infinite goodness of God, and that such be also the bright beams of his most just judgments, that whensoever He taketh into his protection, by the covenant of his Word, any realm, nation, province, or city, so that of mercy He becometh to them conductor, teacher, protector, and father; that He never casteth off the same care and fatherly affection which in his word He doth once pronounce, until they do utterly declare themselves unworthy of his presence;

when this (I say) I did consider and weigh, I was in judgment somewhat reformed. For I find that such was his care and constant love to the whole seed of Abraham (I mean of those descended of Jacob) that albeit in many things they provoked Him to anger, yet did his infinite goodness ever find and make a way by the which his mercy was sensibly felt of that people even in their greatest extremities. . . . For this prerogative had ever the Jews, that first to them were offered the glad tidings of the Kingdom, unto such times as they declared themselves, by open blasphemies, continual resistance, and cruel persecution, most worthy to be deprived of that honour.

"The same order, I see, doth God keep with thee, O thou happy and most unhappy England. Happy not only because thy God, by his own hand, hath oft delivered thee from corporal bondage of divers and strange nations, as of Romans, Saxons, Goths, and Danes, but especially for that, that by the power of his eternal verity (and that of his free grace without thy deserving) He did of late years break and destroy the intolerable yoke of thy spiritual captivity, and brought thee forth as it had been from the bottom of Hell and from the thraldom of Satan, in which thou wast holden, blinded by idolatry and superstition, to the fellowship of his angels and to the possession of that rich inheritance prepared to his dearest children with Christ Jesus, his Son. But O unhappy, and more than unhappy, that hast declared thyself so unthankful and rebellious to so loving and so merciful a Father, who first gave thee life, when thou didst lie polluted in blood and dead in thy sin, and now doth offer Himself to be thy God, Governor, and Father, after that thou, most traitorously conspiring with Satan by solemn oath, hast renounced his verity—O unhappy and more than unhappy art thou (I say) if that this thy treasonable defection, and God's loving kindness yet calling thee to his favours, doth not pierce thy heart with unfeigned repentance. For as this mercy and love of thy God far surmounteth the reach of all men's understanding, so cannot his just judgments long delay to pour forth those horrible vengeances which thy monstrous unthankfulness hath long deserved, if now (as God forbid!) thou shut up thine ears, blind thine eyes, and so harden thy heart, that neither thou wilt hear, see, nor understand the gravity of thy fall, and that inestimable goodness of thy God thus lovingly calling thee to thy ancient honour and dignity again.

"I neither dare nor will cease now by my pen (be it never so rude) to cry unto thee that which sometimes, from the mouth of my Master, Christ Jesus, I have pronounced in the hearing of many, that if thou shalt not know this merciful visitation of the Lord thy God, and so prepare thyself with a penitent and thankful heart to receive, yet while time is, his large graces offered, that then thy habitation shall be left desolate ; and whereas thou hast of long time been the delectable garden, planted by the Lord's hand, thou shalt become a barren wilderness, apt for nothing but to be brent and consumed by fire."

The national sins and the national catastrophes of the people of Israel, he goes on to say, were "a glasse for England." "This is the glass, this is the mirror, O England, in which I would that daily thou shouldst behold what shall be the final end of those that do abuse the long-suffering of God calling all to repentance. If thou shalt think thyself pure and clean from any of the crimes which before are noted in that people, alas! thou shalt declare thyself more than impudent. For all other your iniquities omitted, this your last and universal turning from God by the open denial of his Gospel professed, declareth you, from the highest to the lowest, manifest traitors against his Godly Majesty. It is you all together who most cruelly have shed the blood of a number of your brethren and sisters, which from under the altar cry to be revenged. There is no person guiltless in God's presence who hath bowed their knees to idolatry (whatsoever excuse they list to pretend), but as all are idolaters, so are they, and shall be reputed murtherers before God, which do not wash away that infamy and innocent blood by unfeigned repentance. . . . Absolve and flatter you whoso list, God the Father, his Son Jesus Christ, his holy angels, the creatures sensible and insensible in heaven and earth, shall arise in judgment and shall condemn you, if in time ye repent not. . . . And albeit my blood should be shed for this my affirmation ; yet, having the testimony of a good conscience that I speak not nor write not of private malice against any person, I will still cry as before ; for at your hands (unless that speedily and unfeignedly ye repent) shall God require all the blood, not only which lately hath been shed by your most wicked permission, but also of all those that for the same cause have suffered from the beginning. Tremble, therefore, fear, confess, and unfeignedly repent, that ye may escape the vengeance prepared. Your humiliation, confession, and repentance may now obtain no less of God's great mercy than did Josias, his nobles and people, in the same case, to whom in all things you are so like as one bean is to another. For no crime is so heinous which God will not cast in the bottom of the sea and bring in perpetual oblivion if you, with unfeigned hearts, turn to the Lord your God, whom so grievously you have offended."

Never before or since was England addressed by such a prophet-like voice as this! But Knox was not only a preacher all aglow with prophetic fire. He was thoroughly practical, even when he was most inspired and exalted by his faith in "the eternal veritie" of the Most High. He gives quite a homely matter-of-fact turn to the national repentance and conversion to which he summons the kingdom as with a trumpet blast :—

"This conversion and repentance requireth, no doubt, a reformation, removing, and suppressing of all abuses, all wrongs, all violence, all oppression and fraud—how long, in whom, and by whomsoever they have been maintained, practised, or permitted. But remitting all such things as lie outside of the religion to such as God shall further move with his Holy Spirit to instruct you, I say that your conversion unto God and unfeigned repentance requireth two things : First, that the religious and true honouring of God may be at once brought to that purity which his word requireth ; Secondarily, that order may be taken, so far as in you lieth, that the same religion which God approveth may be kept inviolably amongst you for ever, and that the people universal may be instructed in the same."

Then follows his remarkable programme of ecclesiastical and educational reform, too long to be inserted here, which it is interesting to compare with the numerous programmes of a similar kind which were urged and opposed, re-urged and re-opposed, throughout the whole reign of Elizabeth—all substantial reiterations of the demands which were thus early made by Knox, and which claim the historical importance of being the first printed outline of reform ever published by the Puritan party of the National Church.

The programme is undoubtedly pitched in a key much too high, in some important points, for practical statesmanship, either ecclesiastical or political. Its intolerance in particular is extreme; and it cannot but excite astonishment that a man who had himself suffered so much as Knox had done from the persecution both of Papists and Protestants, should have inculcated the principle that " none ought to be freed from the yoke of Church discipline, nor permitted to decline from the religion of God"—yea, that "Prince, king, or emperor who should go about to destroy God's true religion once established, and to erect idolatry, which God detesteth (meaning Romish superstition), be adjudged to death according to God's commandment."

In maintaining such a principle as this, Knox was, it must be confessed, behind many of the best men of his own age, and went to a tragical extreme of opinion, of which none of the other leading Reformers had set an example. But it is only justice to him to remember that this extreme opinion was only a mistaken theory of Christian duty, and nothing worse; it was in no degree the outcome of a hard or cruel nature; never, even in the days of his greatest power in his own country, could the guilt of shedding blood in the name of religion be laid to his charge. It was entirely due to the too consequential logic with which he carried out to its farthest issues the erroneous principle that the Law of Moses was still binding, politically as well as morally, upon Christian nations. He failed to apprehend and apply the fundamental distinctions which obtain between the administration of a theocracy and that of a Christian kingdom—an error which lay at the root of much of the intolerance of that age, Catholic as well as Protestant.

It is more pleasing to notice in his programme a remarkable instance of moderation in his demand for ecclesiastical reform, and an anticipation of the same enlightened zeal and large-mindedness in the interests of national education, which he displayed in after years in his native country. He was no lover of bishops, as we have seen, but he makes no proposal for the abolition of Episcopacy in the English Church; he will be content to see ten bishops of moderate income substituted for one lordly prelate; and each of the present overgrown dioceses broken up into ten manageable ones, that so in every city and great town there may be placed a godly learned man, with so many joined with him for preaching and instruction as shall be thought sufficient for the bounds committed to their charge. He was much more zealous for schools and learning than he was for bishops and bishoprics, and the last article of his programme for Church and school reform in England was that, "for the preservation of religion, it is most expedient that schools be universally erected in all cities and chief towns, the oversight whereof to be committed to the magistrates and godly learned men of the said cities and towns; that of the youth godly instructed amongst them, a seed may be reserved and continued for the profit of Christ's Church in all ages."

Knox was called back to Scotland in this same year—1559, and had no opportunity or call in duty to bear any part in the work of restoring the Reformation in England. In fact, he was not suffered by Elizabeth, either then, or for a good many years afterwards, to set foot in her realm, so deeply had he offended and disgusted her by his "First Blast against the Monstrous Regiment [Government] of Women." He had sowed the seed of Reformation broadcast in England, and among Englishmen out of England, but he was not permitted to reap personally what he had sown. Others were to reap it, and enter into his labours. But that grieved him not a jot. His hands were full of glorious work in his own country; and, meanwhile, much of what was best in his spirit and principles had passed into many English hearts. His burning words were still as "coals of fire" in many souls from Berwick to Buckinghamshire and London. And, though Elizabeth's settlement of the Reformation lagged far behind the goal which he would have reached out to himself, still his programme of a full and thorough Reformation was not forgotten. It was cherished by many, by an ever-growing number of English minds, as a prophecy of the future, it might be, even, of the near future. For we have been struck with a supplication presented to Queen Elizabeth, as early as 1562-63 (which may be seen in the same Collection alongside of the Knox papers here published), running in the name of the Queen's "obedient and faithful subjects, the main part of the commons of this your realm of England, Wales, and Ireland, and the marches of the same," which bears a striking resemblance to the tone and demands of Knox's own programme. They single out for complaint the very same evils, still suffered to remain unhealed, and they ask almost literally the very same reforms "of the miserable injuries" in the condition of the Church, "which still unjustly and painfully they sustain and suffer." One almost imagines he hears the echoes of Knox's voice still reverberating from "the commons of England, Ireland, and Wales;" so truly was the reform he sketched and pleaded for, the people's reform —not, indeed, to the liking of Queen and courtiers and high prelates, but very much after the heart of "the commonalty of the realm."

With all these facts before us of Knox's life and labours among the English Protestant exiles abroad, and for the religious benefit of English Protestants at home, down to the date of Queen Elizabeth's accession, what are we to think of his place and relations to the great English Puritan party, which immediately afterwards revealed its presence and power in the Elizabethan Church?

Mr. Carlyle considers Knox to have been "chief priest and founder of the Faith that became Scotland's, New England's, Oliver Cromwell's—that is, of Puritanism;" and "brave and remarkable" as the man was in himself, still more important was he as standing in such a relation to Puritanism, "the most interesting phasis," he deems, "which the Reformation anywhere assumes, especially for us English. In Luther's own country Protestantism soon dwindled into a rather barren affair; not a religion or faith, but rather now a jangling of argument; the proper seat of it not the heart; the essence of it sceptical contention. . . . But in our island there arose a Puritanism which even got itself established as a Presbyterianism and National Church among the Scotch, which came forth as a real business of the heart, and has produced in the world very notable fruit. In some senses, one may say it is the only phasis of Protestantism that ever got to the rank of being a Faith, a true heart-communication with Heaven, and of exhibiting itself in history as such; and history will have something to say about this Puritanism for some time to come." "Puritanism was only despicable, laughable," when the Pilgrim Fathers "clubbed their small means together" to hire the little ship *Mayflower;* but nobody can manage to laugh at it now. Puritanism has got weapons and sinews; it has firearms, war-navies; it has cunning in its ten fingers, strength in its right arm; it can steer ships, fell forests, remove mountains; it is one of the strongest things under this sun at present."[*] Was John Knox, then, what Mr. Carlyle claims for him to have been—the founder and chief priest of this mighty Puritanism in England, Scotland, and America? If he was, he was a much greater man—a much more important man—a much more imposing figure in the world's history—than the world has ever yet taken him for.

The only other name that can be supposed to dispute with him

---

[*] "On Heroes, Hero-Worship, and the Heroic in History," p. 133. Edition 1872.

the honours of such a paternity is that of John Hooper. But Knox had precedence of Hooper, in point of date, as a preacher of Puritan Protestantism in the Church of England. Hooper did not return to England from Zurich till about the middle of May, 1549, and we hear of him in June as already "reading a public lecture twice in the day, in London, to so numerous an audience that the church could not contain them." But Knox had already been engaged for several months in similar work in Berwick, and was not only preaching Puritanism, but practising it, conducting the public worship of God without any prescribed liturgy, and administering the Sacraments in the manner of Zurich and Geneva instead of Lambeth and St. Paul's.

It is true also that Hooper preached Puritan doctrine before the King and Council as early as in Lent, 1550,* whereas Knox did not succeed him in that high place till the autumn of 1552. But it is a curious coincidence that Hooper had not quite finished his Seven

---

* In addition to the passages formerly quoted from these remarkable sermons, it may be well to give the following sentences from Hooper's Prefatory Epistle to Edward VI. and his Highness's Privy Council:—

"If the priesthood and ministry of Christ, with his notes and marks, be true, holy, and absolutely perfect, receive it; in case it be not, follow the Pope. Christ cannot abide to have the leaven of the Pharisees mingled with his sweet flour. He would have us either hot or cold; the lukewarm he vomiteth up, and not without a cause. For he accuseth God of ignorance and foolishness that intendeth to adorn and beautify his doctrine and decrees with human cogitations. What king or prince of the world would suffer his statutes, laws, and testament to be cut off and set on at every man's liberty and pleasure? Should not the same glory, majesty, and honour be given unto the laws and testament of Christ, that is sealed with his precious blood? The Word of God, wherewith He governeth and ruleth his Church, is a sceptre of iron (Ps. ii.), and not a rod of willow, to be bowed with every man's finger; either a reed to be broken at man's will; no, neither a piece of leather, to be stretched and reached out with any man's teeth. . . . And a thousand times the rather shall your Majesty restore again the true ministry of the Church, in case ye remove and take away all the monuments, tokens, and leavings of Papistry; for as long as any of them remain, there remaineth also occasion of relapse unto the abolished superstition of Antichrist. . . . I can do no less, howsoever the world shall take my doings, but exhort and pray the magistrates to bring the Church to her first perfection. . . . Help ye, therefore, O ye bishops and priests, the King's Majesty's and his noble Council's proceedings, that all things may be brought to a perfect and apostolical reformation. It is not enough to lay the foundation of the temple, but there must be builded upon it gold, silver, and precious stones. But in any case we must take heed we lay no straw nor stubble upon the foundation; if we do, it will be burned" (1 Cor. iii.).—"Early Writings," pp. 436–39.

Sermons upon the Book of Jonas before the King and Council in the South, when Knox stood forth before the Council of the North to vindicate in the same vehement tone and style " the doctrine that the Sacrament of the Mass is idolatry." Nor were the results that followed Knox's preaching at Court, in 1552, inferior in importance to those which followed Hooper's. The result in Hooper's case was merely to give to the diocese of Gloucester a Puritan bishop; the result in the case of Knox was to add to the English Prayer-book the "Declaration on Kneeling," one of the most Protestant things in the book, which would never have been there but for the boldness and energy of that redoubtable Puritan.

In estimating the comparative influence of these two eminent Puritans upon the Puritan party as afterwards developed and organized, we must also bear in mind that, while Hooper accepted a bishopric, Knox thought it his duty to decline one; and that while the latter stood unflinchingly true to the reasons which he assigned for his declinature, Hooper did not find himself able to maintain his struggle against the episcopal vestments beyond a certain point, but succumbed at last to the antagonism of Cranmer and Ridley. Hooper was a man of heroic spirit, and fought a hard, though a losing battle. Knox was a hero all over, "who never feared the face of man;" and, unconquerable himself, he was the very man to inspire other men who thought as he did with the courage of their convictions, and to become their chosen leader and champion.*

In Hooper's hands, Puritanism never got beyond the stage of a doctrine, or a mode of thought and feeling on Church questions. It never passed into the more advanced stage of an organization

---

* What was the impression made upon Puritan minds by the submission of Hooper to the use of the vestments, appears from a letter of Utenhovius to Bullinger, written at the time : "After a long struggle, Hooper was committed to prison, and about a fortnight after, overcome by the obstinacy of the bishops, the good man submitted himself and his cause to the judgment of the Privy Council ; the result of which was that he was inaugurated in the usual manner, about the middle of Lent, yet not without the greatest regret both of myself and of all good men, nor without affording a most grievous stumbling-block to many of our brethren ; a circumstance which I am unwilling to conceal from you, though, from my affection for Hooper, I am very unwilling to make the communication ; and indeed I should not now do it were I not aware of your sincere regard for Hooper, and that you look upon him as another self."— "Original Letters of the Reformation," p. 586.

and realized form of Church-life. The first beginnings of this took place in Berwick and Newcastle, under the hand of Knox, and the first attempts to carry it out in a shape more complete and typical were also made under his direction in Frankfort and Geneva. Supported by his colleague, Christopher Goodman, assisted by a choice body of elders, including men like Coverdale, Whittingham, Williams, and Bodley, and surrounded by a congregation numbering nearly a hundred souls, all "perfectly joined together in one mind and one judgment," Knox was for several years unquestionably the most conspicuous and influential man among the English Puritans. More than any other single man, looking to all that he did for the cause, both in England and on the Continent, he deserves to be regarded as the Father and Founder of English as well as Scottish Puritanism. It was the men who had been most closely associated with him as exiles in the churches of Frankfort and Geneva, who formed the staunchest section of the Elizabethan Puritans on their return to England. These men, who, in an ecclesiastical sense, might be called the sons of Knox, were the best representatives of the oldest generation of English Puritans—the generation which was succeeded by that of Frith and Wilcox, Travers, and Cartwright. By the Puritans of that older generation, to whom he was known by face and personal fellowship, he was never forgotten; and proof will be produced, before we close, of the affection with which, to his dying day, their old leader continued to refer to them, and to the days when "he lived amongst them in quietness of conscience and contentment of heart." And if his return to Scotland, in 1559, and his long enforced absence from England, had not broken his connection with the English Church, his name would naturally have become more familiar and current among the Puritans of the younger generation; although proof will also be forthcoming that among them too his name, though not, perhaps, "familiar as a household word," was held in high veneration.

Nor was this state of feeling among the elder and the younger Puritans towards Knox only a matter of sentiment. We are fortunately able to produce evidence from one of the Papers printed for the first time in this volume, that, in the time of need, the Puritans of London turned to their old leader in Scotland for practical succour and advice; and that, full as his hands now were and had long been of the business of another kingdom, they did not

CH. VI.] INTERCESSION OF THE CHURCH OF SCOTLAND. 225

turn to him in vain; but he was able to bring to their aid the support and interposition of a whole National Church, though unhappily without effect.

In the year 1566 the troubles to which the Puritan ministers of the Church of England had begun to be subjected by the Court of High Commission, on account of their non-conformity in the use of the surplice, the sign of the Cross in Baptism, etc., became known to their brethren of the Reformed Church of Scotland, and excited among them the liveliest sympathy and concern. Some of "the deprived ministers" had repaired to Scotland, either to solicit aid, or in hope of employment in the ministry; and had acquainted Knox with the melancholy severities which were used by Archbishop Parker and other prelates, against many of the godliest and most learned ministers of the Church in London and other places. Wherefore, "notwithstanding the domestic troubles," as Knox himself writes, "that the Church of God had in Scotland in this turbulent time within the kingdom" (it was the time of the Rizzio and Darnley tragedies), "yet were they not unmindful of the affliction of Jacob, everywhere upon the face of the earth; especially they had before their eyes the state and condition of the Church of God in England. Witness this letter from the General Assembly to the Rulers of the Church of God in England." The letter was drawn up by Knox himself, and ran in the following strain of earnest intercession, and frank yet courteous remonstrance:—

"The Superintendents, Ministers, and Commissioners of Kirks within the Realm of Scotland, to their Brethren the Bishops and Pastors in England, who have renounced the Roman Antichrist, and do profess with them the Lord Jesus in sincerity, desire the perpetual increase of the Holy Spirit, the truth of Jesus Christ.

"By word and writ it is come to our knowledge, reverend brethren, pastors of God's word in the Church of England, that divers of our dearest brethren (amongst whom are some of the best learned within that realm) are deprived from ecclesiastical function and are forbidden to preach, and so by you are stayed to promote the Kingdom of Jesus Christ, because their conscience will not suffer them to put on, at the commandment of authority such garments as idolaters in time of blindness have used in their idolatry. Which report cannot but be most dolorous to our hearts, mindful of that sentence of the Apostle, 'If ye bite and devour one another take heed lest ye be consumed one of another.'

"We purpose not at the present to enter into the ground, which we hear is agitated and handled with greater vehemency by either party than well liketh us, to wit, whether such apparell is to be counted among things which are simply indifferent or not. But in the bowels of Jesus Christ, we crave that Christian charity may so prevail in you (in you, we say, the pastors and leaders of the flock in that realm) that ye do not to others that which ye would not others to do to you. You cannot be ignorant how tender a thing the conscience of man is. All that have knowledge are not alike persuaded. Your consciences reclaimeth not at the wearing of such garments; but many thousands, both godly and learned, are otherwise persuaded, whose consciences are continually stricken with these sentences, 'What hath Christ to do with Belial? What fellowship is there betwixt darkness and light?' If surplice, corner-cap, and tippet, have been the badges of idolaters in the very act of their idolatry, what hath the preacher of Christian liberty, and open rebuker of all superstition, to do with the dregs of that Roman beast? Yea, what is he that ought not to fear either to take in his hand or on his forehead the print and mark of that odious beast? Our brethren who refuse of conscience that unprofitable apparell, do neither condemn nor molest you who use such vain trifles. If ye shall do the like to them, we doubt not but therein ye shall please God and comfort the hearts of many who are wounded with the extremity which is used against these godly and our beloved brethren. Colour of rhetoric or human persuasion we will use none, but charitably we desire you to call that sentence of Peter to mind : 'Feed the flock of God which is committed to your charge, caring for it, not by constraint, but willingly ; not as though ye were lords over God's heritage, but that ye may be examples to the flock.' Further, we desire you to meditate upon that sentence of the Apostle : 'Give no offence, neither to Jew nor to Grecian, nor to the Kirk of God.'

"In what condition of time ye and we both travell, in promoting of Christ's kingdom, we suppose ye be not ignorant ; therefore we are the more bold to exhort you to walk more circumspectly than to trouble the godly for such vanities, for all things which may seem lawful edify not. If the commandment of the authority urge the consciences of you and your brethren with further than they can bear, we unfeignedly crave of you that ye remember that ye are called the 'light of the world,' and the 'salt of the earth; all that are in civil authority have not the light of God shining before their eyes, in their statutes and commands, but their affections savour over much of the earth, and of wordly wisdom ; and therefore we think that ye should boldly oppose yourselves not only to all that power that will or dare extol itself against God, but also against all such as dare burthen the consciences of the faithful farther than God hath burdened them by his own Word.

"But herein we may confess an offence, in that we have entered in reasoning farther than we purposed and promised in the beginning. And therefore we shortly return to our former humble supplication, which is that our brethren who among you refuse the Romish rags may find of you the prelates such favour as our Head and Master commandeth every one of his members to shew one to another; which we look to receive of your gentleness, not only for ye fear to offend God's majesty in troubling of your brethren for such vain trifles, but also because ye will not refuse the humble request of us your brethren and fellow-preachers of Christ Jesus ; in whom, albeit there appeareth no great wordly pomp, yet we suppose ye will not so far despise us but that ye will esteem us to be of the number of those that fight against that Roman Antichrist, and travell that the kingdom of Christ Jesus may be universally advanced. The days are evil ; iniquity aboundeth ; Christian charity groweth cold. Therefore we ought the more diligently to watch, for the hour is uncertain when the Lord Jesus shall appear, before whom ye, our brethren, and we must give account of our administration.

"And thus, in conclusion, we once again crave favour to our brethren, which granted, ye in the Lord shall command us in things of double more importance. The Lord Jesus rule your hearts in his true fear to the end, and give to you and to us victory over that conjured enemy to all true religion, to wit, over that Roman Antichrist, whose wounded head Satan by all means laboureth to cure again. But to destruction shall he and his maintainers go, by the power of the Lord Jesus, to whose mighty protection we heartily commit you.

"From Edinburgh, out of our General Assembly, and third session thereof, the 27th of December, 1566. Your loving brethren and fellow-preachers in Christ Jesus.

" JOHNE CRAIG.	" JAMES MELVILL.
ROBERT PONT.	WILLIAM CHRISTESONE.
NICOL SPITTELL.	JOHNE ROW.
DAVID LINDSAY.	JOHN ARESKINE.
JOHNE WYNRAME.	JOHNE SPOTSWOD."*

It is worth remembering, that though this characteristic letter proceeded from the pen of Knox, he was the only one of the leading ministers of the Church of Scotland who did not sign it. How was this? No doubt because he feared that his name appended to it would make it less agreeable and more unacceptable to some of the Bishops to whom it was addressed. He had been in unpleasant collision with not a few of them in Frankfort—with Grindal, Jewel, Sands, Horne and Cox—and was, no doubt, aware that the addition of his name to the document would be no great recommendation of it to their regard. But, unhappily, neither what he wrote, nor what he abstained from writing, proved of any avail on this sad occasion. We hear no more of the letter, either in English or Scottish chronicles; and we are not aware of any abatement of the severities used against the Puritans, in that evil time, which might have indicated that the remonstrance and intercession of a whole church had been of the least effect.

It is probable that Knox carried the letter into England with his own hand, for at that same meeting of the General Assembly he obtained leave of absence for six months, in order to visit his two sons, who were then at school near Richmond, in Yorkshire, and to attend to some family affairs in which they, in their mother's right, had an interest. Unfortunately, nothing has been recorded of his movements in England on that occasion. It would have been interesting to hear of his visits to old friends and followers in Berwick and Newcastle, on his way to Aske, near Richmond, the seat of his first wife's mother's family. And we can scarcely doubt that he revisited London, where he had so many friends; though,

---

* We have copied this letter from the text of "Calderwood's History," vol. ii. pp. 332-35, in preference to the text of it given in "Knox's History of the Reformation," vol. ii., which is much less accurate, and the vitiations of which detract not a little from the courtesy of the authentic text.

for prudential reasons, it is highly improbable that he would make any public appearance there, in a time of so much ecclesiastical excitement and irritation.

But it is an interesting fact, now for the first time brought to light, that in these very years 1567 and 1568, he was in personal communication and correspondence with the oppressed Puritans of London; whether this arose out of personal intercourse with some of them on occasion of this visit to England, in the first of these years, or whether it was the result only of written applications made to him after his return to Scotland, for his opinion and advice. In either case, the document, which reveals to us this hitherto unknown incident in his later life, is a valuable illustration of the cordial relations in which he stood to the Puritan party, in the first decade of the reign of Elizabeth; and throws unexpected light upon a quality of character for which he does not usually get much or any credit, although his life is not without many other examples of it, namely, his *moderation*—a quality which, in his case, however unusual the case may be, was often found in co-existence with all the perfervid genius attributed to Scottish temperament in general, and with a vehemence of speech and sentiment and opinion which was specifically his own.

The document is a letter which contains ample internal evidence of having been written to Knox by one of the ministers of the first secession which took place from the National Church of England, in the years 1566 and 1567, in consequence of the suspension and subsequent deprivation of a large number of the godliest and most efficient of the London clergy. These painful incidents are narrated in Neal's "History of the Puritans," in the following paragraph:—

"At length, after having wasted about eight weeks, in 1566, to see if the Queen would have compassion upon them, several of the deprived ministers had a solemn consultation with their friends, in which, after prayer and a serious debate about the lawfulness and necessity of separating from the Established Church, they came to this agreement, 'that since they could not have the Word of God preached, nor the sacraments administered without idolatrous geare, (as they called it), and since there had been a separate congregation in London, and another at Geneva, in Queen Mary's time, which used a book and order of preaching, administration of sacraments, and discipline, that the great Mr. Calvin had approved of, and which was free from the superstitions of the English service; that, therefore, it was their duty, in their present circumstances, to break off from the public churches, and to assemble, as they had opportunity, in private houses or elsewhere, to worship God in a manner that might not offend against the light of their consciences."*

"Here was the era and date of the separation—a most unhappy event," says Mr. Strype, "whereby people of the same country, of the same religion, and of the same judgment in doctrine parted communions; one part being obliged to get aside into secret houses and chambers to serve God by themselves, which begat strangeness between neighbours, Christians, and Protestants." "And not only strangeness," adds Neal, "but unspeakable mischiefs to the nation in this and the following reigns."

The chief leaders of the separation among the deprived ministers were Messrs. Colman, Button, Halingham, Benson, White, Rowland, and Hawkins, who had all been beneficed within the diocese of London. "These had their followers of the laity, who forsook their parish churches, and assembled with the deprived ministers in woods and private houses to worship God, without the offensive habits and ceremonies of the Church." It was probably one of these ministers who wrote to Knox the letter of which we are now to make use, as an illustration of Knox's relations, as late as the year 1568, to the London Puritans, and of the view he took and the advice he gave, on occasion of that first disruption of the Church of England which has never since been healed. The reader will find the complete letter in the second part of the volume. In this place we confine ourselves to its most interesting parts, those of a personal and historical nature. It is entitled, in the manuscript which has preserved it, "A letter written to Mr. Knox," and begins thus:—

"Grace and peace and all spiritual and heavenly feeling be with you for ever.

"Dearly beloved in the Lord. After most humble wise, with most hearty thanks for your great kindness and heavenly comfort (the Lord reward you for it), it is no small grief to my heart to hear the news that is with you, how that the Queen is broken forth of prison, and hath 4,000 men with her. The Lord our God, for

* "Neal's History," vol. i. p. 230.

Christ's sake, turn it to the best, and to the comfort of his poor flock, and give grace to the Rulers, with all wisdom to consider well, with all speed."

We have here an interesting allusion to the escape of Mary Queen of Scots, from the Castle of Lochleven, an event which took place early in 1568, which determines approximately the date of the letter, and helps, with other references to matters of known fact in it, to establish its genuineness.

"Our brethren," the writer goes on, "do give hearty thanks for your gentle letter written unto them; but, to be plain with you, it is not in all points liked; and for my part, if I had known the tenor of it *when I was with you*, I would have said many words that I never spake." The writer of this must, it would seem, have been recently in Knox's society; he must have paid him a visit, in Edinburgh, on the affairs of "the congregation or church," and on that occasion Knox must have held language more or less different from the tenor of his last letter to which this was a reply.

What follows is still more curious. Having referred to the Church of the Secession as a Reformed Church, from which he and his fellow members "had no mind to go back to mixtures"—or what he calls, in another place, "a mingle-mangle ministry,"—he continues in the following strain: "Although it be but a poor church, and under perils and persecutions, and have many enemies, both open and familiar friends against it, and have no authority to defend it; and since our departure from you more enemies we have a great many, which seem somewhat to take hold of you for the defence of them, that they may the more cruelly handle us, as some of our brethren feeleth it, and is grown by the party that went away from us, which is now in great favour of the Bishop, which never was before, and hath told him and all others that you are flat against us, and condemn all our doings. At his coming home he did openly stand against the whole Church with many reviling words, and no gentle or honest means could persuade him, whereupon the Church hath excommunicated him."

Here is a curious revelation of a secession from the earliest English Secession, and of an excommunication hurled at the head of the offensive seceder, whose name we should well have liked to know. He, too, had been with Knox, apparently after the writer of the letter had been with him; and apparently, too, had put the circumstances of the case, and the question submitted to Knox's judgment, in a different light from that in which his first visitor had represented it; to which may have been owing the different tenor of Knox's letter from what had been expected. But it is curious to see the use which the deserter referred to so bitterly had made of Knox's name and opinion; how he had gone off to Bishop Grindal to tell him—not very accurately we may be sure—that John Knox himself was flat against the Secessionists, and condemned all their doings; and what serious harm had come of this to the poor outsiders, who had now more enemies than ever, and were more cruelly handled than before, since Knox was reported to have turned his back upon them.

We add one extract more from the letter: "Dearly beloved, in the first letter that ye wrote in answer to our letter when we were in the Fleete, it seemeth that ye are not well contented that we did not communicate with other churches. That is known both to God and man, and other good churches, and for four years what troubles a great many godly suffered in that space; how we were handled by the Popish Court, both in Popish excommunication and imprisonment, for that we would not go back again to the wafer-cake and kneeling, and to other knackles of Popery. That persecution grew so fast as that it brought many a hundred to know one another that never knew before; and we joined, all with one heart and mind, to serve God with pure hearts and minds according to his Word."

It was on the 19th of June, 1567, that the imprisonments in the Counter and the Fleete began, the Sheriffs of London having, on that day, detected and broken up an illegal assembly of worshippers in Plumbers' Hall, numbering about 100 souls, most of whom were taken into custody and carried off to these prisons. "The next day seven or eight of the chief were brought before the Bishop of London, the Lord Mayor, and others. On Grindal's telling them that by their proceedings in absenting themselves from their parish churches, and setting up separate assemblies for prayer and preaching and ministering the sacraments, they condemned the Church of England, which was well reformed according to the Word of God, and those martyrs that had shed their blood for it; one of them replied in the name of the rest, that they condemned them not, but only stood for the truth of God's Word. Another, Mr. John Smith, the ancientest of them, added that they thanked God for the Reformation; and as for the Book of Geneva, which they used in their private assemblies, he offered, in the name of the rest, to yield and do penance at St. Paul's Cross, if the Bishop and the Commissioners with him could reprove that book or anything else that they held by the Word of God. The Bishop told him they could not reprove the book, but that was no sufficient answer for not going to church. One of them delivered to Justice Harris their Book of Order—the Geneva Book, and challenged any of the Commissioners to disprove it by the Word of God, and they would give it over. Again the Bishop replied, that they reproved it not, but they liked not their separate assemblies to trouble the common quiet of the realm against the Queen's will. But the others insisted on their superior regard to the Word of God. In conclusion, the prisoners not yielding to the Bishop, were sent to Bridewell, where they, with their brethren and sundry women, were kept in durance above a year."*

It is interesting to learn, for the first time, from the letter to Knox, that these heroic admirers of the Book of Geneva bethought themselves, in their miserable imprisonment, of its chief author, and put themselves into communication with him, by letters and messengers, in order to receive the benefit of his advice. They knew that they could calculate on his sympathy with their views, for were not these the principles which he had himself embodied in his Book of Common Order? They knew, also, that he could not but honour and appreciate their sufferings in such a cause, for had not he been a sufferer in the same cause himself? In truth, the very spirit of Knox himself seemed to have entered into many of these men of conscience and godly courage. They were Puritans in his very image and likeness, and confessors of the truth quite after his own heart. And they were not mistaken in their hope. His first letter to them was written while they were yet in the Fleet; and it is much to be regretted that neither that letter nor the later one has come down to us; for, no doubt, like the "Two Comfortable Epistles sent to his afflicted Brethren in England," in 1554, "exhorting them to bear Christ's Cross with patience, looking every hour for his coming again to the great comfort and consolation of his chosen," they were "a word in season' to the sufferers, full of strong consolation in Christ, and bountiful in the supply of the "strong meat" drawn from the word of righteousness, "which belongeth to them that are of full age."

* "Neal's History," vol. i. pp. 242-3.

All we know of them is, that they called forth "most hearty thanks for his great kindness and heavenly comfort." "Our brethren do give hearty thanks for your gentle letter." Might the Lord reward him for it. He did for them, by his pen, the same office of fatherly love, as a comforter, which his former colleague at Frankfort, the learned and godly Thomas Lever, did for them by his personal visits to the Fleete and other prisons. But it is remarkable that neither from Lever nor from Knox were the persecuted prisoners able to obtain, notwithstanding all their sympathy with them in their affliction, an approval of their action in separating from the National Church. The proof of this, in the case of Lever, will be found in a "writing which he delivered to the prisoners of Bridewell, on the 5th of December, 1568," which is mentioned by Mr. Neal in his "History of the Puritans,"* and, in the case of Knox, the proof is forthcoming, in abundance, from the letter before us. As his correspondent frankly tells him, his letter to the Secessionist Church "was not in all points liked." In one particular of his judgment, indeed, they all agreed with him, viz., that "certain men should not escape the judgments of God, without hearty repentance for molesting and troubling the hearts and consciences of the godly, and for maintaining things in the Church for which, by the Word of God, they have no ground." This judgment had always been a chief point in his public and private testimony. But in separating themselves entirely from the National Church, on account of certain things retained in it without a Divine warrant, and in still keeping up that separation, they had adopted a course which he was not prepared to approve of, or to recommend others to follow. "God forbid," he had written to them, "that we should damn all for false prophets and heretics that agree not with us in apparell and other opinions, who yet preach the substance of doctrine and salvation in Christ Jesus." He "could not allow or approve of those that obstinately do refuse to hear the message of salvation at such men's mouths as please not us in all things." He had reminded them that "though Paul was offended with Peter and sharply rebuked him, and in that did very well, yet for all that he dissuaded none of his auditors from his preaching; and that though Paul and Barnabas had a contention about John Mark, yet they both held the truth and might both be

* Vol. i. p. 250.

very well heard, for neither of them preached false doctrine, neither maintained anything against the ordinance of Christ." He had also, it seems, drawn an argument from the conduct of Paul in performing the ceremonial act of purification in the temple of Jerusalem. On the whole, he had not been able to see that their consciences had sufficient ground, in the Scriptures, for the view which they had taken of their duty in the circumstances; he wished that their consciences had a better ground. "The matter," also was weighty, "for it condemned the public ministry of England, and he was not well contented that, before taking so grave a step, they did not first communicate with other Churches."

Such appear to have been some of the reasonings of Knox in his second letter, revealing to us the remarkable fact that, however much he loved and admired the Secessionists, and appreciated some of the principles and motives which had impelled them to take a step which had involved them in so much loss and suffering, still, in his deliberate judgment, he could not approve of their deed of secession. It was at least premature; the time for it, to say the least, was not yet full come. A further Reformation was yet to be hoped for, and it was the duty of all the members of the Church who prayed for it, to stay patiently in the Church, and do their utmost there to obtain it. Such was Knox's *moderation*. He had exhibited the same before, when, in 1552, he had counselled his followers in Berwick to submit, without resistance, to the imposition of the Prayer-book, notwithstanding their objection to kneeling in the Lord's Supper and other remains of Romish practice, because the progress already made towards perfection, beyond expectation, in that very Prayer-book, encouraged the hope of still further purity. And why despair any more now than then? Much indulgence had been shown, for a good many years back, on points of Non-Conformity. Were men at once to abandon all hope of seeing a return, in the Church's rulers, to a milder and wiser policy than was now pursued? Were they not rather to possess their souls in patience; to work on and fight on in the cause of reform, giving God thanks for the victories of the past, and taking courage for the future?

All honour to these religious heroes and heroines, martyrs to the cause of truth and liberty! So felt, with all their hearts, men like Knox and Lever; and they were not wanting to their oppressed brethren in the hour of need, oft refreshing them with their sympathy, and "not ashamed of their chain." But none the less there was room for difference of judgment, even among the most staunch and conscientious Puritans, on the question of the requirements of duty, under the conditions and circumstances in which they were then placed. The Bishop of London had some good grounds for urging, in his remarkable interview with the leaders of the Secession, "Have you not the Gospel truly preached and the Sacraments duly ministered, though we differ from other Churches in indifferent ceremonies, which the Prince has power to command for the sake of order." And the very same argument, as we have seen, was urged by Knox. It was this argument, in fact, which weighed with the great bulk both of the Puritan ministers and people at that trying time, who disapproved of the secession and kept aloof from it, however much they, no doubt, sympathized with the afflictions of their persecuted brethren. None of the ministers most eminent for ability and learning, deeply as they too were suffering for their Non-Conformity, took part in the separation. "Most of the Puritans," as Neal observes, "were unwilling to separate from a Church where the Word and Sacraments were truly administered, though defiled with some Popish superstitions. Of this number were Dr. Humphrey, Sampson, Foxe the martyrologist, Lever, Whittingham, Gilby, and others, who continued preaching up and down, as they had opportunity, and could be dispensed with for the habits, though they were excluded all parochial preferment." Dr. Turner, also, the learned Puritan Dean of Wells, wrote, in the same sense, an "Examination of the proposition that no parishioner ought to hear the preaching of his pastor or other common preachers that keep any abrogated ceremonies, or use any several kind of garments which Popes and other superstitious men have devised and brought into the Church without any authority of the Word of God, although the same pastor and preachers do preach that Jesus is Christ and the only Saviour of the world, and that the Pope is the right Antichrist, and that the Mass is abominable and full of foul idolatry."[*]

Nor was it only the chief men of the older generation of Puritans who stood aloof from the Separatists, but the men also of most mark and likelihood of the younger generation now coming into prominence. It does not appear that the group of Secessionist

[*] A copy of this "Examination" is preserved in the "Second Part of a Register," among the "Morrice Papers" in Dr. Williams's library, side by side with Lever's "Writing delivered to the Prisoners of Bridewell."

ministers before named were men of much standing or weight among their Puritan brethren. All the ablest men of the new race of Elizabethan Puritans—Field, Wilcox, Cartwright, Travers, Fulk, Rainolds, and many more—took a different view of their duty, viz., to abide in the Church, though often forbidden to preach in it, and to do their utmost to obtain a more thorough and satisfactory reform. These men, taking rank among the ablest and best men in the Church, were all, ecclesiastically, the children of the Presbyterian Puritans of Frankfort and Geneva—the children of Knox; and it was gratifying to come upon the unexpected evidence supplied by this letter, that Knox, now of venerable age, was of the same mind and judgment as his sons at this crisis of the history of that great Party, when so much of the future, both of the Party and of the Church embracing it in its bosom, depended upon the line of action now followed.

The moderation which Knox manifested on this occasion was all the more remarkable that his dislike to the Prayer-book had not been on the decrease, but very much the contrary, during the thirteen years which had elapsed since the conflict in which it had engaged him with Dr. Cox and others, in Frankfort, in 1555. It is far from correct to allege that the painful issue of that conflict had anything to do with that unfavourable change in the *substance* of his opinion of the Book, which he publicly announced on that occasion, inasmuch as his announcement of it took place some days before that issue was reached;* but it no doubt had much to do with the bitterness of tone in which, for several years afterwards, he gave expression to his altered and much more hostile views. Nor, of course, was that bitterness diminished by the treatment which he received at the hands of Queen Elizabeth and her Council in 1559, when his urgent request to be allowed to land in England, on his way to Scotland—*i.e.*, simply to have a letter of safe-conduct through the country—was repeatedly and peremptorily refused; treatment which, however much Knox had provoked it by his injudicious and ill-timed " First Blast of the Trumpet against the

* Such an allegation is made by Bishop Wordsworth, of St. Andrew's, in his " Discourse on the Scottish Reformation," in the interesting chapter on " Knox and the English Reformers," where he calls attention to the change which passed over Knox's mind in regard to the English Liturgy, and throughout which he does not distinguish sufficiently, we think, between change of opinion and change of tone.

Monstrous Regiment of Women," might fairly and with no loss of dignity to the Queen, have been abstained from, in consideration of the important services which he had rendered to the English Church and nation during King Edward's reign. It was under the sting of these repeated mortifications that he wrote a letter, in 1559, to Mrs. Locke, of London, in which, in answer to her inquiries, he told her his opinion of the "Great Book of England," in language of a more vehement kind than he had ever before used, and which he was himself aware "would be judged extreme and rigorous," even by Mrs. Locke and others of his English friends. "England hath refused me," he exclaimed, in much bitterness of heart, "and yet have I been a secret and assured friend to thee, O England! in cases which thyself could not have remedied. God grant that their ingratitude may not be punished with severity, and that ere they be aware! And thus, with sorrowful heart, I commit thee to the Omnipotent." This bitterness of tone, however, gradually gave way under the softening influence of the alliance which was soon after formed between the two kingdoms for the defence of their common faith against France and the other Catholic powers, and under the genial operation of gratitude, which he expressed very warmly, for the seasonable aid which was sent by Elizabeth to the relief of the Scottish Protestants. But the substance of his opinion of the Liturgy remained the same as before, and all the rather that the Elizabethan revision of it had been the reverse of an improvement, from the Puritan point of view, and that he must have noted with especially high disapprobation the omission, by way of concession to the Papists, of that very "Declaration on Kneeling" which was obtained with so much difficulty by his own efforts in 1552. And hence the language—only not strong enough to be vehement—which he used in referring to the Prayer-book, in the letter sent by the Superintendents of the Scottish Church to the English bishops. In these circumstances it would not have been surprising if he had approved of the course taken by the London Secessionists in 1566, and encouraged them to persevere in it, as the Secessionists themselves evidently expected that he would have done. So great, indeed, is the apparent inconsistency of his action on this occasion with his declared opinion of the Liturgy, and no less with his action in relation to the use of it in Frankfort and Geneva, that it is necessary to remind the reader of the explanation which he gave in his "Epistle to the Congregation of Berwick" of the course which he prescribed to himself and recommended to them in anticipation of conformity to the Rubric on Kneeling being insisted upon by "the upper powers." It is in what he held to be due to "the upper powers," when these powers were, on the whole or in the main, on the side of Reformation-truth, that we find the reconciling principle, which redeems him from inconsistency, and harmonizes his action on all these occasions. "The counsel of all godly, as also the testimony of my own conscience, is that less offence it is to bear this one thing (with dolour of your hearts, daily calling unto God for reformation of the same) than to provoke the magistrates to displeasure, seeing that in principals we all agree." In Berwick and Newcastle and London, he and his brother Puritans were under authority of "the magistrates," the rulers of Church and State; and they must all bear patiently the things which they disapproved of, praying and labouring for a farther reformation. But, in Frankfort and Geneva, he and his brother Puritans were no longer bound by English rulers, and were left free by the magistrates of those cities to worship God according to their own conscientious convictions: why, then, should they not avail themselves of that liberty? To be conformists in the one case and nonconformists in the other involved no inconsistency or contradiction, either in him who advised both these courses, or in those who followed his advice. The difference of conditions in the two cases warranted—and, in conscience, demanded—a difference of action and conduct. Not, indeed, that it was meant by Knox that the "conditions" of the question of the duty of conformity might not be so far changed in the lapse of time, that non-conformity might become the duty of Puritans, even at the risk, or . with the certainty, of "provoking the magistrates to displeasure," and of making themselves amenable to pains and penalties. That change of conditions would arrive when there was no longer any hope remaining of a farther reformation of the National Church, after long and patient waiting and striving for it. All that Knox counselled on the side of conformity was counselled *provisionally*,—for the time then present, in the hope of a better time coming, when the work of reformation would be carried to more perfect issues. His words were—"not to break or trouble common order, thought meet to be kept for unity and peace in the congregations *for a time*."

Knox's communications with the London Secessionists are a fresh proof how lovingly he continued to interest himself in the Puritans of the South, in the midst of all his labours and struggles, as the hero of the triumphant though still menaced Presbyterianism of the Northern Kingdom. Indeed, at this very time, we have it under his own hand that his heart and his thoughts were with his English brethren in a more than ordinary degree, for only a few months before the date of the letter on which we have been commenting, he expressed himself to a friend then living in England, Mr. John Wood, secretary to the Regent Murray, in the following singularly warm-hearted and interesting terms:—

Having referred, in his letter, to the religous troubles of France at that epoch,—" God for his great mercies' sake put such end to the troubles of France, as the purity of his Evangel may have free passage within that realm"—he adds : " In my opinion England and Scotland have both no less cause to fear than the faithful in France, for what they suffer in present action is laid up in store, let us be assured, for both countries. The ground of my assurance is not the determination of the Council of Trent, for that decree is but the utterance of their own malice ; but the justice of God is my assurance, for it cannot spare to punish all realms and nations that are or shall be like to Jerusalem, against whose iniquity God long cried, by his servants the prophets, but found no repentance. The truth of God hath now, of some years, been manifested to both ; but what obedience the words, works, and behaviour of men give sufficient testimony. The defence and maintenance of superstitious trifles produced never better fruit, in the end, than I perceive is budding amongst you—*schism*—which, no doubt, is a forerunner of greater desolation, unless there be speedy repentance. God comfort that dispersed little flock (alluding to the English congregation at Geneva) amongst whom I once lived with quietness of conscience and contentment of heart, and amongst whom I would be content to end my days, if so it might stand with God's good pleasure ; for seeing it hath pleased His Majesty, above all men's expectation, to prosper that work, for the performing whereof I left that company, I would even as gladly return to them, if they stood in need of my labours, as ever I was glad to be delivered from the rage of mine enemies. I can give you no reason that I should so desire other than that my heart so thirsteth.

" *14th Feb.*, 1567-68."

It was thus, that—when the battle of his warrior life was well nigh over, and his great conquest for his own beloved country well assured, and when he was now, like the worn war-horse, beginning to long for and to dream of the quiet green paddock where he was to rest and be thankful, after so many sore campaigns—his fancy wandered in its fond musings, not, as might have been thought, to his native fields in East Lothian and to the green banks of Tyne, flowing softly by the beautiful old church of Haddington, on its smiling way to the Firth of Forth, but turned back to the hills and vales of England, which he had so often and so long traversed, from sea to sea, as one of her earliest evangelists. "God comfort," he exclaimed, "that dispersed little flock." He foresaw coming troubles in England, and he desired once more, before he died, to be their comforter. Just as, many years before, at the moment of his flight from England, he had written to Mrs. Bowes, at the end of his Exposition of the 6th Psalm: "My daily prayer is for the sore afflicted in those quarters." He meant the terrified Protestants of England, under Mary. "Sometime I have thought that impossible it had been so to have removed my affection from the realm of Scotland; that any realm or nation could have been equally dear unto me. But God I take to record in my conscience that the troubles present and appearing to be in the realm of England, are double more dolorous unto my heart than ever were the troubles of Scotland."

In this feature of love, so deep and so touchingly expressed, for England and her people, especially her godly people, Knox was as singular, in that age of constant wars and enmities between the two kingdoms, as he was rare and original in so many other respects. He had evidently quite got over the first home-born feeling expressed in the old Scottish phrase, "our auld enemies of England." To this grand, rough, heroic Scotsman the "auld enemies" had become "new friends," both loved and loving; and more and more deeply loved, because more and more deeply loving to him for his work's sake.

Nor was his love for England and the godly English unrequited, even by Englishmen who never saw him, and who only knew him by his writings. He complains, indeed, with a dignified brevity, in his last letter to Cecil, written at the beginning of 1570, that he had been "fremmedly handelled," *i.e.*, treated like a stranger or foreigner, "yet was he never enemy to the quietness of England;" but that was in writing his last words to the "Principal Secretary to the Queen's Majesty and Council of England." It was only in the highest places of the realm that he had been so handled—only by the Queen and her Court; but among the bulk of the nation his name was held in high esteem and honour; and we cannot close our narrative better than by producing a remarkable example of this fact, which dates only eleven years after his death in 1572.

The name has already been mentioned of John Field, an able and active man among the Elizabethan Puritans, and, indeed, their leading man, before Thomas Cartwright of Cambridge came to the front. It was Field who wrote the "First Admonition to Parliament," a paper of historical importance, in 1571, and who founded the Presbytery of Wandsworth, the first Presbytery in England, in 1572. Now it is an interesting fact, that it was John Field who first sent to the press what he intituled "The notable and comfortable Exposition of Maister John Knox, upon the 4th of Matthew, concerning the Temptations of Christ; first had in the public church, and then afterwards written for the comfort of certain private friends, but now published for the benefit of all that fear God." This was in 1583. Field had had the loan of the MS. from Mrs. Ann Prouze, of Exeter, who had formerly been the wife of Edward Deering, a famous Presbyterian Puritan, of Cambridge and London, and he had sent it to the press without her knowledge, for which he pleads, in apology, as follows: "And methink it is not meete that that which was first publicly done in the church by so worthy and notable an instrument of God as Mr. John Knox was, it also being a thing that would be so fruitful and comfortable to many, that it should lie any longer in the dust in secret, and not be published to the comfort of all. For, first, amongst the rest, it is a seal of his godly and wonderful labours, carrying in the forehead thereof of what an heroical and bold spirit he was; how faithfully and constantly he stood for the glorious truth and religion of Jesus Christ; and how mightily, in the end, after many and tedious troubles, persecutions, and calamities, God gave him yet a victory, so that he prevailed against all those bulls of Bashan. If ever God shall vouchsafe the Church so great a benefit, when his infinite letters and sundry other treatises shall be gathered together, it shall appear what an excellent man he was, and what a wonderful loss that Church of Scotland sustained when that worthy man was taken from them.

... If, by yourself or others, you can procure any other of his writings or letters, here at home or abroad, in Scotland or in England, be a meane that we may receive them. It was great pitie that any, the least of his writings, should be lost, for he evermore wrote most godly and diligently in questions of divinitie, and also of church pollicie; and his letters, being had together, would together set out an whole history of the Churches where he lived."

Such was the enthusiasm of esteem and love which was once felt in England for this grand old father and founder of English and Scottish Puritanism—for this man, so much above the common mould in head, heart, will, speech and action; for this hero of the pulpit and the pen, who never feared the face of man; this man of true, unsophisticated, undiluted manhood,—John Knox.

> Cura Dei: Romae pestis: Mundi horror, et Orci
> Pernicies; coeli fulmen ab arce tonans.

JOHANNES KNOXUS.

Primus Evangelii Instaurator in Scotia, post superiora cruenta illa tempora, obiit placide Edinburgi. "xxiv. ix *bris, hora undecima*, 1572."

> Hic ille est Scotorum Knoxus Apostolus olim,
>   Cui prior hos ingens Beza dedit titulos;
> Interpres cœli, vero qui numine plenus,
>   Plurima venturi praescia signa dedit.
> Facundum pectus, libertas maxima fandi.
>   Totus inexhausto flagrat amore Dei.
> Quam pia cura Poli, tam humani meta furoris;
> . Tanto plus victor, quo furit iste magis.
> Post varios hostes aggressa calumnia tandem,
>   Hoc didicit, nulli nec sibi habere fidem.
> Heroum Pietas odio est mortalibus. Unum hoc
>   Arguat Heroem hunc coelitus esse datum.*

* From John Johnston's Περὶ Στεφάνων—Sive De Coronis Martyrum in Scotia. MS. in Bibl. Facult. Jurid. Edin. A.

PART SECOND.

KNOX-PAPERS.

INTRODUCTORY NOTE.

"The Morrice Collection of Manuscripts" in Dr. Williams's Library, Grafton Street, London.

THE valuable Collection of Manuscripts, in which the following Knox-Papers have been preserved, is described, in the Preface to the Catalogue of the Manuscripts of Dr. Williams's Library, drawn up by the late Mr. W. H. Black, in the following terms :—

"The Historical Collections of the Rev. Roger Morrice, M.A., one of the ejected ministers, appear to have been the labour of above forty years after his ejectment, and describe and illustrate the history of the Reformation, the persecutions endured by the Puritans, their holy and devout lives, the whole history of the times in which the writer lived ; and appear to have been largely and freely used by Neal, in his "History of the Puritans," and perhaps by other writers, who have not acknowledged the source of their information. To this latter cause is owing the fact, that little is known of the writer. He died in 1701, and was buried in Bunhill Fields. By what means, or when this invaluable Collection was deposited here, has not been yet ascertained."

The volume of this Collection, entitled "A Copy of the Second Part of a Register," and in which I first came in sight of the Knox-Papers, is described by Mr. Black, in his Catalogue, under the letter C, as follows :—

"A large and very thick volume, bound in rough calf, and by the name of the Rough Calf MS. referred to in some of Mr. Morrice's MSS. The contents of the volume consist of transcripts or entries of various tracts and documents, made by Mr. Morrice's amanuensis, in a neat and legible hand ; and they bear references to the sources from which they were transcribed, written (with the word 'Finis') at the end of each separate article or entry. The title, 'A Copy of the Second Part of a Register,' is from the same hand as occurs in others of the Morrice MSS., where the Collection is referred to as 'The Rough Calf MS.'"

Prefixed is a list of the quotations made from the MS. by Neal, amounting to 78. Prefixed, also, is "the inscription on Morrice's tombstone, in Bunhill Fields, flat on the ground :"

" Here lyeth y⁰ Body of Mr. Roger Morrice, M.A., and Chaplain to the late Honble. Denzil Lord Hollis, who departed y⁰ life, y⁰ 17th day of January, 1701, Ætat. 73."

Mr. Neal, in the preface to the first volume of his "History of the Puritans," dated February 1, 1731–32, has the following reference to this MS. volume as one of his principal sources :—

"I have cited my authorities in the margin, and flatter myself that I have had the opportunity of bringing many things to light, relating to the sufferings of the Puritans and the state of the Reformation in those times, which have hitherto been unknown to the world, chiefly by the assistance of a large Manuscript Collection of Papers, faithfully transcribed from their originals in the University of Cambridge, by a person of character employed for that purpose, and generously communicated to me by my ingenious and learned friend Dr. Benjamin Grosvenor, for which I take this opportunity of returning him my own and the thanks of the publick."

In Bishop Maddox's "Vindication of the Government, Doctrine, and Worship of the Church of England, against the injurious Reflections of Mr. Neal, etc.," 1740, he blames Mr. Neal, and not without reason, for not having given a more satisfactory account of a Manuscript upon which he had founded so extensively in his "History." The passage occurs at p. 190 :—

" It ought to be remarked that Mr. Neal's account of their sufferings, and behaviour that occasioned these sufferings, is chiefly taken from themselves; he has obtained, as he acquaints us in his preface, a copy of a large MS. Collection of Papers, the originals whereof are said to be lodged in the University of Cambridge, but he names no particular library or college; nor does he acquaint us when the Papers themselves were wrote, by whom, or who was the collector of them. In short, his account of this MS. Collection of Papers upon which he lays so great stress, is the most unsatisfactory and unscholarlike that can be imagined. This gentleman says (p. 201), 'if we may believe Dr. Whitgift,' etc., and yet gives entire credit to anonymous MS. which ought to have been supported by some unquestionable authority, since, by his own account, it brings many things to light hitherto unknown to the world. This he quotes, upon all occasions, as substantial evidence, though it plainly appears to be a very angry and partial account. A MS. is not to be credited merely for being such; and this, in particular, may be convicted of great mistakes." Farther on Maddox speaks of it as "an unknown Manuscript."

In Neal's "Review of the Principal Facts objected to in the first volume of the History of the Puritans," he has the following remarks, in reply to the above strictures of Maddox :—

"Our author is pleased to pour great contempt on Mr. Neal's Manuscript Collection of Original Papers, because it brings to light some of those unjustifiable severities which the historians of those times had omitted; but its authority shall be left with the reader after he is acquainted that it was collected many years ago at the expense of the Rev. Mr. Humphrey (Roger) Morrice, some time Chaplain to Denzil Lord Hollis, who employed an amanuensis in the University of Cambridge for this purpose, whose name I could mention, if it were proper; but it is sufficient to say that at the foot of most of the Papers there are references to the places from whence they were copied; and the industrious Mr. Strype seemed so well satisfied of the authority of this MS. that, at his own request, he was permitted to transcribe from it several of those papers that are among his records."

It is remarkable that Neal should not have been able to go beyond this small additional amount of information, in reply to the Churchman's challenge. No doubt he fell back upon his friend Dr. Grosvenor, who had lent him the MS., for fuller particulars of its history; but Dr. Grosvenor would not appear to have been able to give him even the correct Christian name of Mr. Morrice, and Mr. Neal remained silent on the subject of the library in Cambridge where "the originals" were to be found.

In this unsatisfactory condition the question continued down to our own time, when much fresh light was thrown upon it by Mr. Black, in his Catalogue of the whole of the Morrice Collection of MSS., which had all, since Neal's time, found their way into Dr. Williams's Library.

Among these is catalogued a MS. volume marked by Mr. Black as B, which he describes as "an inconveniently thick book, consisting of a great number of transcripts, made in the time of Queen Elizabeth, chiefly by one hand, bound together in a coarse and insufficient wrapper of parchment. There are two series of numerations, first by pages, afterwards by folios; accordingly, the contents are referred to in Mr. Morrice's books [meaning Mr. Morrice's original writings, still in MS., founded in part upon his MSS. collection] as vols. i. and ii. of the MSS. It is a Collection of Ecclesiastical Documents relative to the state of Religion in England, in the reign of Queen Elizabeth, the proceedings of the Puritan Ministers, and the persecutions which they endured from the hierarchy, designed as a continuation or second part of the old printed book, entitled 'A Parte of a Register containing sundry memorable matters, written by divers godly and learned men in our time, etc.,' consisting altogether of 127 numbered articles."

Here, then, is the "original collection," of which the MS. collection used by Mr. Neal was a copy, as it bears to have been on its title, "A Copy of the Second Parte of a Register." The references at the end of all the Papers found in the "copy" correspond exactly with the papers and pagination of the older collection, which goes back to the days of Elizabeth.

Mr. Morrice himself left a description of this earlier collection, at page 126 of a MS. volume, described as "his largest parchment-covered folio," as follows:—

"These Papers treat of transactions in Queen Elizabeth's reign. They are very fair and free from any interlineations or alterations. *They are in my possession.* They contain the copies of divers Bills that were presented, debated or past in divers Parliaments, and of others drawn up to be printed; and of divers original letters; and of the proceedings against divers persons, written by them that were ear-witnesses thereof while they were fresh on memory, or taken out of the Registers of the said Courts; and of many other considerable matters not in print. They seem to be as worthy of credit as anything we have relating to that reign. I have, in many instances, compared them with the best and truest accounts we have of ecclesiastical matters in that Queen's time, and find them exactly agreeing with, and sometimes perfecting those."

In another place Mr. Morrice characterizes this Collection, as having been brought together " by a most faithful, understanding, observing gentleman, who died about the end of Elizabeth's reign," but the name of the collector was not known to him, otherwise he would have given it.

Mr. Neal, then, was clearly mistaken in the statement which he twice over made, that "the originals," from which his "large Manuscript Collection of Papers" was copied, were in the University of Cambridge at the time he wrote. They may, indeed, have been there at the date when the " copy of the Second Parte of a Register" was made, but if so, they had subsequently come into the possession of Mr. Morrice, nobody can tell how; they were in his possession at the time he wrote the description of them just given, and it is remarkable that Mr. Morrice, who knew best where he obtained them, says nothing of their ever having been in Cambridge.

Mr. Neal appealed, in proof of the authority of his "large Manuscript Collection," to the use which Strype had made of several of the Papers contained in it, and the appeal was a very relevant one in support of that point. Strype was one of Mr. Morrice's correspondents, and refers to him in his edition of Stowe's " Survey of the Cities of London and Westminster," vol. II., p. 57, as "a very diligent collector of ecclesiastical MSS., relating to the later history of the English Church, whereof he left vast heaps behind him, and who favoured me with his correspondence." But it is curious that the manner in which Strype refers to the source from which he derived the papers which Neal refers to as having been used by Strype, goes far to discredit the statement of Neal that the "originals of the Morrice copies" had once been, or still were, in the University of Cambridge. When Strype refers, in his margin, to the MS. source from which he drew these papers, he describes it repeatedly as a *private*, not a public one. But Strype was a Cambridge antiquary, and had the best opportunities of knowing the contents of the libraries and archives in that University. He had several indefatigable correspondents there— Mr. Laughton, the University Librarian, Mr. Baker, of St. John's College, and Mr. Harrison, of Sidney-Sussex College—who did all they could to supply him with copies of letters and historical documents preserved in the University Collections. But he had evidently never heard of the "Second Parte of a Register" as existing there. He refers to it always as a *manuscriptum priva-*

tum. It was in the hands of a private collector, meaning Mr. Morrice, his correspondent.

Not a few of the papers contained in the older collection, described by Mr. Morrice, are "originals" in the strictest sense; but the "Knox-Papers," now published for the first time, are not of the number. On being submitted to the judgment of the heads of the MSS. Department of the British Museum, they were pronounced to be not *originals* but *contemporary transcripts*. They go back, therefore, in date of transcription, to the reigns of Edward VI. and Elizabeth, and, so far as age goes, they lay claim to a historical validity and value scarcely inferior, for practical purposes, to that of originals.

As for the originals themselves, the author has, as yet, searched for them in vain. After several days' hunting in Cambridge, he found that Mr. Neal had certainly put him upon the wrong scent. The most learned librarians of the University had never seen or heard of them. The custodian of the Cecil Papers at Hatfield House, too, could only answer inquiries in the negative; and, though better success is not yet to be despaired of, we must stand prepared to find, in the end, that these writings of the Scottish Reformer have, like many of his other compositions, been saved from oblivion only by the zeal of early friends and admirers, who were more careful to preserve copies of them than he was himself.

I.

JOHNE KNOKKS to the Congregatioun of Bervik, grace be multiplied and peace from God the Father of our Lord Jesus Christ, with all yat unfeynedlie thristis the glorie of his name. Amen.

1.* I have thought it my dewitie (most dearlie beloved bretherin) not onlie to signifie unto you my present estait, bot also in the bowelles of Jesus Christ to require of you bold continuance in that treuthe which ones ye have professede. Ffor ignorant am I not what artes our adversarie the Devill most commonlie useth to draw back such as would go forwarde in the happy journey of life everlasting. Rychteouslie was he compared of Job to that great leviathan, and by the Apostle to a roring lione, for as the one feareth no dart casten or shote by the strenthe of man, and the other hunteth most greedilie for his pray, so cannot our enemye be resisted (much less ordered) by man's pouer or possebilitie; whois vigilantie was such that in maligning against God he cannot wearye, for he is a spreit confirmed with malice against God, against his chosen Church and the verity thereof, in which (veritie, I meane) as that he stuide not, but falling from the samyn became a liear and father of lies, so lacked he nowder practess nor ingine, how that he may cause lies to appear treuth, and simple treuth to appear dampnable lies; and thus most he raige as he hathe done from the begynnyng unto such tyme as the nomber of Goddis elect be fullie compleitt, of whom the most part hes vincust the wicked world by grevous torments and panes, whill by Goddis permissioun they were troden under feit of that cruell enemye who never ceases to accuse Godd's elect.

2. Ffor as of God the Father it is given to the seade of the woman to breik downe the heide of that venemoss serpent, so is it permitted to the samyn serpent to sting and trouble the heill of that holie seade, not in such sort as the most part of men suppose, in tempting and pricking the flesh

---

* The paragraphs of this long letter have been numbered by the Editor to facilitate reference.

with such temptations as commonlie followeth man, but oftentymes so prevailing (after the judgment of creatures earthlie) against the hoile [whole] man that the wicked appeares to have gotten victorie, and God's chosen may seme to be brought to extreme confusioun. As in Cayn and Abell, Esaw and Jacob, Joseph and Phutifer's [Potiphar's] wife, in Pharo and the Israelits, Daniell and Darius' Counsellars, the Princes of the Preestes and Jesus Christ, his Appostles and the Synagogue, and finallie in all martyrs and the malignant church, most manifestlie haith appeared. Ffor who could behold Abell lying under his brother Cayn crying for mercie, whare [where] he never offended, and yet obtenyng nothing but cruellie to be murthered, and shuld not say now haith iniquitie gotten the upper hand, the wicked prevailed, and the just lyeth undder fute. Who, considering simpell Jacob, not onlie fleeing from his father's house and cuntree, with his staff in his hand, for fear of stoutt Esaw, but also return- yng with great substance, sevine tymes to bow and mak homeges before the face of his brother, and his companye; who, I say, considering this, shuld not think Esaw is the lorde and hes gotten the dominione, but Jacob as a slave and remaineth in boundage. And thus may ye reson of the rest, whom ye shall finde so geven over for a tyme in the hands of the ungodlie, yat not onlie are they deprived of honor, libertie, fame and life, but also the best beloved sometymes appears left comfortless, as in Jesus Christ we lerne; who upon the Croce, after ignomynie and most cruell panes susteaned, lamentablie cryed to his heavenlie Father, My God, my God, why hest thou forsacken me? O dolorous voce of the Sone of God, spokin not in secreate place, but in the audience of his raiging and rejosing [rejoicing] enemies, to the establissing of all thair manifest iniquitie! Mycht they not now tryumphe, seeing he had confessed the chief poynts of thair accusatioun, which wes that he had usurped to him- selfe honor and authoritie that God had not granted to him, and that he had made himself God, being butt man; that by false doctrine he deceaved the pepill? Mycht they not now collect and gather of Christis words he is nother God nor yett Goddis chosen, for he compleynes that God has forsaiken him; but God cannot forsaik his elect, and much lesse himself, whairfor this Christ is nother God nor Goddis elect, but a dyssaver, a blas- phemer and a false teacher, as evin we accused him.

3. Thus, deirlie beluived, appeared to prevaill those that in delicatie drinking wine, did oppin thair mouthes against the anoynted of God. Off these thinges put I you in remembrance, dearly beloved, for two causes principall—Ffirst, that by the sufferance of all Goddis elect, and by Christis passioun especiallie, ye shall learn how odious and detestable syn is in the sycht of our hevinlie Father, whose justice is so inviolable yat it most nedes require a satisfactioun of all fleshe whair offence is com- mitted. And because that impossible it was to any sinfull fleshe at any tyme to fulfill the law (muche less to mak reconciliatioun betwene Godd's

justice and man's transgressions bypast, present and to come) God sent his alone Sone in the similitude of sinfull fleshe, that he that knew no syn, by his sacrifice ones offered shuld sanctifie and mak perfitt for ever those that shuld inherit the kingdom prepared. In which sacrifice and oblatioun he alone did satisfie his father's justice; for he, taiking upon his awin back the burden that oppressed all mankind, I meane the synnes of man (not to commit them but to suffer for them), did also taiste the cuppe of his Father's wraithe and indignation most justlie conceaved aginst syn. And this his portioun and cuppe he drank not with silence but oppinlie proclamed in his agonie and paine that his Father haiteth syn and culd not suffire the same unpunist, but loved mankind and thairfor gave to deith the substance of his awin glorie, yat, a satisfactioun maid by him who onlie was able to pay the same, the rest of his sones might be maid free, not to syn and rejose in the same, for that is not propire to Godd's children regenerate. Understand, dear bretherne, what I write unto you. The bitter passioun and grevous panes susteaned by Christ Jesus geveth no libertie to syn, but rychteouslie considered, daylie dothe kille and mortifie syn in these our mortal bodies, that we rejose not in the same. Ffor if we communicatt with Christis deith and passioun by a trewe faith, than are we membres of his bodie and childern of oure hevinlie Father. Bot the membres cannot rejose that they have killed thaire heade, not yett the naturall childern yat thai daylie displease thair loving Father. Membres we are of Christis bodye, so maynie as unfeynedlie beleves upon him, and yet ourselves killed our Heade the only Sone of God. Can we rejose in so cruell acte as daylie to crucifie the Sone of God; and who rejoseth in syn assuredly rejoseth yat he killeth the Son of God. I say not bretherne that we are clene from syn, for suich is no fleshe that liveth on earth; but I say that Godd's elect yat after regeneratioun and embraising of the treuthe, of no loung continuance can rejose or delitte in manifest iniquitie, for the unctioun of the holie Ghost dothe teache to Godd's childern the will of thair hevinlie Father, which albeit they be never able to accomplishe and fulfil as the rigor of the law requyreth, yet when they work expresslie aganst the same they fynd some dolor and compunctioun in hart; as also, if thair syns be manifest, most commonlie they are called to manifest repentance, and do suffer in the fleshe punishment and plagues; which plagues, albeit they be no wyse satisfactorye for man's iniquitie (for yat is propire only to the passioun of him that never offended), yet do they teache us how severlye God doth punishe syn, evin in his elect and chosen vessellis, that by thair examplis admonished we may also lerne to haitt in ourselves the crymes and vicess which God haith declared himself to hait in his most especiall servants. Flatter not yourselves, beloved brethern, God is immutable, and what he hes punished in one age, realme, natioun, citie or person, this same most his just judgments hait and punish in everye realme, natioun, or person that in like manner offended or transgressed. Knowledge of godlinesse without will to live a godlie life is a testimonie and seale of just condemnation.

4. But now to returne unto that from whence we have disgressed; that by the continuall troubles of God's elect, and by the painful death of Jesus Christ we may learn the ire and rage of God most justly conceaved against syn, which is the onlye cause expressed by his holie worde of all calamities that apprehended all fleshe. Ffor albeit that man unjustlie suffer under man, yet under God dothe non suffer without cryme committed. And this I beseeche you, deirly beloved, that when you heire the troubles of Christ or of his Churche that ye will call the cause of the same to mynd, that by the contemplation of God's just judgements ye may cum to the haitreth of yat whiche your Father hath haited ever from the beginning, and so lerne to avode such vicess as God never suffered unpunished. God oppin your eares and illuminatt your understandings that so I ye may do. Amen.

5. The Secund Causs that moved me to putt you in remembrance that Goddes elect hathe ever suffered with most extremites, is that yf such trublesome dayes shall return in your time, as historie and experience witnessed to have passed before us, that than ye be not moved with everie wynde of doctrine, nor yett that ye doubt of the vertue of that relligioun which ye have receaved by knowledge of Christis most Sacred Evangeill preached amongst you by a wretched weak and most feeble man, but receaved of you, and confirmed in the harts of Goddis elect by the omnipotent Spreit of him who never sended his messengers in vane. To this gospell stik fast, bretherne, what truble, chance or varietie that ever happin amongst men. Latt it not offende you that manye which sumtyme appeared most fervent in Christis cause ar now waxen colde, and ar fallen to follow the wickedness of the worlde. If they be of God they shall repent this ther defectioun, and shall with open confessione accuse themselves that as traitors they have declyned from the truthe. And yf they be not of God, but were in thair apperant fervencye dissembled hypochrits, bearing no favor to the treuth, but ether for advantage or for pleasure of men, than hes the wisdom of God, to our most singulair comforte, and to the advancement of his own glorie, begone to tak vengeance upon those pestilent persons, whill [until] that he will compel them to mak manifest unto us whom before thay deceaved, the secrets of thair harts, that we espying thair defectioun may feare to dissemble or play the hypocritis befoir God, whose just judgements may not suffer long unpunished, in anye estaite, the prophanatioun of his name, and abuse of his veritie. And thairfore, bretherne, lett not sum (or many yf thair be) that unthankfullie fallis back from professioun of the treuthe, draw you back with themselves heidlings to dampnatioun. Butt remembring that onlie those that persevere to the end shall be saiffe, latt the defectioun of others sturre and

prick you with trembling and feare to call for assistence of his Holy Spreit. Call to mynd, bretherne, that often ye have harde that hypochrisie cannot long be consealed, albeit for a seîson it shew a fair face. The wheit and dornall growing in one ground, and nurissed with lik moistour and rayne, albeit they be permitted to grow togydder, yitt before the tyme of harvest do bothe shew to the faythfull and vigilant servands of their lorde some tokins and signs how the one is known distinctlie from the other. Even so is it in Christis church; for albeit the wicked shall remane in the Lord's fielde and husbandrie, even to the end, yit be synes [sins] of some that sumtymes appeared godlie so manefest and plane, that we shall cease to wunder when we shall se tham gaddered, bound in faggotts, and so cast in the fyyr to burn for evir. And thairfor, deir bretherne, be not offended, albeit ye se and heare the revolting of manye, for such wes the chance of Christis doctrine deuring the dayes of his dispensatioun. If truble apprehend the preacheors that faythfullie haith labored, under what color or pretext yat evir it be, my hoppe is in you that thairfore ye shall not be offended nor yet ashamed of that veritie that ones ye have professed, but rather I judge that ye, teached by the truthe of God's word yatt judgement begynneth at the houshold of God, and that just men are taking away that place may be gevin to the vengeance and wraith of God, will ye prepaire yourselves with all expeditioun to suffeire with Christ, that with him ye may raign, seing that by manye tribulatiouns most we entere in the kingdom of God. Latt no man judge that presentlie I se any uther apperance of persecutioun than I have oppenlie showin unto your faces, which is the veritie of Christis word, which plainlie affirmes that as the woman after she have conceived, by no means nor medicin can avoide or eshaipe the dolors of her childebirthe, no more can the church of Christ be preserved from tribulatioun by anye art or policye of man. Ffor appoynted it is by Goddis wisdom and providence that the members shalle conforme to the heade who hathe entered into glorie by ignominie and shame. Our hevinlie Father, by Christ his Sone, to encorage us against the dayes of dolour that shall apprehend the wicked world, willeth us amongst tribulatiouns to lift up our heids, that is to be of good comfort and chear, for our redemptioun is at hand; whairby he first wold admonyshe us not to be curious in serching the foreknowledge what tymes be appoynted by God that his elect shall suffer, but rather in the tyme of truble to lucke for hastie and sure deliverance. Secondlie, that certane signes thair be (as contempt of Gods truthe, iniquitie raiging without punissement, the away taiking of godlie magistrates, the multitude of wicked men placed in authoritie) which teacheth God's elect both of the trubles which themselves shall susteane, as also of those horible plagues and distructiouns of ungodlie. But these signes be not observed and marked of all men, but onlie of suche as hath thair eyes oppened by the Holy Ghost to understand and see that the immutable judgements of God in no aige long delayed to tak vengeance upon manefest transgressors, when iniquitie is commed to ripeness and maturitie, albeit a meane [small] number did look for the same.

6. These things are to be seen in the histories and prophecies from the beginning. Ffor in the first aige God cryed, "My Spreit shall not strive with men for evir. I will appoint unto him a hundreth and twentye yeres;" as God would say, "I cry by my prophets, I threaten and strive, even as man wer able to resist me; so will I do no more; my worde shall not thus be mokked; I will revenge the dishonour done against my veritie; I shall destroy all fleshe by watter." Butt, O bretherne, who feared these threatnyngs and eshaipped the plagues? Noe and his familie—aucht persons of the holle world.

In the dayes of the prophets Isaieh, Jeremieh, and Ezechiel, when God by their mouthes did thounder against Israel and Juda manefest plagues to ensew upon their abhominable iniquities, who did repent and turn to the Lord? So meane a nomber of such multitudes that Jeremye himself saide that he would leve the poore sort becaus thai knew not God, and wold go to the cheif reulers and to the riche for thay knew the judgements of thair Lorde; but likewiae had they all brokin the yok, and had heipit transgressioun upon transgressioun; they had denyed the Lorde and saide "It is not He; mischeif shall not chance unto us; we shall nether sweerd [sword] nor hounger." And as for the prophets that most wer honored in the world, their war none amongst them yat boldlye spak of the plagues to cum. And thairfor the prophet of God, in maner despared that anye wer left to heir, cryed thus: "To whom shall I speik? to whom shall I obtest and exhorte, that they may heare? Their eares are incircumcised that they cannot advert; the worde of God is in reproch amangst them; they delighte not in it, from the leist unto the most; every one gapis for advantaege, from the propheit to the preast; every one worked fraudolentlie and with deceate." Thus, bretherne, ye may espye that pure and riche, magistrates and princes, propheits and preasts, when Godd's propheits cryed most plainlie, for the most part wer blinde and inobedient, which unto the godlie prophet was so certane a signe of a miserable and universall plague to fall upon that realme, that he himself in vehemencye of spirit cryeth, "I am replenyshed with the indignatioun of the Lorde, I am vexed in suffering, and thairfore, O Lord, poure furth thy vengeance upon thair children in the streits, and upon the companye of their lustie young men. Latt men and women be taiken prisoners. Latt not the oldyn or decripet in yeres eschaipe. Latt thair housses and feldes be translated to straingers; for they have committed abhominatioun and thay cannot eschame nor repent of mischief." In thiis most feirfull prayer of the propheit wer his eyes oppined that he assuredlye saw all these plagues which short after apprehended this obstinat natioun, albeit in the meane season with contempt thay cried, " Tushe, their words be but wynde. Latt the counsall of the Holy One of Israel cum to pass. We shall have peace and wealthe in our dayes, for we are the pepill yat call upon the Lorde. His law and holie temple are with us." By these meanes did this sinfull natioun persuade themselves of rest, peace and tranquillite, when suddane destructioun approched at hand. But the propheit, and a small number whom God selected from that pestilent multitude, with feare and anguishe looked for truble which followeth that contempt hastilie. Ffor after much contradictioun made to the doctrine of the propheit, he finalle, for a certaine treason wrongfullie laide to his charge, was cast in prison, where he remaned unto that day that the Lorde had performed every worde that was spoken by his mouthe against that stubborn and rebellious peple by his messenger. Nabucadnosar, whoise soldioures burnt their city, defiled thair doightures and wives, killed thair children, young men and aiged, tuik prisoner thair Kyng, put outt his eyes, led himself to Babilon, murthered his sones, distroyed their tempill whairein they gloried against God and his propheit.

And yit, in the myddis of all these plagues forgetteth not God such as feared befoir to offend his majestie, but provided a meane that the propheit wes delivered, and that with honor even by him that punished the inobedient—that Baruch and Abdemelech fand thair life for a prey— that Gedoliah . . . . . and some of all estaites, but most of the poore were left in the land to rest and remaine without all impediment and truble to be maide.

Mark and consider, beloved brethern, that the godlie shall rejose and find favors of God when vengeance shall be executed upon proude contemners. And therefore prepare yourselves to stand in God's feare, not shrynking from the truthe, whidder God strike with plagues (as our synnes deserve) universallie, or begin to whippe and correct his familiares to putt others in mynde that if the less offender eschaipe not punishment (albeit at man's hand he suffer unjustly), what plagues shall they suffer that heipe syn upon syn, and oppin blasphemye upon violent oppressioun. For truble, brethern, shrink not from the treuth, but call earnestlie for Goddi's assistance, knowing that the end of all thinges is at hand.

7. And as for varietie and diversitie of opinions tueching the doctrine and cheife poyntes of relligioun which ye have receaved, God I tak to witness and the Lorde Jesus before whom att ance shall all fleshe appeir, that I never teached unto you nor unto anye others my auditory that doctrine, as necessaary to be beleved, which I did not fynd written in Godds holie law and testament. And thairfor, in that caise, with Paull will I say, " Yf ane angell from heven shall teache unto you another gospell nor ye have harde and externallie receaved, latt him be accursed." Under the Gospell I understande—

What is meant under the Gospell.—Ffirst, the infinitt goodness of God whose mercifull providence hath placed our life and salvation in his only sone Jesus Christ, who, of our God, is maid to us justice, sanctificatioun, wisdom and redemptioun.

2. And our Lorde Jesus, togedder with all such giftes as by Him are gevin to the elect Church of God, as remission of synes, resurrectioun of the fleshe and life everlasting, is the second thing I understand by the Gospell.

3. And the thryde thing is trew fayth, which as it only apprehendeth and understandeth all these precedents, so doth it onlie justifie befoir God, without all respect of works bipast, present or to come; which good warks hath God our Father prepared that we his children, adoptate and chosin in Christ Jesus, befoir the foundation of the world was laide, to life everlasting, shuld walk in them, which is the *ferde* thing I conclude within the Gospell, to witt:

4. A holye and godlye conversatioun wharein we shuld obey our God all the dayes of our life, to the praise and glorie of his holye name who hath appoynted us to be his heares, when yitt we were not.

5. And laste, under the Gospell I undeŕstand Invocatioun unto God alone by Jesus Christ, and thanksgiving unto him for his gret benefits receaved; which sumtymes are private, while man alone, in any tribulatioun, necessitie, or action, incalls the ayde and helpe of his God for Christ his Sones saike; but are commanded oppinlye to be done, in participatioun of Christ's Sacraments, left and commanded to be used in his Church for sealing up and better memorye to be had of those benefitts, that we have resaived by the communion that we have with Christ Jesus in his bodye and bloode.

If in anye of these cheif and principall poyntes any man varie from that doctrine which ye have professed, lett him be accursed.

1. As if anye man teach anye other cause moving God to elect and choose us than his awin infinitt goodnesse and meare mercye.

2. Any other name in hevin or under the hevin, wharein salvation stands, but onlie the name of Jesus Christ.

3. Any other meanes whairby we are justified and absolved from wrath and damnation that our synnes deserve, than by fayth onlye.

4. Any other cause or end of goode works than yat first we are made good trees, and yerafter bringeth forth fruits accordingly, to witnes yat we are lively members of Christ's holye and most sanctified bodye, prepared vesselis to the honor and praise of our Father's glorie.

5. Yf ayne teache prayers to be maid to others than to God alone.

6. Yf any mediator betwixt God and man, but onlie our Lorde Jesus.

7. Yf mo or other Sacraments be affirmed or requyred to be used than Christ Jesus left ordinarye in his Church,—to witt, Baptysm and the Lord's Table or mistycall Supper.

8. Yf ayne denye remissioun of synnes, resurrectioun of the fleshe, and life everlasting to appertaine to us in Christ's blood, which, sprinkled in our harts by fayth, doth purge us from all syn, so yat we neid no more nor other sacrifices than that oblatioun ones offered for all, by the which Goddis elect be fullie sanctifyed and maid perfect. Yf anye, I say, require anye other sacrifice to be maid for syns than Christis death, which ones he suffered, or anye other manner whairby Christis death may be applied to man than by fayth onlie, which also is the gift of God, so that man haithe no cause to glory in warkes. And yett, if anye denye goode warkes to be profitable, as not necessar to a treu Christiane professioun, lett the affirmares teachers or maintenars of such a doctrine be accursed of you, as they are of God unless they repent.

8. Remembring alwayes, beloved bretherne, that dew obedience be given to magistrates reulars and princes, without tumult, grudge or seditioun; for, how wicked yat evir themselves be in life, or how ungodlie that evir thair preceptes or commandementes be, ye most obey thame for conscience saike; except in cheif poynts of relligioun; and than aught ye rather to obey God nor man; not to pretend to defend Godds treuthe or relligioun (ye being subgetts) by violence or sweirde, but patiently suffering what God shall please be laid upon you for constante confessioun of your fayth and beleife. How necessary is such obedience to God and to his appoynted reulars I suppose you not to be ignorant, after so manifest doctrine in that caise, and thairfor that poynt I end. Concluding yet agane yat man or angell yat will teache unto you [on] any cheif poynt abuive rehersed a contrair doctrine to that which ye heave professed, latt him be recompted of you errant from the treuth, and corrupt of judgment, sent of Goddis just judgementes to excecat [blind] and blind such as never delighted in the treuthe of God.

In ceremonies and rites which I used in ministratioun of Christe's sacraments, as I did observe the preceptes and practice of Christ and his apostilles so nye as the Holye Gost did oppin unto me, so this day do I nothing repent of my interprise, and of your obedience; beseeching God, for Christ his Sones saik, that so the harts of magistrates may be inclined to mercye, that what the impyre of Godd's most sacrate worde did worke in your harts, without precept or law appoynted by man, be not now hindred and pulled aback againe by rigour of a law.

9. Heir most I speak of my present estait and what I wold ye estemed of me, notwithstanding rumores and fame which soundeth and bloweth most commonlie to the worst of Goddis messingers, especiallie in thair absence.

First, as tueching my life and conversatioun, I am evin such yit in hart as I was in your presence, when I walked before you, not as ane ypochrite counterfeiting and preferring gravitie before men, and yit lacking Godd's feare in hart; but contrariwise, trembling for my synnes befor the face of my God, I accompanyed with you as your common brother, lik the commone sort of Godd's elect childern, that continuallie lamentis and groanis for syn that remaneth in this our corrupt nature during the dayes of this transitorie life; which my frailtie I never conceled from you, nor from the knowlege of the commone congregatioun; nor yit never pretended I, by policye or craft, to advance myselfe otherwise than God had appoynted by preaching of his treuthe unto men. . By which treuthe if God hath wrought in the harts of anye such favor unto me as displeased some men, I will crave of you, beloved bretherne, in the bowells of Christi's mercie not to suspect crafte or deceate in me, which God knoweth nether wes nor is in me concernyng that mater. These words I writte with dolor of hart. Amongst my uthers grevous offences daylie committed against Godd's majestie, no ane do I more lament than yat I for man's pleasure so long resisted the godlie and just request of such as sought my companye, neither for pleasure of fleshe nor worldlie dignitie, but onlye for increase of hope and desyre of Godd's everlasting kyngdom.

Iff anye man be offended with me that I (willing to avoide Godd's wrayth and vengeance threatned against such as having [no] necessitie despiseth his ordinances) do purpose and intend to obey God, embraising such as he hes offered unto me, than to please and flatter man that unjustlie holded the same from me. Iff anye, I say, for this cause be offended and will seek my displeasure or troubill, latt the same understande that as I have a bodye, which onlie they may hurt (and not unless that God shall so permitt), so have they bodies and soulles which boithe God shall punishe in fyre inextinguishably with the devill and his angellis, unless suddenlie they repent and cease to maling against God and his most holye ordinance. Wythe life and deathe, deir bretherne, I am at poynt, they befoir me in equalle ballances. Transitorie life is not so sweate to me that, for defence thairof, I will jeopard to lose the life everlasting. Nor yit is corporall deathe to me so fearfull that, albeit most certainlie I understand the same shortlie to follow my godlie purpose, that yet, thairfore, I would depone myself to dee in Godd's wrayth and anger for ever and ever, which, no doubt, I did yf for manis pleasur I refused Godd's perfitt ordinance. These things do I signifie unto you (whois offence I more feire than my awin life) that ye be not slandered nor offended as yat same spirit of pryde was lait crepin in to me. Not so, dear bretherne, I unfeynedlie praise God of his free gift, and with teares I pray for continuance of the same. This day I am more vile and of low reputation in my awin ees than I was either that day that my feitt was cheyned in the preson of dolor (the galeis I meane), or yit that day that I was delivered by his only providence from the same. Ffor better now I am taucht of my awin infirmitie which, as it compelleth me frequentlie to grone, so (God be praised) it is a skourge and bridell that administreth me never to glorie in fleshe. And this for my life and present purpose.

10. And as tueching my doctrine, God beareth recorde at this houre to my conscience that I have spoken the treuthe amongst you, and have laboured to instruct you in the same. And thairfor as tueching the chief poynts of relligioun I nether will give place (God assisting my infirmitie) to man or angell teaching the contrair to that which ye have hearde. Bot as for ceremonies or rites, thinges of smaller weyght, I am not minded to move contentioun, so yat with conscience, and without reproche of my former doctrine, I may avoid the same.

To tueche the poynt, kneling at the Lord's Souper I have proved by doctrine to be no convenient gesture for a table, which hath been gevin in that actioun to suche a presence of Christ as no place of Godd's Scriptures dothe teache unto us. And thairfor kneling in that actioun, appering to be joyned with certan dangears no less in manteyning superstitioun than in using Christ's holye institutioun with other gestures than either he used or commanded to be used, I thought good amongst you to avoide, and to use sitting at the Lord's Table, which ye did not refuse, but with all reverence and thanksgiving unto God for his treuthe, knowing, as I suppose, ye confirmed the doctrine with your gestures and confessioun. And this day yet, with a testimonie of good conscience I signifie unto you that as I nother repent nor recant that my former doctrine, so do I (for divers causes long to reherse) muche preferre sitting at the Lord's Table either to kneling standing or goyng at the actioun of that misticall souper.

But because I am but one, having in my contrair magistrates, commone order, and judgements of manye lerned, I am not mynded for maintenance of that one thing to gainstand the magistrates, in all other and cheif poynts of religioun aggreing with Christ and with his true doctrine, nor yet to break nor truble common order, thought meet to be kept for unitie and peace in the congregatiouns for a tyme. And least of all intend I to dampne or lyghtlye regarde the grave judgments of suche men as unfeignedlie I feare, love and will obey in all things by them judged expedient to promote God's glorie—these subsequents granted unto me.

1. Ffirst that the magistrates mak knowin (as that they have done if ministers were willing to do thair dewities) that kneling is not reteyned in the Lord's Souper for maintenance of anye superstitioun, much less that anye adoratioun apperteaneth to anye realle presence of Christ's bodye natural there conteaned, or joyned with those elements of breade and wynne, but onlye for uniforme order to be kept, and that for a tyme, in this Church of England.

2. Secondlie, that commone order clame not kneling in the Lord's Soupper as either necessarie or decent to Christis actioun, but onlye as a ceremonye thought goodely by man and not by Christ himself; for

otherwise shall common order accuse Christ and his actioun of indecencie, or lacking some gestuir necessarie.

3. And last, that my fathers, whom I feare and honor, and my brethren in labors and professioun, whom I unfeynedlie luif, do not truble my conscience imputing upon me anye foolish interprise, for that I have, in ministratioun of Christ's sacraments, more regarded attempting to follow what Christ himself did in his awne perfect actioun than what anye man efter hathe commanded to be done.

These things granted unto me, I nether will gainstand godlie magistrates, nether brak commone order nor yit contend with my superiors or fallow [fellow] preachers, but with patience will I beare that one thing; daylie thirsting and calling unto God for reformatioun of that and others. And this I do beare, bretherne, not for feare of anye truble (as knoweth God) that can apprehend me in my awin persone; for I know who hath the cupp that I most drink in his awin hand, evin God our hevinlie Father, whose mercifull providence so reulleth and gyideth all creatures that neither man nor devil can truble or molest me nor the least of his elect, but as he will, and hath before determined thame and me to be tryed in the furnace of tribulations, for consumyng and burnyng away of vanitie and drosse yat remaneth in this our corrupt nature. And thairfor, brethern, it is not feare of corporall punishment, but the onlye feare that Christian charitie be violated and brokin that swaideth and moves me to give place in this behelf. Albeit I culd with all soberness and dew obedience, shew causes rasonable why sitting at the Lord's Table is to be preferred unto kneling; yett, if the upper powers, not admitting the same, would execute upon me the penaltie of their law (because they may not suffer a commone order to be violated), assuredlie Christian charitie was broken and dissolved upon the one part, ather by me that for so small a mater obstinatlie wuld gainstand suche magistrats as professes themselves earnest promoters of Christs gospell, or elles by them that, persuaded by some manlye rasons [reasons of human wisdom or policy] of certain danger to follow if common order should not universallie be kept in the realme, should trouble the bodie or stope the mouth of him that to his knowledge hath spoken nothing but Christis plane veritie.

11. And besides the breatch of charitie, which alwayes is to be avoided, I have respect to the quieting of your consciences, that if ye shall be compelled by rigour of a law to alter that order, which of Gods assured treuthe ye have learned and received, that nether shall ye dampne yourselves as transgressours of anye law, or violators of any commone order, for that which before ye have godlie used; nether yet that ye shall be accused as declinars or fallen back from the treuthe, for that which ye shall after do; for when ye followed and received Christis sempill institutioun sitting at table, thair wes no law (except the statute of that Roman Antichrist whom

Christ Jesus shall confound and all the manteiners of his abhominatiouns and ydolatrie, contrair your faith), and thairfore did ye not transgress, for where no law is there can be no transgressioun. And if now by especiall commandement of your uppar powars ye shall be compelled to observe the commone order, God forbid that ye shal be dampned or judged as shrinking from Christ; if, first ye rejoiss not that ye are called back againe to a gestuir that is joyned with dangers in that actioun. Secondlie, if oppenlie ye professe that what ye do now, as it proceedeth nether of your will pleasure nor electiouns, so do ye not appear or allow the same, but onlye doith bear and suffer it for obedience unto magistrates, and peice to be kept amongst the congregatiouns; thristing and praying, in the mean season, that God of his great mercy for Christ his Sons saik please so to move and illuminatt the harts and ees of magistrates and rulers that they mott understand and see Christis institutioun to be most perfitt, and men's devises and wisdom in maters of religioun ever to have displeased God; that by contemplation thereof they may studie to eradicat and pull out all such plants as the hevinlie Father hathe not planted. And, lastly, yf hating in your harts all superstitioun and ydolatry, ye likewise oppinlie protest that ye communicatt with such as in that actioun adores any corporall or reall presence of Christis naturall bodye, which is not there but in hevin, which behoveth to receive him till all be compleit that is spokin by the mouths of God's holye propheits. If these things by you be ryghteouslie observed, understand, and believed, God forbid yat of anye ye shall be suspected as that your fervencye towards the treuthe began to abaitt and wax cald, albeit, contrary to your harts' desyre your order be altered; which unto my hart is so dolorus yat yf anye corporall pane that my wicked carcass is able to susteane mycht confirme and establish that order which Godd's treuthe hath planted among you (without truble or danger of you), rather I should suffer the deathe than your quietness and conscience should be molested. But seeing that my resystance shuld rather sturr the magistrates against you than establishe [you] in quietness, the consail of all godliye, as also the testimonie of my owin conscience, is that less offence it is to beare this one thing (with dolor of your harts, dalie calling unto God for reformatioun of the same), than to provoke the magistrates to displeasour, seeing that in principalls we all agree. This for your order, which ye shall not order nor change whill ye be especiallie commanded by such as haith authoritie.

12. And now, brethern, unfeynedlie beloved, for the tender mercies of Jesus Christ and for the honor of that profession which before the world ye have gevin, be thankfull unto God, who of his meare mercie, and not of your deserts, hath called you from ignorancie errors and death, to the knowledge and lycht of his assured veritie and to participatioun of life everlasting. Call unto minde how jealous God is over his awin precepts,

the violatioun whairof his just judgements most nedes punish in all manifest transgressors. Remember that syn can be purged by no other sacrifice but by the onlye deathe of the onlye Son of God; lay befoir your ees the great mercies and liberall goodness of God. And in so doing, first learne to avoide and hait syn, and theirafter shew yourselves myndfull that ye are cled with the white and most cleane garment of Christis justice, and thairfor that ye will not contaminat nor defyle the same by anye manefest iniquitie, which if ye do, remember how fearful it is to fall in the hands of the living God.

Latt Christeane cheritie and brotherlie love be restored and encryse amongst you, one forgeving another, and the strongar bearing with the infirmitie of the weakar, evin as ye wyll that God appardone and bear with your manifold offences. And of this be persuaded, that without brotherlie love and remissioun of offences one against another committed, societie nor fellowship can ye not have with God.

Latt manefest contempnars of God and of godlines be rebuked of you, and convicked by those that beare authoritie, lest, by permissioun and sufferance, at length iniquitie become so familiar that God espye it to be the sin of the citie, and so poure doun plagues without measor in his hot displeasor, because none is found that unfeynedlie regardeth the Lords indignatioun.

Latt not your godlie cair that alwayes ye have had over the poore desist nor cease, but rather let it encrese, knowing that the Lord Jesus hath commanded and committed those that be indigent (not stoutt, stubborn, and idill vagabonds, I meane, but orphanes, widowes, and others impotent) unto your charge, to be provided by you, in testimonye of your gratefull acknowledging of his moste ample benefitts received; which liberalitie towards the poure as he acknowledgeth to be bestowed upon his own bodye, so dothe he reward the same with divers graces, and finallie, with life everlasting. And thairfor, proceide, deir bretheren, and latt the soulles of the pour and neydye by you nourished and fedd, blesse you befoir the presence of your heavenlie Father, throught Jesus Christ his Sone, whose omnipotent and Holye Ghost illuminatt the ees of your senses, and that advisedlye ye may consider what is the riches of that kingdom and glorie whairunto ye are called by grace; and throught the same are ye saved by fayth, that you, revyshed with this desyre of hevinlie thinges, may so travaill throught the stormye sees of this wicked world, that in the day of our Lorde Jesus ye may be found such as oft I have required, and now with my hart wisheth you to be, vesselles prepared to glorie and honor. Amen.

13. I have written unto you, beloved brethern, with such ruide boldness as some tyme I used unto your faces, to lett you understand that albeit I be absent from you in bodye, yet am I present with you in favor and goodwill, which I beare to Christis holle flock, but most especiallie unto

you for that obedience unto the treuthe and that sollempned professioun that God hath wrought in you (I flatter not, for you seik I, not yours) by Jesus Christ, preached by me amongst you in muche weaknes and feare, but yit of good mynd and zeale towards Goddis glorie and your salvatioun. And now, separated from you (the tyme knoweth God, long or short), I unfeynedlie desyre (above the precedents) [in addition to the foregoing] the ayde of your prayers that God, of his meare goodness and mercie for Christ his Sones saik, by his holye Ghost to please to strengthen me to the end of my appoynted ministerie; that the utterance of the veritie may be gevin unto me in such measor and boldness that his holie name may be praised, and the enemies of Christis gospell confounded to their conversioun. And that my life and conversatioun (which, in Godd's presence, I acknowledge wretched, wicked and vane) may be such befoir men, by the regiment [government] of that Spirit that reuleth and guydeth Godd's chosen children, that Christis holye Evangell in me be not slaundered. Amen.

God who of purpose hath called you and justified you by fayth, who also is able and faithful to perform his promesses maid in Christ our Savior, preserve and keipe your harts and mynds in his treue luif and feare; and Jesus Christ, the faythful and onlie goode Sheipherd and Bishope of your soulles, so strengthen you by his holye Spirit, that man nor angell persuade you not to forsaik nor repent that happye society and most blessed communion and fellowshipe which ye have with him in his most precious bodye and bloode ones offered for your offences, and daylie received of us by fayth; whairby also doth Christ remane in our harts, whom he by his own strenth doth carry up to the presence of his hevinlye Father; so that now our conversatioun is in things celestial. To him with the Father and with the holye Ghost, be all praise and honor, ever and ever. Amen.

The peace of our Lord Jesus Christ rest with you all. For the last, goode nycht. So be it.

Your brother,
JOHNE KNOKKS.

NOTE.

The *genuineness* of the above epistle, which bears to be addressed and signed by Knox's own hand, does not admit of a doubt. It bears the strong impress, throughout, of his well-known style, both of thought and language. It corresponds perfectly with the relations which he is otherwise known to have sustained to the Congregation of Berwick; and nobody could have had any conceivable motive or inducement to personate him, in addressing an epistle of such a tenor to his former flock.

The approximate date of this epistle is also, without doubt, one or other of the latest months of the year 1552, as already fixed in the preceding narrative. The *occasion* of it is easily gathered from sections nine and ten, where the writer refers to "rumours and fame" which had been spread abroad, during his absence from the North, to his discredit and disadvantage, both "touching his life and conversation," and the consistency of his present teaching and doctrine with what he had previously professed ; and we can easily understand how the incidents of his visit to London and the Court might give occasion to these rumours, and might readily furnish a handle to the malice of his enemies in Newcastle. A man who had preached with singular acceptance and effect before the King, Court and Council, and who had had the offer of a bishopric by desire of the Duke of Northumberland himself, might easily be supposed to have become less humble than before, and to have allowed a little pride to "creep in ;" and a man who had had large-heartedness enough to acquiesce provisionally in a liturgical rubric, which fell far short of what he strove his utmost to obtain, and to use all his influence, as he was doing, to induce others to acquiesce in it also, was exactly the man to be misunderstood and misrepresented by others less large-hearted than himself, especially by enemies who were waiting for his halting, and ready to put upon his every word and deed the worst construction.

In addition to its own biographical and historical value, the Epistle also serves the important use of helping to establish the Knox-authorship of another document, of much more historical value than itself—that which we have marked No. II.

II.*

COMMANDED by your letters (most honorable) in wrytinge to reporte our judgements and opinyones in suche articles as, exhibited to the kinge's maiestie, ware derected to sartayne learned preacheres, and amonge whome we most unworthie were acompted, that the same by thame and us advisedly consedered, reporte myght be mayde of our opinones to your honores agayne. We, therefore (besydes that our weak and base judgement which we have commytted to wryting in the Latin tonge) most humble do offer unto your honoures this our confessioun uppone the 38 Article, wherein we thinke shall stande most doubtes and contencion; protestinge, ffirst, unto your honores, takinge to recorde in our conscyence the Lorde Jesus, in presence of whose tribunall seate all ffleshe shall ones appere, where shall be disclosed the secretes of heartes, that nether of arrogance nor vayne curyositie, as some maye suspect, nor yet of mynde to have any innovation in thynges that be well ordered (for we are not altogeather ignoraunt what inconvenientes may ensue the ffrequent alteration of religion), [but] do most abhore the same. God we take, therefore, to wytness in our conscience that none of the precedentes do move hus [us] to offere unto you, most honorable, and to afferme this our subsequent conffession, but onely, convicted by manyfest veritie, we are compelled withe all sobernesse to offer and conffesse that which the Screpture of God teacheth unto us, what we truste are persuaded to us to be most true; leste that, commaunded to speake and yet kepe sylence in so weightie a matere, we shalbe accused for betrayer of the trewthe; and yet in this assercion we desyere the honours and auctorytie of all men be saved, in so far as Christien charytie and obedience to Godd's most sacred trewthe shall permett and suffer.

In the 38 Article the Bowke of Common Prayer now last publeshed by the kinge's maiestie, and confirmed by common assent and acte of Parlament, is confirmyd to be holie, godlye, and not onely by Godde's scryptures probable in every rite and ceremonie, but also in no poynt repugnant thereto, as well consernyng common prayers and mynystration

---

* There is no title given to this paper in either of the two copies of it preserved in the " Morrice Collection." In the later copy it is separated from the other three papers, but in the earlier it is placed in one parcel beside the other two papers bearing to be the writings of Knox.

of the Sacrementes, as the orderinge and admyssion of preastes, deacons, busshoppes and archbusshoppes.

This article and assertion in all poyntes not to be tolerable and trewe, us moveth these three reasones subsequents.

Ffirst. No mane, as we suppose, of holie judgement will denye but knelying in the action of the Lorde's Table proceded from a fals and erronious opinion, to wit: That there was Christe's naturall boddy contayned, eyther by waye of transubstanciation, or else by conjunction reall or corporall of his bodye and bloode withe the visyble elements. That the same deceavable opynion doithe yet remayne in the heartes of many, experience itself will well testyfye and playnelie declare.

Then if by a lawe maye be confirmed (Godde's mayestie not offended) that ceremonye that hath spronge furthe from a false opinion, and that feedythe the same in the heartes of men, and that permytteth the idolatere to continue in his idolatrie, we desire the censure of Godde's holie Scriptures.

The holie Ghost, speaking by the mouth of Pawle, affirmythe the contrare in these playne wordes: "Flye idolatrie." Which precept, if we obaye, when we externally do the self same thyng among idolatours that the idolatours do, that yet [then let?] the Scryptures of God, by word and example, pronounce the sentens.

Pawle commanded all thynges of themselves indefferent to be done in the Church to edyfication, and so to be measured by the rewle of charytie that in doyng therof offence neyther be geven to Jew, to Gentile, nor to the Churche of God; but knelyng in this mysticall Supper among such varietie in opyniones edyfieth no man but offereth occasion of slaunder and offence to many.

Ffirst, the idolatour is permytted to do that thinge that his heart most thresteth after, that is, to adore and wershippe suche thynges as, there, be subjecte to his senses—which Christeane charitie no wyse maye abyde. For albeit that in man's powre it lyeth not to porge their hearts from idolatry, yet ought the cyvill magistrate to cut awaye all externall appearance thereof to the uttermost of his powere; ffor so meaneth the streyt commandement geven by God to Moses in these words, "Destroy theyre aultars, cut down theyre groves, beate to powder theyre images, take not the names of theyre idoles in your mouths, contracte no mariages withe them, lest they plucke your hartes ffrom sarving the Lorde;" which thinge, if the people wold not obaye, Joshue dothe threten that then the Lorde shulde not dystroye those nacions before them as that he had begone alreadye to do. These thynges ought to be pondered of us, on whom the endes of the worlde be come, ffor if we offende *in ffygures** we shalbe punyshed, we doubt, as they were.

    * Possibly a mistaken reading of the copyist for *in similibus*.

Secondaryly, by knelyinge in the Lord's Supper the consciences of weyke brethren are not a lyttel offended; ffor by vyolence of a law are they compelled to honore God (their conscience reclaimyng thereto) in suche sorte as in that action nether the example of Christ nor yet any express commandment of his sacred word assured them of [against] evel doing.

Therdely, the Churche of God, that be stronge, and growne to some perfection, is greatly injured; for it is permitted to idolatours to tryumph over the Churche of God, seying that after so longe contention between the professers of the treuth and maintenors of idolatrie, the most part, that is idolatours, hathe vincuste [vanquished] the best, by reason of this law aforsaid; and of their victorye they glorie not a lyttel; for albeit we crie never so lowde, that in that action no adoration ought to be given to no creature, yet whisper they, yea and plainlie do they speak—"crye what they list," saythe the Papistes, "yet are the gospellers compelled to do the self-same thynge that we whom they call idolatours do in every gesture and behaveyor."

If in this case the Holie Ghost were called to judge and discern betwene the Church of Jesus Christ and all the pryncses of the erthe, we are most certanely persuaded, that for no man's favour would he alter or change this his sentens ones pronounsed by Pawle: "Sic autem peccantes in fratres, et vulnerantes conscientiam illorum infirmam, in Christum peccatis." You that so synne agaynst your brethern, woundyng their weyk conscience, do synne agaynst Christ. If any shall object, the cause movyng Pawle so to write and our cause be not alyke, if it please suche to understand that one bodye of idolatrie hathe clothed theself in many cottes, and so by divers garments hathe desaved the worlde from the begynnyng—we thynke he shall find a marvellous congruence between the Corinthiens that sometyme were blynded wythe grosse idolatrie and our Papystes more blynded. They were deceived in that they trusted the meates offered to their goddes to have contracted therebye any holinesse; our Papystes have been more deceived; for what ethnick ever was so mad as to believe and affirme that the fleshe that was offered to their goddes was turned into the substancial nature of the same goddes, as our Papystes have dremed that bread and wine was transubstanciate and changed by their offering and pronouncyng of sartaine words into Christ's naturall bodie. Some of the Corinthiens that did professe Christ's Evangell did not flee the company of idolatours, but with slaunder of the weyke brethern were participiant of the bankettes offered to their goddes. Some this daye appeare to finde no fault will be commytted to bowe and knele amonge the mydst of idolatours. But omyttyng these, dare any deny that in that action hathe not and yet is most horrible idolatrie knowne commytted? And is it not Pawle's commandement that we shall abstayne from apperaunce of evill, yea, and from suche thynges as, althoughe of themselves they be indifferent, yet if our weyke brethern in any maner be offended by our doinge of them, we ought to abstayne by reason of weyke conscience. If these be, as they are, the playne precepts of the Holie Ghost; if then in the action where idolatrie hath bene commytted, where yet idolatours are suffered to adourne and worshipp the visible creatures, and where no small nomber of weyk bretyren are spectatours of our externall works; if with these daungers, we saye, amongst idolatours we knele, howe in Godde's presence we can be excusable, let Godde's Scriptures wytness and pronounce. Men may flatter and desave themselves, but if externally we do the self-same thinge in the action of idolatrie that idolatours dowe, our awin conscience, convick by Godde's word, shall condemp ourselves; for, looke, as to the treue faythe within the heart is requesyte the confession of the mouthe, so to the knowlege and hatred of some idolatries is also required the external avoyding thereof; as wytnesseth Daniel and the Three Children agaynst the lawes of Darius and Nebuchadnezar.

The contempte of Christ's institution and daungers that may ensue if men shuld syt in the Lord's Table, Jesus Christ, our Lord and Master, in whome all treasures of wysdome and knowledge be hidd, did never see nor suspect; for no mencion is mayd in his holie Scriptures that syttyng at the table shuld bryng contempt of his institution. Wonder it is that men are become more circumspect and wyse than God himself. Alas! are we not afrayd of that terrible sentence pronounced in the prophet Esaye, saying, " The wysdome of the wyse shall perishe, and the understandyng of the prudent vanyshe." If the cases be not alyke let Godde's Scriptures it pronounce.

It is greatly to be feared that our wysdome buyld suche strongholds for our enemyes in this case, that hereafter they repayre the walls of Jerico to our owne displeasour; and yet shall he be cursed of God that shall laye the foundation thereof. To be plane, if Papystes hereafter, when this generation shall passe, who lack no eyes to espie their advantage how they maye repayr the decaye of their kingdom, shall inquire of our posteritie, why were the ceremonies devysed by the Church abolyshed and taken awaye nowe of late dayis; and if it shall be answered, because they were Popyshe plants never planted by the Hevinlie Father, whereby the rude and ignorant people were desaved; and if they further shall inquire, why then was kneling left in the action of the Lord's Supper; and if they answer, as we assigne the cause, that by that decent ceremonie the sacrament shuld be kept in estymation, and that the people by knelyng shall avoyde the prophanation and disorder which abowte the holye communion myght else have ensued. In this answere, most strong to our judgments, which we teache our posterityeto geve to their adversaries, have we not mynystered a weppon to wounde, yea utterly to kylle ourselves and posteritye? For this shall be their dartts: " Your knelying, which you have of us," shall the Papystes say, " hath no more firmament [foundation] in Godde's worde than our ceremonies that ye have abolyshed. The profit that cometh of your knelyng is nowhere in Godde's word expressed, but only is the imagination of your awne braynes; lyke dammages and mo [more] are annexed to your knelyng in that actioun, than with the rest of our ceremonies. Wherefore our ceremonies ought equallie to remayne withe your knelyng."

Affections layd asyde, lett indifferent men judge how these dartts can be avoyded. By Godde's Scriptures, assuredly we are not able to declyne them, but if our religion were builded upon that onlye whiche Jesus Christ did and commanded to be done in his remembraunce, then myght not the gates of hell prevayle agaynst the same.

Why the sytting in the action of the Lord's Table is preferred to knelying.

Ffinally, as knelyng is no gesture meete at the Table, so doeth it obscure the joyfull sygnyfications of that holie mysterie. Knelyng is the gesture most commonlye of supplyantes, of beggars, or suche men as, greatly trubled by knowledge of misery or offence committed, seketh help or remission, doubting whether they shall optayne the same or not. But in the Lorde's Supper, chieflye in the action of eatyng and drynkyng, nether shoulde appere in us dolor, povertie, nor syne of any miserye. But commanded to eate and drynke by the Lorde Jesus in remembraunce of hyme, with glad countenance we aught to obbay; and so, calling to our mynde thinges that be past, present, and to come, all signe and feare of servytude and thraldom aught to be removed; to wit, that we somtymes by nature were the sonnes of Godde's wrathe, but now by grace recounted and chossyn in the nomber of the sonnes of Godde through the fayth which is in Jesus our Lord, heyres of God, and fellow heyres with Jesus Christ, in whome we rest, and by whome the Father of Mercy hathe caused us to sit amangs hevinlye thinges, and in the whome, at the end, we shall eate and drinke at his owne table prepared for us in the kingdom of that everlasting Father; of which thinges the Lord's Table is as it were our assurance and seale, in using whereof all signes of dolor aught to be removed. But before we take upon us this great honor and dignytie we aught to take of ourselves approve and tryall; in which we aught not [only] to lament and bewayle our miseries with tears, granyng and sobbes, askyng pardon and mercie for the same, but also aught we to accuse our contynuall ingratitude and great unthankfulness, that neyther can we abyde nor yet at any tyme be suche as it behoveth us to be towarde God and our neighboures. Dejected [cast down, the opposite of "erected" in the next clause] thus in our owne syght, and yet erected and raysed up through God's free promise, and so commaunded by his Sonne to eate and drinke, not as beggars (ffor by grace we are made rich in Chryst), but as sonnes and inherytours whome that victorious Kinge hath placed at his Table—aught we not most gladly to receave the honore and dignytie that is offered to us?—seyng that we canne not do more honore to God then to obbey his voyce, and so to prepare ourselves to that holie action that we appere not betrayours of our own fayth and hope, whiche is, that thraldome is taken away, and that we are the chyldern of God, yea, prests and kinges, united by Chryst's blood; and therfore, without doubting or waverynge, at Christ's commandment passe we to the Table, not as slaves or servants, but as childern of the Kyng and the redeemed people—praysing the goodness of him that hathe called us to that honor and estate. And therefore taught by Christ's example at his holie Table, we syt as men placed in quyetness, and in full possession of our kingdome.

In the propheticall churche, before that Messiah was planely revelat to the world, in that sacrament when every yeare was celebrated by the Israelites the remembraunce of God's benefits, who did deliver their fathers from the thraldome of the Egyptians, amongst manye other rites and ceremonyes, of which the most part did send them unto Chryst, with whome also they had communion and fellowshippe in his bodye and bloode— there was one ceremonye notable, that hastilye they should eate the Lambe standyng, theyr loynes gyrded, with staves in their handes; the Holie Ghost signyfying thereby their sodayne departure from Egypt, the travell and labours they shuld and did susteyne, togyther wythe the defence of God in their journey towards the land of Canaan; in possession whereof albeit Joshua brought their fathers, yet was not the ceremonye chaunged, but did continewe during the generation, because the veray Joshua that was to leade the elect people of God in [into] all rest and full possession of the kyngdom promissed was not then come in fleshe. But at suche tyme as the Sonne of God began to be preached and revealed to the world, not in figures, but even manefestly to be poynted forth by the fynger of his embassador John, from his office named Baptyzor, at that tyme and before a lyttel, began the fygures of the law to evanysshe and to cease; for John began a new ceremonye of baptising, wherewith were signed those who professed repentaunce and remyssion of synes by him that was to come. Which ceremonye Jesus Christ commanded his disciples to kepe and follow, gevyng no charge to circumsyse any; in wytness that blodd shuld cease, by reason that the very perfect sacrifice was already come, whose blood to be shed did all suche rytes, ceremonies and sacryfices as where any blood was used, represented and signyfied. And so, albeit Christ hymself was circumcised, yet after there [that] he beganne to be manefest in the word, the former Sacrement gave place to the latter. Even so do we judge between the Passover and the Lord's Table. The one appereth utterly to have gevin place to the other, even before Christ's deathe. For the nyght before he was to suffer on the morrowe, eatyng the Passover with his disciples, he appereth to have dissolved and disannulled the ceremonye of standing before used at God's commandement in that Sacrement. For evidently it dothe appere by the three Evangelystes, Matthewe, Marke, and Luke, as also by Johne in his Gospell, that the Passover that night was not eatyn standing according to the precept and commandment of the law, but sittynge, to wytness that [He] who is the end of the lawe to every believer by his travall and dolor was shortly to pass before his brethern to the kingdom wherunto they should be fully possessed by Him. For so He manefestly declared: "Desiderio desideravi hoc Pascha manducare vobiscúm antequam patiar;" "most inwardly I have desyred to eate this Passover with you before I suffer." It is to be noted that he sayth *this* Passover, as he wold saye, the ceremonye of other Passovers is here omitted; we sytt as men possessed in rest, and do not stand as men having a long, desysful [fatiguing] and tedious journay; menyng that the journay and travell of the sonnes of God was almost at an end in Himself, as that He dothe witness in these words: "Henceforth," saith Christ, "shall I not eate of it any more untyll it be fulfilled in the kingdom of God." As Christ wold say: "This Passover, as it did remember the corporall deliverance of carnall Israel, did also signifie my blood to be shed and a journay to be taken by Me, which both now be at an end. My journay was my coming from my Father into the world; now I leave the world and go to my Father agane. I that am the Head must pass before you, that ye that be the members may followe after, ffor I go to prepare you a place, yea and to establish you thereinto; and therefore it becomeyth you not to eate and drinke as straungers or foreinars, but as citizens with the saints and householdmen of God." And thus it appereth that immediately after he had said these words, "After this shall I not eate of it until it be fulfilled in the kingdom of God," he took bread and wine and did institute his supper, to be used in remembraunce of hymself; as Christ wold saye, "Nowe and henceforth shall ye not use signs and ceremonyes wherein blood is shed, with present feare, servitude and travell, but you shall eate and drinke as my brethern placed by me in rest."

That the apostles in this wise understand Christes words and the action of his mysticall supper witnesseth the Acts of the Apostles, and Pawle writing to the Corinthians, where the holie action of the supper is called the Lord's Table. Nor yet fyndeth Pawle any fault with his Corinthians that they used this facion of a Table in the congregation. But they used in the same banketting, excesse, ryotous chere and dronkenness, with contempt of the poore, which vices Paul rebuketh most sharply. But the use of the Table, whereat no doubt they used no knelyng, but kept the accustomable manner of the country, did he nather take awaye nor yet inhybit; for he was an obedient dysciple, who wold teache nothing unto them in the Lord's own action, whiche he had not received of his master Jesus Christ.

Thus have we given unto your Honors, most honorable, our plane confession whye, in the Lord's Table, we cannot admit knelyng; yet agayne takyng God to record in our conscience, and Jesus his only Sonne, in whose presence shall the secrets of all hearts be dysclosed that in this case we only seake the glorie of God and the advancement of Christs treuthe. And albeit some withstand us, of zeal also, as we suppose, towards the treuthe, yet when they shall consider the necessity that knelyng be avoyded at the Lord's Table in these perilous dayes, we doubt not but then shall they, according to their excellent gifts and solid judgements, more earnestly and more profoundly persuade unto the Kings Majestie's highness and to your Honors, that in Christs religion, and chiefly in so high a mysterie, ye not bynd that thing under a law, whereof ye neither have commandment nor example of Jesus Christ nor of his apostles, but is the mere imagination of man proceding from a false opinyon; which also hath been the gestures of Idolatours, of whom, alas! no small nomber remaineth unto this daye; as also, because by the said knelyng in that action the weyk brethern and churche of God, brought back agayne extremely to do among the idolatours that which Idolatours [do], are greatly offended; and ffinally, because such gestures, nothing comely for a Table, do obscure the joyfull sygnifications of such things as in that Table we ought to remember, and by very practice to declare to the world. These and mo causes which their wysdoms better can [add?] deeply considered, we doubt not but their fervent desire to Christs glorie shall move them boldly to speak. So shall your Honors' careful dilygence provide that Christs Religion in this realm—all praise and honor be unto God, now tending to perfection and maturitie,—so surely be founded upon Chryste and upon his expresse word, that not only it may abyde the stormy warrs of mens judgment, but also the warfare, the trial of Gods sacrat word we mean, which when it cometh, as it must needs consume and burn away the stuble haye and wood, without respect of persons; so must it try and declare to be fine the gold, silver, and precious stones, how contemned [soever] that other builder appered that builded such fine stuff upon the sure foundement.

Our weke judgements tuchyng the Reformation of other ceremonies contained in the foresaid Bowke we have committed to writing in the Latin tongue, being redy, upon commandment, to put the same also in English. Unfeynedly beseeching the Father of all mercies that so your harts maye be rewled by the holy Ghost that in all the actions of your life you may prefer the will and pleasure of God, contayned within his sacrat word, to longe processe of tyme, and consuettude of man's authority. And so, no doubt, when that great Bishop and onlye Pastor of our souls, Jesus our Saviour, shall appere, at whose presence shall tremble and ever be confounded all tyrannous oppressors of his treuthe, but he shall acknowledge you his true professors, purged with his blood, clad with justice and grace, with him mayde heritours of lyffe everlasting. So be it.

NOTES.

THE historical genuineness of the above document—that it was no after-forgery, but an authentic factor of the sudden movement in high places which issued in the addition of the "Declaration on kneeling," at the last moment, to Edward's Second Prayer-book, may fairly be taken as proved by the observations already offered upon that point in the preceding narrative, pp. 110–11. Its date, also, and all the circumstances which gave rise to it, having already been brought into view, it only remains to determine the question of authorship. As the names of those who drew it up and presented it to the Privy Council do not appear upon the face of the paper itself, how can it be shown that Knox was the principal author of it? and is it possible to determine, with any good degree of probability, the other name or names that were attached to the original document, of which the MS. now printed was only a copy? In the narrative we have assumed that Knox was the chief author; we have now to exhibit the evidence upon which that assumption rests.

The names of the six Royal Chaplains to whom the "Articles" were submitted for their learned judgment were, it will be remembered, "Messrs. Harley, Bill, Horn, Grindal, Perne, and Knox." How many of these reported their judgment to the Council we do not know; we only know, from the Council Book, under date 20th November, of the same year, 1552, that reports were not received from all, as it is recorded there that the Articles had been "considered by certain of His Majesty's Chaplains and others." The whole number of persons, therefore, among whom we have to seek for the authors of the paper before us could not have been considerable, and this diminishes, of course, the difficulty of singling them out.

Confining ourselves, at first, to "certain of His Majesty's Chaplains," Knox is the only man among them, judging from all we know of the rest, who was likely to have taken so stringent a view of the practice of kneeling in the sacrament, and touching the reformation of other ceremonies. Harley, Bill, and Perne were all conservative Reformers; their names never appear among the Protestant exiles whose superior zeal in the cause of reformation had made it dangerous for them to remain in the kingdom, after the accession of Mary; and though other two of the chaplains, Horn and Grindal, shared in that exile, it is well known that they were very far from agreeing with Knox in his dislike of many things still retained in the Prayer-book. In the "troubles of Frankfurt," arising out of the liturgical question, they both sided with Dr. Cox, against their former colleague; and we may be quite certain that they could never have joined in the strong representations against kneeling and other ceremonies, which had been submitted, only two or three years before, to the Privy Council. Knox is thus left standing alone among the chaplains, as the only man among them who can be supposed, with any probability, to have been the author of the document.*

This probability is further very much strengthened by the consideration that nothing was more natural than that that Royal chaplain who had only a few weeks before preached against kneeling in the sacrament before the King and Court, should also have become the author of such a written remonstrance. He would even have failed in the duty he owed to his own convictions, if he had not embraced the opportunity so unexpectedly offered to him, of pressing them upon the Council in this new form.

But, of course, this evidence must be corroborated by the internal characteristics of the document itself, both as to thought and style. Let it then be carefully compared with Knox's Epistle to the congregation of Berwick, written late in 1552. That epistle bears his name, both at the beginning and end, and is indubitably his production. But no one who passes from the one to the other can fail to recognize the strong resemblance between them, in every respect—in sentiment, in tone, in style—in all the marks, in a word, of what he often calls his own "rude hand." The subject is precisely the same in both documents, and in both is considered from precisely the same point of view. The intense conviction, the

---

* It was no doubt the Royal chaplains whom he chiefly alluded to when he spoke of his "fellow preachers," in the "Epistle" given above, as being, along with his superiors—*i.e.*, the Bishops—of a contrary judgment to his own. In relation to all these learned men alike, he was himself, on this point of difference of judgment, "but one"—he stood quite alone.

ardour of feeling, the "perfervidum ingenium" are, throughout, the same in both; the resemblance extends even to the frequent recurrence of the same characteristic single words and phrases.*

Curiously enough, however, there is a good deal of matter in the second part of the document (that in which the writers urge that the gesture of kneeling in the Sacrament "obscures the joyful significations of that holy mystery") which is not to be found in the Epistle or in any of Knox's other writings. We refer, particularly, to the striking and ingenious reasonings put forward on the subject of the analogies and differences between the Feast of the Passover, with its standing posture, and the Lord's Supper, with its gesture of sitting. On noticing this, it occurred to us that, as the document was a joint one, these ideas might have been contributed to the Paper by one or other of the divines who associated themselves with him in drawing it up, and that if the same ideas were to be found in the writings of any of the reformed divines of the period, we might thus come upon probable traces of the learned person or persons who had taken part with Knox in preparing and signing the Paper. Nor was our search for such parallels in vain. We found striking instances of them both in the works of Thomas Becon and Roger Hutchinson of Eton College. Becon was made rector of St. Stephen's, Walbrook, in 1547, and remained in possession of that influential post till the accession of Mary. He was held in high estimation by Cranmer for his learning and godliness, became one of his chaplains, and also chaplain to the Duke of Somerset, and was promoted to a divinity chair in the University of Cambridge. He was, in all respects, a very likely man to be consulted by the Council, in 1552, on the subject of the Articles; and the coincidence of his published views on the subject of the right observance of the Lord's Supper with those of Knox and the "Confession" to the Council, now under consideration, is very remarkable.

In Becon's tract, "The Displaying of the Popish Mass," addressed to the Romish priests, occurs the following passage:—

"And this also is to be noted, that when Christ came in his own usual apparel unto the table he did not kneel, as the Papists do, nor yet stand, as the Jews did in the old law; but he sat down at the

---

* The repeated use of the word *dolor*, and the phrases, "taking God to record in our conscience," "long processe of time," and "consuetude of man's authority," are all characteristic notes of Knox's style.

table. How do ye agree with Christ, at your Mass, in this behalf? Christ sat; ye sometime stand right up, sometime lean upon your elbows, sometime crouch downward, sometime kneel; but sit will ye never, because ye will still contrary Christ, and be one ace above him. And although gestures in this behalf seem, after some men's judgment, to be indifferent, yet the nearer we come to Christs order the better it is; for who can prescribe a more perfect trade for all things to be done at and about the ministration of the Lord's Supper than that which Christ used himself?

"Indeed, the Jews, when they received their sacrament, I mean the Paschal lamb (which was also a figure of Christ to come and to be slain, as ours is a sign and token that he is already come, slain and gone), stood upon their feet, with their loins girded and staves in their hands, to signify not only that they were strangers and pilgrims in this world and had here no dwelling city, but also that there was a farther journey yet to go in the religion of God, and that other sacraments were to be looked for. But Christ and his disciples did sit at their supper, to declare that all things afore figured in the law are now perfectly fulfilled in Christ, the Lamb of God which was 'slain from the beginning of the world;' and that there are no more sacraments to be looked for nor none other doctrine to be inquired for,—neither the Jews' Talmuth, nor Mahomet's Alkaron, nor the Pope's Decretals, nor yet the Emperor's Interim, but that doctrine only which Christ hath already taught and left in writing by the hands of the apostles.

"The Christian religion, both concerning sacraments and doctrine, is now, by Christ, brought unto such a consummate perfection and perfect consummation that nothing ought to be added as necessary also for our salvation. Therefore doth Christ, with his apostles, sit at the receiving of the sacrament, and not stand, after the manner of the Jews; even as they, which travelling by the way are come unto their journey's end, are wont to sit down and to take their rest. Here have we an example of Christ to sit at the Lord's table, when we receive the holy Communion, and not to kneel. But this do ye, Papists, neither observe yourselves nor yet suffer others so to do. . . . But why bind ye the people rather to kneel at the ministration of the Lord's Supper rather than at the ministration of Baptism?—seeing Christ is no less present at the one than at the other, and, by his Holy Spirit, worketh no less effectually in baptism than he doth in the Supper? Why do ye not also compel to kneel at the preaching of God's Word, seeing it is of no less authority than the sacrament of Christ's body and blood?"

In another of his works, "A new Catechism set forth dialoguewise in familiar talk between the Father and the Son," Becon gives still fuller and more pungent expression to his views in the following passage:—

"*Father.*—But what sayest thou concerning the gestures to be used at the Lord's Table? Shall we receive these holy mysteries kneeling, standing, or sitting?

"*Son.*—Albeit I know and confess that gestures of themselves be indifferent, yet I would wish all such gestures to be avoided as have outwardly any appearance of evil, according to this saying of St. Paul, 'Abstain from all evil appearance;' and, first of all, for as much as kneeling hath been long used in the Church of Christ at the receiving of the Sacrament, through the doctrine of the Papists, although of itself it be indifferent to be or not to be used, yet would I wish that it were taken away by the authority of the higher powers.

"*Father.*—Why so?

"*Son.*—Because it hath an outward appearance of evil. When the Papists, through their pestilent persuasions, had made of the sacramental bread and wine a God, and had taught and commanded the people to take and worship it as God, then gave they in commandment, straightways, that all people should with all reverence kneel unto it, worship and honour it. And by this means this gesture of kneeling crept in, and is yet used in the Church of the Papists, to declare that they worship the sacrament as their Lord God and Saviour. But I would wish, with all my heart, that either this kneeling of the sacrament were taken away or else that the people were taught that that outward reverence were not given to the Sacrament and outward sign, but to Christ, which is represented by that sacrament or sign. But the most certain and sure way is utterly to cease from kneeling, that there may outwardly appear no kind of evil, according to this commandment of St. Paul, 'Abstain from all evil appearance,' lest the enemies, by continuance of kneeling, should be confirmed in their error, and the weaklings offended and plucked back from the truth of the Gospel. Kneeling with the knowledge of godly honour is due to none but God alone. Therefore, when Satan commanded our Saviour Christ to kneel down before him and worship him, he answered, 'It is written, Thou shalt worship the Lord.'

"Standing, which is used in the most part of the reformed churches in these our days, I can right well allow it, if it be appointed by common order to be used at the receiving of the holy Communion. And this gesture of standing was also used, at the commandment of God, of the old Jews, when they did eat the Paschal lamb, which was also a sacrament and figure of Christ to come, as our sacrament is a figure of Christ come and gone. Neither did that gesture want his mystery. For the standing of the Jews at the eating of the Lord's Passover signified that they had a farther journey to go in matters of religion, and that there was a more clear light of the Gospel to shine than had hitherto appeared unto them, which were wrapped round about with the dark shadows of ceremonies; again, that other, yea, and those more perfect, sacraments were to be given to Christ's people; which all things were fulfilled and came to pass under Christ, the author of the heavenly doctrine of the Gospel and the Institutor of the holy sacraments, baptism and the Lord's Supper.

"Now, as concerning sitting at the Lord's Table, which is also used at this day in certain reformed churches, if it were received by public authority and common consent, and might conveniently be used in our churches, I could allow that gesture best. For, as it is not to be doubted but that Christ and his disciples sat at the table, when Christ delivered unto them the sacrament of his body and blood, which use was also observed in the primitive church, and long time after; so likely it is most comely that we Christians follow the example of our Master Christ, and of his disciples. Nothing can be more reverently done, that is done after the example of Christ and of his Apostles. We come together to eat and drink the holy mysteries of the body and blood of Christ; we have a table set before us—is it not meet and convenient that we sit at our table? The table being prepared, who standeth at his meat? Yea, rather, who sitteth not down?

"When Christ fed the people, he bade them not kneel down, nor stand upon their feet, but he commanded them to sit down; which kind of gesture is most meet when we assemble to eat and drink, which thing we do at the Lord's Table. Neither doth the sitting of the communicants at the Lord's Table want her mystery. For, as the standing of the Jews, at the eating of the Lord's Passover, signified that there was yet to come another doctrine than the law of Moses, even the preaching of the glorious gospel of our Lord and Saviour Christ Jesus, and other sacraments than circumcision and the passover, even the sacraments of baptism and the Lord's Supper; so, in like manner, the sitting of the Christian communicants at the Lord's Table doth signify, preach and declare unto us, that we are come to our journey's end concerning religion, and that there is none other doctrine, none other sacraments to be looked for than those only which we have already received of Christ the Lord. And therefore, we sitting down at the Lord's Table, shew by that our gesture, that we are come to the perfection of our religion, and look for none other doctrine to be given unto us. Notwithstanding, as I said before, gestures are free, so that none occasion of evil be either done or offered. In all things which we call indifferent, this rule of St. Paul is diligently to be obeyed: 'Abstain from all evil appearance.'

"*Father.*—I do not disallow thy judgment in this behalf."

A divine of King Edward's days who could hold and teach sacramental views like these, could have had no difficulty in joining with Knox in his Memorial to the Privy Council, and must have been quite as much in earnest as he to see effect given to such views in the Reformation of the Church. The Memorial was quite as true an expression of the mind of Becon as of Knox, and, in all probability, was their joint production, if only two hands were concerned in it. But there may have been more than two concerned in it, though two would have sufficed to account for the use of its plural pronouns, "we," and "us," and "our." Can a third man, then, be found who would probably be requested to report his Judgment along with them, and who, if he complied with the request, would as probably have joined with them in drawing up such a Memorial?

In that very year, 1552, Roger Hutchinson, the learned provost of Eton College, preached "Three Sermons on the Lord's Supper," in the College chapel, which he sent soon afterwards to John Day, the printer, "dwelling over Aldersgate," for publication. The tone, the ring of these discourses, would have been thoroughly to Knox's liking; and it is even possible enough that he may have heard them. For that very autumn Knox was preaching in St.

George's Chapel, Windsor, upon the very same subject, and in precisely the same spirit, as Hutchinson in the neighbouring College chapel of Eton.

Here is one passage of the second sermon: "But thou wilt say, 'Tell me how I shall prepare myself to receive this Sacrament.' Many coming to the Lord's Table do misbehave themselves, and so do the lookers-on, in that they worship the Sacrament with kneeling and bowing their bodies, and knocking their breasts, and with elevation of their hands. If it were to be elevated and shewed unto the standers-by, as it hath been used, Christ would have elevated it above his head. He delivered it into the hands of his disciples, bidding them to eat it and not to hold up their hands—to receive it and not to worship it, and he delivered it to them sitting and not kneeling. If either the bread or the wine were to be heaved up, or to be received or hanged up in a pix, as it hath been abused—if it were to be honoured of the receivers, or to be kneeled unto of the lookers-on—undoubtedly Christ would have left us some commandment so to do, or else have taught us by his ensample, or, at the least, he would have left some promise of reward annexed to this outward reverence and homage, or some threatening and punishment for such as will not worship it. Aye, verily; for there is nothing laudable, nothing righteous, nothing honest or acceptable in God's sight, nothing to be done for the which He has not left in his Scriptures either some commandment or some promise of reward, or some example. By his promises, by his threatenings, by his precepts, and through the examples of godly men and women, we know good from evil; we know what is to be done and what is to be left undone; what is to be praised and what is to be dispraised; what delighteth and pleaseth, and what discontenteth and displeaseth the Divine Majesty. God's Book is no imperfect work, but a perfect Book, containing all things to be done—the whole duty of a Christian man, and sufficient doctrine to instruct a God's man in all good works, and to make him perfect, as Paul witnesseth, writing to Timothy; and he must needs accuse God either of ignorancy, or of folly, or of negligence which saith that He hath left any thing untouched and undeclared which concerneth a Christian man's office, and is needful and necessary unto salvation. All such things be expressed in God's book. For in the writing of the prophets He requireth the observation of his law only concerning religion; and He threateneth great plagues and grievous punishments to those that do add any thing to his word, that is to those which teach any other doctrine, or any work to be necessary unto salvation, which is not commanded in his word. But neither Christ nor any of the prophets, nor his disciples, do give us any example to honour the Sacrament; for they kneeled not, neither held up their hands, but sat at the table, as the text witnesseth. Neither doth God promise any benefit, either spiritual or temporal, to such as honour it; nor He doth not give us any precept so to do, neither in the Old nor New Testament. Therefore I say unto you that it is sin to worship the Sacrament, to hold up thy hands, or to bow thy body and kneel to it; for to worship God otherwise than He hath taught us in his holy Book, which is the Bible, is mere idolatry. Be not deceived, good people, nor bewitched with superstition and false holiness; for the Apostle St. Paul saith, *Quicquid non est ex fide, peccatum est.* 'Whatsoever is not of faith' (which cometh, as Paul saith also, by hearing God's word) 'is sin.' If thou wilt honour the Sacrament, I ask thee whether thou do it with faith, or without faith. If thou do it through faith, shew me some text, some testimony, some authority of God's word, or some example in God's Book; for *fides ex auditu.* Faith, saith Paul, cometh by hearing God's word. If thou worship it without God's word—without faith, which cometh only by God's word—hear what Paul saith to thee: 'It is impossible to please God without faith.' For to worship God otherwise than He hath taught us is heresy, is idolatry, is disworship and dishonour of the Divine Majesty. Socrates, a heathen and no Christian man, and yet a learned and a great famous clerk, he in his lifetime held this assertion, that every god is to be honoured and worshipped after such manner and with such ceremonies and rites as he himself teacheth and commandeth. He did attribute more wisdom and more authority to false gods than we do to the God of heaven and earth, who is the fountain of all wisdom, power and authority. It is to be feared that he, at the last day, shall arise to the condemnation of many which profess Christ."

These reasonings, it is true, are addressed to Romanists, not to Protestants; but they are the reasonings of a Protestant like Knox—not of a Protestant like Cranmer. They are the reasonings of a *Puritan* Protestant, directed against "kneeling" in the Sacrament as well as against "knocking"—against kneeling, which Cranmer retained, as much as against knocking, which Cranmer abolished. Hutchinson lays down the fundamental principle of Puritanism, which is that God's Book is a perfect Book, containing the whole duty of a Christian man, and sufficient doctrine, without the addition of Church-doctrine as distinguished from Bible-doctrine, to instruct " a God's man " in all good works, and to make him perfect.

In the Provost of Eton of that day, we see another Edwardian divine who must have sympathized with Knox as thoroughly as Becon has been shown to have done in the question now before us, and who could heartily have joined with him in the representations of the Memorial; and in all probability Hutchinson, who was a man of mark and high place among the reformed clergy of the day, was one of the divines consulted by the Privy Council on this important occasion. But whether this conjecture be accepted or not—for of course it is nothing more than a conjecture—enough has been said to show that there were not wanting, in and near the capital of the kingdom, men who not only were competent men to advise the young King and his Council in such a Church emergency as had arisen, but who were men of Puritan principles and convictions, like John Knox, the royal chaplain, and who could have no difficulty in associating themselves with him in the earnest written remonstrance which he addressed to the Council.

It is impossible to compare the style of the Memorial to the Council with that of these quotations from Becon and Hutchinson without being sensible of a great difference between the two. The former is the rough and uncouth style of the North of England and of all Scotchmen of that age, and of many generations later, who endeavoured to write English; the latter is the much purer, sweeter, and more flowing style of Mid-England and the southern counties. It is manifest that whatever Englishmen may have joined Knox in the Memorial, and whatever they may have contributed to its substance of thought, it was Knox himself who held the pen. They could as little have written in his manner as he could have written in theirs. But if he held the pen, it must have been he also who had taken the initiative. Others joined him— but he was the chief actor—he led the way.

A comparison of these passages from the writings of Becon and Hutchinson with others in the works of John A'Lasco referred to in " Additional Notes " to Chap. III. in Part I. of this volume, leads to the conclusion that these divines had had before them either the Polish theologian's "Brevis et dilucida de Sacramentis Ecclesiae Christi Tractatio," or his "Forma ac Ratio tota Ecclesiastici Ministerii," &c. As Hutchinson's sermons were preached in 1552, and A'Lasco's "Brevis et dilucida Tractatio" appeared in the same year, the latter work must have been that which the learned Provost had before him. Becon's work, quoted above, was not published till a few years later, and either of A'Lasco's two works may have suggested to him the remarkable ideas in which he bears so unmistakable a resemblance to him. In all probability he became acquainted with the earlier of the two works as soon as it appeared, as it was published in London. In this work A'Lasco expatiates at great length upon the *symbolism* of the two attitudes of standing in the Passover and sitting in the Lord's Supper. In his later work of 1555, he repeats many of the same ideas, with more compression, and we prefer on this account to present them in a few paragraphs quoted from that work.

In his account of the "Ritus Coenae Dominicae in Ecclesia peregrinorum Londini," he speaks of the church of the foreigners having adopted the practice of sitting at the Lord's Supper, and of their reasons for preferring this practice to that of kneeling, standing, or walking, in the following terms:—

"Praeterea consessum publicum genuflexioni ac stationi, denique et ambulationi in Coenae usu anteposuimus, ejusque rei nobis multas causas, easque non leves habuisse videmur. Longum autem fuerit commemorare omnes, neque id nostri nunc instituti esse videtur. Sed tamen aliquot recensebimus, ne id temere fecisse existimemur. Hoc interim adjecto, quod nos consessum publicum non ita perpetuum in Coenae usu habemus quin (dum preces funduntur ad Dominum) in genua procumbamus; sed in ipsa actione mystica, in instituta (inquam) a Christo Domino panis et poculi distributione et participatione mensae accumbimus, quicunque illi participamus. Idque eas potissimum ob causas.

"Primum in confesso est omnibus ecclesiae ministris, id potissimum in ipsorum ministerio sequendum esse, quod certo constat magis facere ad ecclesiae aedificationem. Neque dubium est ea ad veram Ecclesiae aedificationem magis multo facere, quorum fontes in verbo Dei palam conspiciuntur, quam quae rationis duntaxat nostrae judicio (extra verbum Dei) speciosa esse videntur. Cum igitur negari non possit, consessum seu accubitum in Coenae actione ipsa, manifestos suos fontes habere in Christi Domini exemplo et Apostolorum observatione, scripturae testimonio; qui fontes alioqui neque in **statione** neque in genuflexione, neque etiam in ambulatione commonstrari possunt. Sane quatenus Ministri Ecclesiae officium suum in suo ministerio praestare volunt, perspicuum est illos (si id eis ullo modo liceat) consessum potius seu accubitum in Coenae Dominicae actione retinere debere, quam aut stationem aut genuflexionem aut ambulationem. Et proinde erat etiam debiti officiique nostri (post permissam nobis praesertim Regia auctoritate nostram libertatem) consessum potius in nostris Ecclesiis in Coenae usu retinere, quam aut stationem aut genuflexionem aut ambulationem.

" Deinde id quoque extra omnem controversiam positum esse constat, magis multo Christianum esse, ut Christum Dominum nihil omnino vane atque otiose vel egisse vel docuisse putemus in Coenae suae institutione; et proinde nihil quoque eorum quae ille tum aut egit aut docuit, immutandum quoquo modo esse, quasi ipsum vane atque otiose egisse docuisseve aliquid, et proinde id nobis pro nostro arbitrio mutandum esse dicamus. Cumque satis constet ex historica Evangelistarum narratione, Christum Dominum exemplo nobis suo, consessum seu accubitum in Coenae suae actione commendasse, certe, quatenus nos eum ipsum consessum neque vane, neque otiose a Christo Domino in Coena sua observatum esse credimus, hactenus illum nobis (quoad ejus fieri queat) retinendum potius quam rejiciendum esse intelligemus. Aut certe re ipsa testabimur (quidquid hic omnino praetendamus) consessum illum vane atque otiose a Christo Domino observatum fuisse, si illum pro nostro arbitrio sine necessitate ulla tolli, aut quoquo modo permutari posse statuamus.

" Imo vero, cum in typica illa Agni olim Paschalis Coena existimandum non est, ullam omnino actionem observatam fuisse quae non suum aliquod, et quidem minime contemnendum mysterium haberet; equidem sine Christi Domini indignitate facere non possumus, ut ea quae ipse in sua cum Apostolis suis Coena (novi testamenti sui obsignaculo) observavit aut suis mysteriis, et quidem multo sublimioribus carere; aut si non careant, abjici a nobis posse arbitremur. Et quemadmodum, cogitandum non est vanum atque otiosum fuisse olim, in Coenae Paschalis apud Iudaeos observatione lumbis accinctis, baculisque in manus sumptis, agnum typicum edere. Nimirum haec testabantur et designabant, magnum adhuc populo iter reliquum fuisse, prius quam typicam suam promissionis terram oculis suis conspecturi essent. Admonebantque praeterea illum populum, ut ad emetiendum iter illud, accinctus semper expeditusque esset, si quidem eo pervenire vellet. Ita et nunc alienum id a nobis maxime esse oportet ut observatum a Christo Domino ejusque demum etiam apostolis consessum in Coena novi testamenti ipsius, vanum, otiosum omnique mysterio vacuum esse imaginemur. Sed est potius nobis summa religione observandum, longe praestantissimum illud, plenumque summae consolationis mysterium, nostrae tam quietis in Christo ipsiusmet Christi Domini verbis nobis commendatum. Nempe, non esse nobis amplius cum Judaeis quaerendam alibi in terris aliam ullam promissionis terram. Sed nos jam per Christum Dominum verum nostrum Josue (mortis suae merito) in vera promissionis terra (saluti videlicet nostra aeterna) collocatos, residere jam prorsusque quiescere debere. Intuentes perpetuo meritum mortis et resurrectionis Christi, ac donatam nobis gratuito salutarem illius communionem, cujus equidem vim ac dignitatem publicus noster in Coenae Dominicae usu consessus symbolo nobis suo adumbrat, attestatur et commendat; quatenus sane Coenam Domini, nostrae cum Christo communionis, et proinde nostrae quoque in illo quietis certum ac salutare obsignaculum esse (juxta ejus institutionem) non dubitamus. Id vero si qui secum animo Christiano perpendere volent, facile intelligent nos in observando circa Coenae usum consessu publico in nostris Ecclesiis, justam satis nostri consilii rationem sequutos esse; facta nobis praesertim potestate ut Christi Domini doctrinam hic atque apostolorum observationem sequeremur. Praeterea ipsae etiam coenae ac mensae Dominicae voces Paulo alioqui apostolo familiares, consessum potius quam aut stationem, genuflexionem aut ambulationem requirere videntur. Nemo enim hac fini coenam aut convivium usquam instituit, neque item convivas ita excipit quisque ut qui convivio sunt adhibendi aut stare, aut ambulare, aut genuflectentes convivari debeant. Sed accumbere considereve jubentur convivae omnes, ut, compositis ad quietem et corporibus et animis pariter, omnes epulentur. Ministrorum est non convivarum, mensis adstare aut circum illas ambulare. Et genuflexio ad altaris adhuc ministerium potius quam ad coenae apparatum videtur pertinere. Ubi dum victimae pro populo offerebantur, vota quoque flexis genibus fiebant, ut oblatio acceptaretur. At vero nullum amplius in terris altare novit Christi Ecclesia. Estque longe alia mensarum ac conviviorum (ut est dictum) et proinde Coenae quoque Dominicae quam altaris ratio. Quam sane sequutus Paulus epulari nos jubet ut convivas, eo quod verus tum demum Agnus noster ille Paschalis Christus Dominus sit pro nobis oblatus; atque in cibum animarum nostrarum (Coenae suae testimonio) propositus, ut illo ad vitam aeternam (per fidem) pascamur, quemadmodum Christus ipsemet apud Ioannem docet. Et vanum id praeterea etiam videri non debet quod Christus Dominus regni nobis coelestis sui felicitatem sub convivii imagine quadam, cum alibi, tum vero etiam in sua Coena adumbrare se nobis voluisse testatur. Quemadmodum enim in Coena sua Apostolis ad mensam accumbentibus panem ac poculum Coenae administravit, ita illis olim etiam nobisque sub eorum nomine omnibus accumbentibus, edentibus ac bibentibus in coelesti sua mensa ministraturum se esse pollicetur. Ut Coenam ipsius hic veluti typum quendam ab ipso institutum esse intelligamus coelestis nostrae olim gloriae, adumbratae nobis sub convivii cujusdam imagine; in quo nobis cum

Abrahamo, Isaaco et Jacobo pariter accumbentibus atque epulantibus ministraturum se esse testatur. Quam sane foelicitatis nostrae aeternae in coelesti olim gloria imaginem (convivialis consessus symbolo nobis ab ipso met Christo Domino ad indicibilem piorum omnium consolationem commendatam), obliterare in Ecclesia velle, sublato (dum retineri potest) illius symbolo; equidem haud scio ad id quisquam gloriae Christi et foelicitatis aeternae illius studiosus, in animum suum inducere possit.

"Postremo vero, non tantum nobis commendatur consessus noster in Coenae Domini usu exemplo Christi Domini, mysteriique sui, quietis (inquam) nostrae hic in Christo designatione, aut futurae olim nostrae in regno Dei gloriae, typica quadam per convivialem accubitum adumbratione; sed praecipi nobis etiam propemodum mandato illo Dominico videtur—*Hoc facite*. Neque enim negari potest hoc mandato comprehendi id totum quod Christus Dominus tum et docuit et fecit. Cumque extra omnem controversiam sit Christum accumbentibus suis Apostolis Coenam suam instituisse, negari sane etiam non potest accubitum illum seu consessum partem fusse omnino actionis in ipsa Coenae institutione, et proinde a mandato illo (Hoc facite) excludi haudquaquam posse. . . . . . .

"Sed non ideo tamen Ecclesias eas omnes violatae divinae institutionis accusamus, quae in Coenae Dominicae usu consessum adhuc publicum non observant. Aliud est enim illum sine ulla necessitate sustulisse; aliud vero, per alios sublatum restituere adhuc non posse sine magna Ecclesiarum perturbatione. Fatemur Filium hominis esse Dominum etiam ipsius Sabbati. Et cum Augustino non putamus scindendas esse Ecclesias propter ea quae nos ex se neque digniores neque indigniores coram Deo facere possunt. Sed officium fidelium in Ecclesia ministrorum esse dicimus ut Divinas omnes Institutiones pro summa virili sua (juxta fidem sui ministerii) ad puritatem illam primaevam doctrinae et observationis Apostolicae reducere semper per omnem occasionem conentur.

"Quod ipsum equidem nos etiam nobis in consessu Coenae Dominicae restituenda sequendum esse existimavimus; praesertim cum illum Christi Domini exemplo, Apostolicaque observatione, mysterii etiam excellentia et typica coelestis nostrae olim gloriae adumbratione, denique et mandato ipso Dominico non temere proculdubio commendatum esse, et proinde etiam ad Ecclesiae aedificationem plurimum facere videremus. Et quidem cum nobis ejus rei potestas Regia autoritate facta esset.

"Haec vero ita de restituto hic per nos in nostris Ecclesiis Coenae Dominicae consessu suo publico commemorare voluimus, ut consilii hac in parte nostri rationem piis omnibus redderemus. Multa autem omisimus quae ad eam rem adferri adhuc poterant, quod his satisfactum piis omnibus fore non dubitemus."

The whole of A'Lasco's views and reasonings in the above extracts from this rare and extremely remarkable work, bear a striking resemblance to those contained in Knox's "Confession," or Memorial to the Privy Council;—so much so, that it would have been almost impossible not to infer that A'Lasco had associated himself with Knox in the preparation of that document, or, at any rate, had been consulted by him about it, if we had not found two English divines at hand who were imbued with the very same ideas derived, it is manifest, from A'Lasco's work on the Lord's Supper. Before publishing that work in 1552, he had preached the whole substance of it in the pulpit of Austin Friars, and in this way his original and very remarkable views of the symbolism of all the parts of Christ's institution may have become known to Becon and Hutchinson by report in 1551. It is not probable that a foreigner would join in presenting a memorial in English to the Privy Council on a matter in which he had no official concern.

III.

The practies of the Lordës Supper yewsed in Barvike-upon-Twyed by Johne Knoxe, precher to that congregation in the Churche there.

Ffyrst, seartan sarmonds [certain sermons] of the benefitts of God by Jesus Chryst, gyven unto us, Johne 13, 14, 15, 16 chapters.

Then after that the principall mynester standing in the pulpit that all the people mycht see, begyns, " In the name of the Father, and of the Sonne, and of the Holye Gost." Amen.

Let us all praye.

Omnypotent and everlasting God, whome all creatures do know and confesse Thee to be Governer and Lorde, but we thy creatures, created to thyne own image and symilitude, ought at all tymes to feare, adore, love and prayse thye godlye Majistie—fyrst for owr creation, but principally for owr redemption when we were dead and lost by sin. Grant unto us thy moist unprofitable servants, that we come together to celebrate the Supper of thy beloved Sonne Jesus Christ our onlye Lord and Saviour, and that we myght do the same with syncere faythe, in remembrance of Him, and thanksgeving unto Thee for thy most lyberall kyndness shewed, graunted, and gevin unto us by thy Sonne our Lorde Jesus, who lyveth and reigneth with Thee in unitie of the Holy Ghost, one God, world without end. Amen.

Then must be red this porcion of Pawlle to the Corinthians, "When they come together," untyll this part, " If we judge ourselves "; with the declaration of the Apostell's mynd upon the same place, for sertyffynge [certifying] the consciences of suche as shall use the Lord's Table without supersticion.

Then must be declaryd what persons be unworthy to be partakers therof; and because no fflesh is juste in the sight of God, commone prayer shall be mayde in fforme of confession, as after followythe :—

Allmyghtie and everlastynge Lord, unyversall but yet most mercifull Father, we have offended and daylye do offend the ees of thy majestie in all the actions of our lyffe. Just cause hast Thou, O Lord, to thrist us into hell for our manyfold offencis, the remembrance wherof is grevous to our conscience, so paynfull and dollorous that easse nor relaxation in ourselves can we fynd none. Whome to shall we call? Whom shall we seke? Who maye release owr sorrow and restore gladnes, but Thou alone, O mercyful Lorde? Thou art the Father of pyttyes, the well of mercye and infinyte goodness, whiche maye not be overcome. We are encoraged to aske mercie of Thee, for when we were Thine enymies, dead by synne, and colde do nothyng but blaspheme Thee in thy face, Thou wast movyd to have mercie; Thou loved and colde not hait us; and *so* Thou loved us that Thou gave thy onlye-begotten Sonne Jesus Chryst for our redemption; and by Him hast Thou mayd unto us one promyse that whensoever two or three gathered in his name asks any thing of thee, the same they shall obtain by Him. We most humblye beseche Thee, by thy Sonne our onlye Savior, fyrst, that Thou wilt mercyfullie forgyve all our synnes and iniquities bypast, which we acknowlege and confess here in thy sight; and that Thou wilt favorably torne awaye from us, throughe the blood and satysfaction of thy Sonne our onlye Savior, thy most just wrath, whyche we have deservyd throughe so manyfold transgressions of thy commandments; and confyrme Thou in us thy Holy Spreit, that we maye utterlye geve ourselves to the obedience of Thee, both nowe and ever; that calling upon Thee alwayes for ourselves and others, we maye obtayne grace and help by Jesus Christ our onlye Lord. Amen.

Some notable place of the Evangell wherein God's mercie is most evidentlye declared shuld as then be rede, planely to assure the penitent of ffull remissyon of all offencyes; and therafter ought the minester openlye to prononce to suche as unfaynydlye repent and belyve in Jesus Christ, to be absolvyd from all dampnacion, and to stand in the favor of God. And therefore ought the mynester to heve [have] there [at that place of the service] prayers mayd not onlye for themselves but also for others; whereupon they owght to begyne to praye for that congregacion.

A Prayer for the Congregacion.

Delyver, O Lorde, thy holye congregacion, thyne own inheryntance, redemyd and bought by the blood of Jesus Chryst, and pryncipally this congregacion of England ffrom all wolves and hyred servants whych ether by tyrannye or proud usurpyd authoritye or domynyon molests and vexes, or throwgh deceipt and avaryce spoyls and doth oppress thy scattered and miserable sheipe. Destroye Thou them, O Lord, and soffer them no longer to prevaille against us. Gyve unto us good and faythfull mynesters, to whome it may please thy goodness to geve the trew spreit of knolyge and understanding, that therby unto us they myght open the secrets of thy Evangell. Encrease with us and them bothe thy Holye Ghost, that we may faythfullye serve Thee, to the good example and provocation of others; that thy scattered sheip throughe the Gospell may be gathered to thy deare Sonne the highe and onlye trew Shepherd and Byshop of oure solles, Jesus Chryst, from all wronge errors; that breffelye we maye be brought agene to the trew communyon of Him, that there may be one flock and one Shepherd.

A Prayer for the Queen's Majestie.

NOTES.

THIS fragment (for it is plainly nothing more) is unquestionably from Knox's own hand. It has the unmistakable signatures of his style of thought and feeling and diction.

It must have been penned by him for his own use in Berwick, either in 1549 or 1550—most probably in the latter year, because he must have been preaching there for some months before the congregation could have been prepared to concur in the new Order of the Communion Service, of which this paper is an interesting though imperfect memorial.

It is singular to find the last item of this "Practies" or Order described as a prayer for the *Queen's* Majestie, instead of the *King's*, as of course it must have stood in Knox's own manuscript. The copy which has come down to us must have been made either early in Queen Mary's reign—before the congregation was compelled to return to the Popish form of worship—or early in Queen Elizabeth's, after the Protestant worship had been restored, and before strict conformity to the Prayer-book began to be enforced. It is well known that, during several of the first years of Elizabeth's reign, such conformity was neither very general nor very much urged by the bishops, who were, in many instances, men of Puritan sympathies; and there were few places where that was so likely to be the case as in Berwick, where Knox's ministry had left so deep a mark, and where its traditions must have long been well remembered.

After the reading 1 Cor. ii. 17-32, the "Order" prescribed that the minister should found upon that passage a declaration of the Apostle's mind on the nature and uses of the Lord's Supper "for certifying the consciences of such as shall use the Lord's Table without superstition." No such "Declaration," however, is included in the fragment, corresponding to "the Exhortation" introduced in the same place in "the Forme of Prayers and Ministration of the Sacraments," drawn up by Knox and others a few years later at Frankfort, and soon afterwards brought into actual use in Geneva. But, curiously enough, we find among Knox's printed works a short piece, entitled "A Summary according to the Holy Scriptures of the Sacrament of the Lord's Supper," which may very well have been the "Declaration" which he was accustomed to use in the Communion Service, both in Berwick and Newcastle. Dr. Laing assigns its date to 1550, though it was not printed till 1556, when it was annexed by the author to his "Vindication of the Doctrine that the Sacrifice of the Mass is Idolatry." That the "Vindication" belonged to 1550 is certain. It was only a happy conjecture of Dr. Laing which assigned the "Summary" to the same year. But the Knox-Papers now before us increase greatly the probability of the truth of that conjecture, as we now know with certainty that Knox was the author of a new "Order of Communion" which prescribed that some such summary should form a part of the service, as it was administered by himself as early as 1549 or 1550.

It will be useful, therefore, to annex this "Summary" here, as being probably in substance the very "Declaration of the Apostle's mind," touching the Lord's Supper, which he was accustomed to make use of, deducting only those forms of expression which were necessary to adapt it for publication under the new title of a declaration of "what opinions we Christians have of the Lord's Supper."

"*A Summary, according to the Holy Scriptures, of the Sacrament of the Lord's Supper.*

"MDL.

"HEIR is brieflie declarit in a Summe, according to the Holie Scriptures, what opinion we Christians haif of the Lordis Supper, callit the Sacrament of the Bodie and Blude of our Savioure Jesus Chryst.

"First, we confess that it is ane holie actioun ordaynit of God, in the whilk the Lord Jesus, by earthlie and visibill thingis sette befoir us, lefteth us up unto hevinlie and invisibill thinges. And that when He had prepareit his spirituall bankett, He witnessit that He Himself was the lyvelie bread, whairwith our saullis be fed unto everlasting life.

"And, thairfoir, in setting furth bread and wyne to eat and drink, He confirmeth and sealleth up to us his promeis and communion (that is, that we salbe partakeris with Him in his kingdome); and representeth unto us, and maketh plane to our senses his hevinlie gifts; and also giveth unto us Himself, to be receavit with faith, and not with mouth, nor yit by transfusioun of substance. But so, through the vertew of the Holie Ghaist, that we, being fed with his fleshe, and refrescheit with his blude, may be renewit both unto trew godliness and to immortalitie.

"And also that heirwith the Lord Jesus gathereth us unto ane visibill bodie, so that we be memberis ane of another, and mak altogether one bodie, whairof Jesus Chryst is onlie heid.

"And, finallie, that by the same Sacrament the Lord calleth us to rememberance of his Death and Passioun, to styrre up our hartis to prais his maist holie name. Farthermore, we acknowlege that this Sacrament ought to be cum to reverentlie, considering thair is exhibited and gevin a testimony of the wonderfull societie and knytting togidder of the Lord Jesus and of the receavers; and also that thair is included and conteanit in this Sacrament, that He will preserve his Kirk, for heirin we be commandit to schaw the Lordis death untill he cum. Also, we beleive that it is a confessioun whairin we schaw what kynd of doctrine we profess, and what congregacion we joyne ourselves unto; and lykwyse that it is a band of mutuall love amangis us.

"And, finallie, we beleive that all the cummeris unto this holie Supper must bring with thame thair conversioun unto the Lord by unfeaned repentance in faith, and in this Sacrament receave the seallis and confirmatioun of thair faith; and yit must in no wyse think that for this workis salle thair synnis be forgevin.*

"And as concerning theis wordis, *Hoc est corpus meum*—This is my bodie—on whilk the Papistis dependis so much, saying that

---

* Probably the "Summary," as spoken from the pulpit of Knox, ended here; the remaining paragraph would in all likelihood be added when it was sent to the press.

ye must neidis beleive that the breid and wyne be transubstantiated into Chrystis bodie and blude, we acknawledge that it is no artikill of our faith whilk can saif us, nor whilk we are bound to beleive upon pane of eternall dampnatioun. For if we suld beleive that his verie naturall bodie, both flesche and blude, wer naturallie in the bread and wyne, that suld not save us, seeing many beleive that, and yit receave it to thair dampnatioun. For it is not his presence in the bread that can save us, but his presence in our hartis thrugh faith in his blude, whilk hath waschit out our synnis, and pacifeit his Fatheris wraith towardis us. And again, if we do not beleive his bodilie presence in the bread and wyne, that sall not dampn us, but the absence out of our hart, throw unbeleif.

"Now, if they wold heir object, that though it be trewth, that the absence out of the bread culd not dampn us, yit are we bound to beleive it because of Godis word, saying 'This is my bodie,' whilk who beleiveth not as muche as in him lyith, maketh God a lier; and thairfoir, of ane obstinat mynd not to beleive his Word, may be our dampnation;—to this we answer, that we beleive Godis word, and confess that it is trew, but not so to be understand as the Papistis grosslie affirme. For in the Sacrament we receave Jesus Chryst spirituallie as did the Fathers of the Old Testament, according to St. Paulis saying (1 Cor. xi.). And if men wold weill wey how that Chryst ordeyning this holie Sacrament of his bodie and blude, spak theis words sacramentallie, doutless thos wold never so grosslie and foolishlie understand thame, contrary to all the Scriptures, and to the expositioun of St. Augustine, St. Hierome, Fulgentius, Vigilius, Origines, and many other godlie wrytteris."

"The Practice of the Lord's Supper used in Berwick-upon-Tweed by John Knox," is extremely interesting as the very earliest sketch or outline of a "Communion office" framed according to the principles and preferences of the English Puritans. Nothing of this kind has hitherto been known to us of an earlier date than "The Forme of Prayer and Ministration of the Sacraments used in the Englische Congregation at Geneva,"—"imprinted at Geneva, by John Crispin, MDLVI., the tenth of February,"—A careful comparison of the earlier and later Sacramental "Formes" brings out the result, that the resemblances and differences between them are neither less nor more than what might have been expected in the different conditions under which they were drawn up—the one by Knox, in Berwick, where he had only his own ideas to carry out; the other by a group of Puritan divines in Frankfort, among whom Knox was only one, though the chief, and who had all their share of influence in moulding the Formulary which was agreed upon by common consent.

It was in the Geneva "Forme of Prayer" that the Puritan Practice in the sacramental "Action"—*i.e.*, in the act of giving and receiving the Sacramental elements—was first published in print. As this, however, was undoubtedly the same, in every important respect, as that previously used by Knox at Berwick, and even earlier at St. Andrew's, it may here be inserted with advantage, so as to complete the reader's impression of the "Practice" which might have been seen in the North of England in those early years, when as yet it was an Order to be seen nowhere else in the kingdom.

" The exhortation ended, the minister cummeth downe from the pulpit, and sitteth at the table, every man and woman in like wise takinge their place as occasion best serveth; then he taketh bread and geveth thankes, either in these woordes following, or like in effect:—' O Father of mercye and God of all consolation,' &c., &c.

" This done, the minister breaketh the breade and delyvereth it to the people, who distribute and divide the same amongst themselves, accordinge to our Saviour Christes commandement, and in likewise geveth the cuppe. Duringe the which tyme some place of the Scriptures is read which doth best set forth the death of Christ, to the intente that our eyes and senses may not only be occupied in these outward signes of bread and wyne, which are called the visible woorde; but that our hartes and myndes also may be fully fixed in the contemplation of the Lord's death, which is by this holy Sacrament represented; and after the action is done, he giveth thanks, saying 'Moste mercifull Father, we render to thee all praise,' &c.

" The action thus ended, the people sing the 103 Psalm, 'My soule give laude,' &c., or some other of thanksgivinge; which ended, one of the blessings beforementioned is recitede, and so they rise from the table and departe."

The action here described corresponds in all points with the form of administration afterwards introduced by Knox into the

Church of Scotland, as described in "The Book of Common Order," published in 1564; and it is to this order that he alludes in his notice of his first Dispensation of the Lord's Supper in St. Andrew's in 1547, when, "not only all those of the castle, but also a great number of the town openly professed, by participation of the Lord's table in the same purity that now it is ministrat in the churches of Scotland, with the same doctrine that he had taught unto them." It cannot be doubted, then, that that part of the service which is omitted from the "Form of the Lord's Supper, used in Berwick by John Knox," bore the closest resemblance to the usage of the English congregation of Geneva and of the Church of Scotland; and the curious fact which emerges from the whole evidence, now for the first time brought together, is that the Lord's Supper, and no doubt the Sacrament of Baptism, were first administered in England in the Puritan and Presbyterian form by the hand of John Knox, the Scottish Reformer, as early as the year 1549 or 1550; and that this form of service was established in Berwick, by a recognized minister of the national Church of England, acting under the implied authority—or allowance at least—of the Government, ten years before it could be introduced, with a similar official recognition, into the national Church of Knox's own native country.

IV.

"*A Letter written to Mr. Knoxe.*"

GRACE and peace, with all spiritual and heavenly feeling be with you for ever.

Dearly beloved in the Lord, after most humble wise, with most harty thanks for your great kindness and heavenly comfort; the Lord reward you for it. It is no small grief to my heart to hear the news that is with you, how that the Queen is broken forth of prison and hath 4,000 men with her. The Lord our God, for Christ's sake, turne it to the best, and to the comfort of his poor flock, and give grace to the rulers with all wisdom to consider well with all speed.

Our brethren do give harty thanks for your gentle letter written unto them; but, to be plain with you, it is not in all points liked; and for my part, if I had known the tenor of it, when I was with you, I would have said many words that I never spake. We all agree well with your judgment that they shall not escape the judgments of God, without harty repentance, for molesting and troubling the hearts and consciences of the godly, and for mainteyning things in the Church for which, by the Word of God, they have no ground. But when you say that you cannot allow those that obstinately do refuse to hear the message of salvation at such men's mouths as please not us in all things; so say we. I know no man in our Congregation that doth obstinately refuse the Word of life. But when you say at such men's mouths, no doubt there be many men that be authorized to preach that are both hereticks and wicked Papists, which the Church of England doth allow; and if you mean them, then we say we utterly refuse to hear them, and also all those that do maintain this minglemangle ministry, Popish order and Popish apparel, which is to the great grief of the godly, and can take no comfort of such doctrine.

Whereas you bring that Paul was offended with Peter and sharply rebuked him, and in that he did very well, you say that for all that he dissuaded none of his auditors from his preaching. Most true it is, and we confess no less with you—but this example toucheth nothing our matter. But if Peter would willingly have maintained, as our men do after a hundred warnings, and brought Christians back from sincerity [purity], sure I am that Paul would not have suffered him, neither would the Apostolic Church have let him remain among them. But Peter yielded and held the true doctrine. And also the contention of Paul and Barnabas; that contention was about Marcus John; but yet they both held the truth, and might both be very well heard, for neither of them preached false doctrine, neither maintained anything against the ordinances of Christ. Although godly men have many infirmities, as I know no man hath not, yet God forbid that any should forsake hearing the Word truly and sincerely taught. But how doth this example touch our time, or doing which is maintained in England?

And also concerning Paul his purifying at Jerusalem. Purifying had his first ground out of the Word of God, and had his end, as all other ceremonies had, in Christ; but it was for confirming the Jews, and therefore Paul, for their infirmities' sake, that he might preach Christ, did it. Sure I am Paul did it not to maintain or allow it to be kept among them, and to persecute for it, and that no man shall preach Christ unless he do it; for many things that are maintained here had never any law of God for them, at any time or in any age, but the law of God ever standing against them. If it were true, as you say, that the Gospel were truly preached, and Sacraments truly administered, and true discipline maintained, it were no matter, neither for the man, neither for the coate. The hearing cannot hurt one, neither his ministry nor any man else.

Whereas you wish that our consciences had a better ground, truly we cannot see by these Scriptures that should alter our consciences from a Reformed Church that hath those marks, to go back to mixtures. Although it be but a poor Church and under perils and persecutions, and have many enemies both open and familiar friends against it, and have no authority to defend it, and since our departure from you more enemies we have a great many, which seem somewhat to take hold of you for the defence of them, that they may the more cruelly handle us, as some of our brethren feeleth it, and is grown by the party that went away from us, which now is in great favour of the Bishop, which never was before, and hath told him and all others that you are flat against us and condemn all our doings. But this is our comfort, the Lord Jesus is with us. At his coming home he did openly stand against the whole Church with many reviling words, and no gentle nor honest means could persuade him, whereupon the Church hath excommunicated him.

Also where you say, "God forbid that we should damn all for false prophets and heretics that agree not with us in our apparel and other opinions, that teacheth the substance of doctrine and salvation in Christ Jesus;" we heartily thank you for your good desire, but we never were of that mind to condemn any man's person; and I trust in the Lord that he will never let us fall in such a gulf. What art thou, saith Paul, that judgest another man's servant? Either he standeth or falleth to his Lord. But this we do; when we see a manifest fact done by any man, either in religion or in manners, that is not good and may be condemned by the Scriptures, we also condemn all such facts; as for the person we leave to God; for Christ saith—The tree is known by the fruit.

Dearly beloved, in the first letter that ye wrote in answer to our letter when we were in the Fleete, it seemeth that ye are not well contented that we did not communicate with other Churches. That is known both to God and men, and other good Churches, and by four years—what troubles a great many godly suffered in that space, how we were handled by the Popish court both in Popish excommunication and imprisonment, for that we would not go back again to the wafer-cake and kneeling, and to other knackles of Popery. That persecution grew so fast as that it brought many a hundred to know one another that never knew before; and we joined all with one heart and mind to serve God with pure hearts and minds according to his Word. And where ye say, The matter is weighty for it condemneth the publicministry of England, let them take heed of that with your Church in Scotland, and the French and Dutch Church in England. We desire no other order than you hold; and to come back from an Apostolical Church, by God's grace we mind not, but rather to take imprisonment, exilement, or what other crosses the Lord shall lay upon us. And if God justify our doings, if all men in the world were against us, it is no matter. And if the Lord condemn us, and all men should justify our doings, we were in a miserable case. I do confess that it is extraordinary and no general rule; but the Lord be praised, we have the testimony of a good conscience, and the open and manifest Word of God to defend our doings, although it be gotten by many tribulations. The God of our fathers direct us in all our doings for his Son Christ his sake, that it may redound to his glory, to the comfort of our own consciences, leaving a good example behind us to posterity. Beseeching you to have us in your hearty prayers.

NOTE.

The date and the occasion of this letter to Knox have already been stated in the Narrative. It would have been well if anything could have been added here touching the name of the writer; but not a single trace has as yet been found that might lead to its discovery. The whole subsequent history of the party which first seceded from the Elizabethan Church is extremely obscure; none of their leaders appear to have risen to any distinction or celebrity.

Compelled to conceal their meetings and movements as much as possible from the eyes of the Church's rulers, and separated by their own act from the counsels of the chief body of their brother Puritans, they came little before the public eye, except on those lamentable occasions when their religious assemblies were discovered to the magistrates by worthless informers, and they were dragged off to prisons and tribunals, to suffer more and worse for being religious and God-fearing after their own manner than ordinary criminals had to endure of condign penalty for their immoralities and crimes.

APPENDIX.

NOTE.

KNOX was so closely associated with William Whittingham for several years in Frankfort and Geneva, and the gifts and career of the latter were in several respects so remarkable, that the author is glad to have had his attention directed to the following authentic sketch of his life, in time to append it to the present work. He is indebted to Mr. Froude's paper on "The Marian Exiles" in the Edinburgh Review for his knowledge of its preservation among the MSS. of Anthony A. Wood, in Oxford; in which paper Mr. Froude included several interesting excerpts from it and a suggestion that it should be published. On examining it in the Bodleian, the author found it suitable in point of bulk to find a place in this work, and made a transcript of it with his own hand.

"*The Life and Death of Mr. William Whittingham, Deane of Durham, who departed this life* A.D. 1579, *June* 10."

He was borne in Westchester and descended from Whittingham, of ye house of Whittingham, in Lancashire neare Preston, which Whittingham did marry ye daughter of Haughton, of Haughton Tower in ye same county. He became a scholler in ye sixteenth year of his age, circa an. 1536, at Oxon, first of Brasen Nose Coll., where he was under a tutor so careful over him to further him in learning as he hath bene often heard to bemoane, y^t his tutor lived not till he was able to requite him for his care and love towards him. From that college he went to All Soules Coll. where he was chose fellow-probationer 1545. From thence he became a fellow of Cardinal Wolsey's Coll. in Oxon, where after he had remained a few years he betooke himself to travell, with purpose to travel through France and soe into Italy. But coming to Lyons in France on his way towards Italy, it pleased God to visit him with sickness, which he took to be a warning to cause him to alter his purpose and to direct his course from that country from which few return the godlier, and soe coming back again he remained for divers years in Orleance, sometimes in Paris, but ever amongst the students in the universities of those cities. In Paris when the Ambassador for England was to go to the court, he desired Mr. Whittingham to accompany him, for which purpose he had his courtly apparel and ornaments lying by him, which at his going to court he used, and at his return became *ut prius* as a student. After some years bestowed in those universities he went to the universities of Germany, and thence to Geneva, and thence, having spent all King Edward the 6's reign in those transmarine universities, returned into England in the very latter end of the same King Edward his reign; presently after whose death Queen Mary being proclaimed, and a taste given of the alteration of religion, he forthwith resolved to go again beyond the seas, and riding over London Bridge on his way to Dover, and thence to take shipping, he met Mr. Harding (who wrote against Jewell) on the bridge, who after salutations asked him whither he was agoing. Mr. Whittingham answered "that he was going beyond the seas." Mr. Harding demanded of him the cause. He answered, "Did ye not hear the proclamation, and how the whole of Roome is again erected amongst us?" to which Mr. Harding replied, "Happy are ye that go for so good a cause." Mr. Whittingham and his company coming to Dover, at night whilst they were at supper, the host of the house told his guests that after supper he must carry them before the magistrate or mayor of the town to be questioned concerning the cause or errand of their going beyond the sea, for the magistrate had received strict command from the Council for the examination of every passenger; and Mr. Mayor had as strictly enjoined them (the innkeepers) to bring their guests to be examined as aforesaid (wherein the host seemed to be more peremptory and precise), it made his news the more distasteful and in part vex his guests. Whilst they were in this anxiety, there being a fair greyhound waiting on the table for relief, Mr. Whittingham chanced to say, "Mine host ye have here a very fair greyhound;" and said the host, "This greyhound is a fair greyhound, indeed, and is of the Queen's kind." "Queen's kind!" said Mr. Whittingham, "what mean ye by that? This is a strange speech which no good subject can endure to hear such words of his sovereign, to have her Majesty to be compared in kind with the kind of a dog," and said that the words were very treasonable, and that he could not see how they could be excused if they should not go and acquaint the magistrate with it, and did further so aggravate the matter even of purpose, as they did drive the host into such a fear as he durst not once mention the carrying of them before the magistrate any more, but was glad to be so freed from their incumbrance. By this means all the company escaping this interruption they proceeded on their journey. And Mr. Whittingham remained in France till he heard of the coming of sundry English bishops, divines, and other good Protestants, who for religion had left their country and were arrived at Frankford, where, after a while, they getting license of the magistrate to establish a church there, and entering into consideration of the particular forms and order of discipline to be used in that church, they did so far vary and dissent amongst themselves as after long contentions no accord could be made between them but were forced to disjoin, and those to remain at Frankford that did best like the form of the government of the Church of England in the days of King Edward 6, and those that liked better of the order of discipline of the Church of Geneva did go to Geneva, amongst whom Mr. Whittingham was one; of which controversy, though here be good occasion given to particulate, yet because the whole matter of that controversie is set forth in a large discourse in an ancient book printed Anno . . . at . . . . I will refer the reader to that book that he may better inform his judgment on the state of the differences between them. And yet withal I have thought good to acquaint the reader with an epistle writ to Mr. Whittingham and Mr. Goodman, being at Geneva, from that worthy, famous, and learned writer, Bishop Jewell, wherein some mention is made of the controversy at Frankford. The letter is thus styled: "Charissimis in Xto fratribus D^{no} Whittinghamo et D^{no} Goodmanno, Genevae." Out of which inscriptions this is referred to the reader's judgment—that seeing amongst graduate scholars not distinguished by preferment antiquity gives the precedence, yet Mr. Jewell, knowing that Mr. Goodman was Mr. Whittingham's ancient in Oxon by much, and had been the Divinity lecturer in Oxon, in King Edward's reign, yet doth he in two directions give to Mr. Whittingham the pre-eminence; the reader, I say, may judge as he pleases, whether he will ascribe it to negligence, or if Mr. Jewell had a greater respect to the difference of their gifts and sufficiency; but the letter followeth :—

(The letter will be found in the Parker Society's edition of "Jewell's Works," Fourth Portion.)

Soon after the arrival at Geneva of Mr. Whittingham, and the rest that went from Frankford, Mr. John Knox, who was a Scotchman, and then the minister of the English congregation, was to leave that place and return to his own country; so as that place was to become void, and they not being so well provided (for the supply of that place) amongst our countrymen as Mr. Calvin (who had the principal care of the church government in that city lying upon him) liked of, moved Mr. Whittingham to take the ministry upon him and to be made minister, which, notwithstanding Mr. Calvin, his many urgencies and pressures, Mr. Whittingham refused to do, alleging that in his former travells and observations, and learning the languages, he had fitted himself for State employments, and had not bended his intentions that way, neither would acknowledge his gifts to be such as to be so worthy as that calling required. But Mr. Calvin resolved not to accept of any refusal, but by continued importunity and urging his gifts and fitness did in the end, rather by conjuring than persuading him, prevail, and so he succeeded Mr. Knox in the ministry of the English Church there, where, after some 2 or 3 years, the learned that were at Geneva, as Bishop Coverdall, Mr. Goodman, Mr. Gilbie, Mr. Samson, Dr. Cole and Mr. Whittingham (and who else I cannot relate), did undertake the translation of the Geneva Bible, which long ere the same was finished (Queen Mary dying, her sister of never dying memory succeeded) whereupon the banished, as well bishops as others of the Church of Frankford, returned unto England. So also did they of the Church of Geneva, saving some of them only, and not all, that were engaged in the translation of the Bible; so as Mr. Whittingham did tarry in Geneva for the finishing of that translation a year and a half after Queen Elizabeth began her reign. He also there turned into metre those psalms of the Geneva psalms which are inscribed with W. W., and then coming into England, Francis Russell, Earl of Bedford, was sent by Queen Elizabeth into France to condole the death of . . . . their late deceased King of France, and Mr. Whittingham, as well for his perfection in that language as former experience of the French Court, was appointed to attend the said Earl thereto. After whose return to England, presently the wars between France and England began at Newhaven, where for the French the Ringrave was the general to oppugn the town, and Ambrose Dudley, Earl of Warwick, was sent by Queen Elizabeth lieutenant of the English forces to defend the same. In which exhibition the said earl procured that Mr. Whittingham should go with him and be their preacher at Newhaven, which he did accordingly; and did so there demean himself, both in his function and in the guise of a soldier's employment, as he, after the experience of the alarums coming on the sudden, even in the midst of the sermons, he used to preach in his armour continually; and as the old captains and soldiers of Berwick would many years after (relate) that when any alarum came whilst he was preaching, he would be on the town walls as soon almost as any man. Nay, if the writer hereof should set down all that he hath heard reported of him in his commendation, not only of the captains and soldiers, but of the most eminent persons, as Sir Henry Sidney, since Lord President of Wales, and even from the Lord Lieutenant himself, not only in his function for his diligence in preaching, and vigilance in discovering a stratagem intended for the surprisal of the town, and the hazard he did daily undergo in going to visit, instruct and comfort, as need required, so many soldiers dying and dead in one great room at once of the plague (the increase whereof caused the loss of the town), but also for his valour and showing himself to be on all occasions as well *tam Marte quam Mercurio;* if, I say, I should so do, I should but fill up too much page, and might be suspected of too much partiality. Yet that the truth of that

that is already alleged of the good opinion that was had of him may the better appear, let it be considered that Mr. Whittingham got not his preferment to the Deanery of Durham by following the Court, nor by such reall gratifications as are said to be the oil that doth facilitate the way to preferment, but only from the commendation of the Lord Lieutenant to the Queen by letters from Newhaven, as by a letter written from the Earl of Leicester, brother to the Lord Lieutenant, from the Court, most plainly appeareth, which letter I have thought good to set down *verbatim* for the better understanding of the truth, directed thus :—

"To my good brother the Earl of Warwick, the Queen's Majesty's Lieutenant at Newhaven.

"My good brother, I have now at last gotten Captain Read's Bill despatched, and the same being delivered under seal to his man, I thought good, likeas to let you understand of that, so of your request to Mr. Whittingham for the Deanery of Durham, whereunto the Queen's Majesty hath also condescended, which she would not, assure ye, do, neither at my or Mr. Secretary's suit, but upon the last letters written on his behalf her Highness hath granted it unto him. He is therefore next unto her Majesty to thank you first. And so with my most hearty commendations I bid you as myself farewell. At the Court the 24 of July 1563.

"Your loving brother,
"R. DUDDLEY.

"Postscript.—I pray you in your next letters give her Majesty thanks for the favour she hath showed to Mr. Whittingham for your sake, and look well to your health, my dear brother."

By this letter it appeareth that the said Queen Elizabeth would not have given the deanery to Mr. Whittingham, neither at the request of the said Earl of Leicester, neither of Mr. Secretary Cecill (then so being) but upon the said Lord Lieutenant's letters from Newhaven. The cause was that she had promised it to one who after became one of the Secretaries of State, and after Mr. Whittingham had enjoyed the deanery 16 years and died, he obtained it, but died within a year and a half after, so as he for a short while enjoyed it. Here, before I proceed any further, I think it meet to mention some things that happened at Newhaven which particularly concern Mr. Whittingham. He being sent from the Lord Lieutenant with a message to the Ringrave, who lay encamped before the town, the Ringrave seeing Mr. Whittingham coming towards him, he spurred his horse, drew his sword or rapier, and came towards Mr. Whittingham in a bravado at a full speed, as though he would have assaulted him; whereupon Mr. W. took out one of the pistols he had at his saddle crutch and held it out towards the Ringrave, who asked him in French if he were in earnest.

He answered, No, only attended to answer what he would put him unto. The Ringrave put up his rapier, and, after kind respects used, Mr. W. having discharged the message, the Ringrave carried him to his tent and caused him to dine with him. And the table being full beset with gentlemen that were Frenchmen, they began to gibe and use broad jests against our nation, which Mr. W. did so return upon them to the touch of the French, that one of them that sat at the lower end of the table did rise in great fury, drew his dagger, and would have stabbed Mr. W. if the waiters and some gentlemen rising from the table had not hindered. Whereat the Ringrave, after having showed great indignation against the Frenchman, caused a great double gilte bowl to be filled with wine, and drank thereof to Mr. Whittingham with these terms, cup and all. Mr. W. pledged the wine, but restored the bowl, which when Mr. W. would by no means accept of, the Ringrave sent it after him to Newhaven, with this message—that if he did refuse to take it and keep for his sake, he would never esteem of him. So Mr. W. took the cup, and left it to his sequeles as a monument of the Ringrave's love, and care the Ringrave had to salve the wrong he had received at his table.

Next it shall be fit to show what course and order was taken and usit at Newhaven in the ecclesiastical government by Mr. Whittingham, and what cautious letters were sent to him out of England concerning the same, and his answer thereunto. Two letters were sent, the one of caution and reprehension from Mr. Secretary Cecill, the other of friendly respects and advertisement from him also. The letters follow :—

" Mr. Whittingham,—

"I cannot but in my small leisure send my complaint unto you. I hear by your meanes the Queen's subjects there forbear the observation of that manner and rite of religion that is here received by authority in this realm. I can surely love you for your good and virtuous gifts, but in this, if it be true, I must needs blame you. I will not argue with you, for my part is much the stronger, and on your part small reasons can be made; but upon singularity, you, nor any born under this kingdom, may be permitted to break the bond of obedience and uniformity. The question is not of doctrine, but of rites and ceremonies. And thus I write lamentably unto you; I have found more letts and impediments in the course of the Gospel here in this ecclesiastical government by certain fond singularities of some men than the most malice the Papists can show. If you knew the crosses I have suffered for stay of religion you might pity me, and ought for God's cause to yield to conformity. I am not learned, but I meane well to learning, and am not insensible of as much as is usually said in this matter. I conclude this variety may not nor must not be suffered, and therefore I require [you] to think and determine thereupon how it may be amended. Setting this apart, I acknowledge myself much

addicted to love you. Deus est Deus pacis mon discordiae. IX. Decemb. 1562.
"Your assured,
"WILL. CECILL."

To which Mr. W. wrote this answer as followeth :—

"I am sorrie that in your great and serious affairs your honour should be troubled with the frivolous complaints of certain which show themselves offended with the manner of ceremonies used here as a thing disagreeing from the order commanded and observed in England. So they drive me to send a reason of that thing which I thought to have been out of controversy and that your honour, with the rest of the godly and learned there, had easily consented unto. And for mine own part, St. Augustine somewhat persuadeth me, who counselleth in such things, to accommodate ourselves to the nature of the place where we are conversant; next, moved by your opinion of this people, who, as they had conceived evil of the infirmity of our rites and cold proceedings in religion, so if they should have seen us but in form, though not in substance, to use the same or like order in ceremonies which the Papists have a little afore observed, against whom they now venture goods and body, they would to our great grief have suspected our doings, and have feared in time to come the loss of that liberty which after a sort they had recovered by the blood-shedding of many thousands. Moreover, as I ever approved this order best, because it is most agreeable to God's Word—nearest approaching to the example of the primitive church, and best allowed of the learned and godly—so I perceived it wrought a marvellous conjunction of minds betwixt the French and us, and brought a singular comfort to all our people. Besides this, Mr. Viron told me that my Lord of London warned and charged that we should use no other order of ceremonies than that which we should find here, which in [my] judgment, considering the place and time, is nothing prejudicial to our order at home, for reformation whereof all the godly have their eyes and hearts bent and directed to your honour, next under God and the Queen's Majesty. For, alas! they are far from perfection, though for gain and advantage they have many patrons, who as I think might with better conscience sustain the reproof of singularity than dissemble these matters of so great importance. Thus, being fully persuaded of your good affection towards me, and for discharge of mine own conscience, I am bold to write plainly, trusting your wisdom will not be offended. For God is my judge, if I knew how to ease you of so many heavy burdens and manifold crosses, which we all acknowledge to lie upon you, I would refuse no pain or travell; but my earnest and continual prayer to God is that He would send you strength and comfort long to serve to the glory of his holy name (for whom no discord is to be feared, and without whom no counsel is to be sought), that as ye have begun to uphold and advance the kingdom of

his Son Jesus Christ, so you may by his mercies continue to perfect and establish the same to his praise, the Queen's honour, and all our comforts.
"Amen."

The second letter, before mentioned, though it concern not this argument, yet that it may show the respect and interchange betwixt them, and the rather for that both Mr. Secretary's letters were all of his own handwriting, I think it not fit to be omitted. It followeth with the direction thus:—

"To my very loving friend, Mr. Whittingham, principal preacher of the Word at Newhaven.

"The peace of God and warr for him be with you. How mighty a stroke was towards is a terrible thought to remember, but to behold his wrathful hand was of late here so fearful, as hitherto I scantly have recovered my heart to take the joy of this merciful benefit. This I write of the Queen's danger and delivery. Almighty God be praised of us all, and give us grace to remember his intended wrath and to enjoy his effectual grace and mercy. Happy were you for that, I think, the tidings of her danger were accompanied with the report of her amendment. Now that my Lord of Warwick is come, I trust every day will amend another. I heartily thank you for your gentle letter, and pray you as your leisure may serve you to write sometimes to me, which shall be my comfort though by my answers I acquit [requite] them not for lack of leisure. The fortunate death of the unfortunate King of Navarre cannot but induce a great blessing of God. XXII. of October, 1562, from London.

"Yours in Christ assured,
"W. CECILL."

Mr. W.'s letter in answer of the former I omit for brevity sake, for that it doth not concern this purpose, but contains advertisements of the then state of affairs, whereof now there can be but small use.

And so Mr. W., returning from Newhaven, and coming to Durham to reside upon his deanery there, Anno. 1563, after he had remained there some years, Secretary Cecil was advanced to be Lord Treasurer, in whose place Mr. Whittingham was nominated amongst others to succeed him in place of Secretary, and was thought fit for that place in respect of his perfection in the French tongue, and his experience he had gathered in 12 years beyond the seas. But the Lord Burleigh, Lord Treasurer, alleged that it was pity to call him to such employment, being so well fitted to discharge his place in his function, neither did he think that he would accept thereof if it were offered him. Against which it was alleged that he having no other church living but the deanery, and it being *sine cura animarum*, as deaneries are said to be, it was only a dignity belonging to the church rather than a place tying on to continual residence. But it took no effect in respect of the incongruity which it cannot but carry in all men's judgments.

And notwithstanding the contents of Mr. W.'s former letter concerning church discipline, after he had remained in the deanery two or three years, and the order of vestures being generally established for churchmen, and so pressed as they that would not use the same should not be permitted to exercise their ministry, he then submitted himself thereunto. And being upbraided therewith for so doing by one that had been with him at Geneva, he answered that they knew and had heard Mr. Calvin say that for these external matters of order they must not neglect their ministry, for so should they for tithing of mint neglect the greater things of the law. And concerning singing in the church, Mr. W. did so far allow of it as he was very careful to provide the best songs and anthems that he could get out of the Queen's chapel to furnish the quire withal, himself being skilful in music. After, when he had lived in the deanery of Durham five or six years more, the rebellion in the North at Durham growing towards, Mr. W. moved the Bishop, divers weeks before the rebellion broke forth into open acts, that he would send for his tenants to come to his castle at Durham with their warlike furniture, which, if he would do, he would cause all the tenants of the church to join likewise with them, which would be a means to awe the collecting rebels, and be a stay and refuge for many gentlemen of the country to repair unto for want whereof many might be driven to adhere to the rebels—which fell out after accordingly, to the utter ruin of many of the gentlemen and their posterities, and the country to this day doth bear the traces of that error. But the Bishop answered that he had a great deal of the Queen's money in his hand, and durst not hazard it. About a week before the rebels rose Mr. W. rid to Newcastle, and calling the Mayor and Aldermen together, did acquaint them with the then present state of the country, and how much it concerned them to look to their own safety, for they must needs think that upon the first rising they would first attempt to surprise them, then (if they should find them unprovided) that they might be lords of their wealth, and that they might be thereby the better enabled to maintain their undertaken enterprise. Whereupon the Mayor caused the gates of the town to be presently shut, the ordinance to be carried to the wall, and such further courses for fortifications to be used as Mr. W. out of his experience in the siege of Newhaven, was able to advise them unto. By means whereof the rebels never dared the attempt of the siege of that town, which was then the refuge for the better affected subjects. Mr. W. himself tarried at Durham till the Thursday next before the Monday that the rebels rose, secret intelligence being brought unto him that if he went not away that night he could not pass southwards, for the bridges would be taken up the next night to prevent all intercourses and intelligences; so that Mr. W. going then unto the south, the rebels entered into his house and spoiled the same, and rent in pieces his books in such sort and abundance as was pitiful to behold. Mr. W. returned within five weeks with the Queen's army, conducted under the government of the afore-named Ambrose, Earl of Warwick, and the Earl of Lincoln. But the rebels hearing of the Lords coming fled, and the Lords, coming no further than to Durham, presently returned.

For eight or nine years after Mr. W. lived in the great love and liking of his neighbours for his affability and bountiful hospitality, which was in such a proportion as is marvelled even to this day how the naked deanery alone (for he had no more) could support his expenses.

After those eight years were expired, the sees of York and of Durham became void both at one time, whereupon the Earl of Leicester (being a great favourite in Court, and he that had formerly moved the Queen for the Deanery of Durham to be bestowed on Mr. W., as appeareth by the letter hereinbefore recited) caused Sir Edward Horsey, who was Captain of the Isle of Wight, a great courtier, and one of Mr. W.'s Newhaven acquaintances, to write to Mr. W. to come to the Court, and he should not fail to have one of those places. Whereunto Mr. W. returned answer by letter, and sent it to the writer hereof, he being then of the Temple, to be delivered; but the letter being delivered and read, the writer hereof got a sight of it, and found the effect of the letter to be that touching the motions contained in his letter, he found himself so declined by age and infirmity, as that he felt himself very unfit to undertake so great a place, with the burden that the good discharge of such a place required; and that her Majesty had so graciously and liberally already recompensed his services, as he should show himself unthankful if he should not seem satisfied with so good a bounty as he had already received, and therefore desired him that he, with all thankfulness and humble acknowledgment in his behalf, would signify to his honour the deep apprehension he conceived of his love towards him, so effectually demonstrated by his lordship's message, which should tie him to a perpetual remembrance of him in his prayers, being not able by any means in his power otherwise to requite so extraordinary a favour.

Then, after a while, the Archbishoprick of York and the Bishoprick of Durham being bestowed at one time, and both of them preferred by the means of one and the self-same noble person as was reported, the Bishop of Durham yielded that the Archbishop should visit the church of Durham, not knowing, belike, or not regarding, the right of his own church. So, after a year or two, the Dean and Prebends of the church of Durham were cited to appear at the visitation. The day appointed being come, the Bishop came to Durham, and after the sermon in the morning, the Bishop going towards the Chapter-house to the visitation, Mr. W. asked the Bishop whether he would visit in his own right or in the

Archbishop of York's right. He answered, in the right of the Archbishop. Whereunto Mr. W. answered, that then he wronged his own jurisdiction, and the clergy and the country in general, and him and the rest of the church more especially, for that they being sworne to maintain the liberties of their church, and by their statutes having no visitor but the Bishop of Durham, if they should yield to be visited in the right of the Archbishop, they should break their oath. All which notwithstanding, and whatsoever could be alleged by Mr. Dean, the Bishop persisted in his former resolution; and by this time being come near the Chapter-house door, Mr. W. called to the doorkeeper to lock the door and give him the keys, which the doorkeeper did forthwith, which the Bishop trusting to prevent, Mr. W. did a little interrupt him, taking hold of his gown, and so the business was concluded. But that accident bred a great indignation both in the Bishop and Archbishop against Mr. W. Yet did that action add (if anything could be added) to the love which the town and country did already bear towards him, and did the more aggravate the displeasure conceived against him by the Archbishop and Bishop, and so incense them, as it appeared by many of their speeches and actions, that they took it for a disgrace offered them, and such as could not be laid aside without a revenge. Hereupon one of the prebends, being one alone, and of a singular factious spirit, and bearing ever a malignity to Mr. W., and spying this opportunity to disgorge himself of his long conceived hatred against him, went to the Bishops and acquainted them with a plott that he had devised, which if they would pursue, he doubted not but it would eject Mr. W. out of his deanery, which they gladly hearkened unto, and did with all forwardness pursue.

The plott was this—that seeing there was one of the Secretaries of the Privy Council to whom the Queen had half given the deanery of Durham before she gave it to Mr. W., and did after alter her purpose by the occasion of Mr. W.'s preferment thereunto by letters of commendation from Newhaven, as aforesaid, he doubted not but he would help, by any means he could, to dispossess him of the deanery, that he might cry quittance with him and gain the deanery to himself. Therefore, if their lordships would write, and would give leave to him to solicit that Secretary to procure a Commission from her Majesty, directed to their lordships and others, to visit the church of Durham, he would prepare such articles against the dean as would procure his deprivation. The Bishop, following the track of his desire, procured a Commission directed to the Lord Archbishop of York, the Earl of Huntingdon, then Lord President and Lord Lieutenant of the North, the Bishop of Durham, the Bishop of Carlisle, the Dean of York, and Sir Thomas Boynton, Sir Robert Stapleton, Sir William Mallorye, Sir Christopher Wandesford, both of Yorkshire, and divers others. They all came to Durham to the visitation, where they sat four days, against when the busy instrument I spoke of before had provided more than fifty articles against Mr. W., and presented them to the visitors (amongst whom there were some that would look to it that they should want no due examination); yet, after four days' sitting, when the rest were found to be frivolous, without purpose, and grounded only upon malice, they were all left as idle and vain saving two, the one that Mr. W. was not capable of the deanery of Durham, being only a Master of Arts, the statutes of the House requiring that the dean should be a Batchelor of Divinity at the least. The second was, that Mr. W. was not capable of the deanery, for that he was not made minister after the order of the Church of England, but after the forme of Geneva, to which point learned Dean Hutton, then of York, afterwards Bishop of Durham, and last Archbishop of York, did then say to those that did most urge against it, that the ministry of Geneva was better than that ministry which was made with these words, "Accipite potestatem sacrificandi pro vivis et mortuis," with which words, it was said, the principal objector was made priest, and therefore had less cause to except against the ministry of Geneva. But to proceed. Mr. W. desired that, because those two articles depended upon points of law, that he might by counsell make his answer, which, though some of the Commissioners would not yield unto, yet it was granted by the greater part and the visitation adjourned to York, against which day appointed Mr. W. had got counsel from London, to strengthen him against both those former objections, whereunto the *non-obstante* in his patent sufficed to free him. The visitation then at York being ended without any certain adjournment, neither any sentence or matter given or done against him, Mr. W. went up to the Privy Council, to move that they would call in the Commission, signifying what had been done in the matter already. But the sure friend that he had of the Council (as is aforesaid) alleged that the Bishop had more matter to urge against him, whereupon letters were sent to the Archbishop to send some to allege against Mr. W., or else the Commission would be called in; whereupon two doctors of the civil law, dependents of the Archbishop's, were sent up to object against Mr. W., who, after two or three hearings before the Privy Council, one of the lords asked them if their master had nothing else to do but to send such a couple to object such idle matters against such a man as Mr. W. was known to be of the most at the board. And so the objectors returned as they came.

But still his true friend, seeing him daily to decline more and more in his health and spirits, and being oppressed with so long troubles, great expenses, and tedious delays, did even then move that Mr. W. (there being then occasion to send an ambassador into France) might be sent thither, whereupon Mr. W. asked the said friend of his if he thought it not sufficient to seek to bereave him of his living, but of his life also, he seeing him in such weakness and debility both of body and spirit, altogether unfit for such employment.

But Mr. W. still labouring to get the Commission called in (having tarried there already a quarter of a year with eight serving men and all their horses, and in winter, to his excessive charge), his true friend had now found out a new colour of delay, to witt, that after Easter (it then being about Candlemas) the Bishop would come up to the Parliament; and so Mr. W. might now go down, and then come up again to hear what the Bishops themselves would object against him, as though the Bishops could allege more than they had given in instructions to the doctors their proxies.

Thus you may see how Mr. W. was oppressed, though having proved himself innocent after so many trials; by which heavy hand so carried over him he was forced to come down, without obtaining his just request, which he took very grievously. And though, at his return to Durham, a great many of the better sort of the city and country went to meet him, the bells rung, and the people came running from all parts of the city in such numbers as the streets were scarcely passable for the multitude, who with doubled and trebled acclamations of joy strived to exhilarate his heart after all his troubles; but yet all was in vain, for within four days after his return he betook himself to his bed, and never left it till he departed this life, being nine weeks after.

And now it is requisite that I should mention what happened concerning him in the time of his so long languishing sickness, how he passed it over, and what was the manner of his death.

The Archbishop, whose malice did not cease to pursue him till death, did certify the Lords of the Council that Mr. W. kept his bed pretending sickness, and had used some words of vaunting, whereof the Council by their letter dated the 3rd of May, 1579 (yet to be shewed), did advertise him. Whereupon, he returning answer to the Lords, Sir Francis Walsingham, the principal secretary, writ to him as followeth :—

"After my hearty commendations. I have received your letters of the 24th of the last, and according to your desire presented the letters, who having seen and read the same have willed me to signify unto you that they take them in good part, allowing so far forth of your answer to the hard suggestions made unto them against you, as that they mind to suspend their judgments of the information of the speeches you were said to have uttered, until ye repair up hither to satisfy them more fully by word of mouth. And the delay of your coming they have resolved by the said letter to grow of the great weakness of your body, which they take to be no matter feigned but a truth, wishing if it please God to send you as perfect recovereth as your self desireth. And so I bid you heartily farewell. From the Court the 1st of June, 1579.

"Your loving friend,
"FRA. WALSINGHAM.

"To the right worshipful my very loving friend,
"Mr. Whittingham, Deane of Durham."

This letter being dated the 1st of June, and he dying the 10th of June, it preceded his death but nine days, whence may be observed, by these letters above mentioned, that the malice of his adversaries did so hotly pursue him as they would not afford him a time of rest from their vexation to die in. And yet all the storm grew only of this (as we have heard) for that he made a conscience to avoide the breach of his oath, and to maintain the liberties of the church whereunto he was sworne. Which case is so strange, that for a matter so good, so just, so conscionable, a man should be so persecuted, and that even by those who by their functions are tied to instruct and to exhort to virtue and to such actions as every good Christian is tied unto, as it cannot be parallelled. And therefore who can hear this and not say with the poet,

> Jupiter hoc cernis? ne vindice fulmine pugnas?
> Tuque Astraea sinis jura sacrata premi?

But neither yet was God wanting to punish the malice and wickedness shewed in this action, neither to take in hand the defence and revenge of the cause of the innocent; for that he shewed such signs of his revenging hand upon five or six of the principal agents in this business against Mr. W., and that so soon after his death, as it grew to be noted of all men and of the best rank as a heavy judgment of God upon them for their malicious plots and pursuits against him. And as he was first in place of the action whom we have before mentioned, so was he the first that was plagued for his iniquities; for being at London, far from home, he fell mad, and in so high degree as he was espied so to be in the street as he went up and down, being at last followed by the boys and children with wonderment as crows do after . . . . And so he went to Ware, and there died in that pitiful case. The rest had great blemishes in their lifetimes, and in their death some of them had a judgment accompanying them. I do of purpose abstain either from particulating those judgments (but of the first which was so notorious to all), or nominating of any of the parties, lest the parties should be easily found out. For I neither desire nor delight in laying aspersions on them, much less on the dead, and so long since, but that the necessity of the history hath enforced me; and therein have I striven to be as obscure as I could, not betraying the history, even for charity sake towards the dead; and so I desire to be construed, lest while I declare other men's malice I should shew myself to want charity. To this I may add, by way of note, that as the former opposite went not scot free who persecuted Mr. W., so Dean Hutton, ever standing with Mr. W., was after advanced to the Bishoprick of Durham, and after to be Archbishop of York.

And having now declared the occasion and process of the crosses which Mr. W. sustained in the cause afore-mentioned, it is fit and convenient that the manner of his death and carriage in his long languishing sickness be also declared. So soon as he kept his bed, he sent for some of his friends, and by their advice he made his will; which after it was done he willed those that were about him that none should henceforth trouble him with any worldly matters. And though he continued languishing about nine weeks after in his bed, he would seldom admit any company to come to him, unless some special friends, and those also rarely; and being divers times asked of his friends why he was so solitary, and would not delight in company, which might help to alleviate his sickness, he would answer them, had he not company enough there? and would take up his Bible and would shew it to them, which lay by him continually on his bed. Sometimes in his sickness, and divers times, he would call all his servants, which were many, to come into his chamber, and would exhort them for an hour together to the fear of God; and privately would call them by one and by one, and tell them of such faults as he had suspected them to be guilty of, and did admonish them to leave them, shewing, withal, that he had been too indulgent or negligent towards them in not carrying a stricter hand over them. For this he did now find as great a burden in conscience as for any other of his sins that he could remember, and did verily think that neglect towards them had as much drawn these his late afflictions and crosses upon him as any other his sins whatsoever.

NOTE.

The above sketch has internal evidence of having been written by a friend of Whittingham at one time resident in the Temple, and who would seem to have been a man of some scholarship. On comparing it with the article on Whittingham in the "Athenæ Oxonienses," it is manifest that Wood, though he made large use of it, omitted several of its most interesting and characteristic passages, and added many particulars to the disadvantage of the Dean's memory—derived by him from an anonymous work, entitled "The Ancient Rites and Monuments of the Monastical and Cathedral Church of Durham," Lond., 1672, 8vo. "Which book," says Wood, "was written by anonymous (one that had belonged to the choir of Durham), and published by John Davis, of Kidwelly."

The MS. here transcribed was formerly in the Ashmolean Museum, but with the rest of Wood's MSS. is now deposited in the Bodleian, numbered Wood, E 4.

FEBRUARY, 1875.

A CLASSIFIED CATALOGUE OF
HENRY S. KING & CO.'S PUBLICATIONS.

CONTENTS.

	PAGE		PAGE
HISTORY AND BIOGRAPHY	1	POETRY	21
VOYAGES AND TRAVEL	4	WORKS OF MR. TENNYSON	22
SCIENCE	6	FICTION	25
ESSAYS AND LECTURES	12	CORNHILL LIBRARY OF FICTION	28
MILITARY WORKS	13	THEOLOGICAL	29
INDIA AND THE EAST	16	MISCELLANEOUS	34
BOOKS FOR THE YOUNG, &c.	18		

HISTORY AND BIOGRAPHY.

JOSEPH MAZZINI: A MEMOIR. By **E. A. V.** With two Essays by Mazzini, "Thoughts on Democracy," and "The Duties of Man." Dedicated to the working classes by **P. A. Taylor, M.P.** Crown 8vo. With Two Portraits. 3s. 6d.

"The author gives, from sources partly public, partly private, an ample and close insight into the mind of the eminent popular leader; touching occasionally at some greater length upon his political doings."—*Examiner.*

SHELLEY MEMORIALS FROM AUTHENTIC SOURCES. Edited by **Lady Shelley.** With (now first printed) an Essay on CHRISTIANITY, by **Percy Bysshe Shelley.** Third Edition. Crown 8vo. With Portrait. Price 5s.

WILLIAM GODWIN (Shelley's Father-in-Law): **AUTOBIOGRAPHY, MEMOIR, AND CORRESPONDENCE.** By **C. Kegan Paul.** 2 vols., demy 8vo. With Portraits. [*Preparing.*

MRS. GILBERT (ANN TAYLOR): AUTOBIOGRAPHY AND OTHER MEMORIALS. Edited by **Josiah Gilbert.** 2 vols. Post 8vo. With 2 Steel Portraits and several Wood Engravings. 24s.

"Mr. Gilbert has succeeded in painting a remarkable and attractive portrait, of which the setting is graceful and appropriate."—*Academy.*

"The autobiography is very beautifully written. It gives the home history of a most interesting and talented family, and it possesses a charm peculiar to the writing of a really clever woman."—*Examiner.*

"The family life was tender and beautiful, . . . but the charm of the group consists in the character of the central figure, which Mr. Gilbert has so firmly yet delicately drawn."—*Nonconformist.*

Second Edition.

A. B. GRANVILLE, M.D., F.R.S.: AUTOBIOGRAPHY. With Recollections of the most Eminent Men of the last Half-Century. Being eighty-eight years of the Life of a Physician who practised his Profession in Italy, Greece, Turkey, Spain, Portugal, the West Indies, Russia, Germany, France, and England. Edited, with a brief account of the last years of his life, by his youngest Daughter, **Paulina B. Granville.** 2 vols. Demy 8vo. With a Steel Portrait. 32s.

"There is a variety of incident and a liveliness of style in Dr. Granville's reminiscences of his long life which make the book pleasant, and even in many respects instructive to read. To few men is it given to tell the tale of a career on which fortune has so uniformly smiled throughout. . . . Of his success with patients, including well nigh every name of mark during two generations, we get an extraordinary abundance of details. Rarely has a physician been more communicative in respect to the names, ailments, fees, or compliments which the case book of fifty years' leading practice must be the means of yielding. Madame de Staël, Lord and Lady Ellenborough, Mrs. Siddons, Bishop Tomlins, Count Woronzow, and a great Persian satrap, are prominent among the list, their maladies and mode of cure giving occasion to many a characteristic anecdote. . . . His autobiography gives us the picture of a gentleman of good parts, restless energy, and prominent self-esteem, intensely fussy, not easily rebuffed, and on the best terms with himself and with the world. The long list of his writings bespeaks his love of work and the versatility of his mind. His services to medicine and the influence he exerted in society will not soon be forgotten ; . . . these memoirs of his lifetime contain a great deal of matter which is well worth the reading."—*Saturday Review.*

65, Cornhill; & 12, Paternoster Row, London.

HISTORY AND BIOGRAPHY—*continued*.

SAMUEL LOVER, R.H.A., THE LIFE OF: Artistic, Literary, and Musical. With Selections from his Unpublished Papers and Correspondence. By **Bayle Bernard.** 2 vols. Post 8vo. With a Steel Portrait. 21s.

"Written in a kindly and generous spirit, exhibiting a tender and sympathetic regard for Lover."—*Art Journal.*

"In this grave age of sorrowful problems we must thank so cheerful a biographer as Mr. Bernard."—*Academy.*

ROWLAND WILLIAMS, D.D.: LIFE & LETTERS. With Extracts from his Note-Books. Edited by **Mrs. Rowland Williams.** With a Photographic Portrait. In 2 vols. Post 8vo. 24s.

"These volumes abound with biographical and literary interest."—*Examiner.*

"Full and instructive. Large as it is, many parts are interesting. Dr. Williams's opinions on

"most subjects come out clearly.... The widow has performed her part lovingly and with taste, presenting the departed husband in all his phases."—*Athenæum.*

JOHN GREY (of Dilston): MEMOIRS. By **Josephine E. Butler.** New and Cheaper Edition. Crown 8vo. 3s. 6d.

"It is not a mere story of success or genius, as far removed as a fairy tale from the experience and imitation of ordinary people; but it is, if we only allow it to be so, an incentive and exemplar to all of us.... Something we must say of the skilful and temperate execution of the memoir

itself: it is impossible to read it without feeling that Mrs. Butler is her father's daughter, and without wishing that she had given us two volumes instead of one."—*From a four-column notice by "The Times" on the First Edition.*

POLITICAL WOMEN. By **Sutherland Menzies.** 2 vols. Post 8vo. 24s.

"Has all the information of history, with all the interest that attaches to biography."—*Scotsman.*

Third Edition, Revised and Corrected. With Index.

SARA COLERIDGE: MEMOIR AND LETTERS. Edited by her **Daughter.** 2 vols. Crown 8vo. With 2 Steel Portraits. Price 24s.

"Sara Coleridge, as she is revealed, or rather reveals herself, in the correspondence, makes a brilliant addition to a brilliant family reputation."—*Saturday Review.*

"These charming volumes are attractive as a memorial of a most amiable woman of high intellectual mark."—*Athenæum.*

Cheap Edition of the above.

SARA COLERIDGE: MEMOIR AND LETTERS. Edited by her **Daughter.** 1 Vol. Crown 8vo. With a Steel Portrait. 7s. 6d.

THE LATE REV. F. W. ROBERTSON, M.A.: LIFE AND LETTERS. Edited by the **Rev. Stopford A. Brooke, M.A.,** Chaplain in Ordinary to the Queen.
 I. In 2 vols., uniform with the Sermons. With a Steel Portrait. Price 7s. 6d.
 II. Library Edition, in demy 8vo, with Two Steel Portraits. Price 12s.
 III. A Popular Edition, in 1 vol. Price 6s.

NATHANIEL HAWTHORNE: A MEMOIR, with Stories now first published in this country. By **H. A. Page.** Post 8vo. Price 7s. 6d.

"Seldom has it been our lot to meet with a more appreciative delineation of character than this Memoir of Hawthorne."—*Morning Post.*

"Exhibits a discriminating enthusiasm for one of the most fascinating of novelists."—*Saturday Review.*

LEONORA CHRISTINA, Daughter of Christian IV. of Denmark: Memoirs written during her Imprisonment in the Blue Tower of the Royal Palace at Copenhagen, 1663–1685. Translated by **F. E. Bunnètt.** With an Autotype Portrait of the Princess. Medium 8vo. Price 12s. 6d.

"A valuable addition to the tragic romance of history."—*Spectator.*

"A valuable addition to history."—*Daily News.*

LIVES OF ENGLISH POPULAR LEADERS IN THE MIDDLE AGES. No. 1.—STEPHEN LANGTON. By **C. Edmund Maurice.** Cr. 8vo. 7s. 6d.

"Very well and honestly executed."—*John Bull.*

"In style it is characterised by the greatest fairness and ability, and the picture of the archbishop

is vigorously and firmly drawn."—*Churchman's Shilling Magazine.*

"Well worth a careful study."—*Jewish World.*

LIVES OF ENGLISH POPULAR LEADERS IN THE MIDDLE AGES. No. 2.—TYLER, BALL, and OLDCASTLE. By **C. Edmund Maurice.** Crown 8vo. Price 7s. 6d.

"The value of this little volume lies in its copious details with regard to the condition of the poorer classes in the Middle Ages, and particularly in the evidence which the author adduces of the close

relationship between the dawning Reformation and the popular movements of the time."—*Daily News.*

65, *Cornhill;* & 12, *Paternoster Row, London.*

HISTORY AND BIOGRAPHY—*continued*.

CABINET PORTRAITS. BIOGRAPHICAL SKETCHES OF STATESMEN OF THE DAY. By T. **Wemyss Reid**. 1 vol. Crown 8vo. Price 7s. 6d.

"We have never met with a work which we can more unreservedly praise. The sketches are absolutely impartial."—*Athenæum*.

"We can heartily commend this work."—*Standard*.

"Drawn with a master hand."—*Yorkshire Post*.

THE CHURCH AND THE EMPIRES: Historical Periods. By the late **Henry W. Wilberforce**. Preceded by a Memoir of the Author by **John Henry Newman, D.D.**, of the Oratory. Post 8vo. With Portrait. 10s. 6d.

"The literary relics preserved by Dr. Newman are varied in subject as in character. They comprise an eloquent, though somewhat empirical, treatise on the formation of Christendom; two masterly reviews of Champigny's too little known works... Henry William Wilberforce was a man of strong opinions, and in all he wrote gave expression to the judgments of a powerful if, possibly, an undetermined mind."—*Standard*.

HISTORY OF THE ENGLISH REVOLUTION OF 1688. By C. D. **Yonge**, Regius Professor, Queen's Coll., Belfast. Crown 8vo. Price 6s.

"A fair, succinct, useful, and masterly summary of the main causes, circumstances, and history of the Revolution, and not without some striking comments on its effects."—*Standard*.

ALEXIS DE TOCQUEVILLE. Correspondence and Conversations with NASSAU W. SENIOR, from 1833 to 1859. Edited by **M. C. M. Simpson**. In 2 vols. Large post 8vo. Price 21s.

"A book replete with knowledge and thought."—*Quarterly Review*.

"An extremely interesting book."—*Saturday Review*.

SORROW AND SONG; or, Studies of Literary Struggle. Henry Mürger —Novalis—Alexander Petöfi—Honoré de Balzac—Edgar Allan Poe—André Chénier. By **Henry Curwen**. 2 vols. Crown 8vo. 15s.

"No one who takes an interest in the lives of authors can read it without sympathy, if not with pleasure."—*Scotsman*.

JOURNALS KEPT IN FRANCE AND ITALY. From 1848 to 1852. With a Sketch of the Revolution of 1848. By the late **Nassau William Senior**. Edited by his Daughter, **M. C. M. Simpson**. In 2 vols. Post 8vo. Price 24s.

"The book has a genuine historical value."—*Saturday Review*.

"No better, more honest, and more readable view of the state of political society during the existence of the second Republic could well be looked for."—*Examiner*.

PERSIA; ANCIENT AND MODERN. By John **Piggot, F.S.A.** Post 8vo. Price 10s. 6d.

"A very useful book."—*Rock*.

"That Mr. Piggot has spared no pains or research in the execution of his work is apparent in the list of authorities, classic and modern, which he continually quotes; his style also, when not recounting history, is lively and pleasant, and the anecdotes which he culls from the writings of travellers are frequently amusing."—*Hour*.

"We are bound to say that in little more than three hundred pages he has succeeded in his aim of giving us 'a fair general view of ancient and modern Persian history, supplemented by chapters on the religion, literature, commerce, art, sciences, army, education, language, sport, &c., of the country.'... He has read up to the level of his subject; old and new authorities have been explored and digested; the style is clear and unambitious; and his compilation is well-planned and is not too long."—*Saturday Review*.

New Edition Revised.

THE HISTORY OF JAPAN. From the Earliest Period to the Present Time. By **Francis Ottiwell Adams, F.R.G.S.**, H.B.M.'s Secretary of Embassy at Berlin, formerly H.B.M.'s Chargé d'Affaires, and Secretary of Legation at Yedo. Volume I. Demy 8vo. With Map and Plans. Price 21s.

"He marshals his facts with skill and judgment; and he writes with an elegance worthy of a very skilled craftsman in literary work... We hope Mr. Adams will not keep the public long without the second volume, for the appearance of which all who read the first will anxiously look."—*Standard*.

"As a diplomatic study, and as referring to a deeply interesting episode in contemporary history, it is well worth reading. The information it contains is trustworthy, and is carefully compiled, and the style is all that can be desired."—*Saturday Review*.

"A most valuable contribution to our knowledge of an interesting people."—*Examiner*.

THE HISTORY OF JAPAN. Volume II. completing the Work. By **Francis Ottiwell Adams, F.R.G.S.** From the Year 1865 to Present Time. Demy 8vo, with Map. Price 21s.

"Pleasant in style, and valuable in substance."—*Standard*.

"Mr. Adams has completed his work well.... It is written in chapters with detailed headings, and the reader has the further aid of a copious index and a glossary."—*Liverpool Albion*.

"May safely be put before all who are interested in foreign politics and foreign manners, who will find it full of valuable information very clearly presented."—*Glasgow News*.

HISTORY AND BIOGRAPHY—*continued.*

THE NORMAN PEOPLE, AND THEIR EXISTING DESCENDANTS IN THE BRITISH DOMINIONS AND THE UNITED STATES OF AMERICA. 8vo. Price 21s.

"A very singular work... We do not accept the consequences to their full extent, but we can cordially recommend the volume as one which is emphatically 'extraordinary.'"—*Notes and Queries.*

"The author has given us a valuable list of mediæval surnames and their origin which demands our best gratitude."—*Standard.*

THE RUSSIANS IN CENTRAL ASIA. A Critical Examination, down to the present time, of the Geography and History of Central Asia. By **Baron F. von Hellwald.** Translated by **Lieut.-Col. Theodore Wirgman,** LL.B. In 1 vol. Large post 8vo, with Map. Price 12s.

"A learned account of the geography of this still ill-known land, of the characteristics of its main divisions, of the nature and habits of its numerous races, and of the progress through it of Russian influence, ... It contains a large amount of valuable information."—*Times.*

"A lucidly written, and apparently accurate account of Turkestan, its geographical features and its history. Its worth to the reader is further enhanced by a well-executed map, based on the most recent Russian surveys."—*Glasgow News.*

BOKHARA: ITS HISTORY AND CONQUEST. By **Professor Arminius Vámbéry,** of the University of Pesth. Demy 8vo. Price 18s.

"We conclude with a cordial recommendation of this valuable book."—*Saturday Review.*

"Almost every page abounds with composition of peculiar merit."—*Morning Post.*

THE RELIGIOUS HISTORY OF IRELAND: PRIMITIVE, PAPAL, AND PROTESTANT; including the Evangelical Missions, Catholic Agitations, and Church Progress of the last half Century. By **James Godkin.** 1 vol. 8vo. Price 12s.

"These latter chapters on the statistics of the various religious denominations will be welcomed."—*Evening Standard.*

"Mr. Godkin writes with evident honesty; and the topic on which he writes is one about which an honest book is greatly wanted."—*Examiner.*

THE GOVERNMENT OF THE NATIONAL DEFENCE. From the 30th June to the 31st October, 1870. The Plain Statement of a Member. By **Mons. Jules Favre.** 1 vol. Demy 8vo. Price 10s. 6d.

"A work of the highest interest. The book is most valuable."—*Athenæum.*
"Of all the contributions to the history of the late war, we have found none more fascinating and,

perhaps, none more valuable than the 'apology,' by M. Jules Favre, for the unsuccessful Government of the National Defence."—*Times.*

ECHOES OF A FAMOUS YEAR. By **Harriet Parr,** Author of "The Life of Jeanne d'Arc," "In the Silver Age," &c. Crown 8vo. Price 8s. 6d.

"Miss Parr has the great gift of charming simplicity of style; and if children are not interested in her book, many of their seniors will be."—*British Quarterly Review.*

VOYAGES AND TRAVEL.

SOME TIME IN IRELAND; A Recollection. Crown 8vo. 7s. 6d.

"The author has got a genuine Irish gift of witty and graceful writing, and has produced a clever and entertaining book."—*Examiner.*
"Clever, brilliant sketches of life and character among the Irish gentry of the last generation..."

The little volume will give to strangers a more faithful idea of Irish society and tendencies still working in that unhappy island than any other we know."—*Literary Churchman.*

WAYSIDE NOTES IN SCANDINAVIA. Being Notes of Travel in the North of Europe. By **Mark Antony Lower,** F.S.A., M.A. Crown 8vo. 9s.

*** This Volume is an Account of Researches prosecuted, during a Tour in Scandinavia, in the Summer of 1873. It contains illustrations of the History, Antiquities, Legendary Lore, and Social Condition of Denmark, Sweden, and Norway, from Ancient to Modern Times.

"A very entertaining volume of light, gossiping matter, written in an easy, agreeable style."—*Daily News.*

VOYAGES AND TRAVEL—*continued.*

ON THE ROAD TO KHIVA. By **David Ker**, late Khivan Correspondent of the *Daily Telegraph.* Illustrated with Photographs of the Country and its Inhabitants, and a copy of the Official Map in use during the Campaign, from the Survey of CAPTAIN LEUSILIN. 1 vol. Post 8vo. Price 12s.

"Though it is a graphic and thoughtful sketch, we refer to it, in some degree, for reasons apart from its intrinsic merits... He (the author) has satisfied us that he was not the impudent impostor he seemed to be; and though he did not witness the fall of Khiva, he travelled through a great part of Central Asia, and honestly tried to accomplish his task... His work, we have said, is an able *résumé* of genuine observation and reflection, which will well repay a reader's attention."—*Times.*

"Very interesting reading... a really good book full of quaint, vivid writing."—*Echo.*
"He is a clever and fluent writer... The book is smartly written."—*Saturday Review.*
"A pleasant book of travels. It is exceedingly smart and clever, full of amusing anecdotes and graphic descriptions."—*Vanity Fair.*
"Mr. Ker knows Russian peasant life very well indeed, and his bits about the Cossacks are full of character."—*Athenæum.*

VIZCAYA; or, Life in the Land of the Carlists at the Outbreak of the Insurrection, with some account of the Iron Mines and other characteristics of the country. With a Map and 8 Illustrations. Crown 8vo. Price 9s.

"Contains some really valuable information, conveyed in a plain unostentatious manner."—*Athenæum.*
"Agreeably written.... People will read with interest what an English party thought and felt when shut up in Portugalete or Bilbao; the sketches will give a good idea of those places and the surroundings, and the map will be useful if they feel inclined to study the recent operations."—*Colburn's United Service Magazine.*

ROUGH NOTES OF A VISIT TO BELGIUM, SEDAN, AND PARIS, in September, 1870-71. By **John Ashton.** Crown 8vo. Price 3s. 6d.

"The author does not attempt to deal with military subjects, but writes sensibly of what he saw in 1870-71."—*John Bull.*
"Possesses a certain freshness from the straightforward simplicity with which it is written."—*Graphic.*
"An interesting work by a highly intelligent observer."—*Standard.*

THE ALPS OF ARABIA; or, Travels through Egypt, Sinai, Arabia, and the Holy Land. By **William Charles Maughan.** Demy 8vo, with Map. 12s.

"Deeply interesting and valuable."—*Edinburgh Daily Review.*
"He writes freshly and with competent knowledge."—*Standard.*
"Very readable and instructive.... A work far above the average of such publications."—*John Bull.*

Second Edition.

THE MISHMEE HILLS: an Account of a Journey made in an Attempt to Penetrate Thibet from Assam, to open New Routes for Commerce. By **T. T. Cooper.** With Four Illustrations and Map. Post 8vo. Price 10s. 6d.

"The volume, which will be of great use in India and among Indian merchants here, contains a good deal of matter that will interest ordinary readers.
It is especially rich in sporting incidents."—*Standard.*

GOODMAN'S CUBA THE PEARL OF THE ANTILLES. By **Walter Goodman.** Crown 8vo. Price 7s. 6d.

"A series of vivid and miscellaneous sketches. We can recommend this whole volume as very amusing reading."—*Pall Mall Gazette.*
"The whole book deserves the heartiest commendation.... Sparkling and amusing from beginning to end."—*Spectator.*

FIELD AND FOREST RAMBLES OF A NATURALIST IN NEW BRUNSWICK. With Notes and Observations on the Natural History of Eastern Canada. By **A. Leith Adams, M.A.** Illustrated. 8vo, cloth. 14s.

"Both sportsmen and naturalists will find this work replete with anecdote and carefully-recorded observation, which will entertain them."—*Nature.*
"Will be found interesting by those who take a pleasure either in sport or natural history."—*Athenæum.*
"To the naturalist the book will be most valuable.... To the general reader most interesting."—*Evening Standard.*

Second Edition. Revised and Corrected.

TENT LIFE WITH ENGLISH GIPSIES IN NORWAY. By **Hubert Smith.** With Five full-page Engravings, 31 smaller Illustrations, and Map of the Country showing Routes. 8vo, cloth. Price 21s.

"Written in a very lively style, and has throughout a smack of dry humour and satiric reflection which shows the writer to be a keen observer of men and things. We hope that many will read it and find in it the same amusement as ourselves."—*Times.*

65, Cornhill; & 12, Paternoster Row, London.

Works Published by Henry S. King & Co.,

VOYAGES AND TRAVEL—*continued*.

FAYOUM; OR, ARTISTS IN EGYPT. A Tour with M. Gérôme and others. By J. Lenoir. With 13 Illustrations. Crown 8vo, cloth. Price 7s. 6d.

"The book is very amusing.... Whoever may take it up will find he has with him a bright and pleasant companion."—*Spectator*.

"A pleasantly written and very readable book."—*Examiner*.

SPITZBERGEN—THE GATEWAY TO THE POLYNIA; OR, A VOYAGE TO SPITZBERGEN. By Captain John C. Wells, R.N. With numerous Illustrations and Map. 8vo, cloth. Price 21s.

"Straightforward and clear in style, securing our confidence by its unaffected simplicity and good sense."—*Saturday Review*.

"Not only a lively narrative, well illustrated, of

an Arctic voyage, it is also a very complete manual of Polar exploration."—*Guardian*.

"A charming book, remarkably well written and well illustrated."—*Standard*.

AN AUTUMN TOUR IN THE UNITED STATES AND CANADA. By Lieut.-Col. J. G. Medley. Crown 8vo. Price 5s.

"Colonel Medley's little volume is a pleasantly-written account of a two months' visit to America."—*Hour*.

"May be recommended as manly, sensible, and

pleasantly written."—*Globe*.

"His impressions of political life in America, as coming from a thoroughly practical man, are worth recording."—*Pall Mall Gazette*.

Second Edition.

THE NILE WITHOUT A DRAGOMAN. By Frederic Eden. In 1 vol. Crown 8vo, cloth. Price 7s. 6d.

"It is a book to read during an autumn holiday."—*Spectator*.

"Should any of our readers care to imitate Mr. Eden's example, and wish to see things with their

own eyes, and shift for themselves, next winter in Upper Egypt, they will find this book a very agreeable guide."—*Times*.

ROUND THE WORLD IN 1870. A Volume of Travels, with Maps. By A. D. Carlisle, B.A., Trin. Coll. Camb. Demy 8vo. Price 16s.

"We can only commend, which we do very heartily, an eminently sensible and readable book."—*British Quarterly Review*.

"Mr. Carlisle's account of his little outing is exhilarating and charming."—*Spectator*.

"Rarely have we read a more graphic description of the countries named, India, China, Japan, California, and South America... The chapters about Japan are especially replete with information."—*John Bull*.

IRELAND. A Tour of Observation, with Remarks on Irish Public Questions. By Dr. James Macaulay. Crown 8vo. Price 7s. 6d.

"We have rarely met a book on Ireland which for impartiality of criticism and general accuracy of information could be so well recommended to the fair-minded Irish reader."—*Evening Standard*.

"A careful and instructive book. Full of facts, full of information, and full of interest."—*Literary Churchman*.

A WINTER IN MOROCCO. By Amelia Perrier. With 4 Illustrations. Crown 8vo. Price 10s. 6d.

"Well worth reading, and contains several excellent illustrations."—*Hour*.

"Miss Perrier is a very amusing writer. She has a good deal of humour, sees the oddity and quaint-

ness of Oriental life with a quick observant eye, and evidently turned her opportunities of sarcastic examination to account."—*Daily News*.

SCIENCE.

THE PHYSICS AND PHILOSOPHY OF THE SENSES; OR THE MENTAL AND THE PHYSICAL IN THEIR MUTUAL RELATION. By R. S. Wyld, F.R.S.E. Illustrated by Several Plates. Demy 8vo. Price 16s.

The author's object is twofold: first, to supply a Manual of the Senses, embracing the more important discoveries of recent times; second, in discussing the subject of Life, Organisation, Sensibility, and Thought, to demonstrate in opposition to the Materialistic Theory, that the Senses, no less than Reason, furnish proof that an immaterial and spiritual element is the operative element in nature.

65, *Cornhill;* & 12, *Paternoster Row, London.*

SCIENCE—*continued*.

SCIENTIFIC LONDON. By **Bernard H. Becker.** 1 vol. Crown 8vo. 5s.

An Account of the History and present Scope of the following Institutions:—

- The Royal Society
- The Royal Institution
- The Institution of Civil Engineers
- The Royal Geographical Society
- The Society of Telegraph Engineers
- The British Association
- The Birkbeck Institute
- The Society of Arts
- The Government Department of Science and Art
- The Statistical Society
- The Chemical Society
- The Museum of Practical Geology
- The London Institution
- The Gresham Lectures.

"Will be useful as a book of reference... The author has certainly done his work well."—*Court Journal.*
"The information is chiefly official, altogether trustworthy, and excellently condensed."—*Standard.*
"An extremely interesting little book."—*Pharmaceutical Journal.*

OBSERVATIONS OF MAGNETIC DECLINATION MADE AT TREVANDRUM AND AGUSTIA MALLEY in the Observatories of his Highness the MAHARAJAH OF TRAVANCORE, G.C.S.I., in the Years 1852 to 1860. Being Trevandrum Magnetical Observations, Volume I. Discussed and Edited by **John Allan Broun, F.R.S.**, late Director of the Observatories. With an Appendix. Imperial 4to, cloth. 3£ 3s.

*** The Appendix, containing Reports on the Observatories and on the Public Museum, Public Park and Gardens at Trevandrum, pp. xii. 116, may be had separately. Price 21s.

"The title of the work, which is a handsome volume, quarto, 600 pages, at first sight would appear to indicate a dry collection of tables and figures. Some of these of course, are necessary; but, in addition to them, there is a considerable amount of most interesting matter to the general reader in the descriptions of the adventures and troubles of a scientific man in Southern India, while the magnetician and physicist will find much to occupy his attention in the various results which Mr. Broun has so clearly brought out in his discussion of the observations, and in the description of the very ingenious instruments he constructed and employed in his researches."—G. M. Whipple, in the *Academy.*

EUCLID SIMPLIFIED IN METHOD AND LANGUAGE. Being a Manual of Geometry on the French System. By **J. R. Morell.**

The chief features of the work are:—The separation of Theorems and Problems—The Natural Sequence of reasoning; areas being treated by themselves and at a later page—The simpler and more natural treatment of ratio—The legitimate use of arithmetical applications, of transposition, and superposition—The general alteration of language to a more modern form—Lastly, if it be assumed to be venturesome to supersede the time-hallowed pages of Euclid it may be urged that the attempt is made under the shelter of very high authorities.

THE QUESTIONS OF AURAL SURGERY. By **James Hinton**, late Aural Surgeon to Guy's Hospital. Post 8vo. With Illustrations. Price 12s. 6d.

"The questions of Aural Surgery more than maintain the author's reputation as a careful clinician, a deep and accurate thinker, and a forcible and talented writer."—*Lancet.*

AN ATLAS OF DISEASES OF THE MEMBRANA TYMPANI. With Descriptive Text. By **James Hinton**, late Aural Surgeon to Guy's Hospital. Post 8vo. Price £6 6s.

"Of Mr. Hinton's Atlas of the Membrana Tympani it is hardly necessary to say more than that it is by far the best and most accurate that has ever yet been published. The drawings are taken from actual specimens, and are all coloured by hand."—*Lancet.*

Second Edition.

PHYSIOLOGY FOR PRACTICAL USE. By various Writers. Edited by **James Hinton.** 2 vols. Crown 8vo. With 50 Illustrations. Price 12s. 6d.

"A more clear, valuable, and well-informed set of treatises we never saw than these, which are bound up into two compact and readable volumes. And they are pleasant reading, too, as well as useful reading."—*Literary Churchman.*
"We never saw the popular side of the science of physiology better explained than it is in these two thin volumes."—*Standard.*
"It has certainly been edited with great care. Physiological treatises we have had in great number, but not one work, we believe, which so thoroughly appeals to all classes of the community as the present. Everything has apparently been done to render the work really practical and useful."—*Civil Service Gazette.*

SCIENCE—*continued.*

Second Edition.

THE PRINCIPLES OF MENTAL PHYSIOLOGY. With their Applications to the Training and Discipline of the Mind, and the Study of its Morbid Conditions. By **W. B. Carpenter, LL.D., M.D., &c.** 8vo. Illustrated. 12s.

"This valuable book . . . . Let us add that nothing we have said, or in any limited space could say, would give an adequate conception of the valuable and curious collection of facts bearing on morbid mental conditions, the learned physiological exposition, and the treasure-house of useful hints for mental training which make this large and yet very amusing, as well as instructive book, an encyclopædia of well-classified and often very startling psychological experiences."—*Spectator.*

SENSATION AND INTUITION. Studies in Psychology and Æsthetics. By **James Sully, M.A.** Demy 8vo. 10s. 6d.

"As to the manner of the book, Mr. Sully writes well, and so as to be understood by any one who will take the needful pains. . . . The materials furnished by a quick and lively natural sense are happily ordered by a mind trained in scientific method. This merit is especially conspicuous in those parts of the book where, with abundant ingenuity and no mean success, Mr. Sully endeavours to throw some light of cosmic order into the chaos of æsthetics. Unhappily for our present purpose, the best qualities of the work are precisely those to which we cannot do justice within the limits of a review."—*Saturday Review.*

"Though the series of essays is by no means devoid of internal connection, each presents so many new points of interest that it is impossible here to note more than one or two particulars. The first essay of all, wherein the author considers the relation of the Evolution-hypothesis to human psychology, may be cited as an excellent specimen of his style of work."—*Examiner.*

". . . In conclusion, we beg to thank Mr. Sully for a meritorious and successful attempt to popularise valuable and not very tractable departments of science."—*Academy.*

Second Edition.

THE EXPANSE OF HEAVEN. A Series of Essays on the Wonders of the Firmament. By **R. A. Proctor, B.A.** With a Frontispiece. Crown 8vo. 6s.

"A very charming work; cannot fail to lift the reader's mind up 'through nature's work to nature's God.'"—*Standard.*

"Full of thought, readable, and popular."—*Brighton Gazette.*

STUDIES OF BLAST FURNACE PHENOMENA. By **M. L. Gruner.** Translated by **L. D. B. Gordon, F.R.S.E., F.G.S.** 8vo. 7s. 6d.

"The whole subject is dealt with very copiously and clearly in all its parts, and can scarcely fail of appreciation at the hands of practical men, for whose use it is designed."—*Post.*

CONTEMPORARY ENGLISH PSYCHOLOGY. From the French of **Professor Th. Ribot.** Large post 8vo. Price 9s. An Analysis of the Views and Opinions of the following Metaphysicians, as expressed in their writings :—

JAMES MILL, ALEXANDER BAIN, JOHN STUART MILL, GEORGE H. LEWES, HERBERT SPENCER, SAMUEL BAILEY.

"The task which M. Ribot set himself he has performed with very great success."—*Examiner.*

"We can cordially recommend the volume."—*Journal of Mental Science.*

HEREDITY: a Psychological Study on its Phenomena, its Laws, its Causes, and its Consequences. By **Th. Ribot,** Author of "Contemporary English Psychology." 1 vol. Large crown 8vo.

"It is generally admitted that "Heredity"—or that biological law by which all living creatures tend to reproduce themselves in their descendants—is the rule in all forms of vital activity. The author devotes his work to the study of the question. "Does the law also hold in regard to the mental faculties?"—*Post.*

A TREATISE ON RELAPSING FEVER. By **R. T. Lyons,** Assistant-Surgeon, Bengal Army. Post 8vo. Price 7s. 6d.

"A practical work, thoroughly supported in its views by a series of remarkable cases."—*Standard.*

65, Cornhill; & 12, Paternoster Row, London.

SCIENCE—*continued.*

Second Edition Revised.

A LEGAL HANDBOOK FOR ARCHITECTS, BUILDERS, AND BUILDING OWNERS. By **Edward Jenkins, Esq., M.P.,** and **John Raymond, Esq.,** Barristers-at-Law. Crown 8vo. 6s.

"This manual has one recommendation which cannot be accorded to more than a very small proportion of the books published at the present day. It proposes to supply a real want.... As to the style of the work, it is just what a legal handbook should be.... We warmly recommend it to our readers."—*Architect.*

"It would be doing it an injustice to class it with the rank and file of legal hand-books. In tone and style it resembles Lord St. Leonards' well-known popular treatise on the law of real property. The writer conceives his subject clearly, and writes in a manner that is pleasant, forcible, and lucid."—*Law Magazine and Review.*

"For all this and much more, about buildings and building contracts, which is not always easy for a layman to understand, but which it is very necessary for an architect to know, the reader will find in the neat little volume just published from the pen of Messrs. Jenkins and Raymond, a very excellent guide."—*Law Journal.*

THE HISTORY OF CREATION, a Popular Account of the Development of the Earth and its Inhabitants, according to the theories of Kant, Laplace, Lamarck, and Darwin. By **Professor Ernst Haeckel** of the University of Jena. The Translation revised, by **E. Ray Lankester, M.A.** With Coloured Plates and Genealogical Trees of the various groups of both plants and animals. 2 vols. Post 8vo.

[*Preparing.*

THE HISTORY OF THE EVOLUTION OF MAN. By **Ernst Haeckel.** Translated by **E. A. Van Rhyn** and **L. Elsberg, M.D.** (University of New York), with Notes and Additions sanctioned by the Author. Post 8vo.

A New Edition.

CHANGE OF AIR AND SCENE. A Physician's Hints about Doctors, Patients, Hygiène, and Society; with Notes of Excursions for Health in the Pyrenees, and amongst the Watering-places of France (Inland and Seaward), Switzerland, Corsica, and the Mediterranean. By **Dr. Alphonse Donné.** Large post 8vo. Price 9s.

"A very readable and serviceable book.... The real value of it is to be found in the accurate and minute information given with regard to a large number of places which have gained a reputation on the continent for their mineral waters."—*Pall Mall Gazette.*

"A singularly pleasant and chatty as well as instructive book about health."—*Guardian.*

"A valuable and almost complete *vade mecum* for the continental tourist seeking health."—*London Quarterly Review.*

New and Enlarged Edition.

MISS YOUMANS' FIRST BOOK OF BOTANY. Designed to cultivate the observing powers of Children. With 300 Engravings. Crown 8vo. Price 5s.

"It is but rarely that a school-book appears which is at once so novel in plan, so successful in execution, and so suited to the general want, as to command universal and unqualified approbation, but such has been the case with Miss Youmans' First Book of Botany.... It has been everywhere welcomed as a timely and invaluable contribution to the improvement of primary education."—*Pall Mall Gazette.*

A DICTIONARY AND GLOSSARY OF THE KOR-AN. With copious Grammatical References and Explanations of the Text. By **Major J. Penrice, B.A.** 4to. Price 21s.

"The book is likely to answer its purpose in smoothing a beginner's road in reading the Kor-ân."—*Academy.*

MODERN GOTHIC ARCHITECTURE. By **T. G. Jackson.** Crown 8vo. Price 5s.

"The reader will find some of the most important doctrines of eminent art teachers practically applied in this little book, which is well written and popular in style."—*Manchester Examiner.*

"This thoughtful little book is worthy of the perusal of all interested in art or architecture."—*Standard.*

CHOLERA: HOW TO AVOID AND TREAT IT. Popular and Practical Notes by **Henry Blanc, M.D.** Crown 8vo. Price 4s. 6d.

"A very practical manual, based on experience and careful observation, full of excellent hints on a most dangerous disease."—*Standard.*

65, *Cornhill;* & 12, *Paternoster Row, London.*

THE INTERNATIONAL SCIENTIFIC SERIES.

The following is a List of the Volumes already published.

Fourth Edition.
I. **THE FORMS OF WATER IN CLOUDS AND RIVERS, ICE AND GLACIERS.** By **J. Tyndall**, LL.D., F.R.S. With 26 Illustrations. Price 5s.

Second Edition.
II. **PHYSICS AND POLITICS**; OR, THOUGHTS ON THE APPLICATION OF THE PRINCIPLES OF "NATURAL SELECTION" AND "INHERITANCE" TO POLITICAL SOCIETY. By **Walter Bagehot**. Price 4s.

Third Edition.
III. **FOODS.** By **Edward Smith, M.D.** Profusely Illustrated. Price 5s.

Third Edition.
IV. **MIND AND BODY**: THE THEORIES OF THEIR RELATION. By **Alexander Bain**, LL.D. With Four Illustrations. Price 4s.

Fourth Edition.
V. **THE STUDY OF SOCIOLOGY.** By **Herbert Spencer**. Price 5s.

Third Edition.
VI. **THE CONSERVATION OF ENERGY.** By **Balfour Stewart, M.A., LL.D.** With Fourteen Engravings. Price 5s.

Second Edition.
VII. **ANIMAL LOCOMOTION**; or, Walking, Swimming, and Flying. By **J. Bell Pettigrew, M.D., F.R.S.** With 119 Illustrations. Price 5s.

Second Edition.
VIII. **RESPONSIBILITY IN MENTAL DISEASE.** By **Henry Maudsley, M.D.** Price 5s.

Second Edition.
IX. **THE NEW CHEMISTRY.** By **Professor Josiah P. Cooke**, of the Harvard University. With Thirty-one Illustrations. Price 5s.

Second Edition.
X. **THE SCIENCE OF LAW.** By **Prof. Sheldon Amos.** Price 5s.

Second Edition.
XI. **ANIMAL MECHANISM.** A Treatise on Terrestrial and Aerial Locomotion. By **Professor E. J. Marey.** With 117 Illustrations. Price 5s.

Second Edition.
XII. **THE DOCTRINE OF DESCENT AND DARWINISM.** By Professor **Oscar Schmidt** (Strasburg University). Illustrated. Price 5s.

Second Edition.
XIII. **HISTORY OF THE CONFLICT BETWEEN RELIGION AND SCIENCE.** By **John William Draper, M.D., LL.D.** Professor in the University of New York; Author of "A Treatise on Human Physiology." Price 5s.

XIV. **FUNGI**; THEIR NATURE, INFLUENCES, USES, &c. By **M. C. Cooke, M.A., LL.D.** Edited by the **Rev. M. J. Berkeley, M.A., F.L.S.** Profusely Illustrated. Price 5s.

XV. **THE CHEMICAL EFFECTS OF LIGHT AND PHOTOGRAPHY**, IN THEIR APPLICATION TO ART, SCIENCE, AND INDUSTRY. By **Dr. Hermann Vogel** (Polytechnic Academy of Berlin). With 74 Illustrations.

XVI. **OPTICS.** By **Professor Lommel** (University of Erlangen). Profusely Illustrated.

65, Cornhill; and 12, Paternoster Row, London.

THE INTERNATIONAL SCIENTIFIC SERIES—*continued*.

Forthcoming Volumes.

Mons. VAN BENEDEN.
    On Parasites in the Animal Kingdom.

Prof. W. KINGDOM CLIFFORD, M.A.
    The First Principles of the Exact Sciences explained to the non-mathematical.

Prof. T. H. HUXLEY, LL.D., F.R.S.
    Bodily Motion and Consciousness.

Dr. W. B. CARPENTER, LL.D., F.R.S.
    The Physical Geography of the Sea.

Prof. WILLIAM ODLING, F.R.S.
    The Old Chemistry viewed from the New Standpoint.

W. LAUDER LINDSAY, M.D., F.R.S.E.
    Mind in the Lower Animals.

Sir JOHN LUBBOCK, Bart., F.R.S.
    The Antiquity of Man.

Prof. W. T. THISELTON DYER, B.A., B.SC.
    Form and Habit in Flowering Plants.

Mr. J. N. LOCKYER, F.R.S.
    Spectrum Analysis: some of its recent results.

Prof. MICHAEL FOSTER, M.D.
    Protoplasm and the Cell Theory.

Prof. W. STANLEY JEVONS.
    Money: and the Mechanism of Exchange.

H. CHARLTON BASTIAN, M.D., F.R.S.
    The Brain as an Organ of Mind.

Prof. A. C. RAMSAY, LL.D., F.R.S.
    Earth Sculpture: Hills, Valleys, Mountains, Plains, Rivers, Lakes; how they were produced, and how they have been destroyed.

Prof. RUDOLPH VIRCHOW (Berlin Univ.)
    Morbid Physiological Action.

Prof. CLAUDE BERNARD.
    Physical and Metaphysical Phenomena of Life.

Prof. H. SAINTE-CLAIRE DEVILLE.
    An Introduction to General Chemistry.

Prof. WURTZ.
    Atoms and the Atomic Theory.

Prof. DE QUATREFAGES.
    The Negro Races.

Prof. LACAZE-DUTHIERS.
    Zoology since Cuvier.

Prof. BERTHELOT.
    Chemical Synthesis.

Prof. J. ROSENTHAL.
    General Physiology of Muscles and Nerves.

Prof. JAMES D. DANA, M.A., LL.D.
    On Cephalization; or, Head-Characters in the Gradation and Progress of Life.

Prof. S. W. JOHNSON, M.A.
    On the Nutrition of Plants.

Prof. AUSTIN FLINT, Jr. M.D.
    The Nervous System and its Relation to the Bodily Functions.

Prof. W. D. WHITNEY.
    Modern Linguistic Science.

Prof. BERNSTEIN (University of Halle).
    Physiology of the Senses.

Prof. FERDINAND COHN (Breslau Univ.)
    Thallophytes (Algæ, Lichens, Fungi).

Prof. HERMANN (University of Zurich).
    Respiration.

Prof. LEUCKART (University of Leipsic).
    Outlines of Animal Organization.

Prof. LIEBREICH (University of Berlin).
    Outlines of Toxicology.

Prof. KUNDT (University of Strasburg).
    On Sound.

Prof. REES (University of Erlangen).
    On Parasitic Plants.

Prof. STEINTHAL (University of Berlin).
    Outlines of the Science of Language.

P. BERT (Professor of Physiology, Paris).
    Forms of Life and other Cosmical Conditions.

E. ALGLAVE (Professor of Constitutional and Administrative Law at Douai, and of Political Economy at Lille).
    The Primitive Elements of Political Constitutions

P. LORAIN (Professor of Medicine, Paris).
    Modern Epidemics.

Prof. SCHÜTZENBERGER (Director of the Chemical Laboratory at the Sorbonne).
    On Fermentations.

Mons. FREIDEL.
    The Functions of Organic Chemistry.

Mons. DEBRAY.
    Precious Metals.

Mons. P. BLASERNA (Professor in the University of Rome.)
    On Sound; The Organs of Voice and of Hearing.

ESSAYS AND LECTURES.

THE BETTER SELF. Essays for Home Life. By the Author of "The Gentle Life." Crown 8vo. 6s.

Second Edition.

A CLUSTER OF LIVES. By **Alice King**. Crown 8vo. 7s. 6d.

CONTENTS.—Vittoria Colonna—Madame Récamier—A Daughter of the Stuarts—Dante—Madame de Sévigné—Geoffrey Chaucer—Edmund Spenser—Captain Cook's Companion—Ariosto—Lucrezia Borgia—Petrarch—Cervantes—Joan of Arc—Galileo—Madame Cottin—Song of the Bird in the Garden of Armida.

"It is not every writer who possesses the faculty of leaving clear impressions of his or her personages upon the minds of readers. This, however, is done, and well done by the writer of the volume before us."—*Pall Mall Gazette.*

"A little collection of historical biographies . . . very gracefully written, . . . brilliant and striking in scenes and costumes, wonderfully accurate as to facts, sensible and correct in reflection."—*Literary Churchman.*

Second Edition.

IN STRANGE COMPANY; or, The Note Book of a Roving Correspondent. By **James Greenwood**, "The Amateur Casual." Crown 8vo. 6s.

"A bright, lively book."—*Standard.*
"Has all the interest of romance."—*Queen.*
"Some of the papers remind us of Charles Lamb on beggars and chimney-sweeps."—*Echo.*

MASTER-SPIRITS. By **Robert Buchanan.** Post 8vo. 10s. 6d.

" Good Books are the precious life-blood of Master-Spirits."—*Milton.*

"Full of fresh and vigorous writing, such as can only be produced by a man of keen and independent intellect."—*Saturday Review.*
"Written with a beauty of language and a spirit of vigorous enthusiasm rare even in our best living word-painters."—*Standard.*

"A very pleasant and readable book."—*Examiner.*
"Mr. Buchanan is a writer whose books the critics may always open with satisfaction . . . both manly and artistic."—*Hour.*

GLANCES AT INNER ENGLAND. A Lecture delivered in the United States and Canada. By **Edward Jenkins, M.P.**, Author of "Ginx's Baby," &c. Crown 8vo. Price 5s.

"These 'glances' exhibit much of the author's characteristic discrimination and judgment."—*Edinburgh Courant.*
"Cleverly written, full of terse adages and rapier-like epigrams it is; thoughtful and just it is in many respects."—*Echo.*
"Eloquent and epigrammatic." — *Illustrated Review.*

OUR LAND LAWS. Short Lectures delivered before the Working Men's College. By **T. Lean Wilkinson.** Crown 8vo, limp cloth. 2s.

"A very handy and intelligible epitome of the general principles of existing land laws."—*Standard.*

AN ESSAY ON THE CULTURE OF THE OBSERVING POWERS OF CHILDREN, especially in connection with the Study of Botany. By **Eliza A. Youmans.** Edited, with Notes and a Supplement, by **Joseph Payne, F.C.P.**, Author of "Lectures on the Science and Art of Education," &c. Crown 8vo. 2s. 6d.

"This study, according to her just notions on the subject, is to be fundamentally based on the exercise of the pupil's own powers of observation. He is to see and examine the properties of plants and flowers at first hand, not merely to be informed of what others have seen and examined."—*Pall Mall Gazette.*

THE GENIUS OF CHRISTIANITY UNVEILED. Being Essays by **William Godwin,** Author of "Political Justice," &c. Edited with a preface by **C. Kegan Paul.** 1 vol. Crown 8vo. 7s. 6d.

"Few have thought more clearly and directly than William Godwin, or expressed their reflections with more simplicity and unreserve."—*Examiner.*
"The deliberate thoughts of Godwin deserve to be put before the world for reading and consideration."—*Athenæum.*

WORKS BY JOSEPH PAYNE, Professor of the Science and Art of Education to the College of Preceptors.

THE TRUE FOUNDATION OF SCIENCE TEACHING. A Lecture delivered at the College of Preceptors. 8vo, sewed, 6d.

THE SCIENCE AND ART OF EDUCATION. A Lecture introductory to a "Course of Lectures and Lessons to Teachers on the Science, Art, and History of Education," delivered at the College of Preceptors. 8vo, sewed, 6d.

FRÖBEL AND THE KINDERGARTEN SYSTEM OF ELEMENTARY EDUCATION. A Lecture delivered at the College of Preceptors. 8vo, sewed, 6d.

MILITARY WORKS.

MINOR TACTICS. By C. Clery, Captain 32nd Light Infantry, Professor of Tactics, Royal Military College, Sandhurst. Demy 8vo. 16s.

This is a treatise on so much of the minor operations of war as every regimental officer ought to be acquainted with. It contains numerous detailed examples from actual warfare, and is illustrated by twenty-six plans.

MOUNTAIN WARFARE, illustrated by the Campaign of 1799 in Switzerland, being a translation of the Swiss Narrative compiled from the works of the Archduke Charles, Jomini, and others. Also of Notes by General H. Dufour on the Campaign of the Valteline in 1635. By **Major-General Shadwell, C.B.** With Appendix, Maps, and Introductory Remarks.

This work has been prepared for the purpose of illustrating by the well-known campaign of 1799 in Switzerland, the true method of conducting warfare in mountainous countries. Many of the scenes of this contest are annually visited by English tourists, and are in themselves full of interest; but the special object of the volume is to attract the attention of the young officers of our army to this branch of warfare, especially of those, whose lot may hereafter be cast, and who may be called upon to take part in operations against the Hill Tribes of our extensive Indian frontier.

RUSSIA'S ADVANCE EASTWARD. Based on the Official Reports of Lieut. Hugo Stumm, German Military Attaché to the Khivan Expedition. To which is appended other Information on the Subject, and a Minute Account of the Russian Army. By **Capt. C. E. H. Vincent, F.R.G.S.** Crown 8vo. With Map. 6s.

"Captain Vincent's account of the improvements which have taken place lately in all branches of the service is accurate and clear, and is full of useful material for the consideration of those who believe that Russia is still where she was left by the Crimean war."—*Athenæum.*

"Even more interesting, perhaps, than Lieutenant Stumm's narrative of one of the most brilliant military exploits of recent years is Captain Vincent's own account of the reconstruction, under Milutin, of the Russian Army. Few books will give a better idea of its progress than this brief survey of its present state and latest achievement."—*Graphic.*

THE VOLUNTEER, THE MILITIAMAN, AND THE REGULAR SOLDIER; a Conservative View of the Armies of England, Past, Present, and Future, as Seen in January, 1874. By **A Public School Boy.** 1 vol. Crown 8vo. Price 5s.

"Deserves special attention. ... It is a good and compact little work, and treats the whole topic in a clear, intelligible, and rational way. There is an interesting chapter styled 'Historical Retrospect,' which very briefly traces all the main steps in the growth of the English army from the time of the Anglo-Saxons. The writer is at great pains to examine the real facts concerning enlistment into the different branches of the army at the present day."—*Westminster Review.*

THE OPERATIONS OF THE GERMAN ENGINEERS AND TECHNICAL TROOPS IN THE FRANCO-GERMAN WAR OF 1870-71. By **Capt. A. von Goetze.** Translated by **Col. G. Graham.** Demy 8vo. With Six Plans.

THE OPERATIONS OF THE FIRST ARMY, UNDER GEN. VON STEINMETZ. By **Major von Schell.** Translated by **Captain E. O. Hollist.** With Three Maps. Demy 8vo. Price 10s. 6d.

"A very complete and important account of the investment of Metz."
"The volume is of somewhat too technical a character to be recommended to the general reader, but the military student will find it a valuable contribution to the history of the great struggle; and its utility is increased by a capital general map of the operations of the First Army, and also plans of Spicheren and of the battle-fields round Metz."—*John Bull.*

THE OPERATIONS OF THE FIRST ARMY UNDER GEN. VON GOEBEN. By **Major von Schell.** Translated by **Col. C. H. von Wright.** Four Maps. Demy 8vo. Price 9s.

"In concluding our notice of this instructive work, which, by the way, is enriched by several large-scale maps, we must not withhold our tribute of admiration at the manner in which the translator has performed his task. So thoroughly, indeed, has he succeeded, that it might really be imagined that the book had been originally composed in English. ... The work is decidedly valuable to a student of the art of war, and no military library can be considered complete without it."—*Hour.*

MILITARY WORKS—*continued.*

THE OPERATIONS OF THE FIRST ARMY UNDER GEN. VON MANTEUFFEL. By Col. Count Hermann von Wartensleben, Chief of the Staff of the First Army. Translated by Colonel C. H. von Wright. With Two Maps. Demy 8vo. Price 9s.

"Very clear, simple, yet eminently instructive, is this history. It is not overladen with useless details, is written in good taste, and possesses the inestimable value of being in great measure the record of operations actually witnessed by the author, supplemented by official documents."—*Athenæum.*

THE GERMAN ARTILLERY IN THE BATTLES NEAR METZ. Based on the official reports of the German Artillery. By **Captain Hoffbauer,** Instructor in the German Artillery and Engineer School. Translated by **Capt. E. O. Hollist.** Demy 8vo. With Map and Plans. Price 21s.

"Captain Hoffbauer's style is much more simple and agreeable than those of many of his comrades and fellow authors, and it suffers nothing in the hands of Captain Hollist, whose translation is close and faithful. He has given the general public a readable and instructive book; whilst to his brother officers, who have a special professional interest in the subject, its value cannot well be overrated."—*Academy.*

THE OPERATIONS OF THE BAVARIAN ARMY CORPS. By **Captain Hugo Helvig.** Translated by **Captain G. S. Schwabe.** With 5 large Maps. In 2 vols. Demy 8vo. Price 24s.

"It contains much material that may prove useful to the future historian of the war; and it is, on the whole, written in a spirit of fairness and impartiality... It only remains to say that the work is enriched by some excellent large scale maps, and that the translator has performed his work most creditably."—*Athenæum.*
"Captain Schwabe has done well to translate it, and his translation is admirably executed."—*Pall Mall Gazette.*

AUSTRIAN CAVALRY EXERCISE. From an Abridged Edition compiled by **Captain Illia Woinovits,** of the General Staff, on the Tactical Regulations of the Austrian Army, and prefaced by a General Sketch of the Organisation, &c., of the Cavalry. Translated by **Captain W. S. Cooke.** Crown 8vo, cloth. Price 7s.

"Among the valuable group of works on the military tactics of the chief States of Europe which Messrs. King are publishing, a small treatise on 'Austrian Cavalry Exercise' will hold a good and useful place."—*Westminster Review.*

History of the Organisation, Equipment, and War Services of

THE REGIMENT OF BENGAL ARTILLERY. Compiled from Published Official and other Records, and various private sources, by **Major Francis W. Stubbs,** Royal (late Bengal) Artillery. Vol. I. will contain WAR SERVICES. The Second Volume will be published separately, and will contain the HISTORY OF THE ORGANISATION AND EQUIPMENT OF THE REGIMENT. In 2 vols. 8vo. With Maps and Plans. [*Preparing.*

VICTORIES AND DEFEATS. An Attempt to explain the Causes which have led to them. An Officer's Manual. By **Col. R. P. Anderson.** 8vo. 14s.

"The young officer should have it always at hand to open anywhere and read a bit, and we warrant him that let that bit be ever so small it will give him material for an hour's thinking."—*United Service Gazette.*
"The present book proves that he is a diligent student of military history, his illustrations ranging over a wide field, and including ancient and modern Indian and European warfare."—*Standard.*

THE FRONTAL ATTACK OF INFANTRY. By **Capt. Laymann,** Instructor of Tactics at the Military College, Neisse. Translated by **Colonel Edward Newdigate.** Crown 8vo, limp cloth. Price 2s. 6d.

"An exceedingly useful kind of book. A valuable acquisition to the military student's library. It recounts, in the first place, the opinions and tactical formations which regulated the German army during the early battles of the late war; explains how these were modified in the course of the campaign by the terrible and unanticipated effect of the fire; and how, accordingly, troops should be trained to attack in future wars."—*Naval and Military Gazette.*

ELEMENTARY MILITARY GEOGRAPHY, RECONNOITRING, AND SKETCHING. Compiled for Non-Commissioned Officers and Soldiers of all Arms. By **Capt. C. E. H. Vincent.** Square cr. 8vo. 2s. 6d.

"This manual takes into view the necessity of every soldier knowing how to read a military map, in order to know to what points in an enemy's country to direct his attention; and provides for this necessity by giving, in terse and sensible language, definitions of varieties of ground and the advantages they present in warfare, together with a number of useful hints in military sketching."—*Naval and Military Gazette.*

65, Cornhill; & 12, Paternoster Row, London.

MILITARY WORKS—*continued*.

THREE WORKS BY LIEUT.-COL. THE HON. A. ANSON, V.C., M.P.

THE ABOLITION OF PURCHASE AND THE ARMY REGULATION BILL OF 1871. Crown 8vo. Price One Shilling.

ARMY RESERVES AND MILITIA REFORMS. Crown 8vo. Sewed. Price One Shilling.

THE STORY OF THE SUPERSESSIONS. Crown 8vo. Price Sixpence.

STUDIES IN THE NEW INFANTRY TACTICS. Parts I. & II.
By **Major W. von Scherff**. Translated from the German by **Colonel Lumley Graham**. Demy 8vo. Price 7s. 6d.

"The subject of the respective advantages of attack and defence, and of the methods in which each form of battle should be carried out under the fire of modern arms, is exhaustively and admirably treated; indeed, we cannot but consider it to be decidedly superior to any work which has hitherto appeared in English upon this all-important subject."—*Standard*.

Second Edition. Revised and Corrected.

TACTICAL DEDUCTIONS FROM THE WAR OF 1870—71.
By **Captain A. von Boguslawski**. Translated by **Colonel Lumley Graham**, late 18th (Royal Irish) Regiment. Demy 8vo. Uniform with the above. Price 7s.

"We must, without delay, impress brain and forethought into the British Service; and we cannot commence the good work too soon, or better, than by placing the two books ('The Operations of the German Armies' and 'Tactical Deductions') we have here criticised in every military library, and introducing them as class-books in every tactical school."—*United Service Gazette*.

THE ARMY OF THE NORTH-GERMAN CONFEDERATION.
A Brief Description of its Organization, of the different Branches of the Service, and their "Rôle" in War, of its Mode of Fighting, &c. By a **Prussian General**. Translated from the German by **Col. Edward Newdigate**. Demy 8vo. Price 5s.

"The work is quite essential to the full use of the other volumes of the 'German Military Series,' which Messrs. King are now producing in handsome uniform style."—*United Service Magazine*.
"Every page of the book deserves attentive study.... The information given on mobilisation, garrison troops, keeping up establishment during war, and on the employment of the different branches of the service, is of great value."—*Standard*.

THE OPERATIONS OF THE GERMAN ARMIES IN FRANCE,
FROM SEDAN TO THE END OF THE WAR OF 1870-71. With large Official Map. From the Journals of the Head-quarters Staff, by **Major William Blume**. Translated by **E. M. Jones**, Major 20th Foot, late Professor of Military History, Sandhurst. Demy 8vo. Price 9s.

"The book is of absolute necessity to the military student.... The work is one of high merit."—*United Service Gazette*.
"The work of Major von Blume in its English dress forms the most valuable addition to our stock of works upon the war that our press has put forth. Our space forbids our doing more than commending it earnestly as the most authentic and instructive narrative of the second section of the war that has yet appeared."—*Saturday Review*.

HASTY INTRENCHMENTS.
By **Colonel A. Brialmont**. Translated by **Lieut. Charles A. Empson, R.A.** With Nine Plates. Demy 8vo. Price 6s.

"A valuable contribution to military literature."—*Athenæum*.
"In seven short chapters it gives plain directions for forming shelter-trenches, with the best method of carrying the necessary tools, and it offers practical illustrations of the use of hasty intrenchments on the field of battle."—*United Service Magazine*.
"It supplies that which our own text-books give but imperfectly, viz., hints as to how a position can best be strengthened by means... of such extemporised intrenchments and batteries as can be thrown up by infantry in the space of four or five hours... deserves to become a standard military work."—*Standard*.

STUDIES IN LEADING TROOPS. Parts I. and II.
By **Colonel von Verdy du Vernois**. An authorised and accurate Translation by **Lieutenant H. J. T. Hildyard**, 71st Foot. Demy 8vo. Price 7s.

*** General BEAUCHAMP WALKER says of this work:—"I recommend the first two numbers of Colonel von Verdy's 'Studies' to the attentive perusal of my brother officers. They supply a want which I have often felt during my service in this country, namely, a minuter tactical detail of the minor operations of war than any but the most observant and fortunately-placed staff-officer is in a position to give. I have read and re-read them very carefully, I hope with profit, certainly with great interest, and believe that practice, in the sense of these 'Studies,' would be a valuable preparation for manœuvres on a more extended scale."—Berlin, June, 1872.

65, *Cornhill*; & 12, *Paternoster Row, London*.

Works Published by Henry S. King & Co.,

MILITARY WORKS—*continued.*

THE OPERATIONS OF THE SOUTH ARMY IN JANUARY AND FEBRUARY, 1871. Compiled from the Official War Documents of the Head-quarters of the Southern Army. By **Count Hermann von Wartensleben,** Colonel in the Prussian General Staff. Translated by **Colonel C. H. von Wright.** Demy 8vo, with Maps. Uniform with the above. Price 6s.

DISCIPLINE AND DRILL. Four Lectures delivered to the London Scottish Rifle Volunteers. By **Capt. S. Flood Page.** Cheaper Edition. Cr. 8vo. 1s.

"The very useful and interesting work."—*Volunteer Service Gazette.*
"An admirable collection of lectures."—*Times.*

CAVALRY FIELD DUTY. By **Major-General von Mirus.** Translated by **Captain Frank S. Russell,** 14th (King's) Hussars. Cr. 8vo, cloth limp. 7s. 6d.

"We have no book on cavalry duties that at all approaches to this, either for completeness in details, clearness in description, or for manifest utility. In its pages will be found plain instructions for every portion of duty before the enemy that a combatant horseman will be called upon to perform, and if a dragoon but studies it well and intelligently, his value to the army, we are confident, must be increased one hundredfold. Skirmishing, scouting, patrolling, and vedetting are now the chief duties dragoons in peace should be practised at, and how to perform these duties effectively is what the book teaches."—*United Service Magazine.*

INDIA AND THE EAST.

Third Edition.

TAMIL PROVERBS, WITH THEIR ENGLISH TRANSLATION. Containing upwards of Six Thousand Proverbs. By the **Rev. P. Percival,** Chaplain Madras Military Female Orphan Asylum, Author of "The Land of the Veda," &c. 8vo., sewed, 9s.

THE THREATENED FAMINE IN BENGAL; How IT MAY BE MET, AND THE RECURRENCE OF FAMINES IN INDIA PREVENTED. Being No. 1 of "Occasional Notes on Indian Affairs." By **Sir H. Bartle E. Frere, G.C.B., G.C.S.I., &c. &c.** Crown 8vo. With 3 Maps. Price 5s.

THE ORIENTAL SPORTING MAGAZINE. A Reprint of the first 5 Volumes, in 2 Volumes, demy 8vo. Price 28s.

"Lovers of sport will find ample amusement in the varied contents of these two volumes."—*Allen's Indian Mail.*
"Full of interest for the sportsman and naturalist. Full of thrilling adventures of sportsmen who have attacked the fiercest and most gigantic specimens of the animal world in their native jungle. It is seldom we get so many exciting incidents in a similar amount of space... Well suited to the libraries of country gentlemen and all those who are interested in sporting matters."—*Civil Service Gazette.*

Second Edition, Revised and Corrected.

THE EUROPEAN IN INDIA. A Hand-book of Practical Information for those proceeding to, or residing in, the East Indies, relating to Outfits, Routes, Time for Departure, Indian Climate, &c. By **Edmund C. P. Hull.** With a MEDICAL GUIDE FOR ANGLO-INDIANS. Being a Compendium of Advice to Europeans in India, relating to the Preservation and Regulation of their Health. To which is added a Supplement on the Management of Children in India. By **R. S. Mair, M.D., F.R.C.S.E.,** late Deputy Coroner of Madras. In 1 vol. Post 8vo. Price 6s.

"Full of all sorts of useful information to the English settler or traveller in India."—*Standard.*
"One of the most valuable books ever published in India—valuable for its sound information, its careful array of pertinent facts, and its sterling common sense. It supplies a want which few persons may have discovered, but which everybody will at once recognise, when once the contents of the book have been mastered. The medical part of the work is invaluable."—*Calcutta Guardian.*

65, Cornhill; & 12, Paternoster Row, London.

INDIA AND THE EAST—*continued.*

MEDICAL GUIDE FOR ANGLO-INDIANS. Being a Compendium of Advice to Europeans in India, relating to the Preservation and Regulation of their Health. With a Supplement on the Management of Children in India. By **R. S. Mair, M.D., F.R.C.S.E.**, late Deputy Coroner of Madras. Post 8vo, limp cloth. Price 3s. 6d.

"It is impossible to speak too highly of the 'Medical Guide,' and the supplementary matter now added to it makes a complete book of family medicine for India."—*Athenæum.*

"The parts devoted to individual hygiene, and to the management (physical and moral) of young children, are judiciously executed."—*Lancet.*

TAS-HĪL UL KALĀM; OR, HINDUSTANI MADE EASY. By **Captain W. R. M. Holroyd,** Bengal Staff Corps, Director of Public Instruction, Punjab. Crown 8vo. Price 5s.

"As clear and as instructive as possible."—*Standard.*
"Contains a great deal of most necessary information, that is not to be found in any other work on the subject that has crossed our path."—*Homeward Mail.*

EASTERN EXPERIENCES. By **L. Bowring, C.S.I.**, Lord Canning's Private Secretary, and for many years Chief Commissioner of Mysore and Coorg. Illustrated with Maps and Diagrams. Demy 8vo. Price 16s.

"An admirable and exhaustive geographical, political, and industrial survey."—*Athenæum.*
"Interesting even to the general reader, but especially so to those who may have a special concern in that portion of our Indian Empire."—*Post.*

"This compact and methodical summary of the most authentic information relating to countries whose welfare is intimately connected with our own."—*Daily News.*

EDUCATIONAL COURSE OF SECULAR SCHOOL BOOKS FOR INDIA. Edited by **J. S. Laurie,** of the Inner Temple, Barrister-at-Law; formerly H.M. Inspector of Schools, England; Assistant Royal Commissioner, Ireland; Special Commissioner, African Settlement; Director of Public Instruction, Ceylon.

"These valuable little works will prove of real service to many of our readers, especially to those who intend entering the Civil Service of India."—*Civil Service Gazette.*

The following Works are now ready:—

	s. d.		s. d.
THE FIRST HINDUSTANI READER, stiff linen wrapper	0 6	GEOGRAPHY OF INDIA, with Maps and Historical Appendix, tracing the growth of the British Empire in Hindustan. 128 pp. cloth	1 6
THE SECOND HINDUSTANI READER, stiff linen wrapper	0 6		

In the Press.

ELEMENTARY GEOGRAPHY OF INDIA.

FACTS AND FEATURES OF INDIAN HISTORY, in a series of alternating Reading Lessons and Memory Exercises.

Second Edition.

WESTERN INDIA BEFORE AND DURING THE MUTINIES. Pictures drawn from life. By **Major-Gen. Sir George Le Grand Jacob, K.C.S.I., C.B.** In 1 vol. Crown 8vo. Price 7s. 6d.

"The most important contribution to the history of Western India during the Mutinies which has yet, in a popular form, been made public."—*Athenæum.*

"Few men more competent than himself to speak authoritatively concerning Indian affairs."—*Standard.*

EXCHANGE TABLES OF STERLING AND INDIAN RUPEE CURRENCY, UPON A NEW AND EXTENDED SYSTEM, embracing Values from One Farthing to One Hundred Thousand Pounds, and at rates progressing, in Sixteenths of a Penny, from 1s. 9d. to 2s. 3d. per Rupee. By **Donald Fraser,** Accountant to the British Indian Steam Navigation Company, Limited. Royal 8vo. Price 10s. 6d.

"The calculations must have entailed great labour on the author, but the work is one which we fancy must become a standard one in all business houses which have dealings with any country where the rupee and the English pound are standard coins of currency."—*Inverness Courier.*

65, *Cornhill; & 12, Paternoster Row, London.*

BOOKS for the YOUNG and for LENDING LIBRARIES.

NEW WORKS BY HESBA STRETTON.

THE WONDERFUL LIFE. With a Map and Illuminated Frontispiece. Fcap. 8vo. 2s. 6d.

This slight and brief sketch is merely the story of the life and death of our Lord. It has been written for those who have not the leisure, or the books, needed for threading together the fragmentary and scattered incidents recorded in the four Gospels. Of late years these records have been searched diligently for the smallest links which might serve to complete the chain of those years of a life passed amongst us as Jesus of Nazareth, the Carpenter, the Prophet, and the Messiah. This little book is intended only to present the result of these close investigations made by many learned men, in a plain continuous narrative, suitable for unlearned readers.

"The style is clear, good, and reverent, and there is a tenderness of diction about the narrative of the events of Him who suffered such contradiction of sinners against Himself as makes the book very profitable reading."—*Literary Churchman.*

CASSY. Twentieth Thousand. With Six Illustrations. 1s. 6d.

THE KING'S SERVANTS. Twenty-eighth Thousand. With Eight Illustrations. 1s. 6d.
Part I.—Faithful in Little. Part II.—Unfaithful. Part III.—Faithful in Much.

LOST GIP. Thirty-sixth Thousand. With Six Illustrations. 1s. 6d.

*** ALSO A HANDSOMELY-BOUND EDITION, WITH TWELVE ILLUSTRATIONS, PRICE HALF-A-CROWN.

SUNBEAM WILLIE, AND OTHER STORIES, for Home Reading and Cottage Meetings. By **Mrs. G. S. Reaney**, author of "Waking and Working." Small square.

DADDY'S PET. By **Mrs. Ellen Ross (Nelsie Brook).** Third Thousand. Small square, cloth, uniform with "Lost Gip." With Six Illustrations. Price 1s.

"We have been more than pleased with this simple bit of writing."—*Christian World.*
"Full of deep feeling and true and noble sentiment."—*Brighton Gazette.*

LOCKED OUT; A Tale of the Strike. By **Ellen Barlee.** Small square. With a Frontispiece. 1s. 6d.

"A tale of the strike in the agricultural districts.... Beautifully written.... Should be bought by all means for parochial libraries, whether in country or in town."—*Literary Churchman.*

PRETTY LESSONS IN VERSE FOR GOOD CHILDREN, with some Lessons in Latin, in Easy Rhyme. By **Sara Coleridge.** A New Edition. Fcap. 8vo. With Six Illustrations. 3s. 6d.

"Both in English and Latin they will pleasantly help little folk through what has been called 'the bitterness of learning.'"—*Saturday Review.*
"A welcome addition to child literature."—*Spectator.*
"lessons in Latin show considerable humour, as well as mastery of rhyme. 'The Warnings of the Weather,' and 'Behaviour at Meals,' are extremely well done."—*Edinburgh Daily Review.*

AUNT MARY'S BRAN PIE. By the Author of "St. Olave's," "When I was a Little Girl," &c. Small crown 8vo. With Five Illustrations. 3s. 6d.

"Amongst its contents, besides various presents, Aunt Mary put in six stories, and here they all are strung together in the happiest way. The stories are exceedingly good, but the 'Blue Rosette' is the best. So, at least, we think the children will say."—*Nonconformist.*

Second Edition.
SEEKING HIS FORTUNE, AND OTHER STORIES. Crown 8vo. With Four Illustrations. Price 3s. 6d.

CONTENTS.—Seeking his Fortune.—Oluf and Stephanoff.—What's in a Name?—Contrast.—Onesta.

"These are plain, straightforward stories, told in the precise, detailed manner which we are sure young people like."—*Spectator.*
"They are romantic, entertaining, and decidedly inculcate a sound and generous moral...."
"We can answer for it that this volume will find favour with those for whom it is written, and that the sisters will like it quite as well as the brothers."—*Athenæum.*

65, Cornhill; & 12, Paternoster Row, London.

BOOKS FOR THE YOUNG AND FOR LENDING LIBRARIES—*continued*.

THREE WORKS BY MARTHA FARQUHARSON.

I. ELSIE DINSMORE. Cr. 8vo. Price 3s. 6d. | III. ELSIE'S HOLIDAYS AT ROSELANDS.
II. ELSIE'S GIRLHOOD. Cr. 8vo. Price 3s. 6d. | Crown 8vo. Price 3s. 6d.

Each Story is independent and complete in itself.
They are published in uniform size and price, and are elegantly bound and illustrated.

"We do not pretend to have read the history of Elsie as she is portrayed in three different volumes. By the help, however, of the illustrations, and by dips here and there, we can safely give a favourable account."—*Westminster Review*.

"Elsie Dinsmore is a familiar name to a world of young readers. In the above three pretty volumes her story is complete, and it is one full of youthful experiences, winning a general interest."—*Athenæum*.

THE LITTLE WONDER-HORN. By Jean Ingelow. A Second
Series of "*Stories told to a Child*." With Fifteen Illustrations. Cloth, gilt. Price 3s. 6d.

"We like all the contents of the 'Little Wonder-Horn' very much."—*Athenæum*.
"We recommend it with confidence."—*Pall Mall Gazette*.

"Full of fresh and vigorous fancy: it is worthy of the author of some of the best of our modern verse."—*Standard*.

Second Edition.
THE AFRICAN CRUISER. A Midshipman's Adventures on the West
Coast of Africa. A Book for Boys. By S. Whitchurch Sadler, R.N., Author of "Marshall Vavasour." With Three Illustrations. Crown 8vo. Price 3s. 6d.

"A capital story of youthful adventure.... Sea-loving boys will find few pleasanter gift books this season than 'The African Cruiser.'"—*Hour*.

"Sea yarns have always been in favour with boys, but this, written in a brisk style by a thorough sailor, is crammed full of adventures."—*Times*.

Third Edition.
BRAVE MEN'S FOOTSTEPS. A Book of Example and Anecdote for
Young People. By the Editor of "Men who have Risen." With Four Illustrations, by C. Doyle. Crown 8vo. Price 3s. 6d.

"A readable and instructive volume."—*Examiner*.
"The little volume is precisely of the stamp to win the favour of those who, in choosing a gift for a boy, would consult his moral development as well as his temporary pleasure."—*Daily Telegraph*.

Second Edition.
PLUCKY FELLOWS. A Book for Boys. By Stephen J. Mac Kenna.
With Six Illustrations. Crown 8vo. Price 3s. 6d.

"This is one of the very best 'Books for Boys' which have been issued this year."—*Morning Advertiser*.

"A thorough book for boys... written throughout in a manly, straightforward manner that is sure to win the hearts of the children."—*London Society*.

Second Edition.
GUTTA-PERCHA WILLIE, THE WORKING GENIUS. By
George MacDonald. With 9 Illustrations by Arthur Hughes. Cr. 8vo. 3s. 6d.

"The cleverest child we know assures us she has read this story through five times. Mr. MacDonald will, we are convinced, accept that verdict upon his little work as final."—*Spectator*.

THE TRAVELLING MENAGERIE. By Charles Camden, Author
of "Hoity Toity." With Ten Illustrations by J. Mahoney. Crown 8vo. 3s. 6d.

"A capital little book.... deserves a wide circulation among our boys and girls."—*Hour*.
"A very attractive story."—*Public Opinion*.

THE DESERT PASTOR, JEAN JAROUSSEAU. Translated from
the French of Eugene Pelletan. By Colonel E. P. De L'Hoste. In fcap. 8vo, with an Engraved Frontispiece. New Edition. Price 3s. 6d.

"A touching record of the struggles in the cause of religious liberty of a real man."—*Graphic*.
"There is a poetical simplicity and picturesqueness; the noblest heroism; unpretentious religion;

pure love, and the spectacle of a household brought up in the fear of the Lord...."—*Illustrated London News*.

THE DESERTED SHIP. A Real Story of the Atlantic. By Cupples
Howe, Master Mariner. Illustrated by Townley Green. Cr. 8vo. Price 3s. 6d.

"Curious adventures with bears, seals, and other Arctic animals, and with scarcely more human Esquimaux, form the mass of material with which the story deals, and will much interest boys who have a spice of romance in their composition."—*Courant*.

65, *Cornhill;* & 12, *Paternoster Row, London.*

BOOKS FOR THE YOUNG AND FOR LENDING LIBRARIES—*continued.*

HOITY TOITY, THE GOOD LITTLE FELLOW. By **Charles Camden.** With Eleven Illustrations. Crown 8vo. Price 3s. 6d.

"Relates very pleasantly the history of a charming little fellow who meddles always with a kindly disposition with other people's affairs and helps them to do right. There are many shrewd lessons to be picked up in this clever little story."—*Public Opinion.*

THE BOY SLAVE IN BOKHARA. A Tale of Central Asia. By **David Ker.** Crown 8vo, with Four Illustrations. Price 5s.

"Ostap Danilevitch Kostarenko, the Russian who is supposed to relate the story, has a great number of adventures, and passes by dint of courage and ability from a state of slavery to one of independence. Will prove attractive to boys."—*Pall Mall Gazette.*

SEVEN AUTUMN LEAVES FROM FAIRY-LAND. Illustrated with Nine Etchings. Square crown 8vo. 5s.

SLAVONIC FAIRY TALES. From Russian, Servian, Polish, and Bohemian Sources. Translated by **John T. Naaké,** of the British Museum. Crown 8vo. With Four Illustrations. Price 5s.

"A most choice and charming selection.... The tales have an original national ring in them, and will be pleasant reading to thousands besides children. Yet children will eagerly open the pages, and not willingly close them, of the pretty volume."—*Standard.*
"English readers now have an opportunity of becoming acquainted with eleven Polish and eight Bohemian stories, as well as with eight Russian and thirteen Servian, in Mr. Naaké's modest but serviceable collection of *Slavonic Fairy Tales.* Its contents are, as a general rule, well chosen and they are translated with a fidelity which deserves cordial praise... Before taking leave of his prettily got up volume, we ought to mention that its contents fully come up to the promise held out in its preface."—*Academy.*

WAKING AND WORKING; OR, FROM GIRLHOOD TO WOMANHOOD. By **Mrs. G. S. Reaney.** Cr. 8vo. With a Frontispiece. 5s.
"A good tale—good in composition, good in style, good in purpose."—*Nonconformist.*

AT SCHOOL WITH AN OLD DRAGOON. By **Stephen J. Mac Kenna.** Crown 8vo. With Six Illustrations. Price 5s.

"Consisting almost entirely of startling stories of military adventure... Boys will find them sufficiently exciting reading."—*Times.*
"These yarns give some very spirited and interesting descriptions of soldiering in various parts of the world."—*Spectator.*
"Mr. Mac Kenna's former work, 'Plucky Fellows,' is already a general favourite, and those who read the stories of the Old Dragoon will find that he has still plenty of materials at hand for pleasant tales, and has lost none of his power in telling them well."—*Standard.*

FANTASTIC STORIES. Translated from the German of **Richard Leander,** by **Paulina B. Granville.** Crown 8vo. With Eight full-page Illustrations, by **M. E. Fraser-Tytler.** Price 5s.

"Short, quaint, and, as they are fitly called, fantastic, they deal with all manner of subjects."—*Guardian.*
"'Fantastic' is certainly the right epithet to apply to some of these strange tales."—*Examiner.*

Third Edition.

STORIES IN PRECIOUS STONES. By **Helen Zimmern.** With Six Illustrations. Crown 8vo. Price 5s.

"A series of pretty tales which are half fantastic, half natural, and pleasantly quaint, as befits stories intended for the young."—*Daily Telegraph.*
"A pretty little book which fanciful young persons will appreciate, and which will remind its readers of many a legend, and many an imaginary virtue attached to the gems they are so fond of wearing."—*Post.*

Fourth Edition.

THE GREAT DUTCH ADMIRALS. By **Jacob de Liefde.** Crown 8vo. With Eleven Illustrations by **Townley Green** and others. Price 5s.

"May be recommended as a wholesome present for boys. They will find in it numerous tales of adventure."—*Athenæum.*
"A really good book."—*Standard.*
"A really excellent book."—*Spectator.*

THE TASMANIAN LILY. By **James Bonwick.** Crown 8vo. With Frontispiece. Price 5s.

"An interesting and useful work."—*Hour.*
"The characters of the story are capitally conceived, and are full of those touches which give them a natural appearance."—*Public Opinion.*

65, *Cornhill; & 12, Paternoster Row, London.*

Works Published by Henry S. King & Co., 21

BOOKS FOR THE YOUNG AND FOR LENDING LIBRARIES—*continued.*

MIKE HOWE, THE BUSHRANGER OF VAN DIEMEN'S LAND. By **James Bonwick**. Crown 8vo. With a Frontispiece. Price 5s.

"He illustrates the career of the bushranger half a century ago; and this he does in a highly creditable manner; his delineations of life in the bush are, to say the least, exquisite, and his representations of character are very marked."—*Edinburgh Courant.*

PHANTASMION. A Fairy Romance. By **Sara Coleridge**. With an Introductory Preface by the **Right Hon. Lord Coleridge of Ottery S. Mary.** A new Edition. In 1 vol. Crown 8vo. Price 7s. 6d.

"The readers of this fairy tale will find themselves dwelling for a time in a veritable region of romance, breathing an atmosphere of unreality, and surrounded by supernatural beings."—*Post.*
"This delightful work... We would gladly have read it were it twice the length, closing the book with a feeling of regret that the repast was at an end."—*Vanity Fair.*
"A beautiful conception of a rarely-gifted mind."—*Examiner.*

LAYS OF A KNIGHT-ERRANT IN MANY LANDS. By **Major-General Sir Vincent Eyre, C.B., K.C.S.I.,** &c. Square crown 8vo. With Six Illustrations. Price 7s. 6d.

Pharaoh Land. | Home Land. | Wonder Land. | Rhine Land.

"A collection of pleasant and well-written stanzas... abounding in real fun and humour."—*Literary World.*
"The conceits here and there are really very amusing."—*Standard.*

BEATRICE AYLMER AND OTHER TALES. By **Mary M. Howard**, Author of "Brampton Rectory." 1 vol. Crown 8vo. Price 6s.

"These tales possess considerable merit."—*Court Journal.*
"A neat and chatty little volume."—*Hour.*
"Considerable skill in portraying character, female character especially, and graphic power describing situations, places, and scenery."—*Daily Review.*

POETRY.

FOUR ELEGANT POETICAL GIFT BOOKS:

LYRICS OF LOVE, From Shakspeare to Tennyson. Selected and arranged by **W. Davenport Adams, Junr.** Fcap. 8vo, cloth extra, gilt edges, 3s. 6d.

"A most excellent collection.... Shows taste and care."—*Westminster Gazette.*
"A charming and scholarly pocket volume of poetry... The editor annotates his pieces just sufficiently for information.... The collection, as a whole, is very choice."—*British Quarterly Review.*
"The anthology is a very full and good one, and represents the robust school of Carew and Suckling better than any other that we know."—*Academy.*

WILLIAM CULLEN BRYANT'S POEMS. Cheap Edition, with Frontispiece. Price 3s. 6d.

"We are glad to possess so neat and elegant an edition of the works of the most thoughtful, graceful, and Wordsworthian of American poets."—*British Quarterly Review.*
"Some of the purest and tenderest poetry of this generation... Undoubtedly the best edition of the poet now in existence."—*Glasgow News.*

ENGLISH SONNETS. Collected and Arranged by **John Dennis.** Fcap. 8vo. Elegantly bound. Price 3s. 6d.

"Mr. Dennis has shown great judgment in this selection."—*Saturday Review.*
"An exquisite selection, a selection which every lover of poetry will consult again and again with delight. The notes are very useful... The volume is one for which English literature owes Mr. Dennis the heartiest thanks."—*Spectator.*

Second Edition.

HOME-SONGS FOR QUIET HOURS. Edited by the **Rev. Canon R. H. Baynes**, Editor of "Lyra Anglicana," &c. Fcap 8vo. Cloth extra, 3s. 6d.

"A tasteful collection of devotional poetry of a very high standard of excellence. The pieces are short, mostly original, and instinct, for the most part, with the most ardent spirit of devotion."—*Standard.*
"A most acceptable volume of sacred poetry; a good addition to the gift books of the season."—*Rock.*
"These are poems in which every word has a meaning, and from which it would be unjust to remove a stanza... Some of the best pieces in the book are anonymous."—*Pall Mall Gazette.*

*** *The above four books may also be had handsomely bound in Morocco with gilt edges.*

65, Cornhill; & 12, Paternoster Row, London.

WORKS BY ALFRED TENNYSON.

THE CABINET EDITION.

Messrs. HENRY S. KING & Co. have the pleasure to announce that they are issuing an Edition of the Laureate's works, in *Ten Monthly Volumes*, foolscap 8vo, at *Half-a-Crown each*, entitled "The Cabinet Edition," which will contain the whole of Mr. Tennyson's works. The first volume is illustrated by a beautiful Photographic Portrait; and the other volumes are each to contain a Frontispiece. They are tastefully bound in Crimson Cloth, and are to be issued in the following order:—

Vol.
1. EARLY POEMS.
2. ENGLISH IDYLLS & OTHER POEMS.
3. LOCKSLEY HALL & OTHER POEMS.
4. LUCRETIUS & OTHER POEMS.
5. IDYLLS OF THE KING.

Vol.
6. IDYLLS OF THE KING.
7. IDYLLS OF THE KING.
8. THE PRINCESS.
9. MAUD AND ENOCH ARDEN.
10. IN MEMORIAM.

Volumes I. to X. are now ready.

Subscribers' names received by all Booksellers.

Reduction in prices of Mr. Tennyson's Works:—

	PRICE.
	s. d.
POEMS. Small 8vo.	6 0
MAUD AND OTHER POEMS. Small 8vo.	3 6
THE PRINCESS. Small 8vo.	3 6
IDYLLS OF THE KING. Small 8vo.	5 0
" " Collected. Small 8vo.	7 0
THE HOLY GRAIL, AND OTHER POEMS. Small 8vo.	4 6
GARETH AND LYNETTE. Small 8vo.	3 0
ENOCH ARDEN, &c. Small 8vo.	3 6
IN MEMORIAM. Small 8vo.	4 0
SELECTIONS FROM THE ABOVE WORKS. Square 8vo, cloth	3 6
" " " " cloth, gilt edges	4 0
SONGS FROM THE ABOVE WORKS. Square 8vo, cloth	3 6
LIBRARY EDITION OF MR. TENNYSON'S WORKS. 6 vols. Post 8vo, each	10 6
POCKET VOLUME EDITION OF MR. TENNYSON'S WORKS. 11 vols., in neat case	31 6
" extra cloth, gilt, in case	35 0
POEMS. Illustrated Edition, 4to	25 0

⁎⁎ *All the above are kept in leather bindings.*

65, *Cornhill; &* 12, *Paternoster Row, London.*

POETRY—*continued*.

WILLIAM CULLEN BRYANT'S POEMS. Collected and Arranged by the Author. Red-line Edition. Handsomely bound. With Illustrations and Portrait. 7s. 6d.

"Of all the poets of the United States there is no one who obtained the same and position of a classic earlier, or has kept them longer, than William Cullen Bryant... A singularly simple and straightforward fashion of verse. Very rarely has any writer preserved such an even level of merit throughout his poems. Like some other American poets, Mr. Bryant is particularly happy in translation."—*Academy*.

THE DISCIPLES. A New Poem. By **Mrs. Hamilton King**. Second Edition, with some Notes. Crown 8vo. Price 7s. 6d.

"Even the most hostile critic could scarcely deny to 'Ugo Bassi' the praise of being a work worthy in every way to live... A poem of great beauty and pathos, full of lofty sentiment and strong religious fervour; evincing a deep appreciation of the beautiful, the tender, and the heroic. ... The book altogether is one that merits unqualified admiration and praise."—*Daily Telegraph*.

"Throughout it breathes restrained passion and lofty sentiment, which flow out now and then as a stream widening to bless the lands, into powerful music."—*British Quarterly Review*.

"A very remarkable poem. The writer does not seem so much to compose, as to breathe it forth; it is the fruit of intense personal feeling; it glows with the fires of an absolute conviction. It is a hymn of praise, a chaunt of sorrow, suffering, and glory.... We feel when we have read a few pages that we are in the presence of something strange to us, of something large and deep, of much more devotion, love, and faith, than we are accustomed to.... That Mrs. King's love for Mazzini has prompted her to write a poem apart from other poems—original, touching, and ennobling—will, we think, be evident to any one who will read the first few pages of her book."—*Saturday Review*.

ASPROMONTE, AND OTHER POEMS. By the same Author. Second Edition. Fcap. 8vo. 4s. 6d.

"The volume is anonymous, but there is no reason for the author to be ashamed of it. The 'Poems of Italy' are evidently inspired by genuine enthusiasm in the cause espoused; and one of them, 'The Execution of Felice Orsini,' has much poetic merit, the event celebrated being told with dramatic force."—*Athenæum*.

"The verse is fluent and free."—*Spectator*.

PRELUDES: a Volume of Poems. By **Alice C. Thompson**. Illustrated by **Elizabeth Thompson**. Demy 8vo.

ARVAN: or, the STORY of the SWORD. A Poem. By **Herbert Todd, M.A.**, late of Trinity College, Cambridge. Crown 8vo. 6s.

Second Edition.
THROUGH STORM AND SUNSHINE. By Adon, Author of "Lays of Modern Oxford." With Illustrations by H. Paterson, M. E. Edwards, A. T., and the Author. Cr. 8vo. Cloth elegant. 7s. 6d.

ROBERT BUCHANAN'S POETICAL WORKS. Collected Edition, in 3 Vols., price 18s. Vol. I. contains, — "Ballads and Romances;" "Ballads and Poems of Life," and a Portrait of the Author.
Vol. II.—" Ballads and Poems of Life;" "Allegories and Sonnets."
Vol. III.—"Coruisskeen Sonnets;" "Book of Orm;" "Political Mystics."

"Holding, as Mr. Buchanan does, such a conspicuous place amongst modern writers, the reading public will be duly thankful for this handsome edition of the poet's works."—*Civil Service Gazette*.

"Taking the poems before us as experiments, we hold that they are very full of promise... In the romantic ballad, Mr. Buchanan shows real power."—*Hour*.

SONGS FOR MUSIC. By **Four Friends**. Square crown 8vo. Price 5s.

CONTAINING SONGS BY
Reginald A. Gatty.   Stephen H. Gatty.
Greville J. Chester.   Juliana H. Ewing.

"A charming gift-book, which will be very popular with lovers of poetry."—*John Bull*.

"The charm of simplicity is manifest throughout, and the subjects are well chosen and successfully treated."—*Rock*.

THOUGHTS IN VERSE. Small crown 8vo. Price 1s. 6d.

This is a Collection of Verses expressive of religious feeling, written from a Theistic stand-point.

"All who are interested in devotional verse should read this tiny volume."—*Academy*.

NARCISSUS AND OTHER POEMS. By **E. Carpenter**. Fcap. 8vo. 5s.

"In many of these poems there is a force of fancy, a grandeur of imagination, and a power of poetical utterance not by any means common in these days."—*Standard*.

POETRY—continued.

ON THE NORTH WIND—THISTLE-DOWN. A volume of Poems. By the Hon. Mrs. Willoughby. Elegantly bound. Small crown 8vo. 7s. 6d.
"Moving is incident and touching in treatment. . . . Her ballads are not without spirit, and a description of a fight between a boy and a stag in 'Euphemia' shows genuine force."—*Athenæum.*
"Very bright, pleasant, and spontaneous verse, . . . altogether natural and unaffected."—*Times.*

PENELOPE AND OTHER POEMS. By Allison Hughes. Fcap. 8vo. 4s. 6d.
"Full of promise. They possess both form and colour, they are not wanting in suggestion, and they reveal something not far removed from imagination. . . . If the verse moves stiffly it is because the substance is rich and carefully wrought. That artistic regard for the value of words, which is characteristic of the best modern workmanship, is apparent in every composition, and the ornament, even when it might be pronounced excessive, is tasteful in arrangement."—*Athenæum.*

COSMOS. A Poem. 8vo. 3s. 6d.
SUBJECT.—Nature in the Past and in the Present.—Man in the Past and in the Present.—The Future.

POEMS. By the Rev. J. W. Augustus Taylor, M.A. Fcap. 8vo. 5s.
"There is a fine spirit of contemplation in these poems, and the imagination of the author, which is singularly chastened from worldly passions, and unsolicited by the love of display, appears to offer a graceful and helpful support to the philosophy which leans upon it with a confidence proper to antique times."—*Pall Mall Gazette.*

AURORA: A Volume of Verse. Fcap. 8vo. 5s.
"This theme (quotation), not remote from that taken up by the Laureate in 'In Memoriam,' is set in many different keys, and is illustrated with considerable power. Much of the imagery employed is equally bold and striking, and the music of some of the lines is admirably fitted to the sense."—*Athenæum.*

POEMS. By Annette F. C. Knight. Fcap. 8vo. Cloth. Price 5s.
". . . . Very fine also is the poem entitled 'Past and Present,' from which we take the song picturing the 'Spirits of the Present.' The verses here are so simple in form as almost to veil the real beauty and depth of the image; yet it would not be easy to find a more exquisite picture in poetry or on canvas of the spirit of the age."—*Scotsman.*
"These poems are musical to read, they give true and pleasant pictures of common things, and they tell sweetly of the deeper moral and religious harmonies which sustain us under the discords and the griefs of actual life."—*Spectator.*
"Full of tender and felicitous verse . . . expressed with a rare artistic perfection. . . . The gems of the book to our mind are the poems entitled 'In a Town Garden.'"—*Literary Churchman.*

METRICAL TRANSLATIONS FROM THE GREEK AND LATIN POETS, AND OTHER POEMS. By R. B. Boswell, M.A. Oxon. Crown 8vo. 5s.
"Most of these translations we can praise as of very high merit. . . . For sweetness and regularity, his verses are pre-eminent."—*Literary Churchman.*
"Mr. Boswell has a strong poetical vein in his nature, and gives us every promise of success as an original poet."—*Standard.*

A TALE OF THE SEA, SONNETS, AND OTHER POEMS. By James Howell. Fcap. 8vo. Cloth, 5s.
"Mr. Howell has a keen perception of the beauties of nature, and a just appreciation of the charities of life. . . . Mr. Howell's book deserves, and will probably receive, a warm reception."—*Pall Mall Gazette.*

EASTERN LEGENDS AND STORIES IN ENGLISH VERSE. By Lieutenant Norton Powlett, Royal Artillery. Crown 8vo. 5s.
"There is a rollicking sense of fun about the stories, joined to marvellous power of rhyming, and plenty of swing, which irresistibly reminds us of our old favourite (Ingoldsby)."—*Graphic.*

Second Edition.
VIGNETTES IN RHYME AND VERS DE SOCIÉTÉ. By Austin Dobson. Fcap. 8vo. 5s.
"Clever, clear-cut, and careful."—*Athenæum.*
"As a writer of Vers de Société, Mr. Dobson is almost, if not quite, unrivalled."—*Examiner.*
"Lively, innocent, elegant in expression, and graceful in fancy."—*Morning Post.*

SONGS FOR SAILORS. By Dr. W. C. Bennett. Dedicated by Special Request to H. R. H. the Duke of Edinburgh. Crown 8vo. 3s. 6d. With Steel Portrait and Illustrations.
An Edition in Illustrated paper Covers. Price 1s.

WALLED IN, AND OTHER POEMS. By the Rev. Henry J. Bulkeley. Fcp. 8vo. 5s.
"A remarkable book of genuine poetry."—*Evening Standard.*
"Genuine power displayed."—*Examiner.*
"Poetical feeling is manifest here, and the diction of the poem is unimpeachable."—*Pall Mall Gazette.*

SONGS OF LIFE AND DEATH. By John Payne, Author of "Intaglios," "Sonnets," etc. Crown 8vo. 5s.
"The art of ballad-writing has long been lost in England, and Mr. Payne may claim to be its restorer. It is a perfect delight to meet with such a ballad as 'May Margaret' in the present volume."—*Westminster Review.*

IMITATIONS FROM THE GERMAN OF SPITTA AND TERSTEGEN. By Lady Durand. Fcap. 8vo. 4s.
"A charming little volume. . . . Will be a very valuable assistance to peaceful, meditative souls."—*Church Herald.*

ON VIOL AND FLUTE. A New Volume of Poems, by Edmund W. Gosse. With Frontispiece by W. B. Scott. Cr. 8vo. 5s.
"A careful perusal of his verses will show that he is a poet. . . . His song has the grateful, murmuring sound which reminds one of the softness and deliciousness of summer time. . . . There is much that is good in the volume."—*Spectator.*

EDITH; OR, LOVE AND LIFE IN CHESHIRE. By T. Ashe, Author of "The Sorrows of Hypsipyle," etc. Sewed. Price 6d.
"A really fine poem, full of tender, subtle touches of feeling."—*Manchester News.*
"Pregnant from beginning to end with the results of careful observation and imaginative power."—*Chester Chronicle.*

65, Cornhill; & 12, Paternoster Row, London.

POETRY—*continued.*

THE INN OF STRANGE MEETINGS, AND OTHER POEMS. By Mortimer Collins. Crown 8vo. 5s.

"Abounding in quiet humour, in bright fancy, in sweetness and melody of expression, and, at times, in the tenderest touches of pathos."—*Graphic.*

"Mr. Collins has an undercurrent of chivalry and romance beneath the trifling vein of good-humoured banter which is the special characteristic of his verse."—*Athenæum.*

GOETHE'S FAUST. A New Translation in Rime. By C. Kegan Paul. Crown 8vo. 6s.

"His translation is the most minutely accurate that has yet been produced..."—*Examiner.*

"Mr. Paul is a zealous and a faithful interpreter."—*Saturday Review.*

AN OLD LEGEND OF S. PAUL'S. By the Rev. G. B. Howard. Fcp. 8vo. 3s. 6d.

"We admire, and deservedly admire, the genuine poetry of this charming old legend as here presented to us by the brilliant imagination and the chastened taste of the gifted writer."—*Standard.*

SONNETS, LYRICS, AND TRANSLATIONS. By the Rev. Charles Turner. Cr. 8vo. 4s. 6d.

"Mr. Turner is a genuine poet; his song is sweet and pure, beautiful in expression, and often subtle in thought."—*Pall Mall Gazette.*

"The light of a devout, gentle, and kindly spirit, a delicate and graceful fancy, a keen intelligence irradiates these thoughts."—*Contemporary Review.*

Second Edition.

SONGS OF TWO WORLDS. First Series. By a New Writer. Fcp. 8vo. 5s.

"These poems will assuredly take high rank among the class to which they belong."—*British Quarterly Review, April 1st.*

"No extracts could do justice to the exquisite tones, the felicitous phrasing and delicately wrought harmonies of some of these poems."—*Nonconformist.*

"A purity and delicacy of feeling like morning air."—*Graphic.*

EROS AGONISTES. By E. B. D. Fcap. 8vo. 3s. 6d.

"It is not the least merit of these pages that they are everywhere illumined with moral and religious sentiment suggested, not paraded, of the brightest, purest character."—*Standard.*

CALDERON'S DRAMAS. Translated from the Spanish. By Denis Florence MacCarthy. Post 8vo. Cloth, gilt edges. 10s.

"The lambent verse flows with an ease, spirit, and music perfectly natural, liberal, and harmonious."—*Spectator.*

"It is impossible to speak too highly of this beautiful work."—*Month.*

THE DREAM AND THE DEED, AND OTHER POEMS. By Patrick Scott, Author of "Footpaths between Two Worlds," etc. Fcap. 8vo. Cloth, 5s.

"A bitter and able satire on the vice and follies of the day, literary, social, and political."—*Standard.*

"Shows real poetic power coupled with evidences of satirical energy."—*Edinburgh Daily Review.*

Second Edition.

SONGS OF TWO WORLDS. Second Series. By a New Writer. Fcp. 8vo. 5s.

"The most noteworthy poem is the 'Ode on a Spring Morning,' which has somewhat of the charm of 'L'Allegro' and 'Il Penseroso.' It is the nearest approach to a masterpiece in the collection. We cannot find too much praise for its noble assertion of man's resurrection."—*Saturday Review.*

"A real advance on its predecessor, and contains at least one poem ('The Organ Boy') of great originality, as well as many of much beauty .... As exquisite a little poem as we have read for many a day . . . but not at all alone in its power to fascinate."—*Spectator.*

"Will be gratefully welcomed."—*Examiner.*

THE GALLERY OF PIGEONS, AND OTHER POEMS. By Theo. Marzials. Crown 8vo. 4s. 6d.

"A conceit abounding in prettiness."—*Examiner.*

"The rush of fresh, sparkling fancies is too rapid, too sustained, too abundant, not to be spontaneous."—*Academy.*

THE LEGENDS OF ST. PATRICK AND OTHER POEMS. By Aubrey de Vere. Crown 8vo. 5s.

"Mr. De Vere's versification in his earlier poems is characterised by great sweetness and simplicity. He is master of his instrument, and rarely offends the ear with false notes."—*Pall Mall Gazette.*

"We have but space to commend the varied structure of his verse, the carefulness of his grammar, and his excellent English."—*Saturday Review.*

ALEXANDER THE GREAT. A Dramatic Poem. By Aubrey de Vere, Author of "The Legends of St. Patrick." Crown 8vo. 5s.

"Undeniably well written."—*Examiner.*

"A noble play. . . . The work of a true poet, and of a fine artist, in whom there is nothing vulgar and nothing weak. . . . We had no conception, from our knowledge of Mr. De Vere's former poems, that so much poetic power lay in him as this drama shows. It is terse as well as full of beauty, nervous as well as rich in thought."—*Spectator.*

FICTION.

LISETTE'S VENTURE. By Mrs. Russell Gray. 2 vols.

HIS QUEEN. By Alice Fisher, Author of "Too Bright to Last." 3 vols. Cr. 8vo.

THE HIGH MILLS. By Katherine Saunders, Author of "Gideon's Rock," &c. 3 vols.

AILEEN FERRERS. By Susan Morley. In 2 vols. Crown 8vo, cloth.

"Her novel rises to a level far above that which cultivated women with a facile pen ordinarily attain when they set themselves to write a story. It is as a study of character, worked out in a manner that is free from almost all the usual faults of lady writers, that 'Aileen Ferrers' merits a place apart from its innumerable rivals."—*Saturday Review.*

FICTION—continued.

MALCOLM: A Scottish Story. By George MacDonald. 3 vols. Second Edition.
"Mr. MacDonald has not only put into his (Malcolm's) mouth much of the fine poetry of which the book is full, but has also given to his part active and passive heroism of the most romantic kind.... Of the other characters, Duncan, the aged and blind Highland piper, is admirably drawn. The intensity of his love and hate, of his pride and prejudice, is brought out with the utmost vividness in his relations with Malcolm and his master .... But these few and slight blemishes are lost in the host of beautiful images with which Mr. MacDonald delights his readers."—*Pall Mall Gazette.*
"Full of high teaching; the author's individuality is pervasive; he colours all that he touches with the fine light of his character, and most often generously transforms it."—*Nonconformist.*

THE NEGLECTED QUESTION. By B. Markewitch. Translated from the Russian, by the Princesses Ouroussoff. 2 vols. Crown 8vo. 14s.
"The rights and interests of the children of women 'who change one affection for another, ruthlessly treading every obstacle under foot'—that is to say, the deserted children of guilty wives—are advocated and urged by the Russian novelist in strong terms, and enforced by a striking and terrible example."—*Spectator.*

WOMAN'S A RIDDLE; OR, BABY WARMSTREY. By Philip Sheldon, 3 vols.
"In the delineation of idiosyncrasy, special and particular, and its effects on the lives of the personages of the story, the author may, without exaggeration, be said to be masterly. Whether in the long-drawn-out development of character, or in the description of peculiar qualities in a single-pointed sentence, he is equally skilful, while, where pathos is necessary, he has it at command, and subdued, sly humour is not wanting."—*Morning Post.*

IDOLATRY. A Romance. By Julian Hawthorne, Author of "Bressant." 2 vols.
"A more powerful book than 'Bressant'.... If the figures are mostly phantoms, they are phantoms which take a more powerful hold on the mind than many very real figures..... There are three scenes in this romance, any one of which would prove true genius."—*Spectator.*
"Made to fix the attention and interest of the reader in a very remarkable degree. ... His descriptions are very clever; his turn of thought original and often striking, as in the dialogue in the dark on the deck of a steamer; and he has a subtle perception of moral and mental phases of character."—*Times.*

BRESSANT, A Romance. By Julian Hawthorne. 2 vols. Crown 8vo.
"One of the most powerful with which we are acquainted."—*Times.*
"We shall once more have reason to rejoice whenever we hear that a new work is coming out written by one who bears the honoured name of Hawthorne."—*Saturday Review.*

VANESSA. By the Author of "Thomasina," "Dorothy," &c. 2 vols. Second Edition.
"But the book has other characters besides Amy Mertoun, plenty of subsidiary heroines, with heroes to match; and they all fit comfortably into a very pretty and interesting story."—*Times.*

THOMASINA. By the Author of "Dorothy," "De Cressy," &c. 2 vols. Crown 8vo.
"A finished and delicate cabinet picture; no line is without its purpose."—*Athenæum.*

ISRAEL MORT: OVERMAN. The Story of the Mine. By John Saunders, Author of "Hirell," &c. 3 vols. Crown 8vo.

LADY MORETOUN'S DAUGHTER. By Mrs. Eiloart. In 3 vols. Crown 8vo.
"Carefully written .... The narrative is well sustained."—*Athenæum.*
"An interesting story .... Above the run of average novels."—*Vanity Fair.*
"Will prove more popular than any of the author's former works .... Interesting and readable."—*Hour.*
"The story is well put together, and readable."—*Examiner.*

WAITING FOR TIDINGS. By the Author of "White and Black." 3 vols.
"An interesting novel."—*Vanity Fair.*
"A very lively tale, abounding with amusing incidents."—*John Bull.*

TWO GIRLS. By Frederick Wedmore, Author of "A Snapt Gold Ring." 2 vols.
"A carefully-written novel of character, contrasting the two heroines of one love tale, an English lady and a French actress. Cicely is charming; the introductory description of her is a good specimen of the well-balanced sketches in which the author shines."—*Athenæum.*

CIVIL SERVICE. By J. T. Listado. Author of "Maurice Rhynhart." 2 vols.
"A very charming and amusing story ... The characters are all well drawn and life-like .... It is with no ordinary skill that Mr. Listado has drawn the character of Hugh Haughton, full as he is of scheming and subtleties ... The plot is worked out with great skill and is of no ordinary kind."—*Civil Service Gazette.*
"A story of Irish life, free from burlesque and partisanship, yet amusingly national ... There is plenty of 'go' in the story."—*Athenæum.*

MR. CARINGTON. A Tale of Love and Conspiracy. By Robert Turner Cotton. In 3 vols. Cloth, crown 8vo.
"A novel is so many ways good, as in a fresh and elastic diction, stout unconventionality, and happy boldness of conception and execution. His novels, though free spoken, will be some of the healthiest of our day."—*Examiner.*

TOO LATE. By Mrs. Newman. 2 vols.
"The plot is skilfully constructed, the characters are well conceived, and the narrative moves to its conclusion without any waste of words . . . The tone is healthy, in spite of its incidents, which will please the lovers of sensational fiction. . . . The reader who opens the book will read it all through."—*Pall Mall Gazette.*

REGINALD BRAMBLE. A Cynic of the 19th Century. An Autobiography. 1 vol.
"There is plenty of vivacity in Mr. Bramble's narrative."—*Athenæum.*
"Written in a lively and readable style."—*Hour.*

CRUEL AS THE GRAVE. By the Countess Von Bothmer. 3 vols.
"Jealousy is cruel as the Grave."
"Interesting, though somewhat tragic."—*Athenæum.*
"Agreeable, unaffected, and eminently readable."—*Daily News.*

65, Cornhill; & 12, Paternoster Row, London.

Works Published by Henry S. King & Co., 27

FICTION—continued.

SEPTIMIUS. A Romance. By Nathanial Hawthorne. Second Edition. 1 vol. Crown 8vo, cloth, extra gilt. 9s.
"The *Athenæum* says that 'the book is full of Hawthorne's most characteristic writing.'"

EFFIE'S GAME; How she Lost and how she Won. By Cecil Clayton. 2 vols. Crown 8vo.
"Well written. The characters move, and act, and, above all, talk like human beings, and we have liked reading about them."—*Spectator.*

JUDITH GWYNNE. By Lisle Carr. In 3 vols. Cr. 8vo, cloth. Second Edition.
"Mr. Carr's novel is certainly amusing .... There is much variety, and the dialogue and incident never flag to the finish."—*Athenæum.*
"Displays much dramatic skill."—*Edinburgh Courant.*

CHESTERLEIGH. By Ansley Conyers. 3 vols. Crown 8vo.
"We have gained much enjoyment from the book."—*Spectator.*

HONOR BLAKE: The Story of a Plain Woman. By Mrs. Keatinge. 2 vols.
"One of the best novels we have met with for some time."—*Morning Post.*
"A story which must do good to all, young and old, who read it."—*Daily News.*

HEATHERGATE. A Story of Scottish Life and Character. By a new Author. 2 vols.
"Its merit lies in the marked antithesis of strongly developed characters, in different ranks of life, and resembling each other in nothing but their marked nationality."—*Athenæum.*

THE QUEEN'S SHILLING. By Captain Arthur Griffiths. 2 vols.
"Every scene, character, and incident of the book are so life-like that they seem drawn from life direct."—*Pall Mall Gazette.*

MIRANDA. A Midsummer Madness. By Mortimer Collins. 3 vols.
"Not a dull page in the whole three volumes."—*Standard.*
"The work of a man who is at once a thinker and a poet."—*Hour.*

SQUIRE SILCHESTER'S WHIM. By Mortimer Collins. 3 vols.
"We think it the best (story) Mr. Collins has yet written. Full of incident and adventure."—*Pall Mall Gazette.*
"So clever, so irritating, and so charming a story."—*Standard.*

THE PRINCESS CLARICE. A Story of 1871. By Mortimer Collins. 2 vols.
"Mr. Collins has produced a readable book, amusingly characteristic."—*Athenæum.*
"A bright, fresh, and original book."—*Standard.*

JOHANNES OLAF. By E. de Wille. Translated by F. E. Bunnètt. 3 vols.
"The art of description is fully exhibited; perception of character and capacity for delineating it are obvious; while there is great breadth and comprehensiveness in the plan of the story."—*Morning Post.*

A GOOD MATCH. By Amelia Perrier, Author of "Mea Culpa." 2 vols.
"Racy and lively."—*Athenæum.*
"This clever and amusing novel."—*Pall Mall Gazette.*

THE STORY OF SIR EDWARD'S WIFE. By Hamilton Marshall, Author of "For Very Life." 1 vol. Cr. 8vo.
"A quiet, graceful little story."—*Spectator.*
"Mr. Hamilton Marshall can tell a story closely and pleasantly."—*Pall Mall Gazette.*

HERMANN AGHA. An Eastern Narrative. By W. Gifford Palgrave. 2 vols. Crown 8vo, cloth, extra gilt. 18s.
"There is a positive fragrance as of newly-mown hay about it, as compared with the artificially perfumed passions which are detailed to us with such gusto by our ordinary novel-writers in their endless volumes."—*Observer.*

LINKED AT LAST. By F. E. Bunnètt. 1 vol. Crown 8vo.
"The reader who once takes it up will not be inclined to relinquish it without concluding the volume."—*Morning Post.*
"A very charming story."—*John Bull.*

OFF THE SKELLIGS. By Jean Ingelow. (Her First Romance.) In 4 vols.
"Clever and sparkling."—*Standard.*
"We read each succeeding volume with increasing interest, going almost to the point of wishing there was a fifth."—*Athenæum.*

SEETA. By Colonel Meadows Taylor, Author of "Tara," etc. 3 vols.
"Well told, native life is admirably described, and the petty intrigues of native rulers, and their hatred of the English, mingled with fear lest the latter should eventually prove the victors, are cleverly depicted."—*Athenæum.*
"Thoroughly interesting and enjoyable reading."—*Examiner.*

WHAT 'TIS TO LOVE. By the Author of "Flora Adair," "The Value of Fosterstown." 3 vols.
"Worthy of praise: it is well written; the story is simple, the interest is well sustained; the characters are well depicted."—*Edinb. Courant.*

MEMOIRS OF MRS. LETITIA BOOTHBY. By William Clark Russell. Crown 8vo. 7s. 6d.
"Clever and ingenious."—*Saturday Review.*
"Very clever book."—*Guardian.*

HESTER MORLEY'S PROMISE. By Hesba Stretton. 3 vols.
"Much better than the average novels of the day; has much more claim to critical consideration as a piece of literary work,—very clever."—*Spectator.*
"All the characters stand out clearly and are well sustained, and the interest of the story never flags."—*Observer.*

THE DOCTOR'S DILEMMA. By Hesba Stretton. 3 vols. Crown 8vo.
"A fascinating story which scarcely flags in interest from the first page to the last."—*British Quarterly Review.*

THE SPINSTERS OF BLATCHINGTON. By Mar. Travers. 2 vols.
"A pretty story. Deserving of a favourable reception."—*Graphic.* [*Examiner.*
"A book of more than average merits."—

PERPLEXITY. By Sydney Mostyn. 3 vols. Crown 8vo.
"Written with very considerable power, great cleverness, and sustained interest."—*Standard.*
"The literary workmanship is good, and the story forcibly and graphically told."—*Daily News.*

65, Cornhill; & 12, Paternoster Row, London.

THE CORNHILL LIBRARY OF FICTION.
3s. 6d. per Volume.

It is intended in this Series to produce books of such merit that readers will care to preserve them on their shelves. They are well printed on good paper, handsomely bound, with a Frontispiece, and are sold at the moderate price of 3s. 6d. each.

HALF-A-DOZEN DAUGHTERS. By J. Masterman.

THE HOUSE OF RABY. By Mrs. G. Hooper.

"A work of singular truthfulness, ingenuity and power."—*Morning Post.*
"Exceedingly well written."—*Examiner.*
"A well told and interesting story."—*Academy.*

A FIGHT FOR LIFE. By May Thomas.

"An unpretentious history."—*Daily News.*
"All the ups and the downs enough the sea."—*Scotsman.*
"... there cannot be two opinions."—*Athenæum.*

ROBIN GRAY. By Charles Gibbon.

"..."—*Athenæum.*
"A pretty tale, prettily told."—*Athenæum.*
"An interesting, characteristic, and entertaining novel."—*John Bull.*

KITTY. By Miss M. Betham-Edwards.

"..."—*Globe.*
"Very pleasant and amusing."—*Globe.*
"A charming novel."—*John Bull.*

HIRELL. By John Saunders.

"A powerful novel. A tale written by a poet."
"An extraordinary merit."—*Post.*
"We have nothing but words of praise to offer for its style and composition."—*Examiner.*

ONE OF TWO; or, The left-handed Bride. By J. H. Friswell.

"..."
"Admirably narrated, and intensely interesting."—*Public Opinion.*

READY-MONEY MORTIBOY. A Matter-of-Fact Story.

"There is not a dull page in the whole story."—*Vanity Fair.*
"..."
"One of the most remarkable novels which has appeared of late."—*Pall Mall Gazette.*

GOD'S PROVIDENCE HOUSE. By Mrs. G. L. Banks.

"..."
"Possesses the merit of ease, industry, and local knowledge."—*Athenæum.*
"Remarkably readable. The style is very simple and natural."—*Morning Post.*

FOR LACK OF GOLD. By Charles Gibbon.

"A remarkably written nervous story."—*Examiner.*
"..."
"A tour of very genuine workmanship."—*Daily Literary Extra.*

ABEL DRAKE'S WIFE. By John Saunders.

"A striking book, deep, interesting, and loyal, and so touching in its simple pathos."—*Standard.*
"..."

OTHER STANDARD NOVELS TO FOLLOW.

65, Cornhill; & 12, Paternoster Row, London.

THEOLOGICAL.

RUGBY SCHOOL SERMONS. By the **Rev. Henry Hayman, D.D.**, late Head Master of Rugby School. Crown 8vo.

THE LIFE, TIMES, AND TRAVELS OF ABRAHAM. By a Master of Arts of Trinity College, Cambridge.
The results of recent discoveries in Babylonia, Assyria, and Egypt; of the latest Biblical researches; of travels and surveys in Eastern lands, have been concentrated on the life and surroundings of Abraham, to whom, as the author holds, the world owes more than to any save One. Abraham's greatness is shown to have been the result of faith, and the downfall of his descendants to be attributable to the want of it.

HOME WORDS FOR WANDERERS: Sermons. By the Rev. **Arthur S. Thompson**, Chaplain to the British Embassy at St. Petersburg. Crown 8vo. 6s.

THE NEW TESTAMENT, TRANSLATED FROM THE LATEST GREEK TEXT OF TISCHENDORF. By **Samuel Davidson, D.D., LL.D.**
The desirableness of presenting a single text, especially if it be the best, instead of one formed for the occasion under traditional influences, is apparent. From an exact translation of Tischendorf's final critical edition, readers will get both the words of the New Testament writers as nearly as possible, and an independent revision of the authorised version. Such a work will shortly appear, with an Introduction embodying ideas common to Dr. Davidson and the famous Professor at Leipzig.

STUDIES OF THE DIVINE MASTER. By the **Rev. T. Griffith**. Demy 8vo. 12s.
This book depicts the successive phases of the public life of Jesus, so far as is needful to the bringing out into full relief his mission, character, and work, as the Christ; and it comprises a thorough exposition of his teaching about the nature of his Kingdom—its privileges—its laws—and its advancement, in the soul, and in the world.

CHRIST AND HIS CHURCH. A Course of Lent Lectures, delivered in the Parish Church of Holy Trinity, Paddington. By the **Rev. Daniel Moore, M.A.** Small crown 8vo. 3s. 6d.

JOHN KNOX AND THE CHURCH OF ENGLAND: His work in her Pulpit and his influence upon her History, Articles, and Parties. A monograph founded upon several important papers of Knox, never before published. By the **Rev. P. Lorimer, D.D.** Demy 8vo. 12s.

THE PRIVILEGE OF PETER LEGALLY AND HISTORICALLY EXAMINED, AND THE CLAIMS OF THE ROMAN CHURCH COMPARED WITH THE SCRIPTURES, the Councils and the Testimony of the Popes themselves. By the **Rev. R. C. Jenkins, M.A.**, Rector of Lyminge, and Honorary Canon of Canterbury. Fcap. 8vo. 3s. 6d.

THE PARACLETE: An Essay on the Personality and Ministry of the Holy Ghost, with some Reference to Current Discussions. By the **Rev. Joseph Parker, D.D.**, Author of "Ecce Deus." Demy 8vo. 12s.

SERMONETTES: On Synonymous Texts, taken from the Bible and Book of Common Prayer, for the Study, Family Reading, and Private Devotion. By the **Rev. Thomas Moore**, Vicar of Christ Church, Chesham. Small crown 8vo. 4s. 6d.

SERMONS AND EXPOSITIONS. By the **Rev. R. Winterbotham.** Crown 8vo. Cloth. 7s. 6d.

SERMONS. By the late **Rev. Henry Christopherson.** Cr. 8vo, cloth. 7s. 6d.

THE SPIRITUAL FUNCTION OF A PRESBYTER IN THE CHURCH OF ENGLAND. By **John Notrege, A.M.**, for fifty-four years a Presbyter in "that pure and Apostolical Branch of Christ's Holy Catholic Church established in this Kingdom." Small crown 8vo. Red edges. Price 3s. 6d.

THEOLOGICAL—*continued.*

WORDS OF FAITH AND CHEER. A Mission of Instruction and Suggestion. By the **Rev. Archer T. Gurney.** 1 vol. Crown 8vo. Price 6s.

"Speaks of many questions with a wise judgment and a fearless honesty, as well as with an intellectual strength and broad human catholicity. | which command respect."—*British Quarterly Review.*

THE GOSPEL ITS OWN WITNESS. Being the Hulsean Lectures for 1873. By the **Rev. Stanley Leathes, M.A.** 1 vol. Crown 8vo. Price 5s.

THE CHURCH AND THE EMPIRES: Historical Periods. By the late **Henry W. Wilberforce.** Preceded by a Memoir of the Author, by J. H. Newman, D.D. 1 vol. Post 8vo. With a Steel Portrait. Price 10s. 6d.

Second Edition.

THE HIGHER LIFE. Its Reality, Experience, and Destiny. By **James Baldwin Brown, B.A.** Crown 8vo. Price 7s. 6d.

"Very clearly and eloquently set forth."—*Standard.*
"Full of earnest expositions of truth set forth with great eloquence.... Most heartily do we commend it to our readers."—*Rock.*
"One of the richest volumes of sermons that intelligent persons."—*Baptist.*
| we have yet had from the pen of this eloquent preacher."—*Christian World.*
"Full of thought, beauty, and power, and will repay the careful study, not only of those who have a *penchant* for theological reading, but of all

HARTHAM CONFERENCES; OR, DISCUSSIONS UPON SOME OF THE RELIGIOUS TOPICS OF THE DAY. By the **Rev. F. W. Kingsford, M.A.**, Vicar of S. Thomas's, Stamford Hill; late Chaplain H.E.I.C. (Bengal Presidency). "Audi alteram partem." Crown 8vo. Price 3s. 6d.

CONTENTS:—Introductory.—The Real Presence.—Confession.—Ritualism.
"Able and interesting."—*Church Times.*

STUDIES IN MODERN PROBLEMS. FIRST SERIES. Edited by the **Rev. Orby Shipley, M.A.** By Various Writers. Crown 8vo. 5s.

CONTENTS: Sacramental Confession—Abolition of the Thirty-nine Articles. Part I.—The Sanctity of Marriage—Creation and Modern Science—Retreats for Persons Living in the World—Catholic and Protestant—The Bishops on Confession in the Church of England.

STUDIES IN MODERN PROBLEMS. SECOND SERIES. Edited by the **Rev. Orby Shipley, M.A.** By Various Writers. Crown 8vo. 5s.

CONTENTS: Some Principles of Christian Ceremonial—A Layman's View of Confession of Sin to a Priest. Parts I. & II.—Reservation of the Blessed Sacrament—Missions and Preaching Orders—Abolition of the Thirty-nine Articles. Part II.—The First Liturgy of Edward VI., and our own Office, contrasted and compared.

UNTIL THE DAY DAWN. Four Advent Lectures delivered in the Episcopal Chapel, Milverton, Warwickshire, on the Sunday Evenings during Advent, 1870. By the **Rev. Marmaduke E. Browne.** Crown 8vo. Price 2s. 6d.

"Four really original and stirring sermons."—*John Bull.*

Second Edition.

A SCOTCH COMMUNION SUNDAY. To which are added Certain Discourses from a University City. By **A. K. H. B.**, Author of "The Recreations of a Country Parson." Crown 8vo. Price 5s.

"Some discourses are added, which are couched in language of rare power."—*John Bull.*
"Exceedingly fresh and readable."—*Glasgow News.*
| "We commend this volume as full of interest to all our readers. It is written with much ability and good feeling, with excellent taste and marvellous tact."—*Church Herald.*

EVERY DAY A PORTION: Adapted from the Bible and the Prayer Book, for the Private Devotions of those living in Widowhood. Collected and Edited by **Lady Mary Vyner.** Square crown 8vo, elegantly bound. 5s.

"Now she that is a widow indeed, and desolate, trusteth in God."
"An excellent little volume."—*John Bull.*
"Fills a niche hitherto unoccupied, and fills it with complete fitness."—*Literary Churchman.*
"A tone of earnest practical piety runs through | the whole, rendering the work well suited for its purpose."—*Rock.*
"The adaptations are always excellent and appropriate."—*Notes and Queries.*

THEOLOGICAL—*continued*.

ESSAYS ON RELIGION AND LITERATURE. By Various Writers. Edited by the **Most Reverend Archbishop Manning**. Demy 8vo. 10s. 6d.

CONTENTS :—The Philosophy of Christianity,—Mystical Elements of Religion.—Controversy with the Agnostics.—A Reasoning Thought.—Darwinism brought to Book.—Mr. Mill on Liberty of the Press.—Christianity in relation to Society.—The Religious Condition of Germany.—The Philosophy of Bacon.—Catholic Laymen and Scholastic Philosophy.

Fifth Edition.

WHY AM I A CHRISTIAN? By **Viscount Stratford de Redcliffe**, P.C., K.G., G.C.B. Small crown 8vo. Price 3s.

"Has a peculiar interest, as exhibiting the convictions of an earnest, intelligent, and practical man."—*Contemporary Review*.

THEOLOGY AND MORALITY. Being Essays by the **Rev. J. Llewellyn Davies, M.A.** 1 vol. Crown 8vo. Price 7s. 6d.

"The position taken up by Mr. Llewellyn Davies is well worth a careful survey on the part of philosophical students, for it represents the closest approximation of any theological system yet formulated to the religion of philosophy... We have not space to do more with regard to the social essays of the work before us, than to testify to the kindliness of spirit, sobriety, and earnest thought by which they are uniformly characterised."—*Examiner*.

THE RECONCILIATION OF RELIGION AND SCIENCE. Being Essays by the **Rev. T. W. Fowle, M.A.** 1 vol. 8vo. Price 10s. 6d.

"A book which requires and deserves the respectful attention of all reflecting Churchmen. It is earnest, reverent, thoughtful, and courageous..." "There is scarcely a page in the book which is not equally worthy of a thoughtful pause."—*Literary Churchman*.

MISSIONARY ENTERPRISE IN THE EAST. By the **Rev. Richard Collins, M.A.** With Four Illustrations. Crown 8vo. Price 6s.

"A very graphic story told in lucid, simple, and modest style."—*English Churchman*.
"A readable and very interesting volume."—*Church Review*.
"We may judge from our own experience, no one who takes up this charming little volume will lay it down again till he has got to the last word."—*John Bull*.

MISSIONARY LIFE IN THE SOUTHERN SEAS. By James Hutton. 1 vol. Crown 8vo. With Illustrations. 7s. 6d.

This is an historical record of Mission work by the labourers of all denominations in Tahiti, the Hervey, the Austral, the Samoa or Navigators', the Sandwich, Friendly, and Fiji Islands, &c.

THE ETERNAL LIFE. Being Fourteen Sermons. By the **Rev. Jas. Noble Bennie, M.A.** Crown 8vo. Price 6s.

"The whole volume is replete with matter for thought and study."—*John Bull*.
"We recommend these sermons as wholesome Sunday reading."—*English Churchman*.
"Mr. Bennie preaches earnestly and well."—*Literary Churchman*.

THE REALM OF TRUTH. By **Miss E. T. Carne.** Cr. 8vo. 5s. 6d.

"A singularly calm, thoughtful, and philosophical inquiry into what Truth is, and what its authority."—*Leeds Mercury*.
"It tells the world what it does not like to hear, but what it cannot be told too often, that Truth is something stronger and more enduring than our little doings, and speakings, and actings."—*Literary Churchman*.

LIFE: Conferences delivered at Toulouse. By the **Rev. Père Lacordaire.** Crown 8vo. Price 6s.

"Let the serious reader cast his eye upon any single page in this volume, and he will find there words which will arrest his attention and give him a desire to know more of the teachings of this worthy follower of the saintly St. Dominick."—*Morning Post*.

Second Edition.

CATHOLICISM AND THE VATICAN. With a Narrative of the Old Catholic Congress at Munich. By **J. Lowry Whittle, A.M.**, Trin. Coll., Dublin. Crown 8vo. Price 4s. 6d.

"We may cordially recommend his book to all who wish to follow the course of the Old Catholic movement."—*Saturday Review*.

Second Edition.

THE PUBLIC WORSHIP REGULATION ACT, 1874. With an Introduction, Notes, and Index. Edited by **W. G. Brooke, M.A.**, Barrister-at-Law, Author of "Six Privy Council Judgments," &c. Crown 8vo. 3s. 6d.

"A very useful and convenient manual, and deserves to be studied by all who are interested or concerned in the working of this important Act.... The introduction gives a succinct history of the Act in its passage through Parliament. The notes, which follow, are appended to the several clauses of the Bill, and contain very copious remarks, references, and illustrations."—*Guardian*.

THEOLOGICAL—*continued.*

Third Edition.
SIX PRIVY COUNCIL JUDGMENTS—1850-1872. Annotated by W. G. Brooke, M.A., Barrister-at-Law. Crown 8vo. Price 9s.

"The volume is a valuable record of cases forming precedents for the future."—*Athenæum.*
"A very timely and important publication. It brings into one view the great judgments of the last twenty years, which will constitute the unwritten law of the English Establishment."—*British Quarterly Review.*

HYMNS AND SACRED LYRICS. By the Rev. Godfrey Thring, B.A. 1 vol. Crown 8vo. Price 5s.

"Many of the hymns in the charming volume before us have already been published in the principal hymnals of the day, a proof, as we take it, that they have become popular, and that the merits are not superficial or ordinary.... There is an inexpressible charm of quiet and soothing beauty in his verses which we cannot resist if we would, and would not if we could, and what is still better, so penetrating and peaceful is the devotional spirit which breathes through his poems and from them, that we feel all the better—less in a worldly frame of mind, and more in a heavenly mood—after reading them."—*English Churchman.*

HYMNS AND VERSES, Original and Translated. By the Rev. Henry Downton, M.A. Small crown 8vo. Price 3s. 6d.

"Considerable force and beauty characterise some of these verses."—*Watchman.*
"Mr. Downton's 'Hymns and Verses' are worthy of all praise."—*English Churchman.*
"Will, we do not doubt, be welcome as a permanent possession to those for whom they have been composed or to whom they have been originally addressed."—*Church Herald.*

THE MOST COMPLETE HYMN BOOK PUBLISHED.
HYMNS FOR THE CHURCH AND HOME. Selected and Edited by the Rev. W. Fleming Stevenson, Author of "Praying and Working."

The *Hymn-book* consists of *Three Parts*:—I. For Public Worship.—II. For Family and Private Worship.—III. For Children; and contains Biographical Notices of nearly 300 Hymn-writers, with Notes upon their Hymns.

*** Published in various forms and prices, the latter ranging from 8d. to 6s. Lists and full particulars will be furnished on application to the Publishers.

WORKS BY THE REV. H. R. HAWEIS, M.A.
Second Edition.
SPEECH IN SEASON. A New Volume of Sermons. Cr. 8vo. Price 9s.

Eighth Edition.
THOUGHTS FOR THE TIMES. Crown 8vo. Price 7s. 6d.

"Mr. Haweis writes not only fearlessly, but with remarkable freshness and vigour. In all that he says we perceive a transparent honesty and singleness of purpose."—*Saturday Review.*
"Bears marks of much originality of thought and individuality of expression."—*Pall Mall Gazette.*

UNSECTARIAN FAMILY PRAYERS, for Morning and Evening for a Week, with short selected passages from the Bible. Square crown 8vo. Price 3s. 6d.

"These prayers are tender, devotional, and helpful, and may be used with great profit in any household. They are brief, but very beautiful."—*Christian World.*

WORKS BY THE REV. CHARLES ANDERSON, M.A.
Second Edition.
CHURCH THOUGHT AND CHURCH WORK. Edited by the Rev. Charles Anderson M.A., Vicar of St. John's, Limehouse. Containing articles by the Revs. J. M. Capes, Professor Cheetham, J. LL Davies, Harry Jones, Brooke Lambert, A. J. Ross, the Editor, and others. Demy 8vo. 7s. 6d.

"Mr. Anderson has accomplished his task well. The brief papers with which his book is filled are almost of necessity sketchy, but they are none the less valuable on that account. Those who are contending with practical difficulties in Church work, could hardly do better than study Mr. Anderson's suggestions for themselves."—*Spectator.*
"This new series of papers, edited by Mr. Charles Anderson, will be heartily welcomed. A healthy moral earnestness is conspicuous in every one of them."—*Westminster Review.*
"It is a book which may be profitably studied by all, whether clergymen or laymen, members of the established or other churches, who attempt any kind of pastoral work, for it is full of wise practical suggestions, evidently the result of earnest observation and long experience, and not the mere guesses of an à *priori* speculator."—*Nonconformist.*

Second Edition.
WORDS AND WORKS IN A LONDON PARISH. Edited by the Rev. Charles Anderson, M.A. Demy 8vo. Price 6s.

"It has an interest of its own for not a few minds. 'to whom the question 'Is the National Church worth preserving as such, and if so, how best increase its vital power?' is of deep and grave importance."—*Spectator.*

65, *Cornhill;* & 12, *Paternoster Row, London.*

THEOLOGICAL—*continued.*

THE CURATE OF SHYRE. A Record of Parish Reform, with its attendant Religious and Social Problems. By the **Rev. Charles Anderson, M.A.**, Vicar of St. John's, Limehouse. Editor of "Church Thought and Church Work," and "Words and Works in a London Parish." Demy 8vo. 7s. 6d.

"The story of a country-town clergyman's endeavours to shake his people out of their semi-barbarous ways. The author fully succeeds in inspiring the reader with that interest which he himself feels in his characters; the timid old-fashioned rector, the high-minded energetic young curate; the thoughtful but enthusiastic doctor, &c., are drawn to the life. The plans for uniting civilization and religion are sound and practical."—*Westminster Review.*

WORKS BY THE REV. G. S. DREW, M.A.
VICAR OF TRINITY, LAMBETH.

THE SON OF MAN. His Life and Ministry. Crown 8vo. 7s. 6d.
Second Edition.

SCRIPTURE LANDS IN CONNECTION WITH THEIR HISTORY. Bevelled Boards, 8vo. Price 10s. 6d.

"Mr. Drew has invented a new method of illustrating Scripture history—from observation of the countries. Instead of narrating his travels, and referring from time to time to the facts of sacred history belonging to the different countries, he writes an outline history of the Hebrew nation from Abraham downwards, with special reference to the various points in which the geography illustrates the history. . . . He is very successful in picturing to his readers the scenes before his own mind."—*Saturday Review.*

NAZARETH: ITS LIFE AND LESSONS. Crown 8vo, 5s.
Second Edition.

"We have read the volume with great interest. It is at once succinct and suggestive, reverent and ingenious, observant of small details, and yet not forgetful of great principles."—*British Quarterly Review.*

"A very reverent attempt to elicit and develop Scripture intimations respecting our Lord's thirty years' sojourn at Nazareth. The author has wrought well at the unworked mine, and has produced a very valuable series of Scripture lessons, which will be found both profitable and singularly interesting."—*Guardian.*

THE DIVINE KINGDOM ON EARTH AS IT IS IN HEAVEN. 8vo, 10s. 6d.

"Entirely valuable and satisfactory. . . . . There is no living divine to whom the authorship would not be a credit."—*Literary Churchman.*
"Thoughtful and eloquent. . . . . Full of original thinking admirably expressed."—*British Quarterly Review.*

WORKS BY THE REV. C. J. VAUGHAN, D.D.

THE SOLIDITY OF TRUE RELIGION AND OTHER SERMONS PREACHED IN LONDON DURING THE ELECTION AND MISSION WEEK, FEBRUARY, 1874. Crown 8vo. 3s. 6d.

Third Edition.

WORDS OF HOPE FROM THE PULPIT OF THE TEMPLE CHURCH. Crown 8vo. Price 5s.

"Quiet, scholarly, ingenious, natural, spiritual, evangelical, and earnest. The charm of their pleasantness and goodness does not weary. They are the natural products of a cultured, industrious, vigorous mind."—*British Quarterly Review.*

FORGET THINE OWN PEOPLE. An Appeal for Missions. Crown 8vo, 3s. 6d.

"Faithful, earnest, eloquent, tender, and large-hearted."—*British Quarterly Review.*

Fourth Edition.

THE YOUNG LIFE EQUIPPING ITSELF FOR GOD'S SERVICE. Being Four Sermons Preached before the University of Cambridge, in November, 1872. Crown 8vo. Price 3s. 6d.

"Has all the writer's characteristics of devotedness, purity, and high moral tone."—*London Quarterly Review.*
"As earnest, eloquent, and as liberal as everything else that he writes."—*Examiner.*

WORKS OF THE LATE REV. F. W. ROBERTSON, M.A.
NEW AND CHEAPER EDITIONS.

SERMONS.
Vol. I. Small crown 8vo. Price 3s. 6d.
Vol. II. Small crown 8vo. Price 3s. 6d.
Vol. III. Small crown 8vo. Price 3s. 6d.
Vol. IV. Small crown 8vo. Price 3s. 6d.

LECTURES AND ADDRESSES, WITH OTHER LITERARY REMAINS. With Introduction by the Rev. Stopford A. Brooke, M.A. Crown 8vo. 5s.
[*Preparing.*

EXPOSITORY LECTURES ON ST. PAUL'S EPISTLE TO THE CORINTHIANS. Small crown 8vo. 5s.

THE EDUCATION OF THE HUMAN RACE. From the German of Gotthold Ephraim Lessing. Fcap. 8vo. 2s. 6d.

AN ANALYSIS OF MR. TENNYSON'S "IN MEMORIAM." Fcap. 8vo. 2s.

☞ The above works can also be had Bound in half morocco.

₀ A Portrait of the late Rev. F. W. Robertson, mounted for framing, can be had, price 2s. 6d.

65, *Cornhill;* & 12, *Paternoster Row, London.*

THEOLOGICAL—*continued.*

WORKS BY THE REV. STOPFORD A. BROOKE, M.A.
Chaplain in Ordinary to Her Majesty the Queen.

THE LATE REV. F. W. ROBERTSON, M.A.: LIFE AND LETTERS. Edited by the Rev. Stopford A. Brooke, M.A.
I. In 2 vols., uniform with the Sermons. With a Steel Portrait. 7s. 6d.
II. Library Edition, in demy 8vo, with Two Steel Portraits. 12s.
III. A Popular Edition, in 1 vol. 6s.

Second Edition.
THEOLOGY IN THE ENGLISH POETS.—COWPER, COLERIDGE, WORDSWORTH, and BURNS. Post 8vo. 9s.
"Apart from its literary merits, the book may be said to possess an independent value, as tending to familiarise a certain section of the English public with more enlightened views of theology."—*Athenæum.*
"The volume is scholarlike, and evidently the result of study and discrimination."—*Hour.*
"... An admirable example of interpretative criticism. It is clear, adequate, eloquent, and there are many such morsels of thought scattered throughout the book. We have read Mr. Brooke's volume with pleasure—it is fresh, suggestive, stimulating, and we cordially recommend it."—*Nonconformist.*

FREDERICK DENISON MAURICE: THE LIFE AND WORK OF. A Memorial Sermon. Crown 8vo, sewed. 1s.

SERMONS Preached in St. James's Chapel, York Street. Second Series. Crown 8vo. Price 7s.

Eighth Edition.
SERMONS Preached in St. James's Chapel, York Street, London. Crown 8vo. 6s.
"No one who reads these sermons will wonder that Mr. Brooke is a great power in London, that his chapel is thronged, and his followers large and enthusiastic. They are fiery, energetic, impetuous sermons, rich with the treasures of a cultivated imagination."—*Guardian.*

Eighth Edition.
CHRIST IN MODERN LIFE. Sermons Preached in St. James's Chapel, York Street, London. Crown 8vo. 7s. 6d.
"Nobly fearless, and singularly strong. . . . carries our admiration throughout."—*British Quarterly Review.*

Second Edition.
FREEDOM IN THE CHURCH OF ENGLAND. Six Sermons suggested by the Voysey Judgment. Cr. 8vo, 3s. 6d.
"A very fair statement of the views in respect to freedom of thought held by the liberal party in the Church of England."—*Blackwood's Magazine.*
"Interesting and readable, and characterised by great clearness of thought, frankness of statement, and moderation of tone."—*Church Opinion.*

MISCELLANEOUS.

FOR SCEPTRE AND CROWN. A Romance of the Present Time. By **Gregor Samarow.** Translated by **Fanny Wormald.** 2 vols. Cr. 8vo, 15s.
This is the celebrated "Um Szepter und Kronen," which was published about a year ago in Germany, when it created a very great sensation among all classes. It deals with some of the prominent characters who have figured and still continue to figure in European politics, and the accuracy of its life-picture is so great that it is presented to the English public not as a novel, but as a new rendering of an important chapter in recent European history.
"Contains some humorous and careful studies of places and people made famous by the great German War. The author's pen is wielded with considerable power."—*Daily News.*

FRAGMENTS OF THOUGHT. Being Wayside Notes and Fireside Scraps. By T. **Bowden Green.** Dedicated by permission to the Poet Laureate. Crown 8vo, 7s. 6d.

THE ROMANTIC ANNALS OF A NAVAL FAMILY. By Mrs Arthur Traherne. Crown 8vo. 10s. 6d.
"Some interesting letters are introduced, amongst others, several from the late King William IV."—*Spectator.*
"Well and pleasantly told."—*Evening Standard.*

STUDIES IN POLITICAL ECONOMY. By **Anthony Musgrave,** C.M.G., Governor of South Australia. Crown 8vo.

65, Cornhill; & 12, Paternoster Row, London.

MISCELLANEOUS—*continued.*

A GRAMMAR OF POLITICAL ECONOMY. By **Maj.-Gen. W. F. Marriott, C.S.I.** Crown 8vo, 6*s.*

The author's aim in presenting this new elementary treatise to the world is, firstly, to restrict it to truly elementary considerations in each branch of the subject; secondly, to adopt a perfectly precise and unambiguous use of terms in the sense which most nearly agrees with common use; thirdly, to offer reasonable proof of every proposition; and fourthly, to use the utmost brevity consistent with proof, so as to invite and facilitate the judgment of the student as well as of the critic.

" . . . . These qualities of precision in conception and accuracy in statement possessed in so eminent a degree by this grammar, will render it most acceptable to the student of political economy."—*Hour.*

THE ASHANTEE WAR. A Popular Narrative. By **The " Daily News' " Special Correspondent.** Crown 8vo. Price 6*s.*

"Trustworthy and readable, and well fitted to serve its purpose as a popular narrative. . . . The *Daily News'* Correspondent secures interest chiefly by bringing together suggestive incidents, and by clearing up points that his readers would naturally be desirous of knowing."—*Examiner.*

SOLDIERING AND SCRIBBLING. By **Archibald Forbes**, of the *Daily News.* Crown 8vo. Price 7*s.* 6*d.*

"All who open it will be inclined to read through for the varied entertainment which it affords."—*Daily News.*

"There is a good deal of instruction to outsiders touching military life, in this volume."—*Evening Standard.*

'ILÂM ÊN NÂS. Historical Tales and Anecdotes of the Times of the Early Khalifahs. Translated from the Arabic Originals. By **Mrs. Godfrey Clerk**, Author of "The Antipodes and Round the World." Crown 8vo. Price 7*s.*

"Those who like stories full of the genuine colour and fragrance of the East should by all means read Mrs. Godfrey Clerk's volume."—*Spectator.*

"As full of valuable information as it is of amusing incident."—*Evening Standard.*

HAKAYIT ABDULLA. The Autobiography of a Malay Münshi, between the years 1808 and 1843, containing Sketches of Men and Events connected with the English Settlements in the Straits of Malacca during that period. Translated by **J. T. Thomson, F.R.G.S.** Demy 8vo. Price 12*s.*

"The chief interest of the work consists in its singular revelation of the inner life of a native of Asia—of the way in which his mind was affected by contact with Europeans, and of the estimate which he formed as to English rule in India, and English ways generally. . . . The book is written in the grave and sedate, yet amusing style, peculiar to Orientals, and is enriched by the translator's additional matter."—*Daily News.*

GLIMPSES OF THE SUPERNATURAL. Being Facts, Records, and Traditions, relating to Dreams, Omens, Miraculous Occurrences, Apparitions, Wraiths, Warnings, Second-sight, Necromancy, Witchcraft, &c. By the **Rev. Frederick George Lee, D.D.**, Vicar of All Saints, Lambeth. 2 Vols. Crown 8vo.

ANTIQUITIES OF AN ESSEX PARISH; OR, PAGES FROM THE HISTORY OF GREAT DUNMOW. By **W. T. Scott.** Crown 8vo. Sewed, 4*s.*; cloth, 5*s.*

SHAKSPERE; a Critical Study of his Mind and Art. By **Professor Edward Dowden.** Post 8vo. 12*s.*

The chief design of this work is to discover the man—Shakspere—through his works, and to ascertain his course of mental and moral development as far as this is possible. This thread running through the work will make it a continuous study, written for such intelligent readers of Shakspere who are not specialists in Shakspere scholarship, and intended to be an introduction to the study of Shakspere, popular in the sense of being attractive to all intelligent lovers of literature, but founded upon the most recent and accurate Shakspere scholarships, English, German, and American.

RUSSIAN ROMANCE. By **Alexander Serguevitch Poushkin.** Translated from the Tales of BELKIN, &c. By **Mrs. J. Buchan Telfer** (*née* **Mouravieff**). Crown 8vo.

CONTENTS.—The Pistol Shot.—The Snowstorm.—The Undertaker.—The Station-Master.—The Lady-Rustic.—The Captain's Daughter.—The Moor of Peter the Great.—The Queen of Spades, &c.

Miscellaneous—continued.

THE SHAKESPEARE ARGOSY: containing much of the wealth of Shakespeare's Wisdom and Wit, alphabetically arranged and classified by **Capt. A. F. P. Harcourt.** Crown 8vo. Price 6s.

SOCIALISM: its Nature, its Dangers, and its Remedies considered. By the **Rev. M. Kaufmann, B.A.** Founded on the German work "Kapitalismus and Socialismus," by Dr. A. E. F. Schäffle. Crown 8vo. 7s. 6d.

"Of great importance and full of instructive matter. . . . We do not hesitate to recommend it to all readers interested in the important subjects of which it treats."—T. E. Cliffe Leslie, in the *Academy*.

"A really complete theory upon the question. . . . Without assuming the authority of all he (Dr. Schäffle) urges, as explained by his English editor, we feel it would be difficult to recommend to those more especially interested a better or more conscientious summing up of the entire arguments on both sides."—*Standard*.

"Valuable in many respects. There is in it much of sound teaching and wise exposition of economic principles."—*Scotsman*.

"He has given us a valuable book at the very time when it was wanted."—*Edinburgh Daily Review*.

Second Edition.
J. H. NEWMAN, D.D.; CHARACTERISTICS FROM HIS WRITINGS: Selections, Personal, Historical, Philosophical, and Religious. Arranged by **W. S. Lilly**, Barrister-at-law, with the Author's approval. With a Steel Portrait. Crown 8vo. Price 6s.

CREMATION; THE TREATMENT OF THE BODY AFTER DEATH: with a Description of the Process and necessary Apparatus. Crown 8vo, sewed. Third Edition. Price 1s.

THE PLACE OF THE PHYSICIAN. Being the Introductory Lecture at Guy's Hospital, 1873-74; to which is added Essays on the Law of Human Life, and on the Relation between Organic and Inorganic Worlds. By **James Hinton**, Author of "Man and His Dwelling-Place." Crown 8vo, cloth. Price 3s. 6d.

"Very remarkable. There is not a sentence in them that is not pregnant with high meaning."—*Brighton Herald*.

"A thoughtful volume."—*John Bull*.

"Full of suggestive thoughts and scientific generalisation. To partake of this feast of reason the book must be purchased and thought over, which advice we conscientiously give to everyone who wishes to keep up with the intellectual progress of the age."—*Brighton Gazette*.

Seventh Edition.
LITTLE DINNERS; HOW TO SERVE THEM WITH ELEGANCE AND ECONOMY. By **Mary Hooper.** Crown 8vo. Price 5s.

"Given the means and the heart to put her knowledge in practice—she undeniably knows what is good."—*Saturday Review*.

"A capital help to any housekeeper who interests herself in her kitchen and her cook."—*Vanity Fair*.

"To read this book gives the reader an appetite."—*Notes and Queries*.

OUR INVALIDS: HOW SHALL WE EMPLOY AND AMUSE THEM? By **Harriet Power.** Fcap. 8vo. Price 2s. 6d.

"A very useful little brochure. . . . Will become a universal favourite with the class for whom it is intended, while it will afford many a useful hint to those who live with them."—*John Bull*.

REPUBLICAN SUPERSTITIONS. Illustrated by the Political History of the United States. Including a Correspondence with M. Louis Blanc. By **Moncure D. Conway.** Crown 8vo. Price 5s.

"A very able exposure of the most plausible fallacies of Republicanism, by a writer of remarkable vigour and purity of style."—*Standard*.

"Mr. Conway writes with ardent sincerity. He gives us some good anecdotes, and he is occasionally almost eloquent."—*Guardian*.

THE PORT OF REFUGE; OR, COUNSEL AND AID TO SHIPMASTERS IN DIFFICULTY, DOUBT, OR DISTRESS. By **Manley Hopkins.** Cr. 8vo. 6s.

SUBJECTS :—The Shipmaster's Position and Duties.—Agents and Agency.—Average.—Bottomry, and other Means of Raising Money.—The Charter-Party, and Bill-of-Lading. Stoppage in Transitu; and the Shipowner's Lien.—Collision.

"A most useful book."—*Westminster Review*.

"Master-mariners will find it well worth while to avail themselves of its teachings."—*United Service Magazine*.

"Combines, in quite a marvellous manner, a fulness of information which will make it perfectly indispensable in the captain's book-case, and equally suitable to the gentleman's library."—*Iron*.

65, Cornhill; & 12, Paternoster Row, London.

Works Published by Henry S. King & Co., 37

MISCELLANEOUS—*continued.*

Sixth Edition.

LOMBARD STREET. A Description of the Money Market. By **Walter Bagehot.** Large crown 8vo. Price 7s. 6d.

"Mr. Bagehot touches incidentally a hundred points connected with his subject, and pours serene white light upon them all."—*Spectator.*
"Anybody who wishes to have a clear idea of the workings of what is called the Money Market should procure a little volume which Mr. Bagehot has just published, and he will there find the whole thing in a nut-shell."—*Saturday Review.*
"Full of the most interesting economic history."—*Athenæum.*

THE ENGLISH CONSTITUTION. By **Walter Bagehot.** A New Edition, Revised and Corrected, with an Introductory Dissertation on Recent Changes and Events. Crown 8vo. Price 7s. 6d.

"No writer before him had set out so clearly what the efficient part of the English Constitution really is."—*Pall Mall Gazette.*
"A pleasing and clever study on the department of higher politics."—*Guardian.*

NEWMARKET AND ARABIA; AN EXAMINATION OF THE DESCENT OF RACERS AND COURSERS. By **Roger D. Upton,** Captain late 9th Royal Lancers. Post 8vo. With Pedigrees and Frontispiece. 9s.

"It contains a good deal of truth, and it abounds with valuable suggestions."—*Saturday Review.*
"A remarkable volume. The breeder can well ponder over its pages."—*Bell's Life.*
"A thoughtful and intelligent book.... A contribution to the history of the horse of remarkable interest and importance."—*Baily's Magazine.*

MOUNTAIN, MEADOW, AND MERE: a Series of Outdoor Sketches of Sport, Scenery, Adventures, and Natural History. By **G. Christopher Davies.** With 16 Illustrations by BOSWORTH W. HARCOURT. Crown 8vo. Price 6s.

"Pervaded throughout by the graceful melody of a natural idyl, and the details of sport are subordinated to a dominating sense of the beautiful and picturesque."—*Saturday Review.*
"Mr. Davies writes pleasantly, graphically, with the pen of a lover of nature, a naturalist, and a sportsman."—*Field.*

STREAMS FROM HIDDEN SOURCES. By **B. Montgomerie Ranking.** Crown 8vo. Price 6s.

"We doubt not that Mr. Ranking's enthusiasm will communicate itself to many of his readers, and induce them in like manner to follow back these streamlets to their parent river."—*Graphic.*
"The effect of reading the seven tales he presents to us is to make us wish for some seven more of the same kind."—*Pall Mall Gazette.*

MODERN PARISH CHURCHES; THEIR PLAN, DESIGN, AND FURNITURE. By **J. T. Micklethwaite, F.S.A.** Crown 8vo. Price 7s. 6d.

"Any one about to build a church we strongly recommend to study it carefully."—*Notes and Queries.*
"Will be a valuable addition to all clergymen's libraries, whether they have to build churches or not."—*Literary Churchman.*
"We strongly counsel the thinking man of any committee now formed, or forming, to restore or to build a church, to buy this book, and to read out portions of it to his colleagues before allowing them to come to any conclusion on a single detail of the building or its fittings."—*Church Times.*
"A fund of sound remarks and practical suggestions on Church Architecture."—*Examiner.*

Third Edition, Revised and Enlarged.

LONGEVITY; THE MEANS OF PROLONGING LIFE AFTER MIDDLE AGE. By **John Gardner, M.D.** Small crown 8vo. Price 4s.

"We are bound to say that in general Dr. Gardner's directions are sensible enough, and founded on good principles. The advice given is such that any man in moderate health might follow it with advantage, whilst no prescription or other claptrap is introduced which might savour of quackery."—*Lancet.*
"Dr. Gardner's suggestions for attaining a healthy and so far a happy old age are well deserving the attention of all who think such a blessing worth trying for."—*Notes and Queries.*
"The hints here given are to our mind invaluable."—*Standard.*

Fourth Edition.

THE SECRET OF LONG LIFE. By **Mortimer Collins,** Author of "The Princess Clarice," &c. Dedicated by Special Permission to Lord St. Leonards. Large crown 8vo. Price 5s.

"A charming little volume."—*Times.*
"A very pleasant little book, cheerful, genial, scholarly."—*Spectator.*
"Entitled to the warmest admiration."—*Pall Mall Gazette.*

65, *Cornhill; & 12, Paternoster Row, London.*

MISCELLANEOUS—*continued.*

WORKS BY EDWARD JENKINS, M.P.

Thirty-Fourth Edition.
GINX'S BABY: HIS BIRTH AND OTHER MISFORTUNES. Crown 8vo. Price 2s.

LUCHMEE AND DILLOO. A Story of West Indian Life. 2 vols. Demy 8vo. Illustrated. [*Preparing.*

Fourteenth Thousand.
LITTLE HODGE. A Christmas Country Carol. With Five Illustrations. Crown 8vo. Price 5s.
A Cheap Edition in paper covers, price 1s.

Seventh Edition.
LORD BANTAM. Cr. 8vo. Price 2s. 6d.

PANDURANG HARI; or, MEMOIRS OF A HINDOO. A Tale of Mahratta Life sixty years ago. With a Preface by **Sir H. Bartle E. Frere, G.C.S.I.**, &c. 2 vols. Crown 8vo. Price 21s.

"There is a quaintness and simplicity in the roguery of the hero that makes his life as attractive as that of Guzman d'Alfarache or Gil Blas, and so we advise our readers not to be dismayed at the length of Pandurang Hari, but to read it resolutely through. If they do this they cannot, we think, fail to be both amused and interested."—*Times.*

TALES OF THE ZENANA, OR A NUWAB'S LEISURE HOURS. By **W. B. Hockley**, Author of "Pandurang Hari." With an Introductory Preface by **Lord Stanley of Alderley.** In 2 vols. Crown 8vo. Price 21s.

"Love, warlike adventures, and a thirst for wealth form the substantial motives of each tale, but there is no sameness of incident or character. ... The *couleur locale* is carefully preserved, the incidents are characteristic of Hindoo and Mohammedan life, the scenes and adventures are varied, while the interest is so artfully sustained that the reader is not wearied, nor is he often able to guess at the climax. ... Finally, we may fairly rank this as an original book, more abidingly entertaining and instructive than many works by brilliant authors of fifty times its pretensions."—*Spectator.*

MADEMOISELLE JOSEPHINE'S FRIDAYS, AND OTHER STORIES. By **Miss M. Betham-Edwards**, Author of "Kitty," &c. Crown 8vo. 7s. 6d.

A CHEQUERED LIFE: Being Memoirs of the Vicomtesse de Léoville-Meilhan. Edited by the Vicomtesse Solange de Kerkadec. Crown 8vo. Price 7s. 6d.

"There are numerous passages of a strongly dramatic character, describing conventual life, trials for murder, death-bed marriages, village bridals, revolutionary outrages, and the other familiar aspects of those times; and we must say that the *vraisemblance* is admirable."—*Standard.* "Easy and amusing reading."—*Hour.*

GIDEON'S ROCK, and other Stories. By **Katherine Saunders.** In 1 vol. Crown 8vo. Price 6s.

CONTENTS.—Gideon's Rock.—Old Matthew's Puzzle.—Gentle Jack.—Uncle Ned.—The Retired Apothecary.

"The tale from which the volume derives its title, is especially worthy of commendation, but the other and shorter stories comprised in the volume are also well deserving of reproduction."—*Queen.*

JOAN MERRYWEATHER, and other Stories. By **Katherine Saunders.** In 1 vol. Crown 8vo. Price 6s.

CONTENTS.—The Haunted Crust.—The Flower-Girl.—Joan Merryweather.—The Watchman's Story.—An Old Letter.

MARGARET AND ELIZABETH. A Story of the Sea. By **Katherine Saunders**, Author of "Gideon's Rock," &c. Crown 8vo. 6s.

"Simply yet powerfully told. ... This opening picture is so exquisitely drawn as to be a fit introduction to a story of such simple pathos and power. ... A very beautiful story closes as it began, in a tender and touching picture of homely happiness."—*Pall Mall Gazette.*

STUDIES AND ROMANCES. By **H. Schütz Wilson.** Cr. 8vo, 7s. 6d.

"Open the book, at what page the reader may, he will find something to amuse and instruct, and he must be very hard to please if he finds nothing to suit him, either grave or gay, stirring or romantic, in the capital stories collected in this well-got-up volume."—*John Bull.*

THE PELICAN PAPERS. Reminiscences and Remains of a Dweller in the Wilderness. By **James Ashcroft Noble.** Crown 8vo. Price 6s.

"Written somewhat after the fashion of Mr. Helps's 'Friends in Council.'"—*Examiner.* "Will well repay perusal by all thoughtful and intelligent readers."—*Liverpool Leader.*

MISCELLANEOUS—*continued*.

BRIEFS AND PAPERS. Being Sketches of the Bar and the Press. By **Two Idle Apprentices.** Crown 8vo. Price 7s. 6d.

"Written with spirit and knowledge, and give some curious glimpses into what the majority will regard as strange and unknown territories."—*Daily News*.

"This is one of the best books to while away an hour and cause a generous laugh that we have come across for a long time."—*John Bull*.

BY STILL WATERS. A Story for Quiet Hours. By **Edward Garrett**, Author of "Occupations of a Retired Life," &c. Cr. 8vo. With Seven Illustrations. 6s.

"We have read many books by Edward Garrett, but none that has pleased us so well as this. It has more than pleased; it has charmed us."—*Nonconformist*.

COL. MEADOWS TAYLOR'S INDIAN TALES.
1. **THE CONFESSIONS OF A THUG.** 2. **TARA.**

Are now ready, and are the First and Second Volumes of A New and Cheaper Edition, in 1 vol. each, Illustrated, price 6s. They will be followed by "RALPH DARNELL" and "TIPPOO SULTAN."

BRADBURY, AGNEW, & CO., PRINTERS, WHITEFRIARS.

www.ingramcontent.com/pod-product-compliance
Ingram Content Group UK Ltd.
Pitfield, Milton Keynes, MK11 3LW, UK
UKHW020659250925
8075UKWH00047B/1162